SEX EQUALITY

LESBIAN AND GAY RIGHTS

CATHARINE A. MACKINNON
Elizabeth A. Long Professor of Law,
The University of Michigan Law School
Visiting Professor (long-term),
The University of Chicago Law School

NEW YORK, NEW YORK

FOUNDATION PRESS

2003

Reprinted from MacKinnon, Sex Equality
Pages 1 to 50, 551, 1057 to 1190

COPYRIGHT © 2003 by Catharine A. MacKinnon

FOUNDATION PRESS
395 Hudson Street
New York, NY 10014
Phone Toll Free 1–877–888–1330
Fax (212) 367–6799
fdpress.com

All rights reserved
Printed in the United States of America

ISBN 1–58778–563–3

 *TEXT IS PRINTED ON 10% POST CONSUMER RECYCLED PAPER*

In memory of Elizabeth Davis MacKinnon

*

INTRODUCTION

This book investigates social inequality between and among women and men, legal sex equality guarantees, and the present and possible relation between the two. In attempting to grasp the life and the law of sex discrimination together, the inquiry attends to inequalities of race, economic class, sexual orientation, and to some extent age as well. By providing a critical grasp of the legal tools of the field, it aspires to narrow the gap between the law's promise and performance in this domain by promoting change toward equality goals.

Centered on case law in the United States, the inquiry encompasses constitutional, statutory, comparative, and international materials.* Legislation, policy initiatives, and litigation strategies are considered. Materials and references from political theory, social science, and history provide context and perspective. The investigation proceeds concretely through areas of social life that evidence and scholarship identify as significant in gender status. The first half of the book, Foundations, examines conventional sex equality law and theory; the second half, Applications, extends the analysis onto social terrain not generally recognized by law as posing sex discrimination questions.

Part I explores the received legal equality theory of sameness and difference and its doctrinal tools. It ranges from the topic of work, where the sexes are thought most "the same," to pregnancy, where they are considered most "different." An alternate theory of equality centering on dominance and subordination is used as comparison and critique. Both mainstream and alternate theories are then deployed as Part II analyzes questions largely uncharted by sex equality law—including rape, abortion, gay and lesbian rights, and trafficking in women—or reached by it only recently, such as sexual harassment. Whether an issue of sex inequality exists, whether it should be addressed by law, by sex equality principles, and if so how, are left to you.

The analysis is structured to treat law as first substantive then abstract on the view that, in this sphere and perhaps others, law is interpreted and practiced on the basis of substantive experiences and material commitments, from which doctrinal and formal positions inevitably derive. Put

---

* Cases are cut for space and focus; all omissions are indicated by ellipses except for citations and internal headings, which are omitted without notice. Every citation has been checked, but this is not a reference work; lawyers in particular should consult the original sources. Some inaccuracies inevitably remain. I will appreciate being informed of any so they can be corrected. Foreign law examples are highly selective and are not necessarily representative of their legal systems as a whole. Translations are my own unless otherwise credited.

another way, if views on substantive realities like rape and abortion determine legal positions and authoritative outcomes of doctrinal, textual, structural, and interpretive disputes, then engaging the views of others productively and examining one's own positions critically requires engagement with the concrete realities on which both are predicated.

This text accordingly provides a thick reality context in which to analyze issues and dissect doctrine. Hypotheticals are used infrequently and are based on real events. Perhaps, contrary to the usual view that substantive disagreements are inherently unbridgeable, denying the real grounds for dissension and precluding addressing them in court has precluded change. Perhaps the case for sex equality would be stronger if discrimination doctrine revolved less around abstractions and permitted confronting in court more of the reality of sex inequality directly.

In 1861, John Stuart Mill observed:

> The entire history of social improvement has been a series of transitions, by which one custom or institution after another, from being a supposed primary necessity of social existence, has passed into the rank of a universally stigmatized injustice and tyranny. So it has been with the distinctions of slaves and freemen, nobles and serfs, patricians and plebeians; and so it will be, and in part already is, with the aristocracies of color, race, and sex. John Stuart Mill, *Utilitarianism* 56 (Humboldt Publishing Co. 1890) (1861).

If, as I believe, equality is the pivotal issue of the twenty-first century—as freedom, unachievable without equality, was of the twentieth—*Sex Equality*'s readers may help end the aristocracy of sex.

CATHARINE A. MACKINNON

12 December 2000

ACKNOWLEDGMENTS

My view of what law is, whether it matters, and what equality would mean has taken shape primarily in work with clients and lawyers on cases since 1974.* The students who took the course that grew into this book over twenty years have been my collaborators in this project. From those in the original seminar at Yale Law School in 1979 to the last decade at the University of Michigan, including students at Harvard, Stanford, Minnesota, UCLA, Chicago, Osgoode Hall (Toronto), and Basel (Switzerland), their engagement, reactions, and insights are reflected throughout. Scholarship and case law in the area burgeoned during this period as well, making more detailed inquiry possible even as the topics remained the same.

Over time, I become ever more aware of what my early teachers gave me. From Leo Weinstein of Smith College, Robert Dahl of Yale University's Department of Political Science, and Thomas I. Emerson of Yale Law School, I learned more than can be conveyed. Paul Brest first imagined me (over my dissent) as a law professor. Cass Sunstein has been my most constant colleague.

Susanne Baer helped develop comparative materials for *Sex Equality* at an early stage. Lisa Cardyn's historical suggestions at a late stage deepened and sharpened every chapter. Victoria Brescoll researched social science literatures with skill. Research assistants who contributed to this project as colleagues also include Karen E. Davis, Margaret Baldwin, Kaethe Hoffer, Natalie Nenadic, Lila Lee, and Diane Rosenfeld.

Martha Nussbaum's classical erudition improved Chapter 1. Larry W. Sager's bibliographical suggestions helped Chapter 2. Steve Schulhofer and Janine Benedet contributed beneficial readings of Chapter 7.1. Presentation at a student seminar at the Yale Law School and a Law and Philosophy workshop at the University of Chicago Law School, and perceptive critical readings by Marc Spindelman, Christopher Kendall, Susanne Baer, Jim Madigan, John Stoltenberg, Cass Sunstein, Wendy Adams, Martha Nussbaum, and Karen E. Davis, improved Chapter 8. Carl Seele's research on surrogacy was indispensable to Chapter 9. Melissa Farley, Dorchen Leid-

---

* In approximate order of their appearance in this book, cases that were particularly formative in this process were: *Andrews v. Law Society of British Columbia, Pennsylvania NOW v. Commonwealth of Pennsylvania, R. v. Keegstra, Tomen v. Ontario Teachers Federation, Queen v. Seaboyer, Meritor Savings Bank v. Vinson, Alexander v. Yale, United States v. Lanier, Jane Doe v. Police Commissioners, Kadic v. Karadžić, Oncale v. Sundowner Off-shore Services, Borowski v. Canada, Daigle v. Trembley, R. v. Sullivan & Lemay, Thoreson v. Guccione, Hudnut v. American Booksellers, Village Books v. Bellingham, Estates of French & Mahaffey v. Ontario, United States v. Alkhabaz (a/k/a Jake Baker), R.A.V. v. St. Paul, Robinson v. Jacksonville Shipyards, R. v. Butler,* and *Little Sisters Book & Art Emporium v. Canada Customs.* This list will also serve as disclosure.

holdt, and Jessica Neuwirth gave helpful comments on Chapter 10.1. Cass Sunstein commented on many chapters and engaged ideas large and small.

The exceptional law library research staff at the University of Michigan, particularly Barbara Vaccaro Garavaglia and Nancy Vettorello, located sources with expertise and resourcefulness. Skilled secretarial support of the highest quality was provided by Lu Ann Carter at Stanford, David Rayson at Minnesota, and most of all by Rita Rendell at Michigan. John Stoltenberg's world-class editorial and technical skills improved every page. Paula Payton and Christine Killen persisted in tracking down permissions where others would have given up.

A small army of students checked the citations. I am profoundly grateful to each of them for caring to get this right. Maia B. Goodell's sustained and multifaceted contributions approach the heroic. Brian Lehman, Michelle F. Seldin, and Eileen Kiernan each came through at especially difficult times. Valerie Hletko and Rabeha Shereen Kamaluddin pursued elusive foreign citations. Rebecca Brandman and Jane Larrington performed challenging flyspecking. A team of students at the University of Michigan that, at one time or another, also included Patience Atkin, Laura A. Biancke, Rebecca M. Brandman, Heather V. Burror, Huiya Helen Chen, Aaron A. Fate, Michelle Foster, Jennifer Frauson, David Gubbini, Christie J. Hartley, Lawrence S. Hashima, Monika Jeetu, Amy E. Nordeng, Tracey G. Parr, Christina Parker, Colette B. Routel, Robert Alexander Sanders, Michelle F. Seldin, Christina Thacker, Agnieszka Was, Dennis Westlind, and Gillian Wood applied themselves with devotion to accuracy. Paul Hunt pulled this laboring oar the longest, cite-checking case extracts and more for four years. All sacrificed their own projects for this one.

The University of Chicago Law School generously supported the many students there who gave so much to this volume. Brian Lehman, Catharine Clark, Sonia Katyal, Jennifer Thornton, and Claudia Halbac made particularly substantive contributions. Exacting cite-checking was also done by Rachel Brown, Brian Butler, Elizabeth Derbes, Yolanda Gamboa, Chrystal Jensen, Mary M. Kimura, Michelle Lawner, Julia Lee, Laura McFarland-Taylor (at DePaul), Melinda Patterson, and (as an undergraduate) Laura Sjoberg.

A valuable year at the Institute for Advanced Study, Berlin, provided the opportunity to reconceive the book as a whole, to add comparative depth, and to begin final writing. Dick Fenton envisioned *Sex Equality* as a Foundation Press book; the guidance of Steve Errick made it one. I thank them both. Little of the work that went into this book would have been possible without the constant support of Lee Bollinger and Jeffrey Lehman, successive Deans of the University of Michigan Law School. Their generosity and steadfastness have my gratitude always.

Special friends gave love and hope. I would never have made it without them.

I realized I had to write this book when one of my best students, Christine Littleton (Professor of Law at UCLA), said she couldn't teach the materials by themselves because the course was "just too big intellectually." If she couldn't, likely no one else could either. About fifteen years later, when I described the almost finished volume to my friend Kathleen Sullivan (now

Dean of Stanford Law School), she exclaimed, "Great, you put your life's work in a book!" Blessedly, I hadn't seen that before. I hope the result approaches what Chris wanted and Kathleen saw.

PERMISSIONS

Foundation Press and the author gratefully acknowledge the authors and publishers who gave us permission to excerpt and quote from the following copyrighted works:

Abrams, Kathryn, "Complex Claimants and Reductive Moral Judgments: New Patterns in the Search for Equality," 57 *U. Pitt. L. Rev.* 337 (1996), by permission of the *University of Pittsburgh Law Review*.

Abrams, Kathryn, "Gender Discrimination and the Transformation of Workplace Norms," 42 *Vand. L. Rev.* 1183 (1989), by permission of the author and the *Vanderbilt Law Review*.

Allard, Sharon Angella, "Rethinking Battered Woman Syndrome: A Black Feminist Perspective," 1 *UCLA Women's L.J.* 191 (1991). Copyright 1991, the Regents of the University of California. All rights reserved. By permission of the UCLA School of Law.

Allen, Anita L., "Privacy, Surrogacy, and the *Baby M*. Case," 76 *Geo. L.J.* 1759 (1988), © 1988, by permission of Georgetown University and *Georgetown Law Journal*.

Allen, Anita L., "Surrogacy, Slavery, and the Ownership of Life," 13 *Harv. J.L. & Pub. Pol'y* 139 (1990), by permission of the *Harvard Journal of Law & Public Policy*.

Almodovar, Norma Jean, "For Their Own Good: The Results of the Prostitution Laws as Enforced by Cops, Politicians and Judges," 10 *Hastings Women's L.J.* 119 (1999), © 1999 by the University of California, Hastings College of the Law. By permission.

American Association of University Women Educational Foundation, *How Schools Shortchange Girls—The AAUW Report* (1992), by permission of the American Association of University Women.

Anderson, Karen, *Changing Woman* (1996), by permission of Oxford University Press.

Andrews, Lori B., *Between Strangers: Surrogate Mothers, Expectant Fathers, and Brave New Babies* (1989), copyright © 1989 by Lori Andrews, by permission of HarperCollins Publishers.

Andrews, Lori B., "Beyond Doctrinal Boundaries: A Legal Framework for Surrogate Motherhood," 81 *Va. L. Rev.* 2343 (1995), by permission of the *Virginia Law Review*.

Antioch College Community, The Antioch College Sexual Offense Prevention Policy (June 1996), by permission of Antioch College.

Aristotle, *The Nicomachean Ethics* (J.L. Ackrill & J.O. Urmson eds., David Ross trans., Oxford Univ. Press 1980), by permission of Oxford University Press.

Aristotle, *The Politics of Aristotle* (Ernest Barker trans., Oxford Univ. Press 1946), by permission of Oxford University Press.

Becker, Mary E., "The Abuse Excuse and Patriarchal Narratives," 92 *Nw. U. L. Rev.* 1459 (1998), by special permission of Northwestern University School of Law, *Law Review*.

Becker, Mary E., "The Politics of Women's Wrongs and the Bill of Rights: A Bicentennial Perspective," 59 *U. Chi. L. Rev.* 453 (1992), by permission of *The University of Chicago Law Review*.

Bell, Derrick, *Race, Racism and American Law* (3d ed. 1992), by permission of Aspen Publishers, Inc.

Bem, Sandra L. & Daryl J. Bem, "Homogenizing the American Woman: The Power of an Unconscious Ideology," *in Feminist Frameworks: Alternative Theoretical Accounts of the Relations Between Women and Men* 7 (Alison Jagger & Paula Rothenberg Struhl eds., 1978), by permission of Daryl J. Bem.

Benedet, Janine, "Hostile Environment Sexual Harassment Claims and the Unwelcome Influence of Rape Law," 3 *Mich. J. Gender & L.* 125 (1995), by permission of the University of Michigan Law School.

Beneke, Timothy, *Men on Rape* (1982), copyright © 1982 by Timothy Beneke, by permission of St. Martin's Press, L.L.C.

Bennoune, Karima, "S.O.S. Algeria: Women's Human Rights Under Siege," *in Faith and Freedom: Women's Human Rights in the Muslim World* 184 (Mahnaz Afkhami ed., 1995), by permission of I.B. Tauris & Co. Ltd.

Berger, Vivian, "Review Essay—Not So Simple Rape," 7 *Crim. Just. Ethics* 69 (1988), by permission of the author and the Institute for Criminal Justice Ethics, 555 West 57th Street, Suite 601, New York, New York 10019-1029.

Berns, Sandra, *To Speak as a Judge: Difference, Voice and Power* (1999), by permission of Ashgate Publishing.

Bernstein, Elizabeth, "What's Wrong with Prostitution? What's Right with Sex Work? Comparing Markets in Female Sexual Labor," 10 *Hastings Women's L.J.* 91 (1999), © 1999 by the University of California, Hastings College of the Law, by permission.

Bersani, Leo, "Is the Rectum a Grave?," 43 *October* 197 (1987), by permission of the author.

Bird, Robert C., "More Than a Congressional Joke: A Fresh Look at the Legislative History of Sex Discrimination of the 1964 Civil Rights Act," 3 *Wm. & Mary J. Women & L.* 137 (1997), by permission of the *William and Mary Journal of Women and the Law*.

Boserup, Ester, "Economic Change and the Roles of Women," *in Persistent Inequalities: Women and World Development* 14 (Irene Tinker ed., 1990), by permission of Oxford University Press.

Boswell, John, *Christianity, Social Tolerance and Homosexuality: Gay People in Western Europe from the Beginning of the Christian Era to the Fourteenth Century* (1980), © 1980 by the University of Chicago, by permission of the University of Chicago Press.

Brake, Deborah & Elizabeth Caitlin, "The Path of Most Resistance: The Long Road Toward Gender Equity in Intercollegiate Athletics," 3 *Duke J. Gender L. & Pol'y* 51 (1996), by permission of the *Duke Journal of Gender & Policy*.

Brodsky, Gwen & Shelagh Day, *Canadian Charter Equality Rights for Women: One Step Forward or Two Steps Back?* (1989), by permission of the authors.

Brown, Jennifer K., "The Nineteenth Amendment and Women's Equality," 102 *Yale L.J.* 2175 (1993), by permission of the Yale Law Journal Company and Fred B. Rothman & Company.

Brownmiller, Susan, *Against Our Will: Men, Women and Rape* (1975), by permission of Simon & Schuster. Copyright © 1975 by Susan Brownmiller.

Brownmiller, Susan, "Speaking Out on Prostitution," *in Radical Feminism* 72 (Anne Koedt et al., 1973), by permission of the author.

Brownworth, Victoria A., "An Unreported Crisis," *Advocate*, Nov. 5, 1991, by permission of the author.

Bryden, David P. & Sonja Lengnick, "Rape in the Criminal Justice System," 87 *J. Crim. L. & Criminology* 1194 (1997), by permission of Northwestern University School of Law.

Bunch, Charlotte, "Not for Lesbians Only," *Quest*, Fall 1975, at 50, by permission of the author.

Burgess-Jackson, Keith, *Rape: A Philosophical Investigation* (1996), by permission of the author.

Burkett, Elinor, " 'God Created Me to Be a Slave,' " *N.Y. Times Mag.*, Oct. 12, 1997, at 56, by permission of *The New York Times*.

Caldwell, Gillian et al., Global Survival Network, *Crime and Servitude: An Exposé of the Traffic in Women for Prostitution from the Newly Independent States* (1997), by permission of the Global Survival Network.

Callahan, Joan C. & Dorothy E. Roberts, "A Feminist Social Justice Approach to Reproduction-Assisting Technologies: A Case Study on the Limits of Liberal Theory," 84 *Ky. L.J.* 1197 (1995–96), by permission of the authors.

Capers, I. Bennett, Note, "Sex(ual Orientation) and Title VII," 91 *Colum. L. Rev.* 1158 (1991), by permission of the *Columbia Law Review*.

Carter, Vednita & Evelina Giobbe, "Duet: Prostitution, Racism, and Feminist Discourse," 10 *Hastings Women's L.J.* 37 (1999), © 1999 by the University of California, Hastings College of the Law. By permission.

Case, Mary Anne C., "Disaggregating Gender from Sex and Sexual Orientation: The Effeminate Man in the Law and Feminist Jurisprudence," 105 *Yale L.J.* 1 (1995) by permission of the Yale Law Journal Company and Fred B. Rothman & Company.

Cerullo, Margaret, "Hidden History: An Illegal Abortion in 1968," *in From Abortion to Reproductive Freedom: Transforming a Movement* 87 (Marlene Gerber Fried ed., 1990), by permission of South End Press.

Chamallas, Martha, "The Architecture of Bias: Deep Structures in Tort Law," 146 *U. Pa. L. Rev.* 463 (1998), by permission of the *University of Pennsylvania Law Review* and William S. Hein & Company, Inc.

Chandler, Joan M., "The Association of Intercollegiate Athletics for Women: The End of Amateurism in U.S. Intercollegiate Sport," *in Women in Sport: Sociological and Historical Perspectives* 5 (Amy L. Reeder and John R. Fuller eds., West Georgia College Studies in the Social Sciences, vol. 24, 1985), by permission of West Georgia College.

Chavkin, Wendy, Barbara Katz Rothman & Rayna Rapp, "Alternative Modes of Reproduction: Other Views and Questions," *in Reproductive Laws for the 1990s* 405 (Sherrill Cohen & Nadine Taub eds., 1989), by permission of Humana Press, Inc.

Cherry, April L., "A Feminist Understanding of Sex-Selective Abortion: Solely a Matter of Choice?," 10 *Wis. Women's L.J.* 161 (1995), by permission of the *Wisconsin Women's Law Journal*.

Chesler, Phyllis, *Sacred Bond: The Legacy of Baby M* (1988), by permission of Random House, Inc.

Chinery-Hesse, Mary, Bina Agarwal, Jamilah Ariffin, Tendai Bare, Dharam Ghai, Marjorie Lamont Henriques, Richard Jolly, Iola Mathews, Carolyn McAskie & Frances Stewart, *Engendering Adjustment for the 1990s: Report of a Commonwealth Expert Group on Women & Structural Adjustment* (1989), by permission of the Commonwealth Secretariat [London].

Clark, Homer H., The Law of Domestic Relations in the United States (2nd ed. 1987), by permission of the West Group.

Clark, Lorenne M.G., "Liberalism and Pornography," *in Pornography and Censorship* 52–53 (David Copp & Susan Wendell, eds. 1983), copyright 1983, by permission of the publisher, Prometheus Books, Amherst, New York.

Cline, Victor, "An Introduction," *in Where Do You Draw the Line* 3 (Victor Cline ed., 1974), by permission of the author.

Cole, Susan, *Pornography and the Sex Crisis* (1989), by permission of Second Story Press, Toronto.

Coles, Robert & Jane Hallowell Coles, *Women of Crisis* (1978), by permission of Robert Coles, M.D.

Collins, Patricia Hill, "It's All in the Family: Intersections of Gender, Race, and Nation," *Hypatia: J. Feminist Phil.*, Summer 1998, at 62, by permission of the author.

Colker, Ruth, "An Equal Protection Analysis of U.S. Reproductive Health Policy: Gender, Race, Age and Class," 1991 *Duke L.J.* 324, by permission of *Duke Law Journal*.

Colker, Ruth, "Whores, Fags, Dumb-Ass Women, Surly Blacks, and Competent Heterosexual White Men: The Sexual and Racial Morality Underlying Anti-Discrimination Doctrine," 7 *Yale J.L. & Feminism* 195 (1995), by permission of the *Yale Journal of Law and Feminism*.

Combahee River Collective, "A Black Feminist Statement," *in Capitalist Patriarchy and the Case for Socialist Feminism* 362 (Zillah R. Eisenstein ed., 1979), by permission of Monthly Review Press.

Cook, Blanche Wiesen, "The Historical Denial of Lesbianism," 20 *Radical Hist. Rev.* 60 (1979), by permission of Cambridge University Press.

Coombs, Mary, "Comment: Between Women/Between Men: The Significance for Lesbianism of Historical Understandings of Same-(Male)Sex Sexual Activities," 8 *Yale J.L. & Human.* 241 (1996), by permission of the author and the *Yale Journal of Law & the Humanities*.

Corea, Gena, *The Mother Machine: Reproductive Technologies from Artificial Insemination to Artificial Wombs* (1985). Copyright © 1985 by Gena Corea. By permission of HarperCollins Publishers.

Corea, Gena, "The Reproductive Brothel," *in Man-Made Women: How New Reproductive Technologies Affect Women* 38 (Gena Corea et al. eds., 1987), by permission of Indiana University Press, Bloomington & Indianapolis.

Cornell, Stephen, *The Return of the Native: American Indian Political Resurgence* (1988), by permission of Oxford University Press.

Cott, Nancy F., *The Grounding of Modern Feminism* (1987), by permission of Yale University Press.

Cott, Nancy F., *Bonds of Womanhood: "Woman's Sphere" in New England, 1780–1835* (2d ed. 1997), © 1977 by Yale University, by permission of Yale University Press.

Crenshaw, Kimberlé W., "Demarginalizing the Intersection of Race and Sex: A Black Feminist Critique of Antidiscrimination Doctrine, Feminist Theory and

Antiracist Politics," 1989 *U. Chi. Legal F.* 139 (1989), by permission of the University of Chicago Law School.

Crocker, Phyllis L., "Childhood Abuse and Adult Murder: Implications for the Death Penalty," 77 *N.C. L. Rev.* 1143 (1999), © 1999 by the North Carolina Law Review Association. By permission.

Crocker, Phyllis L., "Annotated Bibliography on Sexual Harassment in Education," 7 *Women's Rts. L. Rep.* 91 (1982), by permission of the author and the *Women's Rights Law Reporter*.

Crocker, Phyllis L. & Anne E. Simon, "Sexual Harassment in Education," 10 *Cap. U. L. Rev.* 541 (1981), by permission of the *Capital University Law Review*.

Czapanskiy, Karen, "Domestic Violence, the Family, and the Lawyering Process: Lessons from Studies on Gender Bias in the Courts," 27 *Fam. L.Q.* 247 (1993), by permission of ABA Publishing.

Dahl, Robert, "Equality versus Inequality," 29 *PS: Political Science & Politics* 639 (1996), by permission of the author.

Daniels, Roger, "Why It Happened Here," *in Racism in California: A Reader in the History of Oppression* 177 (1972), by permission of the author.

Darrow, Whitney Jr. & Kraus, Robert, *I'm Glad I'm a Boy! I'm Glad I'm a Girl!* (1970), by permission of Robert Kraus.

Davis, Angela Y., "Outcast Mothers and Surrogates: Racism and Reproductive Politics in the Nineties," *in American Feminist Thought at Century's End: A Reader* 355 (Linda S. Kauffman ed., 1993), by permission of Blackwell Publishers.

Davis, Angela Y., *Women, Race & Class* (1983), © 1981 by Angela Davis, by permission of Random House, Inc.

De Beauvoir, Simone, *The Second Sex* (H.M. Parshley ed. & trans., 1974), copyright 1952 and renewed 1980 by Alfred A. Knopf, Inc. By permission of Alfred A. Knopf, a division of Random House, Inc.

Dershowitz, Alan, "False Equality for Swept-up Johns," *L.A. Times*, Jan. 24, 1985, part 2, at 5, by permission of the author.

Diduck, Alison & Helena Orton, "Equality and Support for Spouses," 57 *Mod. L. Rev.* 681 (1994), by permission of Blackwell Publishers.

Ditmore, Melissa, Network of Sex Projects, "Addressing Sex Work as Labour," *in Trafficking and The Global Sex Industry: Need for Human Rights Framework* 34 (Geneva, June 21–22, 1999), by permission of the author.

Dobash, R. Emerson & Russell P. Dobash, "Wives: The Appropriate Victims of Marital Violence," 2 *Victimology* 426 (1978), by permission of Rebecca Dobash.

Dobkowski, Michael N., *The Tarnished Dream: The Basis of American Anti-Semitism* (1979), by permission of Greenwood Publishing Group Inc.

Dolgin, Janet L., "Status and Contract in Surrogate Motherhood: An Illumination of the Surrogacy Debate," 38 *Buffalo L. Rev.* 515 (1990), © 1990 *Buffalo Law Review*, by permission of the *Buffalo Law Review*.

Dominga Trapasso, Rosa, "Clandestine Prostitution in Peru," address at Trafficking in Women Conference (1988), by permission of the author.

Douglas, William O., *The Court Years: 1939–1975* (1980), by permission of Random House, Inc.

Drexler, Jessica N., "Government's Role in Turning Tricks: The World's Oldest Profession in the Netherlands and the United States," 15 *Dick. J. Int'l L.* 201 (1996), by permission of the *Dickinson Journal of International Law*.

Dunlap, Mary C., "Toward Recognition of 'A Right to be Sexual,'" 7 *Women's Rts. L. Rep.* 245 (1982), by permission of the author and the *Women's Rights Law Reporter*.

Dworkin, Andrea, "Against the Male Flood: Censorship, Pornography and Equality," 8 *Harv. Women's L.J.* 1 (1985), by permission of the author.

Dworkin, Andrea, *Intercourse* (1987), copyright © 1987, 1997 by Andrea Dworkin, by permission of The Free Press, a division of Simon & Schuster.

Dworkin, Andrea, *Letters from a War Zone* (1988), copyright © 1993, 1988, published by Lawrence Hill Books, an imprint of Chicago Review Press, Inc. 814 North Franklin Street, Chicago, Illinois 60610, by permission of the Elaine Markson Literary Agency and Lawrence Hill Books.

Dworkin, Andrea, *Our Blood: Prophecies and Discourses on Sexual Politics* (1975), by permission of the Elaine Markson Literary Agency.

Dworkin, Andrea, "Pornography Is a Civil Rights Issue for Women," 21 *U. Mich. J.L. Reform* 55 (1987/1988), by permission of the author.

Dworkin, Andrea, *Pornography: Men Possessing Women* (E.P. Dutton, 1989) (1981), by permission of the author.

Dworkin, Andrea, "Prostitution and Male Supremacy," 1 *Mich. J. Gender & L.* 1 (1993), by permission of the author and the *University of Michigan Journal of Gender and the Law*.

Dworkin, Andrea, *Right-wing Women* (1983), by permission of the author and the Elaine Markson Literary Agency.

Dworkin, Andrea, *Life and Death* (1977), by permission of the author.

Eaton, Mary, "At the Intersection of Gender and Sexual Orientation: Toward Lesbian Jurisprudence," 3 *S. Cal. Rev. L. & Women's Stud.* 183 (1994), by permission of the author and the *USC Review of Law and Women's Studies*.

Editors of the *Harvard Law Review, Sexual Orientation and the Law* (1990), copyright © 1989, by permission of Harvard Law Review Association.

Edwards, Susan, "The Legal Regulation of Prostitution: A Human Rights Issue," in *Rethinking Prostitution: Purchasing Sex in the 1990s*, at 57 (Graham Scambler & Annette Scambler eds., 1997), by permission of International Thomson Publishing Services.

Eichler, Margrit, "The Limits of Family Law Reform or, The Privatization of Female and Child Poverty," 7 *Canadian Fam. L. Q.* 59 (1990–91), by permission of Carswell, a division of Thomson Canada Limited.

Elizabeth Fry Society of Toronto, *Streetwork Outreach with Adult Female Prostitutes: Final Report* (1987), by permission of the Elizabeth Fry Society of Toronto.

Ellman, Ira Mark, "The Theory of Alimony," 77 *Cal. L. Rev.* 1 (1989), © 1989 by California Law Review, Inc., by permission of the University of California Press.

El Saadawi, Nawal, *The Hidden Face of Eve: Women in the Arab World* (Sherif Hetata ed. & trans., 1980), by permission of Zed Books.

England, Paula & Barbara Stanek Kilbourne, "Markets, Marriages, and Other Mates: The Problem of Power," in *Beyond the Marketplace: Rethinking Economy and Society* 163 (Roger Friedland & A.F. Robertson eds., 1990), by permission of Walter DeGruyter Inc.

Engels, Friedrich, *The Origin of the Family, Private Property, and the State* (Alec West trans., 1972) (1884), by permission of International Publishers Co., Inc.

English, Deirdre, "The Politics of Pornography," *Mother Jones*, Apr. 1980, at 48, © 1980 Foundation for National Progress, by permission of *Mother Jones*.

Epstein, Cynthia Fuchs, "Multiple Myths and Outcomes of Sex Segregation," 14 *N.Y.L. Sch. J. Hum. Rts.* 185 (1998), by permission of the *New York Law School Journal of Human Rights.*

Epstein, Richard Allen, *Forbidden Grounds: The Case Against Employment Discrimination Laws* (1992), Cambridge, Massachussets: Harvard University Press, copyright © 1992 the President and Fellows of Harvard College, by permission of the publishers.

Epstein, Richard A., "Gender Is for Nouns," 41 *DePaul L. Rev.* 981 (1992), by permission of the *DePaul Law Review.*

Erickson, Nancy, "Women and the Supreme Court: Anatomy Is Destiny," 41 *Brook. L. Rev.* 209 (1974), © 1974 by Nancy Erickson, by permission of the *Brooklyn Law Review.*

Estrich, Susan, *Real Rape* (1987), copyright © 1987 by the President and Fellows of Harvard College, by permission of Harvard University Press.

Estrich, Susan, "Rape," 95 *Yale L.J.* 1087 (1986), by permission of the Yale Law Journal Company and Fred B. Rothman & Company.

Estrich, Susan, "Sex at Work," 43 *Stan. L. Rev.* 813 (1991), by permission of the Copyright Clearance Center.

Faculty Affairs Committee, Univ. of Minn., *Sexual Harassment Policy & Procedure* (Spring 1984), by permission of the University of Minnesota.

Fajer, Marc A., "Can Two Real Men Eat Quiche Together?: Storytelling, Gender-Role Stereotypes, and Legal Protection for Lesbians and Gay Men," 46 *U. Miami L. Rev.* 511 (1992), by permission of the *University of Miami Law Review.*

Fallon, Richard H. Jr., "Sexual Harassment, Content Neutrality, and the First Amendment Dog That Didn't Bark," 1994 *Sup. Ct. Rev.* 1, © 1995 by the University of Chicago, by permission of the author and the University of Chicago Press.

Faludi, Susan, *Backlash* (1991), by permission of Random House, Inc.

Farley, Melissa, Isin Baral, Merab Kiremire & Ufuk Sezgin, "Prostitution in Five Countries: Violence and Post-traumatic Stress Disorder," 8 *Feminism and Psychol.* 405 (1998), by permission of Melissa Farley and Sage Publications.

Feminist Anti-Censorship Task Force, "Amici Curiae Brief in *American Booksellers Ass'n v. Hudnut*," 21 *Mich. J.L. Reform* 69 (1988), by permission of the *Michigan Journal of Law Reform.*

Field, Martha, "Killing 'the Handicapped,'" 16 *Harv. Women's L.J.* 79 (1993), © 1993 by permission of the President and Fellows of Harvard College and the *Harvard Women's Law Journal.*

Field, Martha A., "Surrogacy Contracts—Gestational and Traditional: The Argument for Nonenforcement," 31 *Washburn L.J.* 1 (1991), by permission of the *Washburn Law Journal.*

Fitzgerald, Louise F., S. Swan & K. Fischer, "Why Didn't She Just Report Him?," 51 *J. Soc. Issues* 117 (1995), by permission of Blackwell Publishers.

Fortune Magazine, Advertisement, Feb. 17, 1989, copyright © 1989 Time Inc. All rights reserved. By permission.

Foucault, Michel, 1 *The History of Sexuality* (Robert Hurley trans., New York: Random House). Originally published in French as *La Volonté de Savoir.* Copyright © 1976 by Editions Gallimard. By permission of Georges Borchardt, Inc.

Franklin, John Hope, "History of Racial Segregation in the United States," *Annals Am. Acad. Pol. Soc. Sci.*, Mar 1956, at 1, by permission of Sage Publications Inc.

Goldhagen, Daniel Jonah, *Hitler's Willing Executioners: Ordinary Germans and the Holocaust* (1996), by permission of Random House, Inc., a Knopf Imprint.

Goldberg, Susan, "Medical Choices During Pregnancy: Whose Decision Is It Anyway?," 41 *Rutgers L. Rev.* 591, (1989), by permission of the author.

Goldstein, Anne Tierney, Center for Reproductive Law & Policy, *Recognizing Forced Impregnation as a War Crime Under International Law* (1993), by permission of the Center for Reproductive Law and Policy.

Goldstein, Anne B., Comment, "History, Homosexuality, and Political Values: Searching for the Hidden Determinants of *Bowers v. Hardwick*," 97 *Yale L.J.* 1073 (1988), by permission of the Yale Law Journal Company and Fred B. Rothman & Company.

Gordon, Linda, *Woman's Body, Woman's Right: A Social History of Birth Control in America* (1976), by permission of the author.

Graham, Katharine, *Personal History* (1997), by permission of the author.

Gray, C. Boyden, "Disparate Impact: History and Consequences," 54 *La. L. Rev.* 1487 (1994), by permission of the *Louisiana Law Review*.

Graycar, Regina & Jenny Morgan, *The Hidden Gender of Law* (Regina Graycar & Jenny Morgan eds., 1990), by permission of Federation Press.

Guinier, Lani, Michelle Fine & Jane Balin, *Becoming Gentlemen: Women, Law School, and Institutional Change* (1997), by permission of Beacon Press.

Gutek, Barbara A., *Sex and the Workplace* (1985), by permission of the author.

Hacker, Helen, "Women as a Minority Group," 30 *Soc. Forces* 60 (Oct. 1951), by permission of the University of North Carolina Press.

Hadfield, Gillian K., "An Expressive Theory of Contract: From Feminist Dilemmas to a Reconceptualization of Rational Choice in Contract Law," 146 *U. Pa. L. Rev.* 1235 (1998), by permission of the copyright holder, the *University of Pennsylvania Law Review*.

Haney López, Ian F., *White by Law: The Legal Construction of Race* (1996), by permission of New York University Press.

Harris, Melody, "Hitting 'Em Where It Hurts: Using Title IX Litigation to Bring Gender Equity to Athletics," 72 *Denv. U. L. Rev.* 57 (1994), by permission of the *Denver University Law Review*.

Hartmann, Heidi, "Capitalism, Patriarchy, and Job Segregation by Sex," 1 *Signs* 137 (1976), © 1976 by the University of Chicago Press, by permission of the University of Chicago Press.

Halttunen, Karen, "Humanitarianism and the Pornography of Pain in Anglo-American Culture," 100 *Am. Hist. Rev.* 303 (1995), by permission of the author.

Herman, Judith Lewis, M.D., *Trauma and Recovery* (1992). Copyright © 1992 by BasicBooks, a division of HarperCollins Publishers Inc. By permission of BasicBooks, a member of Perseus Books, L.L.C.

Hochschild, Arlie with Anne Machung, *The Second Shift* (1989), © 1989 by Arlie Hochschild, by permission of Viking Penguin, a division of Penguin Putnam.

hooks, bell, *Yearning: Race, Gender and Cultural Politics* (1990), by permission of South End Press.

Holsopple, Kelly, "Strip Clubs According to Strippers: Exposing Workplace Sexual Violence," *in Making the Harm Visible: Global Sexual Exploitation of Women and Girls* 252 (Donna Hughes & Claire Roche eds., 1999), by permission of Kelly Holsopple.

Hunter, Nan, "Marriage, Law, and Gender: A Feminist Inquiry," 1 *Law & Sexuality* 9 (1991), by permission.

Lee, Lila, "FACT's Fictions and Feminism's Future: An Analysis of the FACT Brief's Treatment of Pornography's Victims," 75 *Chi.-Kent L. Rev.* 785 (2000), by permission of the *Chicago-Kent Law Review*.

Lees, Sue, *Carnal Knowledge: Rape on Trial* (1996) (Penguin Books, 1996), copyright © Sue Lees, 1996, by permission of the publisher.

Leidholdt, Dorchen, "Prostitution: A Violation of Women's Human Rights," 1 *Cardozo Women's L.J.* 133 (1993), by permission of the *Cardozo Women's Law Journal*.

Lemaire, Lyn, "Women and Athletics: Toward a Physicality Perspective," 5 *Harv. Women's L.J.* 121 (1982), ©1982 by the President and Fellows of Harvard College and the *Harvard Women's Law Journal*, by permission of the *Harvard Women's Law Journal*.

Li, Xiaorong, "License to Coerce: Violence Against Women, State Responsibility, and Legal Failures in China's Family-Planning Program," 8 *Yale J.L. & Feminism* 145 (1996), by permission of the Yale Journal of Law & Feminism, Inc.

Littleton, Christine A., "Reconstructing Sexual Equality," 75 *Cal. L. Rev.* 1279 (1987), © 1987 by California Law Review, Inc., by permission of the author and the University of California Press.

Lorde, Audre, *Zami: A New Spelling of My Name* (1982), © 1982, published by The Crossing Press, Freedom, California, by permission.

MacKinnon, Catharine A. & Andrea Dworkin, *In Harm's Way: The Pornography Civil Rights Hearings* (1997), by permission of Catharine A. MacKinnon, Andrea Dworkin, Linda Borman, R.M.M., and Carole laFavor.

MacKinnon, Catharine A., *Toward a Feminist Theory of the State* (1989), by permission of the author.

MacKinnon, Catharine A., "Reflections of Sex Equality Under the Law," 100 *Yale L.J.* 1281 (1991), by permission of the author and the Yale Law Journal Company and Fred B. Rothman & Company.

Madigan, Lee & Gamble, Nancy C., *The Second Rape* (1991), by permission of University Press of America.

Mahoney, Martha R., "Legal Images of Battered Women: Redefining the Issue of Separation," 90 *Mich. L. Rev.* 1 (1991), copyright 1991 by the Michigan Law Review Association, by permission of the *Michigan Law Review* and the author.

Maine, Sir Henry Sumner, *Ancient Law: Its Connection with the Early History, and Its Relation to Modern Ideas* (new ed., John Murray 1930) (1861), copyright © 1986 the Arizona Board of Regents, by permission of the University of Arizona Press.

Malveaux, Julianne, "Comparable Worth and Its Impact on Black Women," 14 *Rev. Black Pol. Econ.* 47 (1985-1986), by permission of the *Review of Black Political Economy*.

Massaro, Toni M., "Experts, Psychology, Credibility, and Rape: The Rape Trauma Syndrome Issue and Its Implications for Expert Psychological Testimony," 69 *Minn. L.R.* 395 (1985), by permission of the author.

Matsuda, Mari J., "Standing Beside My Sister, Facing the Enemy: Legal Theory Out of Coalition," *in Where Is Your Body? And Other Essays on Race, Gender & The Law* 61 (1996), by permission of Beacon Press.

Mazur, Amy G., *Gender Bias and the State: Symbolic Reform at Work in Fifth Republic France* (1995), © 1995, by permission of the University of Pittsburgh Press.

McCaffery, Edward, "Slouching Towards Equality: Gender Discrimination, Market Efficiency, and Social Change," 103 *Yale L.J.* 595 (1993), by permission of the Yale Law Journal Company and Fred B. Rothman & Company.

McCaw, Jodee M. & Charlene Y. Senn, "Perceptions of Cues in Conflictual Dating Situations," 4 *Violence Against Women* 609 (1998), © 1998 by Sage Publications Inc., by permission of Sage Publications Inc.

McDougal, Myres S., Harold D. Lasswell & Lung-chu Chen, "Human Rights for Women and World Public Order: The Outlawing of Sex-Based Discrimination," 69 *Am. J. Int'l L.* 497 (1975), © The American Society of International Law, by permission.

McIntosh, Mary, "The Homosexual Role," 16 *Soc. Probs.* 182 (1968), ©1968 by the Society for the Study of Social Problems, by permission of the author and the University of California Press.

Messer, Ellen & Kathryn E. May eds., *Back Rooms: Voices from the Illegal Abortion Era* (Amherst, New York: Prometheus Books, 1994), copyright 1988, 1994, by permission of the publisher and Ellen Messer.

Michael, Robert T., *Pay Equity: Empirical Inquiries* vii (Robert T. Michael et al. eds., 1989), by permission of National Academy Press.

Mill, John Stuart, "The Subjection of Women," *in Three Essays* 425 (Oxford Univ. Press 1975) (1869), by permisson of Oxford University Press.

Mill, John Stuart, *On Liberty* (Liberty Arts Press 1956) (1859), by permission of Hackett Publishing Company, Inc. All rights reserved.

Miller, Jody, "Researching Violence Against Street Prostitutes: Issues of Epistemology, Methodology, and Ethics," *in Researching Sexual Violence Against Women: Methodological and Personal Perspectives* 144 (Martin D. Schwartz ed., 1997), copyright © 1997 by Sage Publications Inc., by permission of Sage Publications Inc.

Millett, Kate, *Sexual Politics* (New York: Simon & Schuster, 1969), copyright © 1969, 1970, 1990 by Kate Millet, by permission of Georges Borchardt, Inc., for the author.

Millett, Kate, *The Prostitution Papers* (Kate Millett ed., Paladin Books 1975) (1973), copyright © 1973, 1976 by Kate Millett, copyright © 1971 by Basic Books, by permission of Georges Borchardt, Inc., for the author.

Mirhosseini, Akran, "After the Revolution: Violations of Women's Human Rights in Iran," *in Women's Rights/Human Rights: International Feminist Perspectives* 72 (Julie Peters & Andrea Wolper eds., 1995), by permission of Julie Peters and Andrea Wolper.

Monnin, Paul Nicholas, "Proving Welcomeness: The Admissibility of Evidence of Sexual History in Sexual Harassment Claims Under the 1994 Amendments to Federal Rule of Evidence 412," 48 *Vand. L. Rev.* 1155 (1995), by permission of the *Vanderbilt Law Review.*

Minow, Martha, "Learning to Live with the Dilemma of Difference: Bilingual and Special Education," 48 *L. & Contemp. Probs.* 158 (1985), by permission of *Law and Contemporary Problems.*

Morgan, Denise C., "Finding a Constitutionally Permissible Path to Sex Equality: The Young Women's Leadership School of East Harlem," 14 *N.Y.L. Sch. J. Hum. Rts.* 95 (1998), by permission of the *New York Law School Journal of Human Rights.*

Morris, Danielle Keats, "*Planned Parenthood v. Casey*: From U.S. 'Rights Talk' to Western European 'Responsibility Talk,'" 16 *Fordham Int'l L.J.* 761 (1993), by permission of the *Fordham International Law Journal.*

Mossman, Mary Jane, "Feminism and Legal Method: The Difference It Makes," *in At the Boundaries of Law: Feminism and Legal Theory* 283 (Martha Fineman & Nancy S. Thomadsen eds., 1991), copyright © 1990, by permission of Routledge, Inc.

Myers, John E.B., Jan Bays, Judith Becker, Lucy Berliner, David L. Corwin & Karen J. Saywitz, "Expert Testimony in Child Sexual Abuse Litigation," 68 *Neb. L. Rev.* 1 (1989), © by the University of Nebraska, by permission of the University of Nebraska.

National Black Feminist Organization, "Statement of Purpose," *Ms.,* May 1974, at 99, by permission of *Ms.* magazine.

National Black Women's Health Project, "Reproductive Rights Position Paper," *in From Abortion to Reproductive Freedom: Transforming a Movement* 291 (Marlene Gerber Fried, ed., 1990), by permission of South End Press.

Needleman, Herbert L. & David Bellinger, "Recent Developments," 46 *Envtl. Res.* 190 (1988), by permission of the authors and Academic Press.

Nelson, Mariah Burton, *The Stronger Women Get, the More Men Love Football: Sexism and the American Culture of Sports* (1994), copyright © 1994 by Mariah Burton Nelson, by permission of Harcourt Brace & Company.

Niles, Donna Marie, "Confession of a Priestesstute," *in Sex Work: Writings by Women in the Sex Industry* 148 (Frédérique Delacoste & Priscilla Alexander eds., 1987), by permission of Cleis Press.

Nowrojee, Binaifer, *Shattered Lives: Sexual Violence During the Rwandan Genocide and Its Aftermath* (1996), by permission of Human Rights Watch.

Obiora, L. Amede, "Bridges and Barricades: Rethinking Polemics and Intransigence in the Campaign Against Female Circumcision," 47 *Case W. Res. L. Rev.* 275 (1997), by permission of the *Case Western Reserve Law Review.*

Offer of Proof Concerning the Testimony of Dr. Rosalind Rosenberg, *E.E.O.C.* v. *Sears,* 628 F. Supp. 1264 (N.D. Ill. 1986), *reprinted in* "Women's History Goes to Trial: [*EEOC v. Sears Roebuck and Company*]," 11 *Signs* 575 (1986), by permission of the University of Chicago Press.

Olsen, Frances, "Statutory Rape: A Feminist Critique of Rights Analysis," 63 *Tex. L. Rev.* 387 (1984), copyright 1984 by the Texas Law Review Association, by permission of the author and the *Texas Law Review.*

Olson, Wendy, "Beyond Title IX: Toward an Agenda for Women and Sports in the 1990's," 3 *Yale J.L. & Feminism* 105 (1990), by permission of the Yale Journal of Law & Feminism, Inc.

O'Melveny, Mary K., "Playing the 'Gender' Card: Affirmative Action and Working Women," 84 *Ky. L.J.* 863 (1995-96), by permission of the author.

Oppenheimer, David Benjamin, "Exacerbating the Exasperating: Title VII Liability of Employers for Sexual Harassment Committed by Their Supervisors," 81 *Cornell L. Rev.* 66 (1995), by permission of the *Cornell Law Review.*

O'Toole, Laura L. & Jessica R. Schiffman, *Gender Violence: Interdisciplinary Perspectives* 173 (Laura L. O'Toole & Jessica R. Schiffman eds., 1997), by permission of the authors.

Overall, Christine, *Human Reproduction: Principles, Practices, Policies* (1993) (Toronto: Oxford University Press Canada, 1993), © Christine Overall 1993, by permission of Oxford University Press.

Overall, Christine, "What's Wrong with Prostitution? Evaluating Sex Work," 17 *Signs* 705 (1992), © 1992 by The University of Chicago, by permission of the University of Chicago Press.

Padilla, Laura M., "Intersectionality and Positionality: Situating Women of Color in the Affirmative Action Dialogue," 66 *Fordham L. Rev.* 843 (1997), by permission of the *Fordham Law Review*.

Pateman, Carole, *The Sexual Contract* (1988), by permission of Stanford University Press.

Pharr, Suzanne, *Homophobia: A Weapon of Sexism* (1988), by permission of Chardon Press. Available from Women's Project, 2224 Main Street, Little Rock, Arkansas 72206

Phillips, Anne, *Engendering Democracy* (1991), by permission of the author.

Pitt, Jonathan B., "Fragmenting Procreation," 108 *Yale L.J.* 1893 (1999), by permission of the Yale Law Journal Company and Fred B. Rothman & Company.

Plummer, Kenneth, *Sexual Stigma: An Interactionist Account* (1975), by permission of the author.

Polikoff, Nancy, "We Will Get What We Ask For: Why Legalizing Gay and Lesbian Marriage Will Not 'Dismantle the Legal Structure of Gender in Every Marriage,'" 79 *Va. L. Rev.* 1535 (1993), by permission of the *University of Virginia Law Review*.

Posner, Richard A., "An Economic Analysis of Sex Discrimination Laws," 56 *U. Chi. L. Rev.* 1311 (1989), by permission of the *University of Chicago Law Review*.

Posner, Richard A., "The Ethics and Economics of Enforcing Contracts of Surrogate Motherhood," 5 *J. Contemp. Health L. & Pol'y* 21 (1989), by permission of the *Journal of Contemporary Health Law and Policy*.

Posner, Richard A., *Law and Literature* (1988), © 1990 by the President and Fellows of Harvard College, by permission of Harvard University Press.

Posner, Richard, "Free Speech in an Economic Perspective," 20 *Suffolk U. L. Rev.* 1 (1986), by permission of the *Suffolk Law Review*.

Powledge, Tabitha M., "Unnatural Selection: On Choosing Children's Sex," *in The Custom-Made Child?: Women-Centered Perspectives* 193 (Helen B. Holmes et al. eds., 1981), by permission of Humana Press, Inc.

Radin, Margaret, *Contested Commodities* (1996), © 1996 by the President and Fellows of Harvard College, by permission of Harvard University Press.

Radin, Margaret Jane, "What, If Anything, Is Wrong with Baby Selling?," 26 *Pac. L.J.* 135 (1995), by permission of *The Pacific Law Journal*.

Raymond, Janice G., "Reproductive Gifts and Gift Giving: The Altruistic Woman," 20 *Hastings Center Report*, Nov/Dec 1990, at 7, © The Hastings Center, by permission of the author and the Hastings Center.

Raymond, Janice G., *Women as Wombs* (1993), by permission of the author.

Reimann, Mathias, "Prurient Interest and Human Dignity: Pornography Regulation in West Germany and the United States," 21 *U. Mich. J.L. Reform* 201 (1987–88), by permission of the *University of Michigan Journal of Law Reform*.

Reist, Melinda Tankard, *Giving Sorrow Words: Women's Stories of Grief After Abortion* (2000), by permission of the author.

Resnik, Judith, "Dependent Sovereigns: Indian Tribes, States and the Federal Courts," 56 *U. Chi. L. Rev. 671 (1989),* by permission of University of Chicago Law School.

Rhode, Deborah L., *Speaking of Sex: The Denial of Gender Equality* (1997), copyright © 1997 by Deborah L. Rhode, by permission of Harvard University Press.

Rich, Adrienne, "Husband-Right and Father-Right," *in On Lies, Secrets, and Silence: Selected Prose 1766–1978,* at 219 (1979), copyright © 1979 by W.W.

Russell, Diana, E.H., *Rape, Child Sexual Abuse, Sexual Harassment in the Work-place: An Analysis of the Prevalence, Causes, and Recommended Solutions*, The Final Report for the California Commission on Crime Control and Violence Prevention (Mar. 1982), by permission of the author.

Russell, Diana E.H., *Rape in Marriage* (1990), by permission of Indiana University Press.

Russell, Diana E.H., "Pornography and Rape: A Causal Model," *in Making Violence Sexy: Feminist Views on Pornography* (1993), by permission of Blackwell Publishers Ltd.

Russo, Ann, "Feminists Confront Pornography's Subordinating Practices: Politics and Strategies for Change," *in Pornography: The Production and Consumption of Inequality* 8 (Gail Dines et al. eds., 1998), by permission of Taylor & Francis, Inc./Routledge, Inc., http://www.routledge-ny.com.

Rutherford, Charlotte, "Reproductive Freedoms and African American Women," 4 *Yale J.L. & Feminism* 255 (1992), by permission of the *Yale Journal of Law and Feminism*.

Sachs, Albie & Joan Hoff Wilson, *Sexism and the Law: A Study of Male Beliefs and Judicial Bias in Britain and the United States* (1978), by permission of the authors.

Sachs, Albie, *Protecting Human Rights in a New South Africa* (1990), by permission of the author.

Sarna, Jonathan D., "American Anti-Semitism," *in History and Hate: The Dimensions of Anti-Semitism* 115 (David Berger ed., 1986), by permission of the Jewish Publication Society.

Schafer, Carolyn M. & Marilyn Frye, "Rape and Respect," *in Feminism and Philosophy* 333 (Mary Vetterling-Braggin et al. eds., 1977), by permission of Littlefield Publishing.

Schnapper, Eric, "Affirmative Action and the Legislative History of the Fourteenth Amendment," 71 *Va. L. Rev.* 753 (1985), by permission of the *Virginia Law Review*.

Schuck, Peter H., "The Social Utility of Surrogacy," 13 *Harv. J.L. & Pub. Pol'y* 132 (1990), by permission of the *Harvard Journal of Law & Public Policy*.

Schulhofer, Stephen, J., *Unwanted Sex: The Culture of Intimidation and The Failure of Law* (1998), © 1998 by the President and Fellows of Harvard College, by permission of Harvard University Press.

Schultz, Marjorie M., "Abortion and the Maternal-Fetal Conflict: Broadening Our Concerns," 1 *S. Cal. Rev. L. & Women's Stud.* 79 (1990), by permission of the *Southern California Review of Law and Women's Studies*.

Schultz, Marjorie Maguire, "Reproductive Technology and Intent-Based Parenthood: An Opportunity for Gender Neutrality," 1990 *Wis. L. Rev.* 297, copyright 1990 by the Board of Regents of the University of Wisconsin System, by permission of the *Wisconsin Law Review*.

Schultz, Vicki, "Reconceptualizing Sexual Harassment," 107 *Yale L.J.* 1683 (1998), by permission of the Yale Law Journal Company and Fred B. Rothman & Company.

Schultz, Vicki & Stephen Petterson, "Race, Gender, Work, and Choice: An Empirical Study of the Lack of Interest Defense in Title VII Cases Challenging Job Segregation," 59 *U. Chi. L. Rev.* 1073 (1992), by permission of the *University of Chicago Law Review*.

Schultz, T. Paul, *World Bank, Women and Development: Objectives, Frameworks, and Policy Interventions* (1989), by permission of the World Bank.

Schur, Edwin, *The Americanization of Sex* (1998), by permission of Temple University Press.

Schwartz, Marilyn, Task Force on Bias-Free Language of the Association of American University Presses, *Guidelines for Bias-Free Writing* (1995), by permission of Indiana University Press, Bloomington & Indianapolis.

Sedgwick, Eve Kosofsky, *Epistemology of the Closet* (1990), copyright © 1990 the Regents of the University of California, by permission of the University of California.

Segrave, Kerry, *The Sexual Harassment of Women in the Workplace, 1600 to 1993* (1994), by permission of the author.

Senauer, Benjamin, "The Impact of the Value of Women's Time on Food and Nutrition," *in Persistent Inequalities: Women and World Development* 150 (Irene Tinker ed., 1990), by permission of Oxford University Press.

Senate Committee on Faculty Affairs, Univ. of Minn., *Policy Statement on Sexual Harassment* (Apr. 16, 1981), by permission of the University of Minnesota.

Shalev, Carmel, *Birth Power: The Case for Surrogacy* (1989), by permission of Yale University Press.

Shanley, Mary L., "Unwed Fathers' Rights, Adoption, and Sex Equality: Gender-Neutrality and the Perpetuation of Patriarchy," 95 *Colum. L. Rev.* 60 (1994), by permission of the publisher and author.

Shanley, Mary Lyndon, " 'Surrogate Mothering' and Women's Freedom: A Critique of Contracts for Human Reproduction," 18 *Signs* 618 (1993), by permission of the University of Chicago Press, © 1993 by The University of Chicago.

Siegel, Reva B., "Home as Work: The First Woman's Rights Claims Concerning Wives' Household Labor, 1850–1880," 103 *Yale L.J.* 1073 (1994), by permission of the Yale Law Journal Company and Fred B. Rothman & Co.

Siegel, Reva B., " 'The Rule of Love': Wife Beating as Prerogative and Privacy," 105 *Yale L.J.* 2117 (1996), by permission of the Yale Law Journal Company and Fred B. Rothman & Company.

Siegel, Reva, "Reasoning from the Body: A Historical Perspective on Abortion Regulation and Questions of Equal Protection," 44 *Stan. L. Rev* 261 (1992), by permission of the *Stanford Law Review* from the Copyright Clearance Center.

Silverstein, Charles, *Man to Man: Gay Couples in America* (1981), © 1981 by Dr. Charles Silverstein, by permission of HarperCollins Publishers, Inc., William Morrow.

Simon, William, & John H. Gagnon, "On Psychosexual Development," *in Handbook of Socialization Theory and Research* 733 (David Goslin ed., 1969), by permission of David Goslin.

Skrobanek, Siriporn, et al., *The Traffic in Women: Human Realities of the International Sex Trade* (1997), by permission of St. Martin's Press.

Snyder, Louis L., *Hitler's Third Reich: A Documentary History* 213 (Louis L. Snyder ed., 1981), by permission of Nelson-Hall Publishers, Inc.

Sohn, Louis, The New International Law: Protection of the Rights of Individuals Rather than State, 32 *Am. U. L. Rev.* 1 (1982), by permission of American University Law Review.

Sorenson, Elaine, *Comparable Worth: Is It A Worthy Policy?* (1994), copyright © 1994 by Princeton University Press, by permission of Princeton University Press.

Spatz, Melissa, "A 'Lesser' Crime: A Comparative Study of Legal Defenses for Men Who Kill Their Wives," 24 *Colum. J.L. & Soc. Probs.* 597 (1991), by permission of the *Columbia Journal of Law and Social Problems*.

Stanton, Elizabeth Cady, *Elizabeth Cady Stanton as Revealed in Her Letters, Diary and Reminiscences* (Theodore Stanton & Harriot Stanton Blatch eds., 1922), by permission of Ayer Company Publishers.

Stimpson, Catharine, "'Thy Neighbor's Wife, Thy Neighbor's Servants': Women's Liberation and Black Civil Rights," *in Woman in Sexist Society: Studies in Power and Powerlessness* 622 (Vivian Gornick & Barbara Moran eds., 1971), by permission of the author.

Stoller, Robert J., "Pornography and Perversion," 22 *Archives Gen. Psychiatry* 490 (1970), copyright 1970 American Medical Association, by permission of the American Medical Association.

Stoltenberg, John, *Refusing to Be a Man: Essays on Sex and Justice* (rev. ed. 2000) (1989), by permission of the author.

Summer, Toby, "Women, Lesbians and Prostitution: A Workingclass Dyke Speaks Out Against Buying Women for Sex," 2 *Lesbian Ethics* 33 (1987), by permission of the author.

Sunstein, Cass, "Neutrality in Constitutional Law (With Special Reference to Pornography, Abortion and Surrogacy)," 92 *Colum. L. Rev.* 1 (1992), by permission of the author and the *Columbia Law Review*.

Sunstein, Cass, "Pornography and the First Amendment," 1986 *Duke L.J.* 589, by permission of the author and the *Duke Law Journal*.

Sunstein, Cass R., "Sexual Orientation and the Constitution: A Note on the Relationship Between Due Process and Equal Protection," 55 *U. Chi. L. Rev.* 1161 (1988), by permission of the author.

Swent, Jeannette F., "Gender Bias at the Heart of Justice: An Empirical Study of State Task Forces," 6 *S. Cal. Rev. L. & Women's Stud.* 1 (1996), by permission of the Southern California Review of Law and Women's Studies.

Thomas, Kendall, "Corpus Juris (Hetero)sexualis: Doctrine, Discourse, and Desire in *Bowers v. Hardwick*," 1 *GLQ* 33 (1993). Copyright 1993. All rights reserved. By permission of Duke University Press.

Tong, Rosemarie, "Feminist Perspectives and Gestational Motherhood: The Search for a Unified Legal Focus," *in Reproduction, Ethics and the Law* 55 (Joan C. Callahan ed., 1995), by permission of Indiana University Press, Bloomington & Indianapolis.

Tribe, Laurence, *American Constitutional Law* (2d ed. 1988), by permission of Foundation Press.

Tussman, Joseph & Jacobus tenBroek, "The Equal Protection of the Laws," 37 *Cal. L. Rev.* 341 (1949), by permission of California Law Review, Inc.

Valdes, Francisco, "Queers, Sissies, Dykes, and Tomboys: Deconstructing the Conflation of 'Sex,' 'Gender,' and 'Sexual Orientation' in Euro-American Law and Society," 83 *Cal. L. Rev.* 3 (1995), ©1995 by California Law Review, Inc., by permission of the author and the University of California Press.

Veléz-Ibáñez, Carlos G., "The Nonconsenting Sterilization of Mexican Women in Los Angeles," *in Twice a Minority: Mexican American Women* 235 (Margarita B. Melville ed., 1980), by permission of the author.

Venter, Christine Mary, "The New South African Constitution: Facing the Challenges of Women's Rights and Cultural Rights in Post-Apartheid South Africa," 21 *J. Legis.* 1 (1995), © 1995 by the *Journal of Legislation*, Notre Dame Law School. By permission.

Victor, Roberta, *in* Studs Turkel, *Working* 91 (Avon Books 1974) (1972), by permission of Donadio & Olson, Inc., copyright 1972, 1974 by Studs Terkel.

Walker, Alice, "What Can the White Man Say to the Black Woman?," *The Nation*, May 22, 1989, at 691, by permission of the author.

Walker, Lenore E., *The Battered Woman* (1979), copyright © 1979 by Lenore E. Walker, by permission of HarperCollins Publishers, Inc.

Walker, Lenore E., *Terrifying Love: Why Battered Women Kill and How Society Responds* (1989), by permission of HarperCollins Publishers, Inc.

Ward, Andrew, "Whites: 140, Blacks: 3," *N.Y. Times,* Feb. 7, 1989, at A29, copyright © 1989 by the New York Times Co. By permission.

Warren, Samuel D. & Louis D. Brandeis, "The Right to Privacy," 4 *Harv. L. Rev.* 193 (1890), copyright © 1890 by the Harvard Law Review Association, by permission of the *Harvard Law Review*.

Washburn, Josie, *The Underworld Sewer: A Prostitute Reflects on Life in the Trade, 1871–1909* (Bison Books 1997) (1909), by permission of the University of Nebraska Press.

Wasserstrom, Richard A., "Racism, Sexism, and Preferential Treatment: An Approach to the Topics," 24 *UCLA L. Rev.* 581 (1977), by permission of the author.

Wechsler, Herbert, "Toward Neutral Principles of Constitutional Law," 73 *Harv. L. Rev.* 1 (1959), copyright © 1959 by the Harvard Law Review Association, by permission of the author and the *Harvard Law Review*.

Weeks, Jeffrey, *Sexuality and Its Discontents: Meanings, Myths, and Modern Sexualities* (1985), by permission of International Thomson Publishing Services on behalf of Routledge, Inc.

Weiner, Robin D., "Shifting the Communication Burden: A Meaningful Consent Standard in Rape," 6 *Harv. Women's L.J.* 143 (1983), © 1983 by the President and Fellows of Harvard College and the *Harvard Women's Law Journal*, by permission of the *Harvard Women's Law Journal*.

West, Robin, "Equality Theory, Marital Rape, and the Promise of the Fourteenth Amendment," 42 *Univ. Fla. L. Rev.* 45 (1990), by permission of the *University of Florida Law Review*.

West German Abortion Decision: A Contrast to *Roe v. Wade*," 9 *John Marshall J. Prac. & Proc.* 605 (Robert E. Jonas & John D. Gorby trans., 1976), by permission of the *John Marshall Law Review*.

Williams, Craig A., *Roman Homosexuality: Ideologies of Masculinity in Classical Antiquity* (1999), © 1999 by Craig A. Williams, by permission of Oxford University Press and the author.

Williams, Wendy, "The Equality Crisis: Some Reflections on Culture, Courts, and Feminism," 7 *Women's Rts. L. Rep.* 175 (1982), by permission of the author and the *Women's Rights Law Reporter*.

Williams, Wendy W., "Equality's Riddle: Pregnancy and the Equal Treatment/Special Treatment Debate," 13 *N.Y.U. Rev. L. & Soc. Change* 325 (1984–85), by permission of the *New York University Review of Law & Social Change*.

Willis, Ellen, "Putting Women Back into the Abortion Debate," *Village Voice*, July 16, 1985, at 16, © V.V. Publishing Corporation, by permission of the *Village Voice*.

Wing, Adrien K. & Eunice P. de Carvalho, "Black South African Women: Toward Equal Rights," 8 *Harv. Hum. Rts. J.* 57 (1995), by permission of the Copyright Clearance Center.

Wittig, Monique, *The Straight Mind and Other Essays* (1992), by permission of Beacon Press.

Women's Legal Education and Action Fund (LEAF), *Equality and the Charter: Ten Years of Feminist Advocacy Before the Supreme Court of Canada* (1996), by permission of the Women's Legal Education and Action Fund.

Woods, Polly S., Comment, "Boys Muscle In on Girls' Sports," 53 *Ohio St. L.J.* 891 (1992), by permission of the author and the *Ohio State Law Journal*.

Woolf, Virginia, *A Room of One's Own* (Harcourt Brace Jovanovich 1981) (1929), copyright 1929 by Harcourt, Inc., and renewed 1957 by Leonard Woolf, by permission of the publisher.

Yale University, Policies on Sexual Harassment and Sexual Relations Between Teachers and Students Proposed by the Yale University Ad Hoc Committee on Faculty-Student Consensual Sexual Relations, Yale Bulletin and Calendar (Nov. 24–Dec. 8, 1997), by permission of Yale University.

York University Senate, Policy on Personal Relationships Between Instructors and Students (1989), by permission of York University.

SUMMARY OF CONTENTS

*

TABLE OF CONTENTS

Chapter 7 Sexual Subordination

Chapter 8 Lesbian and Gay Rights

*

TABLE OF CASES

Principal cases are in bold type. Non-principal cases are in roman type. References are to Pages.

*

Sex Equality

Lesbian and Gay Rights

*

PART I

FOUNDATIONS

[I]f one advances confidently in the direction of his dreams, and endeavors to live the life which he has imagined, he will meet with a success unexpected in common hours. He will put some things behind, will pass an invisible boundary; new, universal, and more liberal laws will begin to establish themselves around and within him; or the old laws be expanded.... If you have built castles in the air, your work need not be lost; that is where they should be. Now put the foundations under them.

Henry D. Thoreau, *Walden* 362 (A. L. Burt 1902) (1854)

Negroes have proceeded from a premise that equality means what it says, and they have taken white Americans at their word when they talked of it as an objective. But most whites in America in 1967, including many persons of good-will, proceed from a premise that equality is a loose expression for improvement. White America is not even psychologically organized to close the gap—essentially it seeks only to make it less painful and less obvious but in most respects to retain it.

Martin Luther King Jr., *Where Do We Go from Here?* 8 (1967)

CHAPTER 1

EQUALITY

Equality in human societies is commonly affirmed but rarely practiced. As a principle, it can be fiercely loved, passionately sought, highly vaunted, sentimentally assumed, complacently taken for granted, and legally guaranteed. Its open detractors are few. Yet despite general consensus on equality as a value, no society is organized on equality principles. Few lives are lived in equality, even in democracies. As a fact, social equality is hard to find anywhere.

Social inequality, by contrast, is seldom defended but widely practiced. Common among men—vast disparities in wealth are one evidence—social inequality is nowhere more apparent than between women and men as groups. The inequality of women relative to men varies in extent, form, and degree by time and place, but the sexes are equal nowhere, by any measure. *See, e.g.,* U.N. Dep't of Int'l Economics & Social Affairs, *The World's Women 1970–1990: Trends and Statistics*, U.N. Doc. ST/ESA/STAT/ SER.K/8, U.N. Sales No. E.90.XVII.3 (1991). The second-class status of women as a group is widely documented to be socially and legally institutionalized, cumulatively and systematically shaping access to life chances on the basis of sex. As a result, women, compared with men, are deprived of access to many measures and markers of social worth, including dignity, respect, resources, security, authority, credibility, speech, power, and full citizenship. The group women, composed of all its variations, has a collective social history of group-based devaluation, disempowerment, exploitation, and subordination that extends to the present. *See* Vern L. Bullough, et al., *The Subordinated Sex: A History of Attitudes Toward Women* (Univ. Ga. Press 1988) (1973) (presenting social history of women's devaluation); *Persistent Inequalities: Women and World Development* (Irene Tinker ed., 1990).

A potent combination of social and political mechanisms enforces this pattern. Political science Professor Robert Dahl observes, "[T]he subordination of women [is] institutionalized and enforced by an overwhelming array of the most powerful forces available [including] individual and collective terror and violence, official and unofficial; law, custom, and convention; and social and economic structures [and is] backed up by the state itself." Robert A. Dahl, "Equality Versus Inequality," 29 *PS: Political Science & Politics* 639, 643 (1996). Given this analysis of interlocking forces supporting sex inequality, what interventions will produce sex equality is an open question.

Unless something is done, even if recent rates of measurable progress for elite women continue, no American now alive will live in a society of sex equality, nor will their children or their children's children. Pamela McCorduck and Nancy Ramsey estimate by linear projection that top corporations will be sex-equal by 2270, Congress by 2500. *See* Pamela McCorduck & Nancy Ramsey, *The Futures of Women: Scenarios for the 21st Century* 7–8 (1996). But will these changes stop rape? end domestic violence against women? produce an equal income for the average woman? integrate combat forces? guarantee that women's voice and experience shapes culture and policy? eliminate discrimination against gay men and lesbian women? make abortions rare? make prostitution wither away? elect a woman President? What must change for sex equality to be achieved? In your answer, are some parts of the problem more central or harder to change than others? If so, why? Should some of these areas be left alone? Do you see a way to accomplish the changes you envision? Is there a role for law in your strategy?

Sex equality is often guaranteed by law, including where sex inequality is pervasive in society. More imagined than real in life, sex equality in law tends to be more formal or hypothetical than substantive and delivered. In legal application, the meaningfulness of sex equality guarantees varies dramatically, its observance ranging from obvious to anathema. Around the world and throughout history, in settings from the institutional to the intimate, sex equality remains more promise than fact.

In the words of philosopher Richard Rorty, to be a woman "is not yet the name of a way of being human." Richard Rorty, "Feminism and Pragmatism," *in The Tanner Lectures on Human Values: 1992* 1, 7 (Grethe B. Peterson ed., 1992) (describing MacKinnon's theory). His formulation at once recognizes that women's lives would not be "human" by the standard set by men, and that women's reality has not been reflected in the standard for what "human" is. It invites redefinition of the human standard in the image of women's realities and unrealized possibilities, as well as proposes change in women's situation to meet the existing standard of a "human" life. Can one challenge the validity of a standard and assert a right to the benefits of its application it at the same time? Are women "human"?

I. EQUALITY UNDER LAW

As a norm, equality animates Western law on several levels. The ideal of "the rule of law" implicitly embodies a kind of equality rule: under law, anyone is entitled to the same consideration as anyone else, to be treated without personal favor or prejudice. In the West since the Enlightenment—building on the Greeks' concept of "isonomia," equality under law—law as law has meant equalization by uniform rules over the inequalities of force and social hierarchy. Overthrowing feudalism's status and caste structures was supposed to produce individual desert, results unaffected by preconceptions or built-in limits based on bias or social location. In the Enlightenment tradition, building on the classics and overthrowing feudalism, law as law embodies a leveling principle that treats everyone the same, no favorites and no exceptions, except when distinctions are real and can be justified. Law as law in this sense is equal, or it is not law at all.

On another level, reasoning through analogy and distinction makes a notion of equality methodological in law. An equality norm of sameness for the same (analogy) and difference for the different (distinction) is built into legal reasoning itself. Elevating this notion of rationality over arbitrary status and preconception, legal method in the Western tradition embodies one equality approach by treating the same that which is the same and differently that which is different. *See* Edward H. Levi, *An Introduction to Legal Reasoning* 2–3 (1948). Separating an equality norm from the rule of law, and equality thinking from legal thinking as such, thus becomes a complex task, since the way one thinks and what one thinks about are simultaneously involved. Can you think legally without asking whether one set of facts is like or not like another? If law were consistently and accurately applied according to these norms, would an explicit equality guarantee ever be needed?

On another level of legal systems, equality is often explicitly guaranteed in positive law. International treaties and conventions structure governments' relations with one another on equal terms. Increasingly, international human rights instruments promise equality. Constitutions typically provide for equality in governments' relations with the governed. Statutes typically guarantee equality in citizens' relations among themselves. Constitutional and international equality law centers on prohibiting official inequality by public acts or actors, principally prohibiting unequal laws and policies, although the problematic line between public and nonpublic inequality is contested and changing. Statutory equality aims to equalize relations among individuals as members of social groups defined on specific social grounds, such as sex or age or race, in specific spheres of civil society, typically education and employment.

On every level of equality thinking, from systemic values to positive law, equality reasoning has meant reasoning from sameness and difference. Most visibly in common law systems that reason from case to case, but just as strongly in civil law systems that rely on legislation and reason from authoritative principles, the foundational formulation that originated with Aristotle of treating likes alike, unlikes unalike, rules.

A.   THE ARISTOTELIAN APPROACH TO EQUALITY

Mainstream equality thinking has descended in an unbroken line from Aristotle's concept that "[e]quality consists in the same treatment of similar persons." Aristotle, *The Politics* 307 (Benjamin Jowett trans., Random House 1943).[1] In the context of constituting a polity, Aristotle took the view that, where citizens rule and are ruled by turns—as contrasted with one individual being above all the others like a god is above mortals—any regime that puts one permanently above the others is unjust and will be unstable. So, at least when a polity is being constituted, equality means that all who are similar in being citizens should enjoy similar basic privileges, such as ruling. Whether Aristotle intended this notion of equality to apply to other settings is questionable. Can the rules that constitute a state be separated from the rules of its daily governance? Aristotle proposed a model from nature to guide the distinctions needed in governance: the rule of the old over the young. *Id. See id.* Are sex and race like age?

For present purposes, what Aristotle thought or meant is less important than what has been made of his equality thinking in law. Under the influence of Aristotle, equality as such in law has come to mean treating likes alike and unlikes unalike. If one is the same, one is to be treated the

---

1. Variance among translations of such passages suggests that the legal version of Aristotle's view may come in part from some of his translators. For example, Ernest Barker translates this passage as: "In a society of peers equality means that all should have the same rights: and a constitution can hardly survive if it ... [gives *different* rights to men who are of the same quality]." *The Politics of Aristotle* 315 (Ernest Barker trans., Oxford Univ. Press 1946).

same; if one is different, one is to be treated differently. The concept is empirical (how one *ought* to be treated is based on the way one *is*) and symmetrical (as if on two sides of an equation, conjoined with a mathematical = sign)—or this is the meaning virtually universally attributed to Aristotle's formulation.

In the modern period, movements for human liberation and the legal changes they have inspired and impelled have used the concept of equality as a legal tool for social change, demanding that it be delivered as well as guaranteed. In this process, the legal concept of equality itself, implicitly transformed in use to challenge diverse social realities, has largely escaped scrutiny. However elaborated and mobilized by law and politics over time, the sameness/difference approach Aristotle originated has been treated as obvious and self-evident, alike by movements claiming it and by law in applying it through constitutions, statutes, and international provisions worldwide, as if there could be no other way of thinking about the subject. The single exception is the constitutional law of Canada since 1989. *See infra Andrews v. Law Soc'y of B.C.*, [1989] 1 S.C.R. 143.

For Aristotle, equality was a moral virtue, a form of justice, which in turn was an "excellence" in the character of the soul of the just man. This man acts instinctively "in the mean," meaning justly, meaning equally. The rules to which such an individual would reflexively conform would display justice in both the distributive form and the rectificatory, or corrective, sense. Aristotle's distributive justice, from which legal mainstream equality primarily flows, is "a species of the proportionate." Aristotle, *Ethica Nicomachea* 113 (J.L. Ackrill & J.O. Urmson eds. & W. Ross trans., 1980).

Aristotle, *Ethica Nicomachea*

v.3 1131a–1131b, 112–17
(J.L. Ackrill & J.O. Urmson eds. & W. Ross trans., 1980)

We have shown that both the unjust man and the unjust act are unfair or unequal; now it is clear that there is also an intermediate between the two unequals involved in either case. And this is the equal; for in any kind of action in which there is a more and a less there is also what is equal. If, then, the unjust is unequal, the just is equal.... And since the equal is intermediate, the just will be an intermediate. Now equality implies at least two things. The just, then, must be both intermediate and equal and relative (i.e. for certain persons). And *qua* intermediate it must be between certain things (which are respectively greater and less); *qua* equal, it involves *two* things; *qua* just, it is for certain people. The just, therefore, involves at least four terms; for the persons for whom it is in fact just are two, and the things in which it is manifested, the objects distributed, are two. And the same equality will exist between the persons and between the things concerned; for as the latter—the things concerned—are related, so are the former; if they are not equal, they will not have what is equal, but this is the origin of quarrels and complaints—when either equals have and are awarded unequal shares, or unequals equal shares. Further, this is plain from the fact that awards should be "according to merit"; for all men agree that what is just in distribution must be according to merit in some sense, though they do not all specify the same sort of merit, but democrats identify it with the status of freeman, supporters of oligarchy with wealth (or with noble birth), and supporters of aristocracy with excellence. ...

This, then, is what the just is—the proportional; the unjust is what violates the proportion. Hence one term becomes too great, the other too small, as indeed happens in practice; for the man who acts unjustly has too much, and the man who is unjustly treated too little, of what is good. In the case of evil the reverse is true. ... This, then, is one species of the just.

The remaining one is the rectificatory, which arises in connexion with transactions both voluntary and involuntary. ... [T]he justice in transactions between man and man is a sort of equality indeed, and the injustice a sort of inequality.... For it makes no difference whether a good man has defrauded a bad man or a bad man a good one, nor whether it is a good or a bad man that has committed adultery; the law looks only to the distinctive character of the injury, and treats the parties as equal, if one is in the wrong and the other is being wronged, and if one inflicted injury and the other has received it. Therefore, this kind of injustice being an inequality, the judge tries to equalize it; for in the case also in which one has received and the other has inflicted a wound, or one has slain and the other been slain, the suffering and the action have been unequally distributed; but the judge tries to equalize things by means of the penalty, taking away from the gain of the assailant.... [T]herefore corrective justice will be the intermediate between loss and gain. This is why, when people dispute, they take refuge in the judge; and to go to the judge is to go to justice; for the nature of the judge is to be a sort of animate justice.... Now the judge restores equality; it is as though there were a line divided into unequal parts, and he took away that by which the greater segment exceeds the half, and added it to the smaller segment. And when the whole has been equally divided, then they say they have "their own"—i.e. when they have got what is equal.... [F]or to have more than one's own is called gaining, and to have less than one's original share is called losing, e.g. in buying and selling and in all other matters in which the law has left people free to make their own terms; but when they get neither more nor less but just what belongs to themselves, they say that they have their own and that they neither lose nor gain.

NOTES AND QUESTIONS ON ARISTOTLE

1. **Formal equality:** The principle that has come to be termed "formal equality," the core of conventional equality law, is predicated on readings of this passage and others of similar import. Its familiar calculus—sameness and difference, identity and distinction—requires same treatment if one is the same, different treatment if one is different. The concept is clearly premised on some original just status quo allocation and presupposes a uniform measuring device for whatever is to be distributed. It permits change, but change that conforms what one receives to what one is or has or had. As equality is like treatment for likes, inequality means different treatment for likes, same treatment for unlikes. The basic idea is, you get what you're worth. Do you think that people get what they're worth? Consider as you read the cases in this book whether the judges who wrote them see themselves as engaging in the process of justice Aristotle envisions.

2. **Why sameness?** Aristotle does not defend his comparative empirical approach on normative grounds: he does not ask why one must *be* the same as someone else before one *ought* to receive equal consideration or benefit. Are there ever times when equality is promoted by treating different people the same, such as when admitting a diverse law school class? Can diversity be a value in Aristotle's equality? He also does not address why those who have been unequally treated should have to be "like" those who do not

have this problem before their inequality should be ended. Members of dominant groups never have to meet any comparative test to acquire or retain their privileges and advantages. Are measures of "likeness" free of bias? Are measures of merit unproblematic? What if measures of merit are infected with inequality? How many of those who have been unequally treated have been permitted to be "like" those who have not been so treated? Is there any basis in Aristotle's text for answering these questions?

3. The same as who? Aristotle often closely attended to empirical reality in his work, but his equality approach does not specify the reference points for sameness of treatment. Can you derive general standards for the relevant comparator from his discussion?

4. Perceiving and creating difference: Aristotle says "if they are not equal, they will not have what is equal." How do we know or measure who "is" equal? If people have been *kept* unequal, they will often *be* unequal, in the sense of not measurably appearing to be the same as people who have not been so treated. At what point will the equal treatment reckoning start? What defines its original distribution, so that we can know inequality—when equals have unequal shares, or unequals equal shares—when we see it? With respect to what standard is valid proportion assessed? How is a fair standard of measurement to be found if resources are empirically and systematically maldistributed along a line of difference as far back as the eye can see, or today from cradle to grave?

Aristotle does not recognize that differences might be socially created and defined, including by social inequality, to the extent other Greeks (Plato, for instance) did. Nor does he interrogate how difference is socially perceived. Aristotle did not see the social rankings he observed around him as artifacts of social power and location, social constructs that are deeply arbitrary rather than emanating from something innate. Can you trace the operation of Aristotle's assumption in his equality theory?

5. Perceiving and creating sameness: How can subordinated groups be *seen as* "like" dominant groups if society has organized its inequalities along lines of socially perceived "unalikeness"? The worst conditions of subordination, such as racially segregated schools or sexually segregated workplaces, place those disadvantaged by them in situations that are the most circumstantially "unlike" the situation of those advantaged by them. These conditions can make their occupants look "different" from those free of such conditions, institutionalizing inequality while breeding as well as demarcating differences between groups. If these situations are seen as people being "different" from one another rather than as conditions being unequal, treating some less favorably than others simply looks like treating unalikes unalike. Applying the Aristotelian paradigm, are such arrangements likely to be made equal?

6. Aristotle in practice: Some progress toward social equality has occurred under the Aristotelian rubric—mostly for elites, those exceptional members of subordinated groups who, despite conditions of inequality, meet dominant standards. At the same time, the conceptual queries in the notes above draw force from some historical applications of the sameness/difference equality concept.

Aristotle himself, his concept of equality apparently undisturbed, defended slavery in at least some forms and lived in a society in which prostitution thrived and no women were citizens. *See* Elizabeth V. Spelman, *Inessential Woman* 37–56 (1988). The Aristotelian approach readily supported racial segregation by law in the United States, African Americans being considered "different" from whites on the basis of the color of their skin. *See Plessy v. Ferguson*, 163 U.S. 537 (1896). (*See* Chapter 2.) The Aristotelian approach was used under Nazi Germany's Third Reich to justify different treatment of Jews from "Aryans," including discrimination and extermination.[2]

Is it possible to oppose these inequalities using the likes-alike/unlikes-unalike approach? If so, why did that approach support them instead? What does it mean that the Aristotelian equality logic was used to rationalize such extremes of inequality, just when law was urgently needed to oppose them?

In light of the fact that legal equality guarantees promise and aim for a social equality they have yet to achieve, consider the fact that the same equality idea that was used to legalize segregation and genocide remains fundamental to an American law that has repudiated racism and a European law that has rejected fascism. The United States today rejects state-enforced racial separation, but not the fundamental approach to equality emanating from Aristotle that legally rationalized it. The German Constitutional Court, repudiating Nazi law, also embraced the traditional approach to equality that the Nazis (and everyone else) used: equal justice means "to treat equals the same [or likes alike], and unequals [or unlikes] differently according to their distinguishing characteristics." 3 BVerfGE 58, 135 (1954) (" 'Gleiches gleich, Ungleiches seiner Eigenart entsprechend verschieden' zu behandeln" in Nazi civil servants case). The sameness/difference approach also remains fundamental to equality under international human rights law, which was created largely to make sure that nothing like the Holocaust ever happens again. It is as if the lesson learned was that Aristotle was not applied rigorously enough, or that redoubled efforts at being the same or seeing all as the same are the solution to never again being perceivable as "different"—not that the sameness/difference equality paradigm itself might be flawed.

Are these historical instances of inequality isolated exceptional excesses? Are they errors in applying the Aristotelian equality approach, or are their results consistent with its basic principles? As long as Blacks can be seen as different from whites, or Jews from Aryans, or women from men, can they be treated differently, according to this equality principle, including by dehumanization, segregation, and liquidation? Does anything in the Aristotelian equality approach define all human beings as presumptively equal? Are these applications abuses or uses of Aristotle's theory? Can equality seekers afford an equality logic that has demonstrably at least adapted to social judgments of who is fully human and who is not?

7. Democracy: As a democrat, Aristotle was at best ambivalent. While he recognized the potential for tyranny and unrest in one-man rule, particularly in democratic polities, he also at times appeared to favor it. According to one scholar, "[T]he monarchy of the perfect man . . . is for Aristotle the ideal constitution." Sir David Ross, *Aristotle* 263 (6th ed. 1995); *see also id.*

---

2. *See* Georg Weippert, *Das Prinzip der Hierarchie* 29 (1932); Ulrich Scheuner, "Der Gleichheitsgedanke in der völkischen Verfassungsordnung," 99 *Zeitschrift fur die gesamte* *Staatswissenschaft* 245, 260–67 (1939). A sign over one extermination camp stated "Jedem das Seine," in an eerie echo of Aristotle's giving "each one's own."

at 258–61. (For Aristotle, however, that perfect man may have been nonexistent, a god.) Should democracies use a legal equality theory consistent with assumptions of natural hierarchy and political elitism?

8. Principled or power-driven? In operation, the substantive judgments that Aristotle left to the "excellences" of individual character, political systems leave to the political realm: the realm of power and force. Yet the presence of the equality principle in law is often presented as both equality-producing and a counterbalance to, rather than a reiteration of, power politics. Does the outcome in any legal situation applying Aristotle's approach depend upon the politics with which its use is infused? Does this happen with all abstract legal approaches, or are some more prone to it than others? Is an approach principled if it is subject to political forces? Is an approach to equality, the principles of which depend on the substantive politics of those who use it, at least as consistent with assumptions and outcomes that are unequal as with those that are equal? Is an equality approach that can produce equality or inequality an equality approach at all?

9. The dangers of "special treatment": Whatever Aristotle intended, same treatment for sameness has been the primary equality rule in every legal equality regime, relegating different treatment for differences to a clear secondary place. The first principle of legal equality has been same treatment based on relevant empirical sameness, equivalence, symmetry with a relevant comparator. In the American law of sex discrimination, this standard is termed "gender neutrality." (*See* Chapter 3.) Different treatment, from the Nazi's *Sönderbehandlung*—"special treatment," a euphemism for extermination—to arguments that women's weakness and incapacity require particular protection, called the "special benefits" rule in American law (*see* Chapter 3.2), has often produced inequality, not equality. American courts see sex discrimination law's "special benefits" rule as being in tension with its fundamental "gender neutrality" rule of equal treatment, not as simply complementary to it. Same treatment is considered equality itself. Different treatment is seen as a double standard, inimical to equality. (*See* Chapter 3.2, 3.3.) Giving women maternity leave when no workers have disability leave, for example, is seen by many as a double standard based on sex. Affirmative action—undoing racism or sexism by taking race or sex into account—is seen by many as special or preferential treatment, at once treating those who are alike differently and those who are unalike the same. (*See* Chapter 2.)

Does Aristotle's approach allow the valuing of differences? Would treating all differences equally well be a social improvement? Once the social world is divided into sameness and difference, such that the standard against which one is the same or different is set by dominant groups, won't all change in an unequal status quo seem like a special benefit, hence stigmatic? Why is equality in law defined more in abstract than substantive terms? What exactly is wrong with noticing which groups, substantively, are harmed by inequality, and remedying that harm? Is this always enforcing "difference"?

Consider this dilemma: While same treatment for sameness offers an illusory equality, different treatment for differences, which has sometimes produced needed remedies, has also proved dangerous, at times catastrophically so. Yet where inequality creates differences, ignoring them is to ignore inequality. Can sameness/difference theory solve this?

10.   Evaluating Aristotle: How should Aristotle's approach be evaluated? by whether it can be made to promote equality in the hands of someone who knows what inequality is and wants to end it? by whether it has given openings to assert equality rights by historically unequal groups? by whether it has ever been used to ignore or promote inequality? by whether or not its logic intrinsically promotes social equality and identifies social inequality? By whether you can make it produce the results you want?

11.   Evaluate this critique: The Aristotelian approach to equality tends to reproduce inequality by seeing the products of dominance as "difference." Its blindness to hierarchy makes it incapable of producing determinate outcomes in opposition to inequality; it will tend systematically to produce outcomes that reinforce and reproduce social inequality. It excels at correcting comparatively minor inequalities. If existing society were structurally equal, the Aristotelian approach would adequately correct minor marginal inequality errors. It recognizes only the *least* unequal situations as unequal, failing to perceive, hence exonerating, the most unequal situations. Against major or structural social inequality, it is impotent, even regressive.

12.   Compare Aristotle with Rousseau: Jean–Jacques Rousseau (1712–1778), a French social contract theorist of the Enlightenment influenced by the Greeks, in turn influenced the French Revolution, was widely read in the United States after 1776, *see* Paul Merrill Spurlin, *Rousseau in America 1760–1809* at 104 (1969), and remains widely regarded as a liberal thinker today. Do people you know tacitly hold the views he expresses?

Jean–Jacques Rousseau, *Discourse on the Origin and Basis of Inequality Among Men*

143–44 (Lowell Bair trans., ed., *The Essential Rousseau*, 1975)

I see two kinds of inequality in the human race. One, which I call natural or physical inequality because it is established by nature, consists in differences of age, health, bodily strength, and qualities of the mind or the soul. The other can be called moral or political inequality because it depends on a kind of agreement and is established, or at least authorized, by the consent of men. It consists in the various privileges which some men enjoy to the detriment of others, such as being richer, more honored, more powerful than they, or even being able to make them obey.

It would be pointless to ask what the source of natural inequality is, because the mere definition of the term supplies the answer. It would be still more pointless to ask whether there is any essential connection between the two kinds of inequality, for that would amount to asking whether those who command are necessarily better than those who obey, and whether strength of body or mind, wisdom or virtue, are always present in the same individuals in proportion to power or wealth. This may be a good question for slaves to discuss within the hearing of their masters, but it is unfit for rational and free men in search of truth.

Is Rousseau's approach to equality more likely to produce equal results in reality than Aristotle's? Are their approaches similar in significant ways? How do you evaluate Rousseau's distinction between kinds of inequality? Do you know any inequality, in the sense of social hierarchy, that is natural in his sense? Are groups that are socially dominant healthier, stronger, and smarter than groups that are socially less powerful? Are children naturally unequal to adults?

How would you describe the role of the concept "nature" in Rousseau's theory? To Rousseau, natural inequality originates in nature; a just society may reflect it. Political inequality, however, is unjust. How do Rousseau's concepts map onto the inequality between the sexes as you see it? As to Rousseau's own views of men and women, in *Emile* he said, inter alia, that the location of women's sex organs determined the extent of their influence, so that "the internal influence continually recalls women to their sex ... the male is male only at certain moments, but the female is female throughout her life." Joan Wallach Scott, *Only Paradoxes to Offer: French Feminists and the Rights of Man* 49 (1996) (quoting Jean–Jacques Rousseau, *Emile*). What does this essentialist analysis imply about his view of whether sex is a natural or a political inequality?

It is often the case that male philosophers' theories can be applied productively to the situation of women, while their own views of women precluded them from doing so. For an analysis of how women's inequality is first granted as artificial then naturalized in Rousseau's theory, see Susan Moller Okin, *Women in Western Political Thought* 99–139 (1979); for the implications for the status of women in contractarian theory, including Rousseau's, see Carole Pateman, *The Sexual Contract* (1988).

Rousseau believed that a "state of nature," in which men were naturally equal, preceded society, in which men were unequal. As he states in *The Social Contract*, "Man is born free; and everywhere he is in chains." Jean–Jacques Rousseau, "The Social Contract, or Principles of Political Right," in *The Social Contract and Discourses* 181, 181 (G.D.H. Cole trans., rev. ed. 1993). How is one to know what is natural, in the sense of presocial, when everyone lives in society? Is it necessary to posit a presocial natural state in which women and men are equal to criticize an inequality as socially imposed? In 1730, Mary Astell retorted, "If *all Men are born Free*, how is it that all Women are born Slaves?" Mary Astell, *Some Reflections upon Marriage* 107 (4th ed. Source Book Press 1970) (1730). Does her question retain force? How might Rousseau answer it? Does one need a theory of equality in nature to oppose slavery as a practice of inequality?

What Rousseau calls "power" in the excerpt above is a social, not natural, form of unequal privilege, such as wealth. Do inequalities of race or class, in your judgment, depend on the "agreement" or "consent" of those who have less, as Rousseau implies? If some men have the privilege, "to the detriment of others," of "being able to *make them* obey" (emphasis added), can those men who are made to obey be said to consent, or agree to, the arrangement? Is this what consent means? Does Rousseau build force into his definition of consent? Is nonresistance to force agreement? Is silence consent?

Rousseau states that it is pointless to ask whether a social inequality is based in nature, because that presumes that men who are socially arrayed above other men *really are* better than those below them. Ask yourself as you read the cases in this book how many of the discussions of whether a given disadvantage to women is sex discriminatory are, in Rousseau's sense, worthy for slaves to use to educate masters but unworthy for free people in pursuit of truth. As you read the cases, ask yourself whether they tacitly assume that men are better than women.

B.   EQUALITY IN THE UNITED STATES CONSTITUTION

The U.S. Constitution did not originally guarantee equality. It was not mentioned. Constitutional equality is not explicit in any text reflecting the original intent of the Framers. The Framers were members of the elite: white male property owners. Many were slaveholders; many were married men in a system that granted them virtual ownership of wives. (*See* Chapter 6.) John Adams, beseeched by his wife Abigail Adams to "[r]emember the ladies," 1 *Adams Family Correspondence* 370 (L.H. Butterfield et al. eds., 1963) (1776), in founding the United States, replied, "[w]e know better than to repeal our Masculine systems." *Id.* at 382. Thomas Jefferson, a founder and drafter of the ringing language of the Declaration of Independence that affirmed "all men are created equal," The Declaration of Independence para. 2 (U.S. 1776), owned slaves and expressed a suspicion that Africans (which included members of his own family) were racial inferiors to whites.[3] Jefferson was not alone in believing that even a pure democracy would exclude women from public life: "Were our State a pure democracy . . . there would yet be excluded from their deliberations . . . [w]omen, who, to prevent depravation of morals and ambiguity of issue, could not mix promiscuously in the public meetings of men." Letter from Thomas Jefferson to Samuel Kercheval (Sept. 5, 1816) *in* 10 *The Writings of Thomas Jefferson* 45–46 n.1 (Paul Leicester Ford ed., 1899). Is speaking in public a sexual activity?

Notwithstanding the Framers' devotion to their "Masculine systems," the Constitution, placed in historical context, may have another story to tell. In a creative gloss on American constitutional history, Justice Ruth Bader Ginsburg of the U.S. Supreme Court has observed that guarantees fundamental to the goal of women's equality impelled the U.S. Constitution from its inception. She writes, "The founding fathers rebelled against the patriarchal power of kings and the idea that political authority may legitimately rest on birth status." Ruth Bader Ginsburg, "Speaking in a Judicial Voice," 67 *N.Y.U. L. Rev.* 1185, 1188 (1992). In this reading, the spirit of the founding included opposition to patriarchy as a form of authority predicated on condition of birth. Opposition to institutionalized male dominance is thus situated within original constitutional values.

---

3. Jefferson wrote: "The improvement of the blacks in body and mind, in the first instance of their mixture with the whites, has been observed by every one, and proves that their inferiority is not the effect merely of their condition of life. . . ." *Thomas Jefferson: Writings* 267 (Merrill D. Peterson ed., 1984). He continued, "I advance it . . . as a suspicion only, that the blacks, whether originally a distinct race, or made distinct by time and circumstances, are inferior to the whites in the endowments both of body and mind. . . . [Their] unfortunate difference of colour, and perhaps of faculty, is a powerful obstacle to the emancipation of these people." *Id.* at 270; *see* David Brion Davis, *The Problem of Slavery in the Age of Revolution: 1770–1823* 166–69, 194 (1975); Mary Beth Norton et al., "The Afro–American Family in the Age of Revolution," *in Slavery and Freedom in the Age of the American Revolution* 175–87 (Ira Berlin & Ronald Hoffman eds., 1983) (discussing Jefferson's slave holdings and economic dependence on them); James Lindgren, "Measuring the Value of Slaves and Free Persons in Ancient Law," 71 *Chi–Kent L. Rev.* 149, 149 n.1 (1995) (reviewing evidence that Jefferson enslaved his relatives). That Jefferson's own family included Black people is discussed and documented in Annette Gordon–Reed, *Thomas Jefferson and Sally Hemings: An American Controversy* (1997) and *Sally Hemings and Thomas Jefferson: History, Memory, and Civil Culture* (Jan Ellen Lewis & Peter S. Onuf eds., 1999). Jefferson's attempt to include a condemnation of slavery and the slave trade in the Declaration of Independence failed. *See* David N. Mayer, *The Constitutional Thought of Thomas Jefferson* 58 (1994) (describing Jefferson's "at best ambivalent" attitude toward the institution of slavery).

After the Civil War, a war fought largely over the institution of slavery of Africans (*see* Chapter 2), the Fourteenth Amendment's guarantee of "equal protection of the laws" was added to the Constitution in 1868 as part of the effort to eliminate legalized racism.

U.S. Constitution, Amendment XIV

Section 1. All persons born or naturalized in the United States and subject to the jurisdiction thereof, are citizens of the United States and of the State wherein they reside. No State shall make or enforce any law which shall abridge the privileges or immunities of citizens of the United States; nor shall any State deprive any person of life, liberty, or property, without due process of law; nor deny to any person within its jurisdiction the equal protection of the laws.

Section 2. Representatives shall be apportioned among the several States according to their respective numbers, counting the whole number of persons in each State, excluding Indians not taxed. But when the right to vote at any election for the choice of electors for President and Vice President of the United States, Representatives in Congress, the Executive and Judicial officers of a State, or the members of the Legislature thereof, is denied to any of the male inhabitants of such State, being twenty-one years of age, and citizens of the United States, or in any way abridged, except for participation in rebellion, or other crime, the basis of representation therein shall be reduced in the proportion which the number of such male citizens shall bear to the whole number of male citizens twenty-one years of age in such State.

Through decisions of courts that gave life to this provision by adjudicating real disputes, the approach Aristotle originated became the tacit bedrock beneath the Fourteenth Amendment. Its threshold requirement became that equality claimants must be "similarly situated" to those undamaged by inequality in order to be entitled to equal treatment. One must first claim to be the same in order to claim entitlement to equality within its constitutional meaning under the Fourteenth Amendment. The first time the U.S. Supreme Court used language to this effect was in construing the "equal protection" provision of the Fourteenth Amendment in 1885, in an adjudication of the constitutionality of a municipal regulation of laundries.

Barbier v. Connolly

Supreme Court of the United States
113 U.S. 27, 30–32 (1885)

There is no invidious discrimination ... in the regulation under consideration.... It is not legislation discriminating against any one. All persons engaged in the same business within it are treated alike; are subject to the same restrictions and are entitled to the same privileges under similar conditions.

The Fourteenth Amendment ... undoubtedly intended ... that equal protection and security should be given to all under like circumstances in the enjoyment of their personal and civil rights; that all persons should be equally entitled to pursue their happiness and acquire and enjoy property; that they should have like access to the courts of the country for the protection of their persons and property, the prevention and redress of wrongs, and the enforcement of contracts; that no impediment should be interposed to the pursuits of any one except as applied to the same pursuits by others under like circumstances; that no greater burdens should be laid upon one than are laid upon others in the same calling and condition, and that in the administration of criminal justice no different or higher punishment should be imposed upon one than such as is prescribed to all for like offenses. [But] [s]pecial burdens are often necessary for general benefits—for supplying water, preventing fires, lighting districts, cleaning streets, opening parks, and many other objects. Regulations for these purposes may press with more or less weight upon one than upon another, but they are designed, not to impose unequal or unnecessary restrictions upon any one, but to promote, with as little individual inconvenience as possible, the general good. Though, in many respects, necessarily special in their character, they do not furnish just ground of complaint if they operate alike upon all persons and property under the same circumstances and conditions. Class legislation, discriminating against some and favoring others, is prohibited, but legislation which, in carrying out a public purpose, is limited in its application, if within the sphere of its operation it affects alike all persons similarly situated, is not within the amendment.

Putting the same concept more concisely, the Court in 1920 again distinguished the wide legislative discretion to classify, seen as basic to legislation as such, from that which the Fourteenth Amendment prohibits: "[T]he classification must be reasonable, not arbitrary, and must rest upon some ground of difference having a fair and substantial relation to the object of the legislation, so that all persons similarly circumstanced shall be treated alike." *F.S. Royster Guano Co. v. Virginia*, 253 U.S. 412, 415 (1920); *see also Hayes v. Missouri*, 120 U.S. 68, 71 (1887) (under state laws regulating preemptory challenges to jurors in capital cases, the Fourteenth Amendment requires that all persons subjected to such legislation be treated alike under like circumstances and conditions).

The application of Aristotle's approach in this body of law makes the conceptual queries more pointed, visible, and urgent. Can what is now termed the "similarly situated" approach produce social equality? Why must socially unequal groups, in order to demand equal treatment, be first situated the same as groups not afflicted by inequality? If one must first be the same to be equally treated, must one first have equality to get it? If so, will anyone who needs equality from law ever receive it? If, in order to be entitled to the benefit of equality law, situated differences must be obscured rather than exposed, how will the situated consequences of inequality, which by definition afflict some differently than others, be exposed in order to be remedied? In other words, if situated differences must be elided to gain access to equal benefits, how will social inequality ever be revealed in order to be rectified? If the principle of equal treatment imposes the same treatment on those who have and those who have not, on those who need and those who are not in need, on those who have been harmed and on those who have inflicted or benefited from that harm, how will the status of some relative to others ever be changed? Is an approach requiring treating oppressed and oppressor the same "reasonable"? Can oppression ever be stopped this way? Must equality be a symmetrical concept? Must it be in some sense asymmetrical in unequal societies to produce socially equal outcomes?

Equal legal treatment for women, in their capacity as members of their gender, was not originally envisioned under either section of the Fourteenth Amendment. The ratification debates in Congress, to the extent they considered women as such, centered on whether the Amendment would mandate women's suffrage. *See The Reconstruction Amendments Debates* (Alfred Avins ed., 1967). In those discussions, supporters of passage reassured skeptics that it guaranteed neither that women would be permitted to vote nor, should they later be argued to be "persons," that they would be treated the same as men under state laws. *Cong. Globe*, 39th Cong., 1st Sess. 1064 (Sen. Hale), 2767 (Sen. Howard) (1866). Section 2 of the Fourteenth Amendment, explicitly acquiescing in the exclusion of women from the franchise, marks the first time the word "male" appears in the U.S. Constitution. Some women's rights advocates who were also abolitionists, appalled that equality would be constitutionally entrenched without including women, resulting in the failure to guarantee full citizenship even to all former slaves, made the anguished decision to urge its defeat. *See* 2 *History of Woman Suffrage* 90–151 (Elizabeth Cady Stanton et al. eds., AYER Co. Publishers 1985) (1882). *See also* Louise Michele Newman, *White Women's Rights: The Racial Origins of Feminism in the United States* 5, 62–65 (1999). It passed.

In 1875, the U.S. Supreme Court, referencing the language of Section 2, ruled unanimously in *Minor v. Happersett*, 88 U.S. (21 Wall.) 162 (1874), that voting, a creature of state law, was not a right of national citizenship protected from denial to women by the Fourteenth Amendment. The Court reasoned, "[I]f suffrage was necessarily one of the absolute rights of citizenship, why confine the operation of the limitation to male inhabitants?" 88 U.S. at 174. *See generally* Norma Basch, "Reconstructing Female Citizenship: Minor v. Happersett," *in The Constitution, Law, and American Life: Critical Aspects of the Nineteenth–Century Experience* (Donald G. Nieman ed., 1992).

In 1920, the women's suffrage movement finally achieved for American women that elementary right of democratic citizenship, the right to vote, through ratification of the Nineteenth Amendment. *See* Aileen S. Kraditor, *Ideas of the Woman Suffrage Movement, 1890–1920* (1981); *see also* Eleanor Flexner & Ellen Fitzpatrick, *Century of Struggle: The Woman's Rights Movement in the United States* (1996). Its passage culminated the movement with roots from 1848 in Seneca Falls, New York, where the "Declaration of Sentiments" stated that woman's inability to vote was central in woman's oppression: "Having deprived her of this first right of a citizen, the elective franchise, thereby leaving her without representation in the halls of legislation, [man] has oppressed her on all sides." "Declaration of Sentiments," *reprinted in* 1 *History of Woman Suffrage* 70 (Elizabeth Cady Stanton et al. eds., AYER Co. Publishers 1985) (1848).

U.S. Constitution, Amendment XIX

The right of citizens of the United States to vote shall not be denied or abridged by the United States or by any State on account of sex.

Congress shall have power to enforce this article by appropriate legislation.

What did the passage of the Nineteenth Amendment mean for women? If prohibition of the franchise was central to women's oppression, did achieving that right end women's oppression? Did it hasten its end? Does the Nineteenth Amendment, read structurally, negate the term "male" in Section 2 of the Fourteenth Amendment? Women did not automatically gain the right to serve on juries, which are based on voting lists, as a structural argument might have suggested. (*See* Chapter 3.2.) How would you evaluate what the vote gained for women? What do women have today that they would not have without the vote? Does voting symbolize full citizenship? Does it constitute self-government? Are women represented wherever they can vote? Do women consent to a regime in which they can vote? *See generally Suffrage and Beyond: International Feminist Perspectives* (Caroline Daley & Melanie Nolan eds., 1994). Does the Nineteenth Amendment have untapped potential as a source of constitutional interpretation? *See* Reva B. Siegel, "Collective Memory and the Nineteenth Amendment: Reasoning About 'the Woman Question' in the Discourse of Sex Discrimination." *in History, Memory and the Law* 131 (Austin Sarat & Thomas R. Kearns eds., 1999) (urging Nineteenth Amendment as source of norm of women's full citizenship).

Not until 1971, in *Reed v. Reed*, 404 U.S. 71 (1971) (*see* Chapter 3.2), was the Fourteenth Amendment guarantee of equal protection of the laws interpreted to prohibit state laws that, in so many words, created different legal rights for women and men. Since then, the Equal Protection Clause has proved to have what Justice Ginsburg termed "growth potential." Ruth Bader Ginsburg, "Speaking in a Judicial Voice," 67 *N.Y.U. L. Rev.* 1185, 1188 (1992). Over time, legal prohibitions against sex-based discrimination have been extended under the Fourteenth Amendment. (*See* Chapter 3.) Through interpretation, sex equality as a principle has become firmly if incompletely entrenched in U.S. constitutional jurisprudence. At the same time, the solidity, meaning, vitality, and reach of sex equality as a constitutional principle are far from settled, its direction far from certain, its development far from over.

The lack of an explicit guarantee of sex equality has limited the U.S. Constitution as a vehicle for securing women's rights and social advancement. In 1923, the first Equal Rights Amendment (ERA) was introduced into Congress, providing that "[m]en and women shall have equal rights throughout the United States and every place subject to its jurisdiction." S.J. Res. 21, 68th Cong., 1st sess. (1923). It got nowhere. On March 22, 1972, Congress passed and sent to the states for ratification a proposed Federal Equal Rights Amendment, H.R.J. Res. 208, 92d Cong., 2d Sess., 86 Stat. 1523 (1972). As revised in 1943, the ERA no longer mentioned women and men, and no longer granted equal rights, but proposed to keep states from, on grounds of sex, taking rights away. *See* S.J. Res. 25, 78th Cong., 1st sess. (1943). Do you see differences in coverage or philosophy between the two versions? in effectiveness? For discussion of the historical context, see Nancy F. Cott, *The Grounding of Modern Feminism* 119–29, 134–42 (1987); Susan D. Becker, *The Origin of the Equal Rights Amendment: American Feminism Between the Wars* (1981).

The Equal Rights Amendment (ERA)

Section 1. Equality of rights under the law shall not be denied or abridged by the United States or by any State on account of sex.

Sec. 2. The Congress shall have the power to enforce, by appropriate legislation, the provisions of this article.

Sec. 3. This amendment shall take effect two years after the date of ratification. H.R.J.Res. 208, 92nd Cong., 2nd sess., 86 Stat. 1523 (1972).

Supporters and opponents debated what an explicit guarantee of sex equality in the Constitution would do: what ERA would mean for women and men and their relations, symbolically and concretely, aspirationally and materially, legally and culturally. Some opponents of ERA feared that this constitutional sex equality guarantee would subject women to the military draft and to combat, eliminate women's private liberal arts colleges, require federal funding for abortions, and recognize same-sex marriages, undermining women's assertedly protected status and the traditional family. After extensive struggle, this attempt to give sex equality explicit constitutional dimension expired, failing of ratification on June 30, 1982. *See* Deborah L. Rhode, *Justice and Gender* 63–77 (1989). For attempts to analyze its demise, see Donald Mathews & Jane Sherron De Hart, *Sex, Gender and the Politics of the ERA: A State and the Nation* (1990) and Jane J. Mansbridge, *Why We Lost the ERA* (1986). What does it mean for sex equality legally and politically to have lost an attempt to enshrine the principle in the Constitution? Should another ratification attempt be mounted? Should the same language be used?

C. Title VII of the Civil Rights Act of 1964

Almost one hundred years after the passage of the Fourteenth Amendment, with racial equality far from realized (*see* Chapter 2), Congress passed the Civil Rights Act of 1964, prohibiting "discrimination . . . on the basis of sex" as well as race in employment. Contrary to widespread myth, the term "sex" appears not to have been included in Title VII by accident or as only a joke or as a racist attempt to defeat the entire bill. *See* 110 Cong. Rec. 2577–84 (floor debate); Jo Freeman, "How 'Sex' Got into Title VII: Persistent Opportunism as a Maker of Public Policy," 9 *J.L. & Ineq.* 163, 176–78 (1991); Robert C. Bird, "More Than a Congressional Joke: A Fresh Look at the Legislative History of Sex Discrimination of the 1964 Civil Rights Act," 3 *Wm. & Mary J. Women & L.*, 137 (1997) (documenting that feminists strongly supported inclusion of sex and secured passage); *but cf.* Charles & Barbara Whalen, *The Longest Debate: A Legislative History of the 1964 Civil Rights Act* 115–18 (1985) (reading floor record to mean that addition of "sex" was a racist joke to defeat the bill that backfired). The most that can be concluded from available historical sources is that some members of Congress who were not friendly to civil rights preferred a bill, if there was to be one, that prohibited discrimination in employment based on sex as well as race.[4] Debate was substantive if brief, including the following opposition from Representative Emmanuel Celler:

4. Adding the term "sex" to Title VII was voted on separately by the House of Representatives twice, passing both times, followed the second time by the passage of Title VII as amended. *See* 110 Cong. Rec. 2585 (1964) (first passage); 110 Cong. Rec. 2804 (1964) (second passage). The "sex" amendment's sponsor, Rep. Smith, a segregationist who had been an ERA sponsor since 1943 and spoke in favor of a "sex" amendment in 1956, *see* Freeman, *supra*, at 182, said he was "serious about this" twice in his introduction, which nonetheless included some inexplicable jocular statements. 110 Cong. Rec. 2577 (1964). A handful of those who spoke or voted for including "sex" in Title VII may have had diverse or perverse motives. This is routinely true without branding legislation as unintended by the bodies that pass it by large margins as Congress did Title VII. Attempts to include "sex" in other titles of the Act had been defeated

You know, the French have a phrase for it when they speak of women and men. When they speak of the difference, they say "vive la difference." I think the French are right. Imagine the upheaval that would result from adoption of blanket language requiring total equality. Would male citizens be justified in insisting that women share with them the burdens of compulsory military service? What would become of traditional family relationships? What about alimony? Who would have the obligation of supporting whom? Would fathers rank equally with mothers in the right of custody to children? What would become of the crimes of rape and statutory rape? Would the Mann Act [prohibiting white slavery, see Chapter 10.1] be invalidated? Would the many State and local provisions regulating working conditions and hours of employment for women be struck down? You know the biological differences between the sexes. In many States we have laws favorable to women. Are you going to strike those laws down? This is the entering wedge, an amendment of this sort. The list of foreseeable consequences . . . is unlimited.

110 Cong. Rec. 2577–78 (1964). Is his theory of gender consonant with the Aristotelian approach? Although his position was rejected in passing Title VII, virtually all of the laws he mentions have been questioned under Fourteenth Amendment sex equality principles, independently of Title VII. Is sex discrimination in employment systematically central to sex-differential rights, as Mr. Celler claimed? What is your view of his parade of horribles?

Representative Margaret Griffiths argued that the inclusion of "sex" was necessary to give white women the same rights in employment that "colored women" would otherwise get under the bill. 110 Cong. Rec. 2579–2580 (1964). So did Mr. Smith. See 110 Cong. Rec. 2583 (1964). It seems not to have dawned on them that women of color could be, and were, discriminated against based on sex (as well as race, often both), thus had at least as much to gain from the inclusion of "sex" in the Act as white women did, and as much or more to lose from a failure to include it. (See Chapter 4.) Why did "sex" have a white image? Does it still? Is it deserved? Is there a connection between one's position on race and sex equality issues?

Title VII of the Civil Rights Act of 1964

(Sec. 703(a) (as amended)) 42 U.S.C. § 2000e–2

It shall be an unlawful employment practice for an employer—

(1) to fail or refuse to hire or to discharge any individual, or otherwise to discriminate against any individual with respect to his compensation, terms, conditions, or privileges of employment, because of such individual's race, color, religion, sex, or national origin; or

---

directly. See 110 Cong. Rec. 1978–79, 2280–81, 2264–65, 2297 (1964). "The overall voting pattern implies that there was a large group of Congressmen (in addition to the Congresswomen) that was serious about adding 'sex' to Title VII, but only to Title VII. That is not consistent with the interpretation that the addition of 'sex' was part of a plot to scuttle the bill." Freeman, *supra,* at 178. Professor Bird says that "Smith was an opponent of civil rights legislation and introduced the sex discrimination provision to scuttle the bill. If the bill was to pass, however, Smith genuinely preferred a bill with a ban on sex discrimination. If the bill granted too many rights to other interest groups, at least the bill would protect white women." Bird, *supra,* at 157–58. "The overwhelming evidence defies the conclusion that 'sex' was added as a mere joke." *Id.* at 161.

(2) to limit, segregate, or classify his employees or applicants for employment in any way which would deprive or tend to deprive any individual of employment opportunities or otherwise adversely affect his status as an employee, because of such individual's race, color, religion, sex, or national origin.

Subsequent legislative action against sex discrimination expressed beyond cavil the determination of Congress to prohibit sex discrimination in many areas of social life, extending to education and the federal workplace. (*See* Chapter 3.) When the Supreme Court has failed to interpret legislative mandates to provide sufficient protection from sex discrimination, most pointedly in the area of pregnancy (*see* Chapter 3.5) and burdens of proof (*see* Chapter 5), Congress has passed specific legislation to guarantee sex equality without ambiguity. These are not the acts of a legislative body that regards sex discrimination as a laughing matter.

Political movements for social equality, especially the American Black civil rights movement and the women's rights movements past and present, have driven and directed these legal developments, constitutional and statutory, in and out of court. The operative concept of "civil rights" that was specifically pioneered by the Black movement, beginning in the middle of the twentieth century, profoundly altered the theory and practice of law as an instrument of social change. Aiming to create social equality through legal equality, this movement exposed white racism as systemic in American society and sought to put legal power of redress into the hands of those harmed by it. Title VII is one product of its activism. This movement saw law as something people do, not just as something governments do to people. The democratic innovation in legal form termed "civil rights" was appropriate to the egalitarian aspiration of this movement to transform social hierarchies from the bottom up. Understanding social inequality as pervasive rather than exceptional, the civil rights movement adopted the view that what law has done, it must undo, and what it has not rectified, it should. The jurisprudential notion was that law *is* society at its point of accountability. Through acts or failures to act, law is a force in social order and social change as well as a reflection of social imperatives.

The insights and innovations in theory and practice of the Black civil rights movement reshaped the legal and social landscape. It redefined the notion of rights as such to encompass not only those asserted on individual and universal grounds, but also those grounded in membership in subordinated social groups. The contemporary women's movement deepened and expanded this concept still further. Yet the Aristotelian sameness-difference concept of equality continued to animate both interpretation of the Fourteenth Amendment, from the "similarly situated" threshold forward, and the parallel legal requirement of comparability under Title VII. Implicit in both the Black civil rights movement and the women's movement has been a deeper and broader critique of both inequality in society and conventional equality thinking than has yet emerged in equality theory and litigation[5], and a more visionary reconstruction of democracy than has yet taken place.

---

5. Some flaws, conceptual and consequential, of the mainstream equality approach have been criticized in the racial context without questioning the basic premises of legal equality as such. *See* Owen Fiss, "Groups and the Equal Protection Clause," 5 *Phil. & Pub. Aff.* 107 (1976) (urging group-disadvantaging principle); Alan Freeman, "Legitimizing Racial Discrimination Through Antidiscrimination Law: A Critical Review of

II. SEX INEQUALITY UNDER LAW

The legal pursuit of sex equality has been shaped in a very specific way by the ruling equality paradigm. The preferred definition of equality as sameness has interacted with the definition of the sexes as different. Women—the sex-defined group considered "different" that has most needed equality through law—have not fared well under this paradigm.

Gender defined as a difference is termed, in common parlance, the sex difference. The notion that women and men are defined as gendered by their differences from one another, and the equation of women's so-called differences with inferiority or naturally lower status, has pervaded philosophy and law. It has also, in diverse forms, been an enforced imperative in many if not most human societies. Gender in most societies has defined women as such in terms of differences, real and imagined, from men— usually to women's detriment in resources, roles, respect, and rights.

Thus, in the received traditions, equality is a sameness and gender is a difference. To define equality in terms of sameness and women as "not the same" thus raises the question whether women will be equal under this approach only when they are no longer women. To consider this question is not to affirm women's sameness to men or women's differences from men, but to face a conflict at the point of intersection between the ruling equality paradigm and the social definition of women as such. Sex equality, so understood, appears to be a contradiction in terms.

Such an outcome is, by the way, consistent with some of Aristotle's own views. He believed, for example, that the "excellence of character . . . the temperance of a man and of a woman, or the courage and justice of a man and of a woman, are not, as Socrates maintained, the same; the courage of a man is shown in commanding, of a woman in obeying. And this holds of all other excellences. . . ." Aristotle, *The Politics* 19 (Stephen Everson ed. & Benjamin Jowett trans., Cambridge Univ. Press 1988).[6] Among relations in which "one rules and the other is ruled," in some editions of Aristotle's *Politics*, in "[t]he relation of the male to the female, . . . the inequality is permanent." *Aristotle's Politics* (Benjamin Jowett trans., Random House, 1943). Such substantive notions of human hierarchy, of how women and men rank, may underlie and determine apparent abstractions, such as limiting equality by difference and vice versa. Which

Supreme Court Doctrine," 62 *Minn. L. Rev.* 1049 (1978) (arguing that discrimination law takes perpetrator perspective); Kimberlé Williams Crenshaw, "Race, Reform and Retrenchment: Transformation Legitimation in Antidiscrimination Law," 101 *Harv. L. Rev.* 1331 (1988) (showing how neutral norms in antidiscrimination law reinforce racism); *see also* Paul Brest, "The Supreme Court, 1975 Term—Foreword: In Defense of the Antidiscrimination Principle," 90 *Harv. L. Rev.* 1 (1976). Much of the law created by the Black civil rights movement went beyond the mainstream paradigm, yet because the equality paradigm was never confronted directly, its

gains may have been particularly vulnerable to reversal under changed political conditions without open break with precedent. (*See* Chapter 3.)

6. This passage has also been translated as: "[T]emperance—and similarly fortitude and justice—are not, as Socrates held, the same in a woman as they are in a man. Fortitude in the one, for example, is shown in connexion with ruling; in the other, it is shown in connexion with serving; and the same is true of the other forms of goodness." *The Politics of Aristotle* 36 (Ernest Barker trans., Oxford Univ. Press 1946).

do you think comes first: experiencing women as unequal to men, so equality rules are constructed so sex equality is difficult for women to claim, or devising abstract equality rules that privilege sameness, only to find that women's circumstances largely preclude equality claims?

In practice, legal systems avoid some of the irrationalities and drawbacks conventional equality logic could impose by carving out factual exceptions. These include providing different treatment for real differences—for example, allowing maternity leaves—although no comparable man exists to need them. The fact that there may be no comparable man is seen not as a reason to reexamine the requirement of comparability more generally; it is seen only as a reason to provide an exception for what is presented as a unique sex-linked need, in order to save the sameness/difference approach in general. (*See* Chapter 3.1, 3.5.) Affirmative action is treated as another such exception. People seen as different (meaning "less qualified") are allowed to be treated as if they were the same (meaning "qualified")—clearly a precarious, perhaps doomed venture so long as neither the standards for qualification (the same as what?) nor the basic equality paradigm (likes alike, unlikes unalike) is called into question.

The problems of "same treatment for sameness" for women are, if anything, exceeded by the problems of "different treatment for differences." For one thing, "being" different can be a consequence of prior discrimination. In addition, women's contributions are notoriously undervalued. Standards of merit created in unequal societies can reify social dominance, making people look "different," say unqualified, who in reality have much that is distinctive to contribute. However, so long as an implicitly socially biased merit standard is left unchallenged, counterbalancing or qualifying it will be stigmatizing.

Fundamentally, the law has often failed to call the problem of discrimination by a real name—say, white supremacy or male dominance. It has instead used more neutral terms like "racism" or "racial classifications" or "race," or "sexism" or "sex classifications" or "sex," terms that fail to specify who is doing what to whom. As a result, while many conditions of actual disadvantage are obscured, situations in which the affected and agentic groups appear reversed can easily be made to look like discrimination. Abstractions (are you treated the same or differently?) may be inverted far more readily than substance (are you victimized by white supremacy or male dominance or both?).

Finally, different treatment where differences are seen to be real, the same principle that animates the so-called exceptions that saves the main equality principle of sameness from absurdity, has animated the worst human rights abuses known to history, including racial segregation in the American South and extermination of Jews and others under Germany's Third Reich. It has consistently been used to justify excluding from equality scrutiny some of the most systematic forms of sex-based subordination—for example, paying women in sex-segregated jobs differently, meaning less, (*see* Chapter 3.1), keeping women poor. Creating such "difference" exceptions to save the "sameness" rule functions to preserve the "sameness" standard from question, scrutiny that could expose the bias of standards of sameness by which women and some minority groups are consistently found to be less deserving, revealing this equality approach as a rationalization for and tool in an unequal status quo.

On a systemic level, equality doctrine's "different treatment for differences" is an expression of a norm that underlies the legal system's structural failure to grasp many issues that arguably are problems of inequality *as* problems of inequality. Sexual violence against women is one example. Because perpetrators are overwhelmingly male and victims predominantly female, and because sexual assault is socially rooted in normative images of sexuality seen as gendered by nature, sexual violence has implicitly been seen as part of the sex difference, therefore not raising issues of sex inequality at all. (*See* Chapter 7.) Reproductive rights provide another example of the same dynamic. Because women and men contribute differently to biological reproduction, the social disadvantages to which women are subjected in connection with gestation, birth, and motherhood have been recognized by equality law belatedly, partially, with severe doctrinal strain, and sometimes, as with abortion rights, almost not at all. (*See* Chapters 3.5 and 9.1.)

Another way of stating these problems is to observe that legal systems since the Enlightenment have recognized rights for individuals one at a time—either as a unique self or as an undifferentiated member of humanity—but rarely as members of social groups. Social groups are seen to make persons "different," while their individuality and common humanity makes them "the same." Human rights are thus seen as individual rights, not rights deriving from group membership, whether ascribed to individuals as members of groups or to groups as such. Group membership has been seen to be in tension with humanity understood in individual or universal terms, not as constitutive of it. Group membership can be used to socially define people as unequal to one another; yet membership in social groups undeniably shapes people in their particularity and in their humanity. Group membership does not simply distinguish humans; it is part of being human. Similarly, each woman who is discriminated against as a woman is personally harmed, certainly, but she is harmed in and because of her status as a member of the group women. The injuries harm each woman but the basis on which the harm is done is group-based and collectively shared.

Law, instead of recognizing this, has divided human status (group-based) from human treatment (individual) in both the legal system and in civil society—as if one could be treated unequally but remain equal in status, and as if those with unequal social status will still be treated equally. In reality, status and treatment constitute each other.

In Aristotle's Greece, women had no collective or concerted voice in contesting his formulation of equality and have had little institutional power in shaping its legal applications since. "All research has pointed to one glaring, undisputed gender difference. Women are minimally represented in the political elite." Marianne Githens, "The Elusive Paradigm: Gender, Politics and Political Behavior," *in Political Science: The State of the Discipline* 471, 483 (Ada W. Finifter ed., 1983). Women have not been represented by women in governments, including democracies. In 1995, women members of parliament held only 11.3 percent of the world's seats. *See* Interparliamentary Union, *Women in Parliaments, 1945–1995: A World Statistical Study* (1995); *see also* United Nations Office at Vienna Centre for Social Development and Humanitarian Affairs, *Women in Politics and Decision–Making in the Late Twentieth Century: A United Nations Study* 9, 10 (1992); Gisbert H. Flanz, *Comparative Women's Rights and Political Participation in Europe* (1983). The percentage of women in parliaments has tended to drop since the collapse of communism in Europe and the rise of democracy in Africa. Women's "numbers rise where the power of the office is less." Anne Phillips, *Engendering Democracy* 60–61 (1991). How do you understand the relation between women's exclusion from politics and the rest of women's condition? What does it mean that the less power inheres in an assembly, the more women are likely to be elected to it?

Yet women have begun, through organizing and litigation, activism and scholarship, to articulate and criticize their unequal situation in public. *See, e.g.*, Susan J. Carroll & Linda M.G. Zerilli, "Feminist Challenges to Political Science," *in Political Science: The State of the Discipline II* 55 (Ada W. Finifter ed., 1993). Beginning in the late 1960s, the women's liberation movement profoundly altered the climate and content of law, attitudes, and social relations between the sexes. Its impact has registered powerfully, including in those areas of social inequality between the sexes that have yet to be effectively reached by legal equality guarantees.

The information that has emerged as a result of this global movement has revealed a grim interlocking system for women of deprivation of nutrition and literacy, exclusion from gainful and fulfilling work and remuneration, grinding exploitation of labor, sexual assault as children and adults, and intimate terror and violence. Women are widely demeaned, denigrated, depersonalized, and dehumanized. They are kept poor and dependent, deprived of reproductive control, exchanged and maintained as chattel, forced into marriage and prostitution, bound to rigid roles and narrow lives, and murdered. These abuses have occurred, in varying forms, for a very long time in most societies. *See, e.g.*, U.N. Dep't of Int'l Economic & Social Affairs, *Compendium of Statistics and Indicators on the Situation of Women 1986*, U.N. Doc. ST/ESA/STAT/SER.K/5, U.N. Sales No. E/F.88.-XVII.6 (1988).

Legal institutions have largely supported or enforced these inequalities, whether women are expressly stripped of legal rights by law, given formal equality in countries where legal rules are not the real rules, or given sex equality where law counts but gender-specific violations of it are ignored. Laws in many countries prevent women from voting or owning property, keep them owned and used in families, permit them to be sexually exploited and possessed and violated, and exclude them from advancement through education and from a voice in public life. In a combined regime of unequal treatment and status, through a seamless web of society and law, women as women—understood as members of a social group defined as gender female—are deprived of avenues for independence and self-development, degraded for profit and entertainment and pleasure, violated with impunity, and exploited without limit. In such regimes, law sees women to limit and control them. Otherwise, it does not see them at all. *See* Eschel M. Rhoodie, *Discrimination Against Women: A Global Survey of the Economic, Educational, Social, and Political Status of Women* (1989); International League for Human Rights, *Human Rights Abuses Against Women: A Worldwide Survey* (1990).

If women's current condition is accepted as being "the sex difference," women merely occupy their side of Aristotle's level line disproportionately divided. A "difference" in this sense gives rise to no equality claim because it is practically unchangeable, not produced by inequality, somehow equal or complementary, needing no rectification. If the reality of women's status merely describes such a difference on the basis of sex, social equality between the sexes already exists. The received equality approach needs no scrutiny. If, on the other hand, these facts are changeable, injurious, socially imposed, and in need of rectification, they form an inequality, not a mere difference. But they cannot be represented as a level line. They are a top-down arrangement of imposed superiority and inferiority, of dominance and subordination. They are better represented as a hierarchy.

When law guarantees equality on the basis of sex, it *assumes* that women and men are equal in some relevant sense. To defend current social reality as consistent with a guarantee of equality of the sexes is to assert that women's current treatment *is* equal. This, in turn, is to defend systematically fewer material resources and systemic victimization through aggression as what equality for women looks like—a notion that can be valid only if women are a different order of being from men. Is this what George Orwell meant when he said, in his famous political satire, "All . . . are equal, but some . . . are more equal than others"? George Orwell, *Animal Farm* 118 (Harcourt, Brace & Co. 1982) (1946). Is the assumption that women are not men's equals present in the defense of current social reality as equal, in spite of the fact that most who take this approach—whether on evolutionary, biological, religious, or other grounds—do not openly defend, for instance, mass rape in war or husbands' slaughtering their wives or sex-unequal pay? The question here is whether treating women as what, for men, would be second-class citizens is what equality for women means.

Questions raised by the Aristotelian approach to be explored throughout this book include: Is an assumption of women's natural inequality to men built into the foundations of conventional equality theory? Is the existing equality theory embodied in most law based on an assumption that half the human race is biologically inferior to the other half? Can equality law become an effective tool for social equality? If the existing approach is inadequate, what would an equality theory built on the assumption of equality of the sexes look like? Would such an equality theory allow Aristotle's logic to work to promote sex equality, or would it make his logic obsolete? What if, reversing current ordering in most places, the main equality model pursued an end to group-based hierarchy and prejudice, and a secondary model treated like individuals alike?

III.   COMPARATIVE LEGAL EQUALITY APPROACHES

A.   A CANADIAN ALTERNATIVE

When the traditional equality approach created in women's silence was measured against the realities of women's lives, as women have begun since 1970 to articulate them, analytical and practical shortcomings of that approach began to emerge. The disparity called for an equality theory capable of addressing the sex inequality problems in women's lives that law had traditionally treated ineffectively if at all. In 1989, a basic critique of the legal concept of equality itself based on these realities, together with a proposed alternative, was first argued to a court in *Andrews v. Law Society of British Columbia*, [1989] 1 S.C.R. 143 (Can.), the first legal challenge to be brought under the equality provisions of the new Canadian Charter of Rights and Freedoms, which came into effect in 1985.

Canadian Charter of Rights and Freedoms
Constitution Act, 1982

Equality Rights

Section 15 (1) Every individual is equal before and under the law and has the right to the equal protection and equal benefit of the law without discrimination and, in particular, without discrimination based on race, national or ethnic origin, colour, religion, sex, age or mental or physical disability.

(2) Subsection (1) does not preclude any law, program or activity that has as its object the amelioration of conditions of disadvantaged individuals or groups including those that are disadvantaged because of race, national or ethnic origin, colour, religion, sex, age or mental or physical disability.

Canadian women, determined to prevent a repetition of the legal inadequacies of prior Canadian or American legal approaches to women's rights, ensured through concerted political action, that an additional guarantee of sex equality became part of the Charter:

28.   Notwithstanding anything in this Charter, the rights and freedoms referred to in it are guaranteed equally to male and female persons.

See Mary Eberts, "Sex-based Discrimination and the Charter," *in Equality Rights and the Canadian Charter of Rights and Freedoms* 183 (Ann F. Bayefsky & Mary Eberts eds., 1985). Section 28 was intended at minimum to sensitize the judiciary to women's inequality, although it remains to be seen whether it has done so. *See* Gwen Brodsky & Shelagh Day, *Canadian Charter Equality Rights for Women: One Step Forward or Two Steps Back?* 81–83 (1989). Compare its language with the American ERA. Which is better? Is the comparatively more concrete language of Section 28 an improvement? Does it go far enough?

In its decision in *Andrews*, the Supreme Court of Canada adopted in large part the approach advocated by the Women's Legal Education and Action Fund (LEAF), a women's activist group litigating for sex equality. Their equality argument, grounded in the unequal situation of women, repudiated Aristotle's formulation of equality and with it hundreds of years of doctrinal abstraction. The *Andrews* decision recognizes the value of formal equality as obvious but rejects it as defining the core meaning and setting the outer limits of legal equality guarantees. It ushers in a concrete context-sensitive test and requires that law and policy "promote equality" in order to be constitutional. The opinion holds that the historical context of the enumerated grounds, including the history of race and sex, is a qualifier built into Section 15 as a whole, limiting the distinctions it forbids "to those which involve prejudice or disadvantage," not difference.

The new equality paradigm adopted by the Supreme Court of Canada in *Andrews* criticizes and clarifies the scope, meaning, assumptions, and limits of existing equality approaches and then provides a grounded context-sensitive method for enhancing the realism of equality law and expanding its reach and potential effectiveness in producing social equality. Explicitly moving beyond the confines of sameness and difference analysis for the first time, expressly rejecting the Aristotelian approach that had gone unquestioned for two thousand years, the *Andrews* Court focuses on advantage and disadvantage rather than equivalence and distinction. Revealing that the opposite of equality is hierarchy, not difference, understanding social inequality as vertical rather than horizontal in nature, the *Andrews* opinion exposes social inequality as hierarchy disguised and rationalized by traditional equality thinking as mistaken differentiation.

Canada, unlike the United States, permits the rights guaranteed in its Constitution to be expressly overridden if the challenged law is found to be justified under Section 1. Section 1 states: "The *Canadian Charter of Rights and Freedoms* guarantees the rights and freedoms set out in it subject only to such reasonable limits prescribed by law as can be demonstrably justified in a free and democratic society." Can. Const. (Constitution Act, 1982) pt. I (Canadian Charter of Rights and Freedoms), § 1. The Supreme Court of Canada unanimously adopted the equality reasoning of Mr. Justice McIntyre's opinion below. However, Justice McIntyre was persuaded that the inequality he found in the provision Mr. Andrews challenged was justified. The majority disagreed on this point, making the McIntyre opinion dissenting but only in the result.

Andrews v. Law Society of British Columbia

Supreme Court of Canada
[1989] 1 S.C.R. 143

■ McINTYRE, J. (dissenting in part) [with whom Lamer, J. concurs]. This appeal raises only one question. Does the citizenship requirement for entry into the legal profession ... contravene s. 15(1)? ... The respondent, Andrews, was a British subject permanently resident in Canada ... and had fulfilled all the requirements for admission to the practice of law in British Columbia, except that of Canadian citizenship....

Section 15(1) of the *Charter* provides for every individual a guarantee of equality before and under the law, as well as the equal protection and equal benefit of the law without discrimination. This is not a general guarantee of equality; it does not provide for equality between individuals or groups within society in a general or abstract sense, nor does it impose on individuals or groups an obligation to accord equal treatment to others. It is concerned with the application of the law....

The concept of equality ... is a comparative concept, the condition of which may only be attained or discerned by comparison with the condition of others in the social and political setting in which the question arises. It must be recognized at once, however, that every difference in treatment between individuals under the law will not necessarily result in inequality and, as well, that identical treatment may frequently produce serious inequality [as stated in] the well-known words of Frankfurter J. in *Dennis v. United States*, 339 U.S. 162 (1950), at p. 184: "It was a wise man who said that there is no greater inequality than the equal treatment of unequals." The same thought has been expressed in this Court ... in *R. v. Big M Drug Mart Ltd.*, [1985] 1 S.C.R. 295, where Dickson C.J. said at p. 347: "The equality necessary to support religious freedom does not require identical treatment of all religions. In fact, the interests of true equality may well require differentiation in treatment." ...

To approach the ideal of full equality before and under the law ... the main consideration must be the impact of the law on the individual or the group concerned. Recognizing that there will always be an infinite variety of personal characteristics, capacities, entitlements and merits among those subject to a law, there must be accorded, as nearly as may be possible, an equality of benefit and protection and no more of the restrictions, penalties or burdens imposed upon one than another. . . .

McLachlin J.A. in the Court of Appeal expressed the view . . . that:

> . . . the essential meaning of the constitutional requirement of equal protection and equal benefit is that persons who are "similarly situated be similarly treated" and conversely, that persons who are "differently situated be differently treated". . . . The reliance on this concept appears to have derived, at least in recent times, from J.T. Tussman and J. tenBroek, "The Equal Protection of Laws" 37 *Calif. L. Rev.* 341 (1949). The similarly situated test is a restatement of the Aristotelian principle of formal equality—that "things that are alike should be treated alike, while things that are unalike should be treated unalike in proportion to their unalikeness."

The test as stated, however, is seriously deficient in that it excludes any consideration of the nature of the law. If it were to be applied literally, it could be used to justify the Nuremberg laws of Adolf Hitler. Similar treatment was contemplated for all Jews. The similarly situated test would have justified the formalistic separate but equal doctrine of *Plessy v. Ferguson*, 163 U.S. 537 (1896), a doctrine that incidentally was still the law in the United States at the time that Professor Tussman and J. tenBroek wrote their much cited article. . . . The test, somewhat differently phrased, was applied in the British Columbia Court of Appeal [upholding a section of the Indian Act] which made it an offence for an Indian to have intoxicants in his possession off a reserve. In his locality there were no reserves. . . . This approach was rejected in this Court . . . in *R. v. Drybones*, [1970] S.C.R. 282, in a similar case. . . . "I cannot agree with this interpretation pursuant to which it seems to me that the most glaring discriminatory legislation against a racial group would have to be construed as recognizing the right of each of its individual members 'to equality before the law,' so long as all the other members are being discriminated against in the same way."

Thus, mere equality of application to similarly situated groups or individuals does not afford a realistic test for violation of equality rights. For, as has been said, a bad law will not be saved merely because it operates equally upon those to whom it has application. Nor will a law necessarily be bad because it makes distinctions.

A similarly situated test focussing on the equal application of the law to those to whom it has application could lead to results akin to those in *Bliss v. Attorney General of Canada*, [1979] 1 S.C.R. 183. In *Bliss*, a pregnant woman was denied unemployment benefits to which she would have been entitled had she not been pregnant. She claimed that the *Unemployment Insurance Act, 1971*, violated the equality guarantees of the *Canadian Bill of Rights* because it discriminated against her on the basis of her sex. Her claim was dismissed by this Court on the grounds that there was no discrimination on the basis of sex, since the class into which she fell under the Act was that of pregnant persons, and within that class, all persons were treated equally. This case, of course, was decided before the advent of the *Charter*. . . .

Consideration must be given to the content of the law, to its purpose, and its impact upon those to whom it applies, and also upon those whom it excludes from its application. . . . It is not every distinction or differentiation in treatment at law which will transgress the equality guarantees of s. 15. . . . It is, of course, obvious that legislatures may—and to govern effectively must—treat different individuals and groups in different ways [and make distinctions]. . . . What kinds of distinctions will be acceptable under s. 15(1) and what kinds will violate its provisions?

In seeking an answer to these questions, the provisions of the *Charter* must have their full effect. In *R. v. Big M Drug Mart Ltd.*, this Court emphasized this point at p. 344, where Dickson C.J. stated: "In *Hunter v. Southam Inc.*, [1984] 2 S.C.R. 145, this Court expressed the view that the proper approach to the definition of the rights and freedoms guaranteed by the *Charter* was a purposive one. The meaning of a right or freedom guaranteed by the *Charter* was to be ascertained . . . in the light of the interests it was meant to protect. . . . The interpretation should be . . . a generous rather than a legalistic one, aimed at fulfilling the purpose of the guarantee and securing for individuals the full benefit of the *Charter*'s protection. At the same time it is important . . . to recall that the *Charter* was not enacted in a vacuum, and must therefore . . . be placed in its proper linguistic, philosophic and historical contexts." . . .

The principle of equality before the law has long been recognized as a feature of our constitutional tradition and it found statutory recognition in the *Canadian Bill of Rights*. . . . The shortcomings of the *Canadian Bill of Rights* as far as the right to equality is concerned are well known. In *Attorney General of Canada v. Lavell*, [1974] S.C.R. 1349, for example, this Court upheld s. 12(1)(*b*) of the *Indian Act* which deprived women, but not men, of their membership in Indian bands if they married non-Indians. The provision was held not to violate equality *before* the law. . . . In *Bliss, supra*, this Court held that the denial of unemployment insurance benefits to women because they were pregnant did not violate the guarantee of equality before the law, because any inequality in the protection and benefit of the law was "not created by legislation but by nature". . . . It is readily apparent that the language of s. 15 was deliberately chosen in order to remedy some of the perceived defects under the *Canadian Bill of Rights*. . . .

It is clear that the purpose of s. 15 is to ensure equality in the formulation and application of the law. The promotion of equality entails the promotion of a society in which all are secure in the knowledge that they are recognized at law as human beings equally deserving of concern, respect and consideration. It has a large remedial component. . . .

It must be recognized, however, as well that the promotion of equality under s. 15 has a much more specific goal than the mere elimination of distinctions. If the *Charter* was intended to eliminate all distinctions, then there would be no place for sections such as 27 (multicultural heritage); 2(*a*) (freedom of conscience and religion); 25 (aboriginal rights and freedoms); and other such provisions designed to safeguard certain distinctions. Moreover, the fact that identical treatment may frequently produce serious inequality is recognized in s. 15(2). . . .

Discrimination is unacceptable in a democratic society because it epitomizes the worst effects of the denial of equality, and discrimination reinforced by law is particularly repugnant. The worst oppression will result from discriminatory measures having the force of law. It is against this evil that s. 15 provides a guarantee.

What does discrimination mean? . . . [T]he general concept of discrimination under [the Human Rights Acts in the provinces] has been fairly well settled. . . . In *Ontario Human Rights Commission & O'Malley v. Simpsons-Sears Ltd.*, [1985] 2 S.C.R. 536, 551, discrimination (in that case adverse effect discrimination) was described in these terms:

> It arises where an employer . . . adopts a rule or standard . . . which has a discriminatory effect upon a prohibited ground on one employee or group of employees in that it imposes, because of some special characteristic of the employee or group, obligations, penalties, or restrictive conditions not imposed on other members of the work force.

It was held in that case, as well, that no intent was required as an element of discrimination, for it is in essence the impact of the discriminatory act or provision upon the person affected which is decisive in considering any complaint.... [T]his proposition was expressed in these terms:

> The Code aims at the removal of discrimination. This is to state the obvious. Its main approach, however, is not to punish the discriminator, but rather to provide relief for the victims of discrimination. It is the result or the effect of the action complained of which is significant. If it does, in fact, cause discrimination; if its effect is to impose on one person or group of persons obligations, penalties, or restrictive conditions not imposed on other members of the community, it is discriminatory.

In [the] *Action Travail des Femmes* case, [[1987] 1 S.C.R. 1114], where it was alleged that the Canadian National Railway was guilty of discriminatory hiring and promotion practices contrary to s. 10 of the *Canadian Human Rights Act* ... in denying employment to women in certain unskilled positions, Dickson C.J. in giving the judgment of the Court said, at pp. 1138–39:

> A thorough study of "systemic discrimination" in Canada is to be found in the Abella Report on equality in employment. ... "Discrimination ... means practices or attitudes that have, whether by design or impact, the effect of limiting an individual's or a group's right to the opportunities generally available because of attributed rather than actual characteristics. ...

> It is not a question of whether this discrimination is motivated by an intentional desire to obstruct someone's potential, or whether it is the accidental by-product of innocently motivated practices or systems. If the barrier is affecting certain groups in a disproportionately negative way, it is a signal that the practices that lead to this adverse impact may be discriminatory." ...

I would say then that discrimination may be described as a distinction, whether intentional or not but based on grounds relating to personal characteristics of the individual or group, which has the effect of imposing burdens, obligations, or disadvantages on such individual or group not imposed upon others, or which withholds or limits access to opportunities, benefits, and advantages available to other members of society. Distinctions based on personal characteristics attributed to an individual solely on the basis of association with a group will rarely escape the charge of discrimination, while those based on an individual's merits and capacities will rarely be so classed.

[In general] ... the principles which have been applied under the Human Rights Acts are equally applicable in considering questions of discrimination under s. 15(1). ... The enumerated grounds in s. 15(1) are not exclusive and the limits, if any, on grounds for discrimination which may be established in future cases await definition. The enumerated grounds do, however, reflect the most common and probably the most socially destructive and historically practised bases of discrimination and must, in the words of s. 15(1), receive particular attention. Both the enumerated grounds themselves and other possible grounds of discrimination recognized under s. 15(1) must be interpreted in a broad and generous manner....

[T]he 14th Amendment to the American Constitution, which provides that no State shall deny to any person within its jurisdiction the "equal protection of the laws," contains no limiting provisions similar to s. 1 of the *Charter*. As a result, judicial consideration has led to the development of varying standards of scrutiny of alleged violations of the equal protection provision which restrict or limit the equality guarantee within the concept of equal protection itself. . . . The distinguishing feature of the *Charter*, unlike the other enactments, is that consideration of such limiting factors is made under s. 1 [which "guarantees the rights and freedoms set out in [the Charter] subject only to such reasonable limits prescribed by law as can be demonstrably justified in a free and democratic society"]. . . . [W]hen confronted with a problem under the *Charter*, the first question which must be answered will be whether or not an infringement of a guaranteed right has occurred. Any justification must be made, if at all, under the broad provisions of s. 1. . . . It is for the citizen to establish that his or her *Charter* right has been infringed and for the state to justify the infringement.

Three main approaches have been adopted in determining the role of s. 15(1), the meaning of discrimination set out in that section, and the relationship of s. 15(1) and s. 1. The first one, which was advanced by Professor Peter Hogg would treat every distinction drawn by law as discrimination under s. 15(1). There would then follow a consideration of the distinction under the provisions of s. 1 of the *Charter*. . . .

The second approach put forward by McLachlin J.A. in the Court of Appeal involved a consideration of the reasonableness and fairness of the impugned legislation under s. 15(1). . . . She assigned a very minor role to s. 1. . . .

A third approach, sometimes described as an "enumerated or analogous grounds" approach, adopts the concept that discrimination is generally expressed by the enumerated grounds. Section 15(1) is designed to prevent discrimination based on these and analogous grounds. The approach is similar to that found in human rights and civil rights statutes which have been enacted throughout Canada in recent times. . . . [Hugessen J.A. illustrates]: " . . . Questions of stereotyping, of historical disadvantagement, in a word, of prejudice, are the focus and there may even be a recognition that for some people equality has a different meaning than for others." The analysis of discrimination in this approach must take place within the context of the enumerated grounds and those analogous to them. The words "without discrimination" require more than a mere finding of distinction between the treatment of groups or individuals. Those words are a form of qualifier built into s. 15 itself and limit those distinctions which are forbidden by the section to those which involve prejudice or disadvantage. . . . The third or "enumerated and analogous grounds" approach most closely accords with the purposes of s. 15 and the definition of discrimination outlined above and leaves questions of justification to s. 1. . . .

Non-citizens, lawfully permanent residents of Canada, are—in the words of the U.S. Supreme Court in *United States v. Carolene Products Co.*—a good example of a "discrete and insular minority" who come within the protection of s. 15. . . . [However, the citizenship requirement] is chosen for the achievement of a desirable social goal: one aspect of the due regulation and qualification of the legal profession. This is an objective of importance and the measure is not disproportionate to the object to be attained. [Therefore s. 1 permits the discrimination.]

■ WILSON, J. [Dickson, C.J. and L'Heureux–Dube, JJ. concur].[7] . . . I am in complete agreement with [Justice McIntyre] as to the way in which s. 15(1) . . . should be interpreted and applied [and] as to the way in which s. 15(1) and s. 1

---

7. In the original reasons, Madam Justice Wilson's opinion, the opinion of the Court, appears first, before Mr. Justice McIntyre's. They are presented here in reversed order.

of the *Charter* interact. I differ from him, however, on the application of s. 1 to this particular case. . . . [I agree that this provision violates s. 15.]

[Concerning non-citizens permanently resident in Canada forming the kind of "discrete and insular minority" as referred to in *United States v. Carolene Products Co.*, r]elative to citizens, non-citizens are a group lacking in political power and as such [are] vulnerable to having their interests overlooked and their rights to equal concern and respect violated. . . . Non-citizens, to take only the most obvious example, do not have the right to vote. Their vulnerability to becoming a disadvantaged group in our society is captured by John Stuart Mill's observation . . . that "in the absence of its natural defenders, the interests of the excluded [are] always in danger of being overlooked. . . ." I would conclude therefore that non-citizens fall into an analogous category to those specifically enumerated in s. 15. I emphasize, moreover, that this is a determination which is not to be made only in the context of the law which is subject to challenge but rather in the context of the place of the group in the entire social, political and legal fabric of our society. While legislatures must inevitably draw distinctions among the governed, such distinctions should not bring about or reinforce the disadvantage of certain groups and individuals by denying them the rights freely accorded to others. . . .

[T]he range of discrete and insular minorities has changed and will continue to change with changing political and social circumstances. . . . It can be anticipated that the discrete and insular minorities of tomorrow will include groups not recognized as such today. It is consistent with the constitutional status of s. 15 that it be interpreted with sufficient flexibility to ensure the "unremitting protection" of equality rights in the years to come. . . .

[This infringement of s. 15 of the *Charter* is not a reasonable limit which can be justified under s. 1.] . . .

■ La Forest, J. [concurs in a separate opinion].

NOTES AND QUESTIONS ON *ANDREWS*

1. Substantive equality:

1.1 The U.S. Supreme Court ushered in contemporary American equal protection doctrine in footnote 4 of *United States v. Carolene Products Co.*, 304 U.S. 144, 152 n. 4 (1938), a constitutional case reviewing economic legislation referred to in both opinions in *Andrews*. Footnote 4 did this sideways, stating that it was "unnecessary to consider now whether legislation which restricts those political processes which can ordinarily be expected to bring about repeal of undesirable legislation, is to be subjected to more exacting judicial scrutiny under . . . the Fourteenth Amendment than are most other types of legislation." Carolene Products, 304 U.S. at 152 n.4. Such considerations were suggested to enter into the review of statutes directed at particular religious, national, or racial minorities: "[P]rejudice against discrete and insular minorities may be a special condition, which tends seriously to curtail the operation of those political processes ordinarily to be relied upon to protect minorities, and which may call for a correspondingly more searching judicial inquiry." *Id.* Subsequent cases openly adopted this framework, giving "more searching judicial inquiry" to inequality claims made by "discrete and insular minorities," contrasted with less searching inquiry into inequality claims such as different treatment of aluminum pop-can manufacturers and steel pop-can manufacturers. Footnote 4 thus defined a limiting principle and inaugurated a doctrinal framework for Fourteenth Amendment equality. (As applied to race, sex, and race and sex together, the subsequent doctrine of varying levels of "scrutiny" is traced in Chapters 2, 3, and 4.) *See* Peter Linzer, "The *Carolene Products* Footnote and the Preferred Position of Individual Rights: Louis Lusky and John Hart Ely vs. Harlan Fiske Stone," *in* 12 *Constitutional Commentary* 277 (1995) (providing a history of scholarly views on footnote 4).

1.2   Building in part on this foundation, the Supreme Court of Canada centers its constitutional definition of equality on the treatment of traditionally "disadvantaged" groups, a substantive and open-ended concept that, like "discrete and insular minorities," is predicated on history and responds to social reality and social change. In *Andrews*, Madam Justice Wilson for the majority wrote that "the entire social, political and legal fabric of our society," rather than distinctions made by law as such, defines Section 15 equality claims. *See also R. v. Turpin* [1989] 1 S.C.R. 1296 (holding that inequalities created purely by legal distinctions are not actionable and broadly socially based discrimination that injures an oppressed group through law is actionable). As a limiting principle, does this distinction include too much or exclude too much? What about legal distinctions that are not based on historical oppression or prejudice? Is the substantivity of the *Andrews* test unprincipled, or does its redefinition of principle open to scrutiny issues of substance that control legal judgments in any event? Should a constitutional principle be open to change by design?

1.3   What guidance does the *Andrews* Court provide for determining what groups are disadvantaged and what groups are not? Gwen Brodsky and Shelagh Day, encouraged by the analysis in the *Andrews* decision, also worry about its relative inexplicitness. They comment that "[t]here is no recognition in the judgments that the term 'sex' in section 15 covers both an advantaged and a disadvantaged group, and that courts will have to distinguish between men's sex equality claims and women's sex equality claims. Moreover, the characterization of disadvantaged groups as 'discrete and insular minorit[ies]' reveals an insensitivity to women's equality which is all too familiar." Brodsky & Day, *supra*, at 207–08. Do you share their concerns?

1.4   How does the advantage/disadvantage language map onto concepts of dominant/subordinate? How do grounds map onto groups? Are all inequalities substantively connected? Is addressing all grounds a necessary condition for adequately addressing each one?

2.   The positive spin: The *Andrews* Court adopts a uniquely proactive criterion for judicial review: to be constitutional, law must *promote* equality, not just sit there and sort the legal world into the same piles the social world has already sorted it into. Does this give courts an Archimedean lever on social inequality, a way to move an unequal world? As you read the chapters to follow, ask what makes the *Andrews* approach distinctive. Surely the U.S. Supreme Court does not interpret the Fourteenth Amendment so as to promote *in*equality? Consider whether the Fourteenth Amendment is neutral between equality and inequality as you proceed and whether there is any such position in any given case.

3.   Equality law in social life: Is equality law unusual in its relation to social life? In *Andrews*, inequality is implicitly understood to be a pervasive social fact; law is to be interpreted with a view to altering that fact. Does law usually make the way society is organized illegal? Does law usually promote social change? Can you think of another body of law that gives rights against a social reality that is pervasive and structural? Is *Andrews* an excessive intrusion on legislative prerogatives? Could it be misused? Could its approach promote change beyond the law?

4. The role of Section 15(2): LEAF's factum (a brief is termed a factum in Canada) to the Supreme Court of Canada in *Andrews* argued that Section 15(2) should be used as an interpretive lens through which to read Section 15(1), indeed that the substantive grounds it enumerates should be basic to the way all inequality is interpreted under Section 15. On its narrowest reading, Section 15(2) constitutionalizes affirmative action in the sense of supporting programs to advance the equality of disadvantaged groups. If Section 15(2) is read more broadly, does the distinction between affirmative action and nondiscrimination disappear? Would you favor this? Did the Supreme Court of Canada adopt LEAF's view on this point in *Andrews*?

5. Comparing *Andrews* to the "similarly situated" approach: In *Andrews*, treating pregnant women or Native women less favorably by law—pregnant women because they are different from nonpregnant persons, Native women who marry outside their nation because all First Nations women are treated the same—is regarded not as nondiscriminatory differentiation but as sex discrimination. Why are *Plessy, Bliss*, and *Lavell* said to exemplify the Aristotelian approach? Can the traditional "similarly situated" approach, properly applied, produce the same result as the *Andrews* approach? If so, why did it consistently not do so in the cases mentioned? Recall that *Andrews* embraces a definition of discrimination that includes systemic and adverse-effect discrimination, including unintended and built-in bias that produces disparity in outcomes. Can Aristotle's approach do that? Is the Aristotelian understanding of inequality essentially a horizontal one, assuming that inequality creates disparity among equals but has not ranked equals above and below one another, while the *Andrews* Court understands inequality as essentially vertical, placing some above others?

6. The role of Section 1: What does it do to separate the determination of whether discrimination has occurred from whether a discriminatory act that has occurred can be justified—as the separation of Section 15 from Section 1 determinations allows? Is it analytically clearer than deciding whether Section 1 values are violated as part of determining whether equality rights are violated, as the *Andrews* Court says is done under the Equal Protection Clause? Should any other value in a free and democratic society ever outweigh an equality violation? Can freedom and democracy exist without equality? Should discrimination ever be justified, or should equality be absolute? Does it promote a vital equality guarantee to first recognize a discrimination and then constitutionalize it? Would it be better for promoting equality to deny that a violation had occurred at all? Create a legal role for Canada's Section 1 in light of your answers.

7. Compound disadvantage: Under *Andrews*, how should combined disadvantages, such as those to which women of color are often subjected, be treated? Should programs to remedy disadvantage be ranked or prioritized? If so, how? If not, why not? How should potential tensions between beneficiaries of various programs be handled? Are some more unequal than others? Can a legislature intervene selectively to solve a severe disadvantage—for example, to create a special program for poor mothers of color—

without at the same time funding remedial programs for all women, all poor women, all mothers, or all poor parents of color? Could it create a special health program for immigrant women who have been genitally mutilated as children, or would such a program discriminate against immigrant and nonimmigrant women with intact genitals who also need sexual or reproductive health care? Could it create a program for one physical disability, say blindness, without also covering deafness? for status Indians only, excluding nonstatus Indians?

8. Dominant groups under *Andrews*: Are men's sex inequality claims distinguished from women's sex inequality claims under the *Andrews* principles? Should they be? Can whites as such be discriminated against under its analysis? Can discriminating against men promote the systemic inequality of women?

9. Strategy: In analyzing the *Andrews* breakthrough, what weight do you give to the fact that Andrews is a white male Oxford-educated British lawyer? What are the implications of these facts for equality theory and litigation strategy? Was this a good case for the principles that emerged from it? Would you have chosen it, if you had a choice?

10. Explaining *Andrews*: Canadian society is said to value its ethnic mosaic. American society has famously seen itself as an ethnic melting pot. Do these cultural differences—starkly drawn, Canada openly respecting diversity, the United States valuing homogeneity, Canada seeking equal respect within pluralism, the United States pursuing an assimilationist ideal—help explain the conceptual achievement of *Andrews*? How important was the fact that Section 15 had no precedent to which it was bound? What weight do you give to the explicit language of the Charter, compared with that of the Fourteenth Amendment, in understanding the departure from standard equality thinking in *Andrews*? How important was the presence of Section 15(2)? Did the fact that the Charter was new give the Canadian Supreme Court an interpretive latitude the United States Constitution, absent amendment, lacks?

11. Future unenumerated grounds: In the "enumerated grounds" approach to equality, the equality principle itself is defined in terms of the equality needs of specific groups disadvantaged historically on the basis of traditional grounds for prejudice and mistreatment: race, sex, and others. The list is open-ended by design. Under this substantive approach, what bases for discrimination would you predict are most likely to be added to the enumerated grounds?

Following major changes in the composition of the Supreme Court of Canada, its decision in *Egan v. Canada*, [1995] 2 S.C.R. 915, suggested that the most basic holding of *Andrews*—that Section 15 equality requires that law promote the equality of socially disadvantaged groups—had not been fully comprehended, or perhaps not fully accepted. Confronting the question whether the term "common law spouse" can legislatively be confined to relations "of the opposite sex" for purposes of old-age benefits, the Court unanimously held that sexual orientation discrimination is prohibited under Section 15 as an "analogous ground." Canada, the respondent, had conceded this. But this was not the end of the case.

For the majority, four justices, purporting to rely on *Andrews*, found the opposite-sex requirement for benefits to be "relevant to the functional values underlying the law," namely its purpose to promote marriage for procreation. This was said to make the benefit restriction nondiscriminatory. The majority, disavowing the "similarly situated" test, further noted that the disputed provision did not discriminate on the basis of sexual orientation because opposite-sex couples like brothers and sisters living together were also excluded. In other words, the law had a benign purpose that incidentally happened to exclude gay men and lesbian women, but they alone were not excluded. A concurring opinion argued that the statute was saved under Section 1 because government should not be forced to benefit all in order to benefit some.

The four dissenters argued that the same-sex–couple exclusion did not even rationally fit Parliament's purpose, which was to mitigate poverty among elderly households. They pointed out that heterosexual couples were not required to have children to qualify. (The dissenters might also have mentioned that supporting opposite-sex couples after they turn 65 is ill-suited to supporting procreation.) The challenged law was seen to deprive homosexual people of "dignity"—as if deprivation of equality were not sufficient constitutional violation. Homosexual people were understood throughout as a socially disadvantaged group, stereotyped, marginalized, and deprived of social regard and social choices. But no opinion simply stated that the law in question promoted the inequality of a historically disadvantaged group, hence was discriminatory and clearly unconstitutional.

Should *Egan* have been an easy case under *Andrews*? On the above account, does the majority in *Egan* apply the "similarly situated" test it purports to reject? What does it mean for women and other socially disadvantaged groups in Canada that the substantive *Andrews* approach proved so elusive in such an application—one in which the historical substantive inequality was essentially uncontested? Building on *Egan* and *Andrews*, the Supreme Court of Canada subsequently found unconstitutional Alberta's failure to prohibit discrimination based on sexual orientation in its human rights law. The Charter applies to legislative omissions as well as positive actions, the Court held, so sexual orientation must be "read in" to the legislation. *See Vriend v. Alberta*, [1998] 1 S.C.R. 493. (For further discussion, see Chapter 8.)

12. Learning from *Andrews*: What can the United States learn from the Canadian experience? Can *Andrews* be applied anywhere there is an equality guarantee? The German Basic Law of 1949 states that men and women have equal rights, no one may be discriminated against or favored because of sex, and equality is generally guaranteed. *See* Grundgesetz [Basic Law] [GG] art. 3 (F.R.G.). It has been interpreted with a recognition that society may need to change to meet sex equality standards. Yet its Constitutional Court has not produced an *Andrews*-like decision. Why? Is more needed to produce an interpretation of law that rectifies systematic group-based social disadvantage? Given that equality is legally guaranteed in many systems around the world, could an *Andrews*-type interpretation, carried through, help close the gap between equality law's promise and performance?

B. The Emerging European Community Approach

Europe, long made up of independent nations, has recently moved toward economic and juridical community. What will this mean for the relative status of women and men in Europe? Because a fundamental dynamic of the union revolves around the handling of differences among Member States, adjudication of equality issues on a Community level both highlights cultural assumptions and raises methodological as well as substantive equality questions. The Court of Justice of the European Communities (ECJ), adjudicating Community treaties and directives, has made some creative contributions to women's rights. At the same time, as with the Supreme Court of the United States, its ability to advance equality of the sexes is limited by adherence to the Aristotelian approach. Confronting the realities of gender injustice may yet enlighten both Courts.

The treaties creating the European Community did not themselves prohibit sex discrimination, and sex equality was not generally recognized as a legal principle in the early years of the Community. More recently, however, the Court of Justice has recognized sex equality as a fundamental right under general principles of Community law. *See Defrenne v. Sabena*, [1978] E.C.R. 1365, 1378; *see* Sacha Prechal & Noreen Burrows, *Gender Discrimination Law of the European Community* (1990); Andrew Clapham, *Human Rights and the European Community: A Critical Overview* 25 (1991). This does not mean, however, that sex equality is embraced by all the Member States, or that it is always mandatory. Similarly, the interpretations of Article 119 of the Treaty of Rome, providing for "equal pay without discrimination based on sex," were initially fairly restrictive, *see Sabbatini v. European Parliament*, [1972] E.C.R. 345; *Bilka Kaufhaus GmbH v. Weber van Hartz*, [1986] E.C.R. 1607. Additional rulings have required the Member States to add real sanctions and damages to antidiscrimination laws, *see Von Colson and Kammann v. Nordrhein–Westfalen*, [1984] E.C.R. 1891, 1910; *Harz v. Deutsche Tradax GmbH*, [1984] E.C.R. 1921, 1944, and repudiated a cap on damages. Crucially, Europe has determined that intent requirements in Member State discrimination laws violate European law. *See Draehmpaehl v. Urania Immobilienservice oHG*, [1997] I E.C.R. 2195 (holding that "fault" requirements in German sex discrimination law, no matter how slight or easy to prove, violate equal treatment directive under *Dekker v. Stichting Vormingscentrum* [1990] I E.C.R. 3941).

The formal equality found wanting in *Andrews* has been relied upon to interpret Article 14 of the European Convention for the Protection of Human Rights and Fundamental Freedoms, which provides that its rights "shall be secured without discrimination on any ground such as sex, race, ... or other status." Convention for the Protection of Human Rights and Fundamental Freedoms, Nov. 4, 1950, art. 14, 213 U.N.T.S. 221, 232. The European Court of Human Rights has held that discrimination is unjustified distinction, that "the principle of equality of treatment is violated if the distinction has no objective and reasonable justification ... [and] when it is clearly established that there is no reasonable [relationship] of proportionality between the means employed and the aim sought to be realised." *Belgian Linguistic Case (No. 2)* 1 Eur. H.R. Rep. 252, 284 (1968). This approach raises all the difficulties *Andrews* confronted so innovatively: whether objectivity, reasonableness, and means-ends rationality necessarily promote equality; whether in some circumstances such norms can promote inequality; whether these standards add anything to "the rule of law" as such; whether a legal distinction exists that cannot be justified somehow; what the purpose of an equality law is.

The European equality rulings, largely in the area of work, with those under the mandatory Equal Treatment Directive, made sex equality more meaningful in European women's lives and made the treaties and directives a focus of women's legal activism in Europe. The Equal Treatment Directive provides, in part:

Council Directive of 9 February 1976

76/207/EEC, 1976 O.J. (L39/40)

Article 1

1. The purpose of this Directive is to put into effect in the Member States the principle of equal treatment for men and women as regards access to employment, including promotion, and to vocational training and as regards working conditions and, on the conditions referred to in paragraph 2, social security. This principle is hereinafter referred to as "the principle of equal treatment." . . .

Article 2

1. For the purposes of the following provisions, the principle of equal treatment shall mean that there shall be no discrimination whatsoever on grounds of sex either directly or indirectly by reference in particular to marital or family status. . . .

4. This Directive shall be without prejudice to measures to promote equal opportunity for men and women, in particular by removing existing inequalities which affect women's opportunities in the areas referred to in Article 1(1).

Article 3

1. Application of the principle of equal treatment means that there shall be no discrimination whatsoever on grounds of sex in the conditions, including selection criteria, for access to all jobs or posts, whatever the sector or branch of activity, and to all levels of the occupational hierarchy. . . .

A particularly dynamic and revealing area of the Directive's implementation is affirmative action. Outside the sex equality context, the European Court of Justice has ruled that the equality principle means that similar situations may not be treated differently, nor may dissimilar situations be treated the same, unless objectively justified. As the Court stated in *Italy v. Commission*, [1963] E.C.R. 165, a case involving protective measures imposed by France on Italian refrigerators: "Discrimination in substance would consist in treating either similar situations differently or different situations identically." *Id.* at 178. Fears that such an approach to equality would infect the Court's interpretation of the Equal Treatment Directive were confirmed in its decision in *Kalanke v. Bremen*, [1995] I E.C.R. 3051, invalidating a "positive action" provision of the Bremen Constitution in Germany. This affirmative action provision required that women with the same qualifications as male applicants for public sector positions in which women were underrepresented be preferred in hiring and promotion until women occupy 50 percent of the affected categories. Although the provision was explicitly designed to remedy past discrimination, it was nonetheless found to violate the Directive's equality principle.

The Canadian Charter's Section 15(2) is designed to protect action to change entrenched inequality from being precluded by the standard anti-discrimination approach. Should the Directive's Art. 234 do the same? In the absence of reading it do so, backhanded saving measures have been used such as Europe's Council Recommendation of 13 December 1984, exempting from invalidation under equality laws a nonmandatory provision on the promotion of positive action for women. Council Recommendation 84/635, 1984 O.J. (L331/34). If Europe were promoting equality, would positive action exemplify equality law rather than conflict with, and require an exception to, it? In an attempt to contain the reach of *Kalanke*, the European Commission of Human Rights attempted to narrow its scope to salvage positive action programs, legal under international law to which much of Europe adheres and seen as effective in ending entrenched systems of sex discrimination. *See* "Communication by the Commission to the Council and the European Parliament on the Interpretation of the Judgement of the European Court of Justice on 17 October 1995" *in Kalanke v. Bremen*, [1995] I E.C.R. 3051.

Judicially confining and clarifying *Kalanke*, the European Court of Justice subsequently upheld a directive providing that, in cases of equal qualification, where there are fewer women than men in a civil service sector, "priority be given to the promotion of female candidates." The Court noted that in promotion, men have tended to be automatically preferred over equally qualified women, so that "the mere fact that a male and a female candidate are equally qualified does not mean that they have the same chances." *Marschall v. Land Nordrhein–Westfalen*, [1998] 1 C.M.L.R. 547, 570. Under the Directive, "status as a woman" may be used as an additional criterion for promotion to help reduce actual instances of inequality, so long as women do not have automatic priority over men. Thus the automatic preference of *Kalanke* was still disallowed, but the saving clause, under conditions of inequality, that allowed preference to women unless specific qualities tip the balance in a particular man's favor was permitted. What would Aristotle think of this? What would he require to break a tie between two equally qualified workers of different sexes, in a context in which men have, in effect, been previously preferred? If there are more men in higher positions, although there are as many qualified women for those positions as men, do you say that men have been preferred and women have been discriminated against? Do you call such a situation equal or unequal?

Despite being burdened by an inherited approach to the equality principle that tends to reinstitutionalize inequality when it is decisively addressed, some European authorities are moving to end the inequality of the sexes through law. *See generally* Anne Peters, *Women, Quotas, and Constitutions: A Comparative Study of Affirmative Action for Women Under American, German, European Community and International Law* 231–57 (1999).

C.   THE SOUTH AFRICAN APPROACH

South Africa of today, unlike the United States, is a nation explicitly founded on racial and sex equality as constitutional values. Emerging from a "deeply inegalitarian past," *President of the Republic of South Africa v. Hugo* 1997 (4) SALR 1, at ¶ 41 (CC), of institutionalized apartheid on the basis of race, the democratic postcolonial but still male-dominant South

Africa aims at fresh and determined solutions to ingrained legal and social inequality problems. Its founding provisions include "the achievement of equality," S.Afr. Const. ch.1, § 1(a), specifically "non-racialism and non-sexism," S.Afr. Const. ch.1, § 1(b). Women's groups were active in pressing gender issues in its formation; consciousness of women's equality needs was to some extent explicit in the process. Albie Sachs, now a member of the Constitutional Court, wrote of the process that "the constitution should permit and require the law to look at the actual lives that women lead and thereby enable women to define for themselves what their expectations and priorities are." Albie Sachs, *Protecting Human Rights in a New South Africa* 57 (1990).

South Africa's Constitution includes a concrete list of grounds on which discrimination is prohibited. It prohibits discrimination not only by state action but also in society among persons. If applied horizontally within society, as Section 9(4) appears to provide, as well as vertically between citizens and the state, South Africa's constitutional equality provisions would combine and surpass the Fourteenth Amendment and Title VII in coverage.

The Constitution of the Republic of South Africa (1996)

As adopted on 8 May 1996 and amended on 11 October 1996 by the Constitutional Assembly

Chapter 2 Bill of Rights

Equality

9. (1) Everyone is equal before the law and has the right to equal protection and benefit of the law.

(2) Equality includes the full and equal enjoyment of all rights and freedoms. To promote the achievement of equality, legislative and other measures designed to protect or advance persons, or categories of persons, disadvantaged by unfair discrimination may be taken.

(3) The state may not unfairly discriminate directly or indirectly against anyone on one or more grounds, including race, gender, sex, pregnancy, marital status, ethnic or social origin, colour, sexual orientation, age, disability, religion, conscience, belief, culture, language and birth.

(4) No person may unfairly discriminate directly or indirectly against anyone on one or more grounds in terms of subsection (3). National legislation must be enacted to prevent or prohibit unfair discrimination.

(5) Discrimination on one or more of the grounds listed in subsection (3) is unfair unless it is established that the discrimination is fair.

Structurally similar to the Canadian Charter's Section 1, and unlike the United States Constitution, the South African Constitution's Bill of Rights contains an express limitation provision:

Limitation of Rights

36. (1) The rights in the Bill of Rights may be limited only in terms of law of general application to the extent that the limitation is reasonable and justifiable in an open and democratic society based on

human dignity, equality and freedom, taking into account all relevant factors, including—

(a) the nature of the right;

(b) the importance of the purpose of the limitation;

(c) the nature and extent of the limitation;

(d) the relation between the limitation and its purpose; and

(e) less restrictive means to achieve the purpose.

(2) Except as provided in subsection (1) or in any other provision of the Constitution, no law may limit any right entrenched in the Bill of Rights.

Equality rights may have a preferred, even primary, place in constitutional interpretation in South Africa. Invalidating a law that allowed unwed mothers but not unwed fathers to block adoptions of their biological children (for further discussion of the substantive issue, *see* Chapter 6), Justice Mohamed wrote that "[t]here can be no doubt that the guarantee of equality lies at the very heart of the Constitution. It permeates and defines the very ethos upon which the Constitution is premised." *Fraser v. Children's Court*, 1997 (2) SALR 272 (CC). The Constitutional Court has not resolved the question of whether the equality provision applies horizontally, among citizens, however. In a case in which the majority declined to apply the Bill of Rights to defamation law, Justice Madala noted in dissent that "the verticality approach is unmindful of the modern day reality—that in many instances the abuse in the exercise of power is perpetrated less by the State and more by private individuals against other private individuals." *Du Plessis v. De Klerk*, 1996 (3) SALR 922 (CC).

As to the meaning of the prohibition on "unfair discrimination," the Constitutional Court, referring to the South African history of the provision, said that "Section 8 was adopted . . . in the recognition that discrimination against people who are members of disfavoured groups can lead to patterns of group disadvantage and harm. Such discrimination is unfair: it builds and entrenches inequality amongst different groups in our society. The drafters realised that it was necessary both to proscribe such forms of discrimination and to permit positive steps to redress the effects of such discrimination. The need to prohibit such patterns of discrimination and to remedy their results are the primary purposes of Section 8." *Brink v. Kitshoff NO*, 1996 (6) BCLR 752, at para. 42 (CC).

Adopting an implicitly substantive approach to equality over an abstract one, the Court, in upholding a general presidential pardon of all mothers, but not fathers, in prison who had children under age twelve, held that whether discrimination is unfair turns on whether the "overall impact" of an action "furthers the constitutional goal of equality." *President of the Republic of South Africa v. Hugo* 1997 (4) SALR 1, at ¶ 41 (CC). A majority of the Court concurred in the statement that "[t]he more vulnerable the group adversely affected by the discrimination, the more likely the discrimination will be held to be unfair. Similarly, the more invasive the nature of the discrimination upon the interests of the individuals affected [by it], the more likely it will be held to be unfair." *Id.* at ¶ 112. The Court also rejected the view that equality means same treatment in all circumstances. See *id.* at ¶ 41. Although not widely applied, the African Charter on Human and People's Rights provides that "[a]ll peoples shall be equal; they shall enjoy the same respect and shall have the same rights. Nothing shall justify the domination of a people by another." African [Banjul] Charter on Human and People's Rights, June 27, 1981, Organization of African Unity, art. 19. Do you predict women will be considered "a people" for this purpose? Are women a people in your mind? How might this provision assist constitutional interpretation for South African women?

NOTES AND QUESTIONS ON THE SOUTH AFRICAN CONSTITUTION

1. "Unfair discrimination":

1.1 Affirmative action: The South African constitutional prohibition on "unfair discrimination," much like Section 15(2) of the Canadian Charter, attempts to ensure that programs to eliminate subordination on group grounds are not invalidated as discriminatory. If successful, the provision would avoid the Aristotelian paradox of so-called reverse discrimination—under which the traditionally privileged cry discrimination when the traditionally disadvantaged are given equality relief that results in an erosion of traditional privileges. Like the Framers of the Charter of Rights and Freedoms, the South African Framers clearly felt the need to guard against the abstractions of traditional equality law. Under Section 9(2), bona fide affirmative action programs would likely be "fair discrimination." *See* S.Afr. Const. ch.2 § 9(2). Might the same end be accomplished by an approach that defined promoting equality or eliminating traditional hierarchies as simply equality, rather than as an exception to it, and promoting equality as the purpose of an equality guarantee? Which approach is more effective? simpler? Do the Constitutional Court's interpretations of "unfair discrimination" meet the *Andrews* standard?

1.2 Potential constitutional conflicts: Any time a sex equality right conflicts with any other arguable constitutional right, might the discrimination against women be rendered "fair"? How do you predict that these possible tensions will be resolved within the South African constitutional design? On what will they depend? Should equality take precedence? Will it?

What discrimination is "fair"? Might differential rules or practices construable in terms of so-called differences between women and men—say parenting patterns, sexuality, the work women mostly do—be seen as "fair discrimination" under some circumstances? What about pregnancy leave? Is it "fair discrimination" against men based on sex, or no discrimination based on sex at all? Is "fair discrimination" a contradiction in terms?

1.3 Sex and culture: Might discrimination against women by traditional cultures, under a constitution in which cultural rights are separately guaranteed, be seen as "fair discrimination"? Section 31(1) of the Constitution provides that "[p]ersons belonging to a cultural, religious or linguistic community may not be denied the right ... (a) to enjoy their culture, practise their religion and use their language...." S.Afr. Const. ch.2 § 31(1). Might women's equality rights be compromised by this section, given the pervasiveness of sex inequality in many practices of traditional cultures, religions, and languages? What does "culture" mean? Suppose that constantly evolving customary practices were replaced with rigid rules institutionalizing male dominance by colonial authorities under the influence of African men seeking to secure their dominant position, as argued by Felicity Kaganas and Christina Murray in their article, "The Contest

Between Culture and Gender Equality Under South Africa's Interim Constitution," 21 *J. L. & Soc'y* 409, 411 (1994). Should such cultural practices take precedence over sex equality claims against them? The constitutional provision on cultural rights provides at subsection (2) that "the rights in subsection (1) may not be exercised in a manner inconsistent with any provision of the Bill of Rights." S.Afr. Const. ch.2 § 31(2). Does this help support the preeminence of the equality provision? *See* Christine Mary Venter, "The New South African Constitution: Facing the Challenges of Women's Rights and Cultural Rights in Post–Apartheid South Africa," 21 *J. Legis.* 1, 6–7 (1995). How might the Limitation Clause, which, unlike Canada's Section 1, explicitly mentions equality as a value to be protected, affect this determination? Will such conflicts be resolved under the Limitations Clause? (For further discussion of tensions between gender and culture, see Chapter 4.)

2. The Eritrean equality initiative: The Constitution of Eritrea, draft of July 1996, in addition to providing that "[a]ll persons are equal before the law" and that "[n]o person may be discriminated against on account of" a list of concrete factors, provides that "[t]he National Assembly shall, pursuant to the provisions of this Article, enact laws that can assist in eliminating inequalities existing in the Eritrean society." Eritrea Const. art. 14 § 3. Would such an explicit constitutional recognition that inequalities do exist in society and need to be overcome improve the delivery of equality under the U.S. Constitution? the South African Constitution?

3. Horizontal discrimination: Section 9(4) requires legislation for equality. Can this provision be used to support an argument that the Constitution itself does not provide claims for inequality in society? Is this constitutional language conducive to initiatives against violence against women? How far does the powerful burden of proof allocation at Section 9(5) go in a consideration of whether such legislation might be said to discriminate against men?

4. Intersection of race and gender: Justice Albie Sachs made the following observation concerning race and gender in the new South Africa:

> It is a sad fact that one of the few profoundly non-racial institutions in South Africa is patriarchy. Amongst the multiple chauvinisms which abound in our country, the male version rears itself with special and equal vigour in all communities. Indeed, it is so firmly rooted that it is frequently given a cultural halo and identified with the customs and personality of different communities. Thus, to challenge patriarchy, to dispute the idea that men should be the dominant figures in the family and society, is to be seen not as fighting against male privilege but as attempting to destroy African tradition or subvert Afrikaner ideals or undermine civilized and decent British values. Men are exhorted to express their manhood as powerfully as possible.... Patriarchy brutalizes men and neutralizes women—across the colour line. Albie Sachs, *Protecting Human Rights in a New South Africa* 53 (1990).

Note that the view that male dominance characterizes South African society across racial lines is a view indigenous to South African society. American law professors Adrien Wing and Eunice de Carvalho, noting the Interim Constitution's many benefits for Black South African women, offer the following assessment: "Black women will not be fully emancipated by a reform of South African law unless such reform is followed by the abolition of patriarchal norms, the spread of education, the absorption of women into remunerative occupations outside the home, and participation in the work of the government. The Interim Constitution fails to accommodate the intersectionality of race and gender, or to attack oppression of black women within the private sphere...." Adrien Katherine Wing & Eunice P. de Carvalho, "Black South African Women: Toward Equal Rights," 8 *Harv. Hum. Rts. J.* 57, 85 (1995); *see also* Celina Romany, "Black Women and Gender Equality in a New South Africa: Human Rights Law and the Intersection of Race and Gender," 21 *Brook. J. Int'l L.* 857 (1996). Does the South African Constitution have adequate language for these needs? Are these valid standards to which to hold constitutional equality guarantees? Consider throughout this book the degree to which United States sex equality law meets these standards for emancipation of women of all ethnic groups.

IV. SEX EQUALITY UNDER INTERNATIONAL LAW

International law has long contained a variety of instruments recognizing women's rights. It has not produced sex equality in the world, however. *See generally Reconceiving Reality: Women and International Law* (Dorinda G. Dallmeyer ed., 1993); *Women's Rights, Human Rights: International Feminist Perspectives* (Julie Peters & Andrea Wolper eds., 1995).

The Universal Declaration of Human Rights of December 7, 1948, although not a treaty, is the founding document of international human rights law. While not all the rights it enunciates have been regarded as binding under all circumstances, "the Declaration, as an authoritative listing of human rights, has become a basic component of international customary law, binding all states." Louis B. Sohn, "The New International Law: Protection of the Rights of Individuals Rather Than States," 32 *Am. U. L. Rev.* 1, 17 (1982). The rights it grants women (and most men) nonetheless remain more aspirational than descriptive.

Universal Declaration of Human Rights

G.A. Res. 217, U.N. GAOR, 3d Sess., at 72–76, U.N. Doc. A/810 (1948)

Article 1. All human beings are born free and equal in dignity and rights. They are endowed with reason and conscience and should act towards one another in a spirit of brotherhood.

Art. 2. Everyone is entitled to all the rights and freedoms set forth in this Declaration, without distinction of any kind, such as race, colour, sex, language, religion, political or other opinion, national or social origin, property, birth or other status....

Art. 3. Everyone has the right to life, liberty and security of person.

Art. 4. No one shall be held in slavery or servitude; slavery and the slave trade shall be prohibited in all their forms.

Art. 5. No one shall be subjected to torture or to cruel, inhuman or degrading treatment or punishment.

Art. 6. Everyone has the right to recognition everywhere as a person before the law.

Art. 7. All are equal before the law and are entitled without any discrimination to equal protection of the law. All are entitled to equal protection against any discrimination in violation of this Declaration and against any incitement to such discrimination. . . .

Art. 16.(I) Men and women of full age, without any limitation due to race, nationality or religion, have the right to marry and to found a family. They are entitled to equal rights as to marriages, during marriage and at its dissolution.

(II) Marriage shall be entered into only with the free and full consent of the intending spouses.

(III) The family is the natural and fundamental group unit of society and is entitled to protection by society and the State. . . .

Art. [21.](II) Everyone has the right of equal access to public service in his country. . . .

Art. [23.](II) Everyone, without any discrimination, has the right to equal pay for equal work. . . .

Art. [25.](II) Motherhood and childhood are entitled to special care and assistance. . . .

NOTES AND QUESTIONS ON THE UNIVERSAL DECLARATION OF HUMAN RIGHTS

1. Equality concepts:

1.1 Does the Universal Declaration embody the Aristotelian approach to equality? Are people who are not already socially equal likely to receive legal equality under its provisions?

1.2 Is the Declaration's language gender-inclusive or gender-biased? Is the reader expected to substitute "she" for "he"? If Article 1 commended all to "act towards one another in a spirit of sisterhood," would men know they were included?

1.3 How do you reconcile the definition of equality as sameness, as without distinction, with the "special care and assistance," art. 25(II), granted to motherhood? Does linking motherhood with childhood imply that motherhood is a helplessness or an incapacity?

1.4 At least since the philosopher Immanuel Kant defined being treated as human as being treated as an end in oneself, rather than a means to another's ends, dignity has been seen to be a central human entitlement.

Immanuel Kant, *Grounding for the Metaphysics of Morals*

39–41 (Akad. 433–35)

(James W. Ellington trans., Hackett Publishing Co. 2d ed. 1983)

For all rational beings stand under the law that each of them should treat himself and all others never merely as means but always at the same time as an end in himself. Hereby arises a systematic union of rational beings through common objective laws, i.e., a kingdom that may be called a kingdom of ends (certainly only an ideal), inasmuch as these laws have in view the very relation of such beings to one another as ends and means. A rational being belongs to the kingdom of ends as a member when he legislates in it universal laws while also being himself subject to those laws. He belongs to it as sovereign, when as legislator he is himself subject to the will of no other....

Hence morality consists in the relation of all action to that legislation whereby alone a kingdom of ends is possible. This legislation must be found in every rational being and must be able to arise from his will, whose principle then is never to act on any maxim except such as can also be a universal law and hence such as the will can thereby regard itself as at the same time the legislator of universal law.... In the kingdom of ends everything has either a price or a dignity. Whatever has a price can be replaced by something else as its equivalent; on the other hand, whatever is above all price, and therefore admits of no equivalent, has a dignity.

Whatever has reference to general human inclinations and needs has a market price; whatever, without presupposing any need, accords with a certain taste ... has an affective price; but that which constitutes the condition under which alone something can be an end in itself has not merely a relative worth, i.e., a price, but has an intrinsic worth, i.e., a dignity.

Now morality is the condition under which alone a rational being can be an end in himself, for only thereby can he be a legislating member in the kingdom of ends. Hence morality and humanity, insofar as it is capable of morality, alone have dignity.... This estimation, therefore, lets the worth of such a disposition be recognized as dignity and puts it infinitely beyond all price, with which it cannot in the least be brought into competition or comparison without, as it were, violating its sanctity.

What is equality under the principles of this passage? What is the relation of dignity to equality? Is dignity part of equality? Is equality part of dignity? Is equality a morality in Kant's passage or something else? Is dignity what makes a human being human? Does everything about a person that is sold for a price diminish one's humanity? If one brings a lawsuit for damages for inequality violations, does putting a price on one's inequality violate one's dignity or affirm it? If a human being is used as a means to another's ends, does that diminish dignity, hence humanity? Do the user and the used lose equally? When society is arranged so that some are used systematically as means to the ends of others, are such arrangements what we mean by "inequality"? What is the relation between the "universal" in Kant's passage and the universality of the Universal Declaration? Is the Universal Declaration attempting to achieve Kant's "legislation"? Does it succeed? If Aristotle's approach were infused with Kantian substance, would the defects the *Andrews* Court identified be remedied?

    1.5 Are women "human" under the Universal Declaration's provisions? Does the Universal Declaration reflect the needs and realities of women in its operative concept of the "human"?

2. Particularity: Might a document so specific as to include a right "to join trade unions," art. 23(IV), and to "rest, ... leisure, ... and periodic holiday with pay," art. 24, have specified some violations of security of the person distinctive (if not unique) to women, such as rape and domestic violence, or some of the forms of servitude that particularly afflict women, such as forced reproduction and prostitution? Might it have spelled out whether the right of "[e]veryone who works" to receive "just and favourable remuneration," art. 23(III), covers housework? If housework has Kantian dignity, is it above price, hence above payment? *See* Chapter 3.

3.   Scope: What might the prohibition on "incitement to discrimination," art. 7, encompass? racist hate speech (*see* Chapter 2)? pornography (*see* Chapter 10.2)? How is discrimination incited? Why is the specific equality provision, art. 7, limited to equality *in law* when so many of the other articles appear directed toward society as well?

Efficacy of international legal principles remains largely to be achieved in the sex equality area as well as in most others. International prostitution, for example, continues unabated in the face of scores of conventions against trafficking in women, almost universally adopted and in effect for decades. (*See* Chapter 10.1.) Strong international humanitarian and human rights laws prohibit many violations distinctive to women; yet women civilians continue to be raped in wars with little accountability; similarly, the undeclared war of pervasive violence against women that characterizes daily peacetime in many nations continues without respite. Women are guaranteed equal pay yet continue to be disproportionately poor, equal literacy yet continue to be disproportionately illiterate, equal representation yet continue to be unrepresented. Despite some good intentions by international bodies and much progressive language in international law, the ways in which women are distinctively deprived of human rights throughout the world have effectively eluded the law of nations—whether because of indifference, inertia, intent, unconsciousness, habit, or because women's needs are a low-to-nonexistent priority.

In recent years, following in the footsteps of women's grassroots organizing for equality throughout the world, *see Sisterhood Is Global: The International Women's Movement Anthology* (Robin Morgan ed., 1984), and international meetings designed to further women's rights globally in Nairobi, Mexico City, Geneva, and Vienna, culminating in Beijing in 1995, *see Report of the Fourth World Conference on Women: Beijing, 4–15 September 1995*, U.N. Doc. A/CONF.177/20/Rev. 1, U.N. Sales No. 96.IV.13 (1996), (*Beijing Declaration and Platform for Action*), innovative and far-reaching provisions of international law and their adoption and interpretation have increasingly aimed at sex equality for women everywhere. *See From Basic Needs to Basic Rights: Women's Claim to Human Rights* (Margaret A. Schuler ed., 1995).

One legal vehicle for this movement has been the Convention on the Elimination of All Forms of Discrimination Against Women (CEDAW), proposed by the United Nations in 1979. As of March 1997, CEDAW had been ratified by 155 countries, although the "reservations" many countries have claimed, usually for reasons termed cultural, customary, or religious, have undermined its terms and meaningfulness. *See* Rebecca J. Cook, "Reservations to the Convention on the Elimination of All Forms of Discrimination Against Women," 30 *Va. J. Int'l L.* 643 (1990) (arguing pattern of reservations to CEDAW is impermissible because contrary to the purpose of the treaty); Christine Chinkin, "Reservations and Objections to the Convention on the Elimination of All Forms of Discrimination Against Women," *in Human Rights as General Norms and a State's Right to Opt Out* 64 (J.P. Gardner ed., 1997). Seven countries, including the United States, have signed but not ratified the Convention. *See Human Rights of*

Women: National and International Perspectives 585 (Rebecca Cook ed., 1994).

Convention on the Elimination of All Forms of Discrimination Against Women

U.N. Doc. A/RES/34/180 (1979)

[Preamble]

The States Parties to the present Convention,

Noting that the Charter of the United Nations re-affirms faith in fundamental human rights, in the dignity and worth of the human person and in the equal rights of men and women,

Noting that the Universal Declaration of Human Rights affirms the principle of the inadmissibility of discrimination and proclaims that all human beings are born free and equal in dignity and rights and that everyone is entitled to all the rights and freedoms set forth therein, without distinction of any kind, including distinction based on sex,

Noting that the States Parties to the International Covenants on Human Rights have the obligation to ensure the equal right of men and women to enjoy all economic, social, cultural, civil and political rights, . . .

Concerned, however, that despite these various instruments extensive discrimination against women continues to exist,

Recalling that discrimination against women violates the principles of equality of rights and respect for human dignity, is an obstacle to the participation of women, on equal terms with men, in the political, social, economic and cultural life of their countries, hampers the growth of the prosperity of society and the family and makes more difficult the full development of the potentialities of women in the service of their countries and of humanity,

Concerned that in situations of poverty women have the least access to food, health, education, training and opportunities for employment and other needs,

Convinced that the establishment of the new international economic order based on equality and justice will contribute significantly towards the promotion of equality between men and women,

Emphasizing that the eradication of apartheid, of all forms of racism, racial discrimination, colonialism, neo-colonialism, aggression, foreign occupation and domination and interference in the internal affairs of States is essential to the full enjoyment of the rights of men and women, . . .

Bearing in mind the great contribution of women to the welfare of the family and to the development of society, so far not fully recognized, the social significance of maternity and the role of both parents in the family and in the upbringing of children, and aware that the role of women in procreation should not be a basis for discrimination but that the upbringing of children requires a sharing of responsibility between men and women and society as a whole,

Aware that a change in the traditional role of men as well as the role of women in society and in the family is needed to achieve full equality between men and women ... [have agreed on the following Convention].

Article 1: [Definition of Discrimination Against Women]

For the purposes of the present Convention, the term "discrimination against women" shall mean any distinction, exclusion or restriction made on the basis of sex which has the effect or purpose of impairing or nullifying the recognition, enjoyment or exercise by women irrespective of their marital status, on a basis of equality of men and women, of human rights and fundamental freedoms in the political, economic, social, cultural, civil or any other field.

CEDAW contains wide-ranging and concrete guarantees, including obligations of states parties to act to eliminate discrimination against women (Art. 2); to ensure women's full development and advancement (Art. 3); to eliminate discriminatory customs and practices, stereotyped notions of the attributes and roles of women and men, or the superiority of either sex (Art. 5); to suppress traffic in women and the exploitation of prostitution of women (Art. 6); to promote equality in political and public life (Art. 7); to eliminate discrimination against women in education (Art. 10), employment (Art. 11–1), health care (Art. 12), economic and social life such as financial credit and recreational activities, sports and the arts (Art. 13). Equality of men and women before the law is provided (Art. 15), and discrimination in marriage and family relations is prohibited (Art. 16), while maternity rights and protections are guaranteed (Art. 11–2,3). For commentary, see Japanese Ass'n of Int'l Women's Rights, *Convention on the Elimination of All Forms of Discrimination Against Women: A Commentary* (1995).

NOTES AND QUESTIONS ON CEDAW

1. Universality versus specificity: What does CEDAW provide that the Universal Declaration of Human Rights does not or cannot? Think about universality compared with particularity in framing sex equality rights effectively and long-term. Is CEDAW too specific? specific enough? What level of generality regarding sex equality issues is appropriate for conventions and other legislation in the sex equality area, and what can be left to common law case-by-case adjudication?

2. Violence against women: In 1992, in its 11th Session, the Committee on the Elimination of All Forms of Discrimination Against Women first explicitly recognized that violence against women, because they are women, constitutes discrimination against women. The Committee issued General Recommendation 19 on Violence Against Women, stating that "[g]ender-based violence is a form of discrimination that seriously inhibits women's ability to enjoy rights and freedoms on a basis of equality with men." *Report of the Comm. on the Elimination of Discrimination Against Women*, 47th Sess., at § I1, U.N.Doc. A/47/38 (1992). The Committee defined gender-based violence as "violence that is directed against a woman because she is a woman or that affects women disproportionately." *Id.* at § 6. Without such clarification, is the language of human rights contained in the provisions of CEDAW adequate to sex-specific aggression against women? Does integrating General Recommendation 19 into CEDAW suggest the need to revise Article 1 in any way? Are there other issues of sex equality that suggest to you the need for more specific language?

3. Lesbian rights: Do the sex equality standards set forth above encompass the ways lesbian women are discriminated against as women? *See* International Gay & Lesbian Human Rights Comm'n, *Unspoken Rules: Sexual Orientation and Women's Human Rights* (Rachel Rosenbloom ed., 1995) (country-by-country reports of discrimination against lesbians and argument that lesbian rights are women's rights are human rights). If lesbian women are not specifically mentioned, is there a danger their rights will be left out? Why or why not? Is there any connection between a woman's right not to be sexually abused and a woman's right to be sexual without men?

4. Equality as a right in itself: Is equality only a derivative right, a guarantee of equal access to all other rights, or is equality also a right in itself? Put another way, does meaningful equality for women require a guarantee of sex equality as such, or is guaranteeing women equal access to all other rights enough? Is there anything one needs in order to be equal that is not included in equal access to all other rights? Does the definition of discrimination in Article 1 of CEDAW define sex equality exclusively in terms of equal access to other human rights? Is this definition adequate to the aspirations of the Preamble?

5. Dignity and equality: Analyze the role of "dignity" in the Preamble. Is it part of equality, or something that goes along with it but needs to be separately mentioned? What is the relationship between equality and dignity in social life? in your theory of equality? in *Andrews*? What is the relationship between the guarantee against deprivation of equality and deprivation of dignity throughout CEDAW?

6. Gender neutrality: Do women need rights as women, defined by their particular experience of second-class status, or is a guarantee to rights under what has been a male standard enough? Does CEDAW solve any potential tension between these two standards? *See* Natalie Hevener Kaufman & Stefanie A. Lindquist, "Critiquing Gender–Neutral Treaty Language: The Convention on the Elimination of All Forms of Discrimination Against Women," *in Women's Rights, Human Rights: International Feminist Perspectives* 114 (Julie Peters & Andrea Wolper eds., 1995). Is there such a thing as "just rights," free of gender referents?

Might women-only colleges be endangered by the gender symmetry of CEDAW's structure? Should they be eliminated? Are there sex equality reasons to support women's schools that do not apply to men's schools? (*See* Chapter 3.4.)

7. U.S. nonratification of CEDAW: The United States Senate has not ratified CEDAW, claiming it does not conform with existing U.S. law. In 1994, the Clinton administration supported ratification but filed four reservations, three understandings, and two declarations to qualify its impact. The reservations are that CEDAW's definition of discrimination against women might regulate private conduct not now covered under U.S. law (*see* Chapters 6 and 7.1); that it might require women to be included in ground warfare (*see* Chapter 3.2); and that it might require a guarantee of equal pay for work of comparable value (*see* Chapter 3.1) and paid maternity leave without loss of employment and benefits (*see* Chapter 3.5). Committee on Foreign Relations, Convention on the Elimination of All Forms of Discrimination Against Women, S. Rep. No. 103–108, at 51 (2d sess. 1994) (proposed reservations, understandings, and declarations of the United States).[8]

Should an international treaty be adopted only if it requires no changes in existing domestic law or practice? Why adopt it if it is redundant? What is the point of an international treaty if national law can trump its authority? One member of Congress stated in the hearings on CEDAW, "[A]s we know from our own experiences in the United States, equality mandated does not always translate into equality practiced." *Convention on the Elimination of All Forms of Discrimination Against Women: Hearing Before the Senate Comm. on Foreign Relations*, 101st Cong., 2d sess. 99 (1990) (statement of U.S. Representative Patricia Saiki). Might the United States have something to learn about sex equality from international human rights law?

8. Impact of CEDAW: Would U.S. ratification of CEDAW, making it part of U.S. federal law, help create sex equality in the United States? Would it compensate for the defeat of ERA to any extent? Do the two different political processes of adoption—for ERA, a constitutional amendment (approval by Congress and state legislatures) and for CEDAW, an international treaty (Senate confirmation)—affect the impact of each legal change on social relations between the sexes? What structures or implementing mechanisms would be needed to make CEDAW effective? Who should be able to make complaints? What bodies should receive complaints and enforce remedies? Does the fact that the United States has not only failed to ratify an Equal Rights Amendment but repeatedly declined to adopt CEDAW suggest that sex equality is not fully accepted as a principle?

---

8. On ratification of CEDAW, *see* Margaret Plattner, "The Status of Women Under International Human Rights Law and the 1995 UN World Conference on Women, Beijing, China," 84 *Ky. L.J.* 1249, 1254–1259 (1995); Julia Ernst, "U.S. Ratification of the Convention on the Elimination of All Forms of Discrimination Against Women," 3 *Mich. J. Gender & L.* 299, 304–14 (1995); *see also* Sara Zearfoss, "The Convention for the Elimination of All Forms of Discrimination Against Women: Radical, Reasonable, or Reactionary?" 12 *Mich. J. Int'l L.* 903 (1991); Laurel Fletcher et al., "Human Rights Violations Against Women," 15 *Whittier L. Rev.* 319, 334–35 (1994).

PART II

APPLICATIONS

Shakespeare had a sister; but do not look for her in Sir Sidney Lee's life of the poet. She died young—alas, she never wrote a word.... Now my belief is that this poet who never wrote a word and was buried at the crossroads still lives. She lives in you and in me, and in many other women who are not here tonight, for they are washing up the dishes and putting the children to bed. But she lives; for great poets do not die; they are continuing presences; they need only the opportunity to walk among us in the flesh. This opportunity, as I think, it is now coming within your power to give her. For my belief is that if we live another century or so—I am talking of the common life which is the real life and not of the little separate lives which we live as individuals—and have five hundred a year each of us and rooms of our own; if we have the habit of freedom and the courage to write exactly what we think; if we escape a little from the common sitting-room and see human beings not always in their relation to each other but in relation to reality ... if we face the fact, for it is a fact, that there is no arm to cling to, but that we go alone and that our relation is to the world of reality ... then the opportunity will come and the dead poet who was Shakespeare's sister will put on the body which she has so often laid down. Drawing her life from the lives of the unknown who were her forerunners, as her brother did before her, she will be born. As for her coming without that preparation, without that effort on our part, without that determination that when she is born again she shall find it possible to live and write her poetry, that we cannot expect, for that would be impossible. But I maintain that she would come if we worked for her, and that so to work, even in poverty and obscurity, is worthwhile.

> Virginia Woolf, *A Room of One's Own* 113–14 (Harcourt Brace Jovanovich 1981) (1929)

*

CHAPTER 8

LESBIAN AND GAY RIGHTS

Women who love women and men who love men, people who have sex with people of the same sex, people whose primary passionate, sexual, and intimate relationships and identifications are with members of their own sex, are among the most stigmatized, persecuted, and denigrated people on earth. Lesbian women and gay men outpace their oppressions in both ordinary and extraordinary ways, but their social and legal subordination remains—and it is the fact of inequality, rather than the famous human ability to evade or overcome it at times, that concerns equality law. Significant numbers of people are gay or lesbian, although existing data inspire little confidence,[1] and vary depending (at least) on definition and methodology (*see* I). Do the numbers matter? In these studies, more men appear to be gay than women are lesbian. Do you think this is true? Are

1. In a nonprobability sample of 11,000 interviews, Alfred C. Kinsey reported finding that 10 percent of males were more or less exclusively homosexual, 13 percent had more homosexual than heterosexual experiences for at least three years between ages sixteen and fifty-five, and 18 percent of males had as much homosexual as heterosexual experience. *See* Alfred C. Kinsey et al., *Sexual Behavior in the Human Male* 650–51 (1948). He also reported finding that of unmarried females ages twenty to thirty-five, 2 to 6 percent had been more or less exclusively homosexual for at least one year, 3 to 8 percent had more homosexual than heterosexual experiences, and 4 to 11 percent had as much homosexual as heterosexual experience. *See* Alfred C. Kinsey et al., *Sexual Behavior in the Human Female* 473–74 (1953). In addition, he reported finding that 37 percent of men and 13 percent of women reported having at least one homosexual experience producing orgasm since puberty. *See* Kinsey (1948), *supra*, at 650; Kinsey (1953), *supra*, at 475. In 1979, researchers from Kinsey's Institute for Sex Research published more of the data from the studies and reanalyzed them using new methods. *See* Paul H. Gebhard & Alan B. Johnson, *The Kinsey Data: Marginal Tabulations of the 1938–1963 Interviews Conducted by the Institute for Sex Research* 428, 432–35 (1979). Although these data have been influential, their reliability is questionable. *See* Edward Stein, *The Mismeasure of Desire: The Science, Theory, and Ethics of Sexual Orientation* Part II (1999); Richard A. Posner, *Sex and Reason* 19, 294–95 (1992) (discussing criticisms of Kinsey and analyzing findings of studies). *See also* Wardell B. Pom-

eroy, *Dr. Kinsey and the Institute for Sex Research* (1982); James H. Jones, *Alfred C. Kinsey: A Public/Private Life* (1997). A more recent study found that 9 percent of men and 5 percent of women could be characterized as homosexual based on frequent and ongoing gay experiences. *See* Samuel S. Janus & Cynthia L. Janus, *The Janus Report on Sexual Behavior* 70 (1993). The figures found by other researchers vary depending on factors including sample size and composition, the definition of being homosexual, and how sex is defined. *See Gay & Lesbian Stats: A Pocket Guide of Facts and Figures* 10–12 (Bennett L. Singer & David Deschamps eds., 1994) (comparing methodologies and results). The smallest figure is found by Edward O. Laumann et al., *The Social Organization of Sexuality: Sexual Practices in the United States* 11–12, 294 (1994), who, in a large representative sample, found that the rates for men vary from 2.7 percent having a same-sex sexual partner in the past year to 4.9 percent having any male partners since age eighteen, with 1.3 percent of sexually active women reporting at least one female partner in the past year to 4.1 percent reporting any female partners since age eighteen. Underreporting is generally thought rife. Histories of sexology that consider that science's treatment of homosexuality include Vern L. Bullough, *Science in the Bedroom: A History of Sex Research* (1994); Janice M. Irvine, *Disorders of Desire: Sex and Gender in Modern American Sexology* (1990); *Science and Homosexualities* (Vernon A. Rosario ed., 1997).

there gender-specific pressures to accept a heterosexual identity? Might the role of sexuality in defining gender differentially affect how identity and sex are experienced, without meaning that fewer women have sex with women than men have sex with men? Few people are unaffected by the issues of sexuality and gender raised by questioning the inevitability and etiology of heterosexuality.

In the United States, gay men and lesbian women, or people thought or said to be gay or lesbian, can without legal recourse be denied citizenship, employment, or housing;[2] sexually harassed at work;[3] excluded from serving their own country in the armed forces;[4] and murdered.[5] They can be prosecuted for sex acts that are legal or effectively permitted for others. *See infra.* Being lesbian or gay can also be an officially permitted reason to be deprived of custody of or contact with one's own children[6] and to be

2. Citizenship cases follow in the text. On employment and housing, see, e.g., *De-Santis v. Pacific Tel. & Tel. Co.*, 608 F.2d 327 (9th Cir. 1979), and III B; *Evangelista Assocs. v. Bland*, 458 N.Y.S.2d 996 (Civ. Ct. 1983); *Singer v. United States Civil Serv. Comm'n*, 530 F.2d 247 (9th Cir. 1976), *vacated and remanded*, 429 U.S. 1034 (1977); *see also Smith v. Liberty Mut. Ins. Co.*, 569 F.2d 325, 326–27 (5th Cir. 1978) (holding that discrimination against man based on his "effeminacy" is not discrimination based on sex); *Valdes v. Lumbermen's Mut. Cas. Co.*, 507 F. Supp. 10 (S.D. Fla. 1980) (holding harassment of nonlesbian woman for being lesbian was sexual orientation discrimination not covered under Title VII, but permitting this reason to be potential pretext for sex-based discrimination if policy against employing homosexuals were not applied uniformly to women and men).

3. *See, e.g., Dillon v. Frank*, 952 F.2d 403 (6th Cir. 1992); *Carreno v. Local Union No. 226 IBEW*, 54 F.E.P. Cas. 81 (D. Kan. 1990). *But cf. Sardinia v. Dellwood Foods, Inc.*, 69 F.E.P. Cas. 705 (S.D.N.Y. 1995) (permitting claim for sexual harassment under Title VII for homophobic harassment).

4. *See, e.g., Ben-Shalom v. Marsh*, 881 F.2d 454 (7th Cir. 1989); *Steffan v. Perry*, 41 F.3d 677 (D.C. Cir. 1994) (en banc); *see also Von Hoffburg v. Alexander*, 615 F.2d 633, 639 (5th Cir. 1980) (requiring discharged female servicemember to petition army for administrative review of determination that marriage to female-to-male transsexual showed "homosexual tendencies" prior to judicial review). *But cf. Cammermeyer v. Aspin*, 850 F. Supp. 910 (W.D. Wash. 1994) (holding that exclusion of homosexuals from military violates equal protection of the laws), 97 F.3d 1235 (9th Cir. 1996) (finding appeal moot and remanding without vacating); *Dahl v. Secretary of the U.S. Navy*, 830 F. Supp. 1319 (E.D. Cal. 1993).

5. *See, e.g., Parisie v. Greer*, 671 F.2d 1011 (7th Cir. 1982) (permitting "gay panic" defense to murder), *aff'd en banc and per curiam*, 705 F.2d 882 (7th Cir. 1983), *cert. denied*, 464 U.S. 950 (1983); *Commonwealth v. Shelley*, 373 N.E.2d 951, 956 (Mass. 1978) (holding that mitigation defense of "dissociative reaction" due to "homosexual panic" at victim's homosexual advances may be submitted to jury). *See generally* Beth Loffreda, *Losing Matt Shepard: Life and Politics in the Aftermath of Anti-Gay Murder* (2000). The following two cases uphold convictions for killings while tolerating the submission below of unsuccessful provocation or self-defense claims based on homosexual advances: *State v. Skaggs*, 586 P.2d 1279, 1284 (Ariz. 1978); *Walden v. State*, 307 S.E.2d 474 (Ga. 1983); *see also People v. Saldivar*, 497 N.E.2d 1138 (Ill. 1986) (upholding conviction for voluntary manslaughter where prosecution stipulated victim made homosexual advance); *see generally* Robert C. Bagnall et al., "Burdens on Gay Litigants and Bias in the Court System: Homosexual Panic, Child Custody, and Anonymous Parties," 19 *Harv. C.R.-C.L. L. Rev.* 497, 498–515 (1984); Robert B. Mison, Comment, "Homophobia in Manslaughter: The Homosexual Advance as Insufficient Provocation," 80 *Cal. L. Rev.* 133 (1992); Joshua Dressler, "When 'Heterosexual' Men Kill 'Homosexual' Men: Reflections on Provocation Law, Sexual Advances, and the 'Reasonable Man' Standard," 85 *J. Crim. L. & Criminology* 726 (1995) (supporting "gay panic" defense as excuse not justification). For documentation of state-sanctioned killings of members of sexual minorities around the world, see James D. Wilets, "International Human Rights Law and Sexual Orientation," 18 *Hastings Int'l & Comp. L. Rev.* 1, 28–34 (1994); *see also* Eve Sedgwick, *Epistemology of the Closet* 19–21, 138–39, 182–212 (1990).

6. *See, e.g.,* Chapter 6 III B 2 (particularly *Van Driel* and *Bottoms* cases); *Roe v.*

denied a legal family with a life partner of one's choice.[7] While these precedents and persecutions are by no means uniform—some authority existing to the contrary in some places for most of them—neither are they exceptional, constitutionally barred in the United States or most other countries (South Africa is an exception), nor yet authoritatively established as clear violations of internationally guaranteed human rights.

Why are gay men and lesbian women discriminated against? What can end it? This chapter inquires into whether the subordination of homosexuals to heterosexuals is a part of the subordination of women to men: whether social hierarchy by sex and sexuality are linked. Does sexuality as it is socially gendered define the second-class status of both gay men and lesbian women in society? Gay men and lesbian women are seen as violating traditional gender rules for sexual expression and customary sexual rules for members of their genders. Are these the same rules through which women are subordinated to men? Gay men and lesbian women are sexually defined; so, arguably, are all women—and all men, although they are not reduced to or by the sexuality that socially defines them. Depending upon whether you see a connection between the sexual dimension of gender per se and the sexual definitions of homosexuality, further gender questions can arise. Are gay men and lesbian women equally disadvantaged, or does gender inequality operate as an axis of power within as well as against the group? Do heterosexual women dominate gay men, or is the reverse more often true? Do some legal approaches to altering homosexuality as a disfavored status favor men over women or contribute to male dominance in the long term? Is this group a community? Is the relevant group or community for these purposes defined more by persecution without and public identification, or is it defined as much by consciousness and identity within and hidden or undeclared facts and feelings? What is learned by analyzing gay men as men and lesbian women as women, socially speaking? Achieving human rights for gay men and lesbian women is a task in its own right. The question here is whether sex equality law has a contribution to make to that project, and whether that project is connected to ending the subordination of women to men.

In the United States, same-sex sexual activity has for some years been criminalized by states through laws against sodomy. *See generally* Byrne Fone, *Homophobia: A History* (2000). "[U]ntil 1961, all 50 states outlawed sodomy." *Bowers v. Hardwick*, 478 U.S. 186, 193 (1986). In 1992, around

---

Roe, 324 S.E.2d 691, 694 (Va. 1985) (overturning trial court award of custody to a father who lived with male partner: "The father's continuous exposure of the child to his immoral and illicit relationships renders him an unfit and improper custodian as a matter of law"); *DiStefano v. DiStefano*, 401 N.Y.S.2d 636, 638 (App. Div. 1978) (conditioning visitation of children with mother on "the total exclusion of [the mother's woman partner] from any contact with the wife and children during such visitation" due to deduction that it would detrimentally affect the children); *In re J.S. & C.*, 324 A.2d 90, 97 (N.J. Super. Ct. Ch. Div. 1974) (conditioning visitation of children with gay-activist father on nonexposure to his lover and gay liberation political activity), *aff'd per curiam* 362 A.2d 54 (N.J. Super. Ct. App. Div. 1976).

7. *See* Julie A. Greenberg, "Defining Male and Female: Intersexuality and the Collision Between Law and Biology," 41 *Ariz. L. Rev.* 265, 296–98 (1999) (collecting state laws so providing and commenting that "man" and "woman" are not legally defined); *see also* The Defense of Marriage Act, 1 U.S.C. § 7 (Supp. II 1996), 28 U.S.C. § 1738C (Supp. II 1996), 110 Stat. 2419 (defining marriage for purposes of federal law as a "legal union between one man and one woman as husband and wife" and the word spouse as a person of the opposite sex who is a husband or a wife).

half of them still did. *See* Ruthann Robson, *Lesbian (Out)law* 47, 58 (1992) ("Robson"). As of 1998, thirteen states banned both heterosexual and homosexual sodomy, six exclusively banned same-sex sodomy, *see* Thomas Earl Pryor, "Comment: Does Arkansas Code Section 5-14-122 Violate Arkansas's Constitutional Guarantee of Equal Protection?" 51 *Ark. L. Rev.* 521, 523 (1998) (citing Lambda Legal Defense and Education Fund); those states that ban both are generally conceded to enforce those bans disproportionately or exclusively against same-sex sexual acts. For documentation on sodomy statutes themselves, see William N. Eskridge Jr., *Gaylaw: Challenging the Apartheid of the Closet*, 328–37 (1999) (compiling historical overview); Richard A. Posner & Katharine B. Silbaugh, *A Guide to America's Sex Laws* 65–71 (1996) (presenting sodomy statutes state by state).

But what "sodomy" is, is far from obvious. Many state laws prohibit "the crime against nature" or the "abominable and detestable crime against nature" or "the infamous crime against nature" without further clarification. *See* Robson, *supra* at 48; Robert F. Oaks, " 'Things Fearful to Name': Sodomy and Buggery in Seventeenth-Century New England," 12 *J. Soc. His.* 268, 268 (1978). One Texas court, in finding the indicted facts—apparently a man orally penetrating a woman's vagina, facts not recounted in the opinion itself—not to be sodomy under state law on a postconviction appeal, adverted to the sodomy charge as "too horrible to contemplate, and too revolting to discuss." *Harvey v. State*, 55 Tex. Crim. 199, 200, 115 S.W. 1193, 1193 (App. 1909). For further illustration *see Prindle v. State*, 21 S.W. 360, 31 Tex. Crim. 551 (1893) (discussing use of common law to resolve vagueness in the Texas prohibition on an "abominable and detestable crime against nature"). Other jurisdictions describe the prohibited acts in terms of contact between various body parts when persons are of the same sex, as well as sex between people and animals. Here are some examples:

> A person commits sodomy if such person performs any act of sexual gratification involving: (1) the penetration, however slight, of the anus or mouth of an animal or a person by the penis of a person of the same sex or an animal; or the penetration, however slight, of the vagina or anus of an animal or a person by any body member of a person of the same sex or an animal. Ark. Code Ann. § 5-14-122(a) (Michie 1997).

> Criminal sodomy is . . . sodomy between persons who are 16 or more years of age and members of the same sex or between a person and an animal. Kan. Stat. Ann. § 21-3505(a) (1995).

> A person commits the crime of sexual misconduct in the first degree if he has deviate sexual intercourse with another person of the same sex. Mo. Rev. Stat. § 566.090(1) (1994). "Deviate sexual intercourse" means any act involving the genitals of one person and the mouth, tongue, or anus of another person or a sexual act involving the penetration, however slight, of the male or female sex organ or the anus by a finger, instrument or object done for the purpose of arousing or gratifying the sexual desire of any person. Mo. Rev. Stat. § 566.010(1) (1994).

Compare the role of penetration in these statutes with its role in heterosexual intercourse. What distinguishes the two such that the former is presumptively criminal, the latter presumptively not? Compare the provisions above with those of rape laws, *see* Chapter 7.1; note the absence of nonconsent and force requirements in the sodomy laws.

Strikingly, sex that many people mutually want is against the law because it is same-sex, while much sexual abuse presumptively heterosexual—sex inflicted through various forms of force and coercion by men on women and girls, *see* Chapter 7—remains in effect legally permitted and socially protected. Might the reasons have anything to do with the place of heterosexuality in gender inequality? Is male dominance as a system at once served by permitting heterosexual sexual abuse on a wide scale and by prohibiting mutually desired same-sex sexual intimacy? Is gender equality more likely between two people of the same sex? What do you think is the purpose and meaning of prohibiting sex with animals in terms similar to those prohibiting sex with someone of one's own sex? Who, in standard heterosexual intercourse, is in the positions prohibited for animals under Arkansas law? What is the legal status under these laws of the penetration of a woman by an animal's penis, a common act in pornography (*see* Chapter 10.2)? Prosecutions for same-sex sodomy are few and far between but not extinct.[8]

It is worth asking what laws are doing on the books that are almost never enforced. One possible answer is that sodomy laws are more effective unenforced than enforced, since each act of enforcement provides standing for a challenge that exposes the laws to judicial scrutiny, potentially resulting in their invalidation.[9] Criminal sodomy prohibitions appear not to

8. *See, e.g., Branche v. Commonwealth*, 489 S.E.2d 692 (Va. Ct. App. 1997); *State v. Chiaradio*, 660 A.2d 276 (R.I. 1995); *Commonwealth v. Nicholas*, 663 N.E.2d 266 (Mass. App. Ct. 1996) (reversing sodomy conviction for inadequate evidence that act occurred in public); *Sawatzky v. City of Oklahoma City*, 906 P.2d 785 (Okla. Crim. App. 1995) (upholding conviction for soliciting sodomy); *Christensen v. State*, 468 S.E.2d 188 (Ga. 1996) (upholding constitutionality of sodomy statute in solicitation case); *but see Powell v. State*, 510 S.E.2d 18 (Ga. 1998) (finding Georgia statute criminalizing private, unforced, noncommercial sex acts between persons legally able to consent infringed Georgia's constitutional privacy right) (*see infra* note 5.3 to *Bowers v. Hardwick*); *People v. Livermore*, 9 Mich. App. 47, 155 N.W.2d 711 (1967); *Missouri v. Walsh*, 713 S.W.2d 508 (Mo. 1986) (en banc); *see also Doe v. Commonwealth's Att'y*, 403 F.Supp. 1199 (E.D. Va. 1975), *aff'd mem.*, 425 U.S. 901 (1976) (denying declaratory injunction, upholding constitutionality of sodomy prohibition as applied to adult, consensual male-male sexual relationships against due process, free expression, and privacy challenges); *Bowers v. Hardwick* (upholding sodomy statute as constitutional under privacy attack in case involving arrest). In the military context, see *United States v. Ford*, 1995 WL 935052 (N-M.Ct. Crim. App. 1995) (unpublished).

Prosecutions of sodomy (acts or solicitation) for money include *State v. Neal*, 500 So. 2d 374 (La. 1987); *State v. Gray*, 413 N.W.2d 107 (Minn. 1987) (finding no fundamental right under state constitution to engage in sodomy for compensation, hence no violation of right to privacy); *see also People v. Lino*, 527 N.W.2d 434 (Mich. 1994) (upholding conviction for procurement of act of "gross indecency between males" and statute against vagueness attack, in case in which defendant (Brashier) procured and paid young boys to inflict abuse on another man (Goike) while that man masturbated); *State v. Richmond*, 708 So. 2d 1272 (La. Ct. App. 1998) (upholding conviction of woman for soliciting undercover male officer for oral sex for money under statute prohibiting "crime against nature" for compensation).

Of the comparatively few prosecutions that have occurred, Professor Sanford Kadish has observed: "Opportunities for enforcement are limited by the [often] private and consensual character of the behavior. Only a small and insignificant manifestation of homosexuality is amenable to enforcement. This is that which takes place, either in the solicitation or the act, in public places. Even in these circumstances, it is not usual for persons to act openly. To obtain evidence, police are obliged to . . . degrade and demean both themselves personally and law enforcement as an institution." Sanford H. Kadish, "The Crisis of Overcriminalization," 374 *Annals Am. Acad. Pol. & Soc. Sci.* 157, 161 (1967).

9. Examples of (so to speak) use it and lose it are: *State v. Smith*, 729 So. 2d 648 (La. Ct. App. 1999) (invalidating Louisiana's sod-

have widely deterred or punished the acts proscribed. The lowest figure reported from a probability sample documents that more than 4 percent of women and 9 percent of men have engaged in at least one sex act with a person of their own sex since puberty, *see* Edward O. Laumann et al., *The Social Organization of Sexuality: Sexual Practices in the United States* 294–96 (1994) ("Laumann"), most of which acts would likely be covered by sodomy prohibitions. Another report found that 22 percent of men and 17 percent of women had had same-sex sexual experiences. *See* Samuel S. Janus & Cynthia L. Janus, *The Janus Report on Sexual Behavior* 69 (1993).[10] What purposes do the laws against sodomy serve? Do criminal laws have to be enforced to have a branding, coercive, *in terrorem* effect? Is this what law as symbol means? Why do rape laws seem to have little such effect? Do criminal laws affect civil status? For the social consequences of criminal laws, does it matter who has power and who does not? Which comes first, the social powerlessness or the differential criminal prohibition? Can legal equality for the affected groups go far as long as criminal sodomy statutes remain in place? To borrow from religious terminology, can law "love the sinner" by granting freedom from discrimination "but hate the sin" by criminalizing the sex acts?

Largely ineffective as criminal prohibitions, sodomy laws are observably effective in rationalizing discrimination against gay men and (if differently at times) against lesbian women in civil society and under civil law. The stigma of homosexuality is often predicated on and justified by the criminality of sodomy. Professor Elvia Arriola argues that sodomy laws "license prejudice" against lesbians and gays. *See* Elvia R. Arriola, "Gendered Inequality: Lesbians, Gays, and Feminist Theory," 9 *Berkeley Women's L.J.* 103, 122 (1994); *see also* Sylvia A. Law, "Homosexuality and the Social Meaning of Gender," 1988 *Wis. L. Rev.* 187, 190. Criminal sodomy laws define the group homosexuals as at once sexual and criminal: the law reduces the group to this act. Their resulting sexual outlaw status then is used to justify imposing a range of further civil disadvantages, *see, e.g.,* *Romer v. Evans*, 517 U.S. 620, 641 (1996) (Scalia, J., dissenting), including as parents, teachers, employees, soldiers, and citizens.[11] Conversely, "being" gay as a sociolegal status, when known, can lead to discrimination for

---

omy law in case of heterosexual "private, consensual, noncommercial acts of sexual intimacy between individuals who are legally capable of giving consent" as infringement of state constitutional privacy right, 729 So. 2d at 654, having rejected prior challenges on other legal grounds in *State v. Baxley*, 656 So. 2d 973 (La. 1995)), *writ granted*, 746 So. 2d 612 (La. 1999); *Commonwealth v. Wasson*, 842 S.W.2d 487 (Ky. 1992) (finding criminal statute proscribing consensual homosexual sodomy violates privacy and equal protection guarantees of Kentucky Constitution, as it denies equal treatment under law without rational basis by imposing "majoritarian sexual preference"; repudiating "punishing people because they are different rather than because of what they are doing," 842 S.W.2d at 500, 501).

10. Reasons for the varied results include that different questions were asked and

different people define "sex" differently, and are permitted to do so by the instruments. Some ask, "Have you had homosexual experiences?" Others ask about "homosexual contact to orgasm" (without specifying whose orgasm). Some specify age or time periods and some do not. The studies do not report possible gender distinctions in perceptions of what sex is. Nothing is asked about affection or lovemaking as such.

11. In *City of Dallas v. England*, 846 S.W.2d 957 (Ct. App. 1993), the Texas sodomy statute was held unconstitutional as applied to private consensual adult homosexual sex in the case of a lesbian woman who had been refused employment as a police officer. Is this a promising strategy for breaking the link between criminal act and civil status? The case relies on *State v. Morales*, 826 S.W.2d 201 (Tex. App. 1992), *rev'd*, 869 S.W.2d 941 (Tex. 1994).

engaging in, or being thought to engage in, acts that are crimes only for that group. Many heterosexuals engage in the same acts, *see* Laumann et al., *supra*, at 98–99 (1994) (finding that three-quarters of those who engage in opposite-sex encounters have engaged in oral sex, one-fifth in anal sex), yet are neither prosecuted for them nor defined by society as who they are on the basis of them. When a group is sexually defined, reduced to a list of prohibited sex acts, and targeted for discrimination socially and legally on this basis, while others perform these same acts without being defined or criminalized or disadvantaged as a result, is the constitutional "guarantee[ ] [of] equal laws," *Personnel Adm'r v. Feeney*, 442 U.S. 256, 273 (1979), met? Professor Andrew Koppelman observes, "[I]f the same conduct is prohibited or stigmatized when engaged in by a person of one sex, while it is tolerated when engaged in by a person of the other sex, then the party imposing the prohibition or stigma is discriminating on the basis of sex." Andrew Koppelman, *Antidiscrimination Law and Social Equality* 154 (1996). Do you agree? When the sex of those who have sex makes them criminals, is that sex discrimination? (For discussion, see III B.)

Legal discrimination against gay men and lesbian women is part of a larger social edifice of ostracism and shunning, stigmatization and psychological terrorism, medicalization, deprivation of positive role models and sex education, invidious stereotyping, enforced invisibility, and economic vulnerability. This edifice is bound together by forcible socialization to heterosexuality as the only way to be and the only human way to relate, to which anyone who does not want or fit the standard heterosexual models for men and women continues to be routinely subject, in one form or another, in most societies. In most cultures, punishment for any sexuality but standard heterosexuality begins very young and continues throughout life in forms that can include withdrawal of love, enforced silencing, forced conversion, psychiatric incarceration and torture, and other overt violence including rape and murder. *See generally* Peter M. Nardi & Ralph Bolton, "Gay–Bashing: Violence and Aggression Against Gay Men and Lesbians," *in Targets of Violence and Aggression* 349 (Ronald Baenninger ed., 1991). Some societies, for example ancient Greece, have been more tolerant of what has come to be called homosexuality—there, mainly as practiced among males, in particular by sexually dominant men with boys. *See* Kenneth James Dover, *Greek Homosexuality* (1978); *see also* John Boswell, *Same-Sex Unions in Premodern Europe* (1994).[12] However, Greek men who prostituted themselves were punished by law by loss of civil status and rights of citizenship, including the right to speak in public. *See* Eva Cantarella, *Bisexuality in the Ancient World* 49 (1992) (citing Aeschines' oration "Against Timarchus"). Most societies, continuing to the present, have not been tolerant of homosexuality. *See generally* Fone, *supra*; Theo van der Meer, "Tribades on Trial: Female Same–Sex Offenders in Late Eighteenth–Century Amsterdam," 1 *J. Hist. Sexuality* 424 (1991). Granting that tolerance is an improvement over intolerance, is it equality?

---

12. For analysis of historical tolerance in indigenous cultures of behavior that defies prevailing gender and sexual stereotypes, see Paula Gunn Allen, "Lesbians in American Indian Cultures," *in Hidden from History: Reclaiming the Gay and Lesbian Past* 106 (Martin Duberman et al. eds., 1989); Evelyn Blackwood, "Sexuality and Gender in Certain Native American Tribes: The Case of Cross–Gender Females," 10 *Signs* 27 (1984); Harriet Whitehead, "The Bow and the Burden Strap: A New Look at Institutionalized Homosexuality in Native North America," *in Sexual Meanings: The Cultural Construction of Gender and Sexuality* 80 (Sherry B. Ortner & Harriet Whitehead eds., 1981).

In Europe in the past, persons considered not heterosexual have been subjected, often with legal and theological support, to beating, whipping, hanging, castration, and burning at the stake. *See* John Boswell, *Christianity, Social Tolerance and Homosexuality: Gay People in Western Europe from the Beginning of the Christian Era to the Fourteenth Century* 267–334 (1980). ("Christianity, Social Tolerance"); Bernadette J. Brooten, *Love Between Women: Early Christian Responses to Female Homoeroticism* 18, 24–25, 162–71, 236 (1996) (documenting cliteridectomy as means of suppressing women's "masculine" desire). Homosexuals were persecuted by the Nazis during the Holocaust along with Jews, Romani (Gypsies), and Communists.[13] *See* Richard Plant, *The Pink Triangle: The Nazi War Against Homosexuals* 441–42 (1986). Gay men were marked by the pink triangle; it appears that some lesbian women, regarded with prostituted women as "antisocial" elements, may have been marked with the black one.

In the United States, legal discrimination, stigmatization, medicalization, and other forms of marginalization and abuse of gay men and lesbian women have deep historical roots extending to the colonial era. *See, e.g.,* Louis Crompton, "Homosexuals and the Death Penalty in Colonial America," 1 *J. Homosexuality* 277 (1976). Homosexuals, real or imagined, were deported with Communists during the "Red Scare" of 1919–1920 and persecuted with Communists during the McCarthy period in the 1950s. *See* John D'Emilio, *Sexual Politics, Sexual Communities: The Making of a Homosexual Minority in the United States 1940–1970*, at 40–53 (2d ed. 1998); John D'Emilio, "The Homosexual Menace: The Politics of Sexuality in Cold War America," *in Passion and Power: Sexuality in History* 226 (Kathy Peiss & Christina Simmons eds., 1989); Patricia Cain, "Litigating for Lesbian and Gay Rights: A Legal History," 79 *Va. L. Rev.* 1551, 1556–57, 1565–66 (1993). In interpreting this history, there is disagreement over whether western law of the past discriminated as viciously against lesbians as it did against gay men, or whether the invisibility of lesbians, the triviality of women, and the unthinkability of sexual expression without a man around, protected lesbian women from legalized oppression, or the worst of it.[14] Perhaps, for women, the oppression simply took equally onerous forms that were not always the same as the forms it took for men. Professor Sheila Jeffreys contends that lesbian sex was historically ignored in English law as the best strategy for eradicating it and eliminating the women who practiced it. *See* Sheila Jeffreys, *The Spinster and Her Ene-*

---

13. *See The Hidden Holocaust: Gay and Lesbian Persecution in Germany 1933–45* (Gunter Grau ed., Patrick Camiller trans., Fitzroy Dearborn Publishers, Inc., 1997) (1993); Erwin J. Haeberle, "Swastika, Pink Triangle, and Yellow Star: The Destruction of Sexology and the Persecution of Homosexuals in Nazi Germany," 17 *J. Sex Res.* 270 (1981); Frank Rector, *The Nazi Extermination of Homosexuals* (1981); Claudia Schoppmann, *Days of Masquerade: Life Stories of Lesbians During the Third Reich* (Allison Brown trans., Columbia University Press 1996) (1993).

14. *Compare* John D'Emilio & Estelle B. Freedman, *Intimate Matters: A History of Sexuality in America* 122 (2d ed., University of Chicago Press 1997) (1988) (stating sexual acts between two women were generally not criminalized in the past), *and* Sylvia A. Law, "Homosexuality and the Social Meaning of Gender," 1988 *Wis. L. Rev.* 187, 202 n.75 ("The traditional common law and religious condemnation of homosexuality did not encompass women") *with* Ruthann Robson, "Lesbianism in Anglo–European Legal History," 5 *Wis. Women's L.J.* 1, 7–13 (1990) (arguing that lesbian sex was criminal under Canadian and British law more complexly than previously thought), *and* Louis Crompton, "The Myth of Lesbian Impunity: Capital Laws from 1270–1791," *J. Homosexuality*, Fall/Winter 1980–1981, at 11.

mies: Feminism and Sexuality 1880–1930, at 114 (1985). Some legalized subordination in the past took standard forms of persecution under facially gender-neutral laws, if applied in sex-conscious ways. In early eighteenth-century Germany, for example, a woman was sentenced to death for sodomy and executed for having sex by means of an artificial penis with another woman, whom she married disguised as a man. *See* "A Lesbian Execution in Germany, 1721: The Trial Records," *in J. Homosexuality* 27 (trans. Brigitte Eriksson, Fall/Winter 1980/81). Sodomy was defined there, inter alia, in discussion of applicable Saxon and canon law, as "the [vice] with the same sex, as man with man and woman with woman." *Id.* at 39.

There is no doubt of the continued viciousness and extent of social discrimination against lesbian women. *See* Lacey M. Sloan & Nora S. Gustavsson, *Violence and Social Injustice Against Lesbian, Gay and Bisexual People* (1998); Dawn Snape et al., *Discrimination Against Gay Men and Lesbians: A Study of the Nature and Extent of Discrimination Against Homosexual Men and Women in Britain Today* (Social & Community Planning Research, 1995); Diane Helene Miller, *Freedom to Differ; the Shaping of the Gay and Lesbian Struggle for Civil Rights* (1998); Shannon Minter, "United States," *in Unspoken Rules: Sexual Orientation and Women's Human Rights* (Rachel Rosenbloom ed. 1996) ("Rosenbloom"); Gary David Comstock, *Violence Against Lesbians and Gay Men* 38–55, 194–95 (1991). In the United States, sexual violence against lesbian women, and women perceived as lesbians, is common. Thirty-seven percent of women who identify as lesbian in one study reported experiencing physical abuse, 41 percent rape or other sexual attack, and 19 percent victimization through incest in childhood. *See* Judith Bradford & Caitlin Ryan, National Lesbian and Gay Health Foundation, *The National Lesbian Health Care Survey: Final Report* 76, 80, 83 (1988). Consider whether injuries to females prior to self-identification as lesbian, and injuries by aggressors who do not perceive their victims as lesbians, should be counted. Compare the figures above with comparable data for all women in Chapter 7. To the extent the figures are similar, does this mean that the lesbian women studied by Ms. Bradford and Ms. Ryan were not abused as lesbians? Lesbian women or gay men battered by their partners, after years of invisibility, are often denied social services and other supportive intervention. *See* Chapter 6 IV.[15] Thirty-one percent of lesbian-identified women questioned in one study in Britain reported experiencing homophobic violence in the last five years and 28 percent had experienced harassment—and lesbian sex acts were never illegal in England. *See* Anya Palmer, "Britain," *in* Rosenbloom at 25, 30–31.

Law and society actively collaborate to enforce the inequality of gay men and lesbian women, *see generally* House of Commons, Parliamentary Committee on Equality Rights, *Equality for All* (Oct. 1985) (esp. Chapter 4), whether as individuals, couples, or collectivities, raising a host of issues. Do the negative legal and social consequences of being gay or lesbian suggest why the majority of the population becomes predominantly heterosexual? Do people have much choice? Why do societies enforce heterosexu-

---

15. For further discussion, see Leslie K. Burke & Diane R. Follingstad, "Violence in Lesbian and Gay Relationships: Theory, Prevalence, and Correlational Factors," 19 *Clinical Psychol. Rev.* 487 (1999); Carolyn M. West, "Leaving a Second Closet: Outing Partner Violence in Same-Sex Couples," *in Partner Violence: A Comprehensive Review of 20 Years of Research* (Jana L. Jasinski et al. eds., 1998); *Violence in Gay and Lesbian Domestic Partnerships* (Claire M. Renzetti & Charles Harvey Miley eds., 1996).

ality so aggressively, including through law? If, as is often said, heterosexuality is "natural," why does it need to be enforced? Why is who a person may sexually love or sexually interact with prescribed and proscribed on the basis of sex? What makes same-sexuality—an experience for many of joy, pleasure, love, intimacy, pride, identity, family, and community—a target for others of hatred, violence, and discrimination?

Early litigation against antigay citizenship standards exposes the convergence of legal and social bias. Citizenship standards define one threshold for entrance to political community. Consider in this light the reasons given in 1967 for excluding one young gay man from the United States and finding him unworthy of American citizenship. Does Michael Boutilier's case suggest that if Congress and the Supreme Court could choose, gay and lesbian Americans would not be citizens? What would an affirmative answer mean for their status as citizens in the community?

Boutilier v. Immigration and Naturalization Service

Supreme Court of the United States.
387 U.S. 118 (1967)

■ JUSTICE CLARK delivered the opinion of the Court.

The petitioner, an alien, has been ordered deported to Canada as one who upon entry into this country was a homosexual and therefore "afflicted with psychopathic personality" and excludable under § 212 (a)(4) of the Immigration and Nationality Act of 1952, 66 Stat. 182, 8 U. S. C. § 1182 (a)(4)....

Petitioner, a Canadian national, was first admitted to this country on June 22, 1955, at the age of 21.... In 1963 he applied for citizenship and submitted ... an affidavit in which he admitted that he was arrested in New York in October 1959, on a charge of sodomy, ... which was ... thereafter dismissed.... In 1964, petitioner ... submitted another affidavit which revealed the full history of his sexual deviate behavior. It stated that his first homosexual experience occurred when he was 14 years of age, some seven years before his entry into the United States. Petitioner was evidently a passive participant in this encounter. His next episode was at age 16 and occurred in a public park in Halifax, Nova Scotia. Petitioner was the active participant in this affair. During the next five years immediately preceding his first entry into the United States petitioner had homosexual relations on an average of three or four times a year. He also stated that prior to his entry he had engaged in heterosexual relations on three or four occasions. During the eight and one-half years immediately subsequent to his entry, and up to the time of his second statement, petitioner continued to have homosexual relations on an average of three or four times a year. Since 1959 petitioner had shared an apartment with a man with whom he had had homosexual relations.

The 1964 affidavit was submitted to the Public Health Service for its opinion as to whether petitioner was excludable for any reason at the time of his entry. The Public Health Service issued a certificate in 1964 stating that in the opinion of the subscribing physicians petitioner "was afflicted with a class A condition, namely, psychopathic personality, sexual deviate" at the time of his admission. Deportation proceedings were then instituted.... [T]he officer found that both of petitioner's psychiatrists "concede that the respondent has been a homosexual for a number of years but conclude that by reason of such sexual deviation the respondent is not a psychopathic personality." Finding against petitioner on the facts, the issue before the officer was reduced to the purely legal question of whether the term "psychopathic personality" included homosexuals and if it suffered illegality because of vagueness.

The legislative history of the Act indicates beyond a shadow of a doubt that the Congress intended the phrase "psychopathic personality" to include homosexuals such as petitioner.... [We] ... conclude that the Congress used the phrase "psychopathic personality" not in the clinical sense, but to effectuate its purpose to exclude from entry all homosexuals and other sex perverts.... For over six years prior to his entry petitioner admittedly followed a continued course of homosexual conduct.... The Government clearly established that petitioner was a homosexual at entry.... [W]e do not now disturb that finding, especially since petitioner admitted being a homosexual *at the time* of his entry. The existence of this condition over a continuous and uninterrupted period prior to and at the time of petitioner's entry clearly supports the ultimate finding upon which the order of deportation was based.

Petitioner says, even so, the section as construed is constitutionally defective because it did not adequately warn him that his sexual affliction at the time of entry could lead to his deportation.... [Section] 212 (a)(4) never applied to petitioner's conduct after entry.... The petitioner is not being deported for conduct engaged in after his entry into the United States, but rather for characteristics he possessed at the time of his entry. Here, when petitioner first presented himself at our border for entrance, he was already afflicted with homosexuality. The pattern was cut, and under it he was not admissible.... [Congress can exclude, unrestricted by the Constitutional requirement of fair warning.] See The Chinese Exclusion Case, 130 U.S. 581 (1889). Here Congress commanded that homosexuals not be allowed to enter. The petitioner was found to have that characteristic and was ordered deported. The basis of the deportation order was his affliction for a long period of time *prior to entry*, i.e., six and one-half years before his entry. It may be, as some claim, that "psychopathic personality" is a medically ambiguous term.... But the test here is what the Congress intended, not what differing psychiatrists may think. It was not laying down a clinical test, but an exclusionary standard which it declared to be inclusive of those having homosexual and perverted characteristics....

But petitioner says that he had no warning [and] was unaware of the fact that homosexual conduct engaged in after entry could lead to his deportation order.... We do not believe that petitioner's post-entry conduct is the basis for his deportation order.... A standard applicable solely to time of entry could hardly be vague as to post-entry conduct.

■ JUSTICE DOUGLAS, with whom JUSTICE FORTAS concurs, dissenting.

The term "psychopathic personality" is a treacherous one like "communist" or in an earlier day "Bolshevik." A label of this kind when freely used may mean only an unpopular person. It is much too vague by constitutional standards for the imposition of penalties or punishment.... Many experts think that it is a meaningless designation.... It is much too treacherously vague a term to allow the high penalty of deportation to turn on it. When it comes to sex, the problem is complex. Those "who fail to reach sexual maturity (hetero-sexuality), and who remain at a narcissistic or homosexual stage" are the products "of heredity, of glandular dysfunction, [or] of environmental circumstances." Henderson, "Psychopathic Constitution and Criminal Behaviour," in Mental Abnormality and Crime 105, 114 (Radzinowicz & Turner eds., 1949). The homosexual is one, who by some freak, is the product of an arrested development:

> All people have originally bisexual tendencies which are more or less developed and which in the course of time normally deviate either in the direction of male or female. This may indicate that a trace of homosexuality, no matter how weak it may be, exists in every human being. It is present in the adolescent stage, where there is a considerable amount of undifferentiated sexuality. Abrahamsen, Crime and the Human Mind 117 (1944)....

It is common knowledge that in this century homosexuals have risen high in our own public service—both in Congress and in the Executive Branch—and have served with distinction. It is therefore not credible that Congress wanted to deport everyone and anyone who was a sexual deviate, no matter how blameless his social conduct had been nor how creative his work nor how valuable his contribution to society. [I agree with the dissenting judge below] that the legislative history should not be read as imputing to Congress a purpose to classify under the heading "psychopathic personality" every person who had ever had a homosexual experience:

> Professor Kinsey estimated that "at least 37 per cent" of the American male population has at least one homosexual experience, defined in terms of physical contact to the point of orgasm, between the beginning of adolescence and old age. Kinsey, Pomeroy & Martin, Sexual Behavior in the Human Male 623 (1948).... The sponsors of Britain's current reform bill on homosexuality have indicated that one male in 25 is a homosexual in Britain. To label a group so large "excludable aliens" would be tantamount to saying that Sappho, Leonardo da Vinci, Michelangelo, Andre Gide, and perhaps even Shakespeare, were they to come to life again, would be deemed unfit to visit our shores.[16] Indeed, so broad a definition might well comprise more than a few members of legislative bodies. 363 F.2d 488, 497–98.

The Public Health Service, from whom Congress borrowed the term "psychopathic personality" admits that the term is "vague and indefinite." If we are to hold, as the Court apparently does, that any acts of homosexuality suffice to deport the alien, whether or not they are part of a fabric of antisocial behavior, then we face a serious

---

16. [3] Sigmund Freud wrote in 1935: Homosexuality is assuredly no advantage, but it is nothing to be ashamed of, no vice, no degradation, it cannot be classified as an illness; we consider it to be a variation of the sexual function produced by a certain arrest of sexual development. Many highly respectable individuals of ancient and modern times have been homosexuals, several of the greatest men among them (Plato, Michelangelo, Leonardo da Vinci, etc.). It is a great injustice to persecute homosexuality as a crime, and cruelty too. If you do not believe me, read the books of Havelock Ellis. Ruitenbeek, The Problem of Homosexuality in Modern Society 1 (1963).

question of due process. By that construction a person is judged by a standard that is almost incapable of definition.... Anyone can be caught who is unpopular, who is off-beat, who is nonconformist.... "Psychopathic personality" is so broad and vague as to be hardly more than an epithet. The Court seeks to avoid this question by saying that the standard being applied relates only to what petitioner had done prior to his entry, not to his postentry conduct. *But at least half of the questioning of this petitioner related to his postentry conduct.*

Moreover, the issue of deportability ... turns on whether petitioner is "afflicted with psychopathic personality." On this I think he is entitled to a hearing ... [including evidence such as that from one report:]

> The patient's present difficulties obviously weigh very heavily upon him. He feels as if he has made his life in this country and is deeply disturbed at the prospect of being cut off from the life he has created for himself.... What emerged out of the interview was not a picture of a psychopath but that of a dependent, immature young man with a conscience, an awareness of the feelings of others and a sense of personal honesty. His sexual structure still appears fluid and immature so that he moves from homosexual to heterosexual interests as well as abstinence with almost equal facility. His homosexual orientation seems secondary to a very constricted, dependent personality pattern rather than occurring in the context of a psychopathic personality. My own feeling is that his own need to fit in and be accepted is so great that it far surpasses his need for sex in any form.

In light of [the evidence] I cannot say that it has been determined that petitioner was "afflicted" in the statutory sense either at the time of entry or at present. "Afflicted" means possessed or dominated by. Occasional acts would not seem sufficient. "Afflicted" means a way of life, an accustomed pattern of conduct. Whatever disagreement there is as to the meaning of "psychopathic personality," it has generally been understood to refer to a consistent, lifelong pattern of behavior conflicting with social norms without accompanying guilt.[17] Nothing of that character was shown to exist at the time of entry. The fact that he presently has a problem, as one psychiatrist said, does not mean that he is or was necessarily "afflicted" with homosexuality. His conduct is, of course, evidence material to the issue. But the informed judgment of experts is needed to make the required finding. We cruelly mutilate the Act when we hold otherwise.

Was the statutory standard of proscribed conduct in *Boutilier*, found not legally vague, a resonant model of clarity? How was a clinical term found not to be applied in a clinical sense? Ponder, too, the legal relevance of whether Mr. Boutilier was "active" or "passive" in sex. Does the majority seem to assume that, in sex, a person is one or the other? Would such an assumption have anything to do with sex roles? The dissent quotes Mr. Boutilier's psychiatrist's report, revealing an arguably unscripted,

---

17. [6] ... [The] legislative history indicates that the term "afflicted with psychopathic personality" was used in a medical sense and was meant to refer to lifelong patterns of action that are pathologic and symptomatic of grave underlying neurosis or psychosis. Homosexuality and sex perversion, as a subclass, are limited to the same afflictions.

gender-unrigid, uncompulsive sexuality on Mr. Boutilier's part. How did such qualities became deportable defects under law? Against what standard does a sexuality that is "fluid" in gender terms make one unworthy of U.S. citizenship? Professor Mary McIntosh's analysis of Kinsey's data on U.S. women suggests that, with increasing age, women's sexual partners become more gender-diverse, men's less. *See* Mary McIntosh, "The Homosexual Role," 16 *Soc. Probs.* 182, 191–92 (1968). Could this have been the standard against which Mr. Boutilier was found wanting? Could whatever social reality generated those data have anything to do with male dominance and sexuality's place in it? Is the standard of heterosexuality adopted in *Boutilier* in any sense not only a narrow sexual standard but a male dominant one?

Both opinions in *Boutilier*, if to varying degrees, take the view that homosexuality is a fact, a state, a condition, a virtually congenital illness, a malady or sickness subject to diagnosis. One difference between the majority and the dissent on this point concerns the indications of whether one is "afflicted" with this so-called condition, and whether the ultimate conclusion facing the court is a matter of statutory interpretation or medical evidence. For the majority, the question is what Congress intended. For the dissent, the relevant determination, to be humane, is for doctors. This opinion was written before homosexuality was no longer considered a psychiatric disorder. *See* Ronald Bayer, *Homosexuality and American Psychiatry: The Politics of Diagnosis* (1981) (recounting history of removal of homosexuality from Diagnostic and Statistical Manual in 1973 after two decades of struggle). Would you rather be seen as a psychopath as a matter of law or as a freak of arrested development as a matter of fact? Do both opinions obscure discrimination against a subordinated group—the majority by interpretation, the dissent by evidence?

Another difference between the opinions, starkly stated, is the degree to which homosexuality is seen to be a course of conduct as opposed to a personal trait or characteristic. The dissenters appear to think that Mr. Boutilier had some choice or control over whether he expressed his homosexuality; for them, homosexuality, to some degree, was constituted by homosexual sex acts, which one could do or not do. For the majority, by contrast, homosexuality was an inborn trait, an essence, evidenced, not constituted, by acts.[18] The question of what makes for homosexuality— what "it is"—remains contested in the cases and materials throughout this chapter. In *Boutilier*, the majority labors to make clear what it believes could not be plainer: Michael Boutilier could not do anything about who he was, and he was this at the time of his entry into the United States, so it made no difference that the statute gave him no notice as to the consequences of his actions, because it was for who he was, not what he did, that he was deported and denied naturalization. This version of the "status not act" analysis of homosexuality is, in this case, a defense for the statute: the statute could not be unconstitutionally vague as to conduct because a

---

18. For analysis of the medicalization of homosexual "deviance," see Jennifer Terry, *An American Obsession: Science, Medicine, and Homosexuality in Modern Society* (2000); Peter Conrad & Joseph W. Schneider, "Homosexuality: From Sin to Sickness to Lifestyle," *in Deviance and Medicalization: From Badness to Sickness* 172 (Temple University Press, 2d ed. 1994) (1980); George Chauncey Jr., "From Sexual Inversion to Homosexuality: Medicine and the Changing Conceptualization of Female Deviance," 58–59 *Salmagundi* 114 (1982–1983); Lillian Faderman, "The Morbidification of Love Between Women by Nineteenth-Century Sexologists," 4 *J. Homosexuality* 73 (1978).

psychopathic personality is something one has, not something one does, a fixed attribute, not a behavior. There was, in other words, nothing Mr. Boutilier could have avoided doing while in the United States that would have helped his case; he was ejected not for anything he did, but for who he was seen as being. In an equal protection context, would this analysis by the Court look like classic status-based discrimination? Is there in *Boutilier* even the semblance of what, in an equality challenge, would be rationality review? The dissent, in contrast, seems to regard homosexuality more as act than essence, and asserts that Michael Boutilier should have had a chance not to be, i.e., act, homosexual (or, as may be more accurate, bisexual), in order to remain in the United States. Does the dissent's approach avoid discrimination, or would it, also invidiously and irrationally under an equality standard, enforce asexuality only on homosexuals as a price for being in America? In this context, is discrimination for acts or for status still discrimination? If the acts injured others, would it be different?

Exclusion of aliens with a "psychopathic personality," or "sexual deviation," was eliminated by Congress in the Immigration Act of 1990, *see* Immigration Act of 1990, Pub. L. No. 101–649, 104 Stat. 4978–5088 (1990), in a revision specifically intended to revoke the history of excluding "homosexuals," *see* William N. Eskridge Jr. & Nan D. Hunter, *Sexuality, Gender & the Law* 186–89 (1997). For historical investigations of "sexual psychopath" campaigns as oppression of gays, see George Chauncey Jr., "The Postwar Sex Crime Panic," *in True Stories from the American Past* 160 (William Graebner ed., 1993); Estelle B. Freedman, " 'Uncontrolled Desires': The Response to the Sexual Psychopath, 1920–1960," 74 *J. Am. Hist.* 83 (1987). However, in theory noncitizens can still be excluded or deported for homosexuality if, for example, found guilty of "crime[s] involving moral turpitude," 8 U.S.C. § 1182(a)(2)(A)(i)(I) (1994), or denied naturalization if found to lack "good moral character," 8 U.S.C. § 1427(a)(3) (1994). As interpreted and applied by the immigration authorities and the courts, same-sex sexual conduct and expression can conform to or violate the moral requirements.[19] Is morality a particularly serviceable instrument and cover for unequal treatment? Was it in *Boutilier*? Since 1994, homosexuals have been considered a potentially persecuted "particular social group" under INS standards for withholding deportation and granting asylum.[20] Does an opinion like *Boutilier* help construct (as well as

---

19. *See Posusta v. United States*, 285 F.2d 533, 534–35 (2d Cir. 1961) (Hand, C.J.) (stating that test of good moral character is "not the personal moral principles of the individual judge or court before whom the applicant may come [but] what [is believed] to be the ethical standards current at the time"); *In re Labady*, 326 F. Supp. 924 (S.D.N.Y. 1971) (naturalizing gay man as of good moral character because conduct was "private," *see* II); Shannon Minter, Note, "Sodomy and Public Morality Offenses Under U.S. Immigration Law: Penalizing Lesbian and Gay Identity," 26 *Cornell Int'l L.J.* 771, 783 (1993).

20. *See* Att'y Gen. Order No. 1895–94 (June 19, 1994); *In re Toboso–Alfonso*, 20 I. & N. Dec. 819 (1990); *In re Tenorio*, No. A72–093–558, (Immigration Ct., S.F., July 26,

1993), *reprinted in* Karen Musalo et al., *Refugee Law and Policy* 713 (1997) (granting asylum to gay Brazilian man on grounds of membership in particular social group subject to persecution); *Pitcherskaia v. INS*, 118 F.3d 641, 647 (9th Cir. 1997) (finding that definition of persecution does not require showing of malignant intent in response to involuntary psychiatric treatments intended to "cure" lesbian woman not to punish her: "Persecution by any other name remains persecution"); Jin S. Park, "Pink Asylum: Political Asylum Eligibility of Gay Men and Lesbians Under U.S. Immigration Policy," 42 *UCLA L. Rev.* 1115 (1995); *see also* Eva N. Juncker, "A Juxtaposition of U.S. Asylum Grants to Women Fleeing Female Genital Mutilation and to Gays and Lesbians Fleeing

reflect) antigay attitudes? Do subsequent developments in immigration law help counter and deconstruct those same attitudes, moving toward altering the definition of political community? Are gay men and lesbian women free of persecution in the United States—as granting them asylum in the United States from persecution elsewhere tends to claim? Consider throughout this chapter whether attitudes on display in *Boutilier* continue to animate their legal and social treatment.

Resistance to discriminatory attitudes and practices like those Michael Boutilier encountered, in mobilization that was accelerating just as his claim was being denied, has produced a movement for gay rights that has become increasingly organized, visible, proud, and legally activist throughout the twentieth century in many countries. The first organization for gay civil rights was formed in Germany in 1897. Beginning in the United States in 1906, extending through the formation and existence of the Mattachine Society and the Daughters of Bilitis in the 1950s, *see* John D'Emilio, *Making Trouble: Essays on Gay History, Politics, and the University* 17–56 (1992); John D'Emilio, *Sexual Politics, Sexual Communities, supra* at 57–74, to the several days of Stonewall Riots in 1969 in resistance to police repression, *see* Martin Duberman, *Stonewall* 195–212 (1993), gay men and lesbian women have become increasingly visible and have organized to assert their full citizenship and human rights.[21]

The legal arm of the movement for gay rights has attempted to address the lack of legal protections for gay and lesbian people and legal threats to gay and lesbian existence, flourishing, and expression. *See generally* Eric Marcus, *Making History: The Struggle for Gay and Lesbian Equal Rights, 1945–1990* (1992); Urvashi Vaid, *Virtual Equality: The Mainstreaming of Gay and Lesbian Liberation* (1995); Andrew Sullivan, *Virtually Normal: An Argument About Homosexuality* (1995). This movement has achieved some success by attempting to meet the requirements of various legal doctrines on their own terms, insisting in effect that same-sexuality cannot disentitle individuals to rights to which they are otherwise legally entitled.[22] An

Physical Harm," 4 *J. Int'l Legal Stud.* 253 (1998).

21. *See* D'Emilio, *Sexual Politics, Sexual Communities, supra*; Jonathan Ned Katz, *Gay American History: Lesbians and Gay Men in the U.S.A.* 335–443 (1976); Barry D. Adam, *The Rise of a Gay and Lesbian Movement* (1987); Eric Marcus, *Making History: The Struggle for Gay and Lesbian Equal Rights, 1945–1990: An Oral History* (1992); Jonathan Ned Katz, *Gay/Lesbian Almanac: A New Documentary* (1983); Dudley Clendinen & Adam Nagourney, *Out for Good: The Struggle to Build a Gay Rights Movement in America* (1999). Early works from this movement in the United States include: Del Martin & Phyllis Lyon, *Lesbian/Woman* (1972); Sidney Abbott & Barbara Love, *Sappho Was a Right-On Woman* (1972); Dennis Altman, *Homosexual: Oppression and Liberation* (1971); Merle Miller, *On Being Different* (1971); Kay Tobin & Randy Wicker, *Gay Crusaders* (1972); *Out of the Closets: Voices of Gay Liberation* (Karla Jay & Allen Young eds., 1972); *The Gay Liberation Book: Writ-* ings by and About Gay Men (Len Richmond & Gary Noguera eds., 1973); Doris Klaich, *Woman + Woman* (1974).

22. *See generally Sexual Orientation and the Law* (Harvard Law Review, 1989). At times, family law has been an example. Same-sex families have been permitted to claim some rights to their children, *see, e.g., In re the Adoption of Evan*, 583 N.Y.S.2d 997 (Sur. Ct. 1992) (permitting legal adoption of biological child of one lesbian mother by the other, her partner); *Thomas S. v. Robin Y.*, 599 N.Y.S.2d 377 (Fam. Ct. 1993) (denying filiation to gay male sperm donor with some relation to child in favor of lesbian mothers), *rev'd*, 618 N.Y.S.2d 356 (App. Div. 1994). So, at times, has free speech law. Attacks on same-sex literature as obscene because it is same-sex have been repudiated under the First Amendment. *See, e.g., One, Inc. v. Olesen*, 241 F.2d 772, *rev'd mem. per curiam*, 355 U.S. 371 (1958) (reversing denial of injunction with result of permitting mailing of homophile publication over obscenity attack). In

example is the creative attempts to use the First Amendment to protect "coming out" as gay or lesbian as a form of political expression, and to prohibit punishing such activity as protected speech, bridging act and status, and at times combining equality with speech theories, in a way that also strikes at the invisibility of gay and lesbian people. *See generally* William Rubenstein, "Since When Is the Fourteenth Amendment Our Route to Equality?," 2 *Law & Sexuality* 19 (1992) (advocating use of First Amendment to gain equality for gays and lesbians); David Cole & William N. Eskridge Jr., "From Hand–Holding to Sodomy: First Amendment Protection of Homosexual (Expressive) Conduct," 29 *Harv. C.R.-C.L. L. Rev.* 319 (1994) (arguing that being gay is protected expressive conduct). The most prominent doctrines employed in arguing for gay and lesbian rights as such, targeting bodies of law and patterns of practice as unconstitutionally punitive or exclusionary or facially biased or virtually always invidious, have been privacy and equal protection on the basis of sexual orientation, with equal protection on the basis of sex a distant third. The choice of tools for addressing the status and treatment of gay and lesbian people raises fundamental issues of social, political, and legal analysis.

Privacy strategies fielded under the legal rubric of substantive due process have historically been preferred, their principal target the criminal sodomy laws. *See* II. These initiatives seek to define an inviolable sphere of safety and sanctuary in which everyone can be sexual and express their personal identities intimately and affectionately and make love without state intrusion, punishment, or constraint. In the current context, the approach is epitomized by the slogan "Get your laws off my body," *see* II, a slogan also used by pro-choice abortion-rights activists. By distinction, the goal of the theory of equality of status without discrimination because of sexual orientation or preference seeks equal entitlements, resources, power, and legitimacy in public and private inseparably. *See* III A. This approach has achieved some legislative success, *see, e.g.*, Wis. Stat. §§ 111.31–36 (1997–98); Cal. Lab. Code § 1102.1 (West Supp. 1999), as well as judicial victories, particularly under rationality approaches in the United States, and under *Andrews* and its progeny in Canada. *See* III A. The attempt to secure gay rights as sex equality rights by challenging discrimination against gay men as men and lesbian women as women, that is, on the basis of sex and gender, is least developed but has received increasing attention. *See* III B.

I. LANGUAGE

The copula between the terms in which gay and lesbian existence is spoken about and the terms on which it is lived has been central to the activism and scholarship flourishing on the subject since the 1970s. Terms and concepts also embody political views and analyses that favor certain

People v. Friede, 133 Misc. 611, 233 N.Y.S. 565 (N.Y.C. Magistrate's Ct. 1929), Radclyffe Hall's *The Well of Loneliness* was found obscene under New York law. The result was reversed by the New York Supreme Court in an unreported opinion. *See* " 'Well of Loneliness' Cleared in Court Here," *N.Y. Times*, Apr. 20, 1929, at 20. *See generally* Diana Souhami, *The Trials of Radclyffe Hall* (1998); Vera Brittain, *Radclyffe Hall: A Case of Obscenity?* (1968); Leigh Gilmore, "Obscenity, Modernity, Identity: Legalizing *The Well of Loneliness* and *Nightwood*," 4 *J. Hist. Sexuality* 603 (1994).

legal approaches over others to the problem of securing gay and lesbian rights.

Although human beings have probably always made love or been sexual with one another in various ways, "sexuality" as a feature of the self or social identity or as a social institution is of relatively recent minting, according to historians. Considerable discussion has taken place on the question whether "homosexuality" and "heterosexuality" have or have not always been recognized as a cultural dualism, producing some concurrence that what is now called "homosexuality" dates from the last century or two. *See* David M. Halperin, *One Hundred Years of Homosexuality* 41–53 (1990). Professor John Boswell, a historian, located one point in the evolution in the way homosexuals were perceived "from the personal preference of a prosperous minority, satirized and celebrated in popular verse, to a dangerous, antisocial, and severely sinful aberration" at sometime between 1150 and 1350. *See* John Boswell, *Christianity, Social Tolerance, supra,* at 295. Western European and American cultures showed a similar shift around the turn of the twentieth century as sexological concepts were disseminated.

The term "homosexual" was created in the late nineteenth century by German psychologists. *See id.* at 42–43 & n.4; *see also* Jonathan Ned Katz, " 'Homosexual' and 'Heterosexual': Questioning the Terms," *in A Queer World* 177 (Martin Duberman ed., 1997) (attributing the first use of term "homosexual" to a German writer); Jonathan Ned Katz, *The Invention of Heterosexuality* 10 (1995). Homosexuality has generally been a diagnostic designation for sex between people of the same sex considered as something gone wrong. Its clinical resonance diagnoses a putatively inborn sexual deviance termed "sexual perversion" or "sexual inversion," complete with negative value judgments and stigma, *see, e.g.,* Richard von Krafft–Ebing, *Psychopathia Sexualis: A Medico–Forensic Study* 470 (Harry E. Wedeck trans., G.P. Putnam's Sons 1965) (1886); 2 Havelock Ellis, *Studies in the Psychology of Sex* 262 (3rd ed. 1930), some analysts having claimed that homosexuals are a "third sex," *see* David F. Greenberg, *The Construction of Homosexuality* 408–09 (1988); Hubert C. Kennedy, "The 'Third Sex' Theory of Karl Heinrich Ulrichs," 6 *J. Homosexuality* 103 (1980–1981); *Third Sex, Third Gender: Beyond Sexual Dimorphism in Culture and History* (Gilbert Herdt ed., 1994). Homosexuality was labeled a psychiatric disorder by the American Psychiatric Association until 1973, when it was removed from the diagnostic canon. *See* Bayer, *supra,* at 40. The term "homosexual" is gender neutral. Might it, like other gender neutral terms, conceal gendered specificities and disparities?

The term "homosexual" was specifically "coined in the nineteenth century to express the new idea that a person's immanent and essential nature is revealed by the gender of his desired sex partner." Anne B. Goldstein, Comment, "History, Homosexuality, and Political Values: Searching for the Hidden Determinants of *Bowers v. Hardwick*," 97 *Yale L.J.* 1073, 1088 (1988). The extent to which this view of same-sexuality remains accepted is unclear. Whatever its determinants, homosexuality has been socially opposed to "heterosexuality"[23] to mean sex between people

---

23. Interestingly, and unlike the meaning the term has come to have, "heterosexuals" was used in 1892 in the United States in a medical journal in reference to Krafft–Ebing's *Psychopathia Sexualis* to mean "inclinations to both sexes . . . as well as to abnormal

not of the same sex, other-sex sexuality—socially widely supposed to be normative, normal, natural, desirable, and right. The notion that homosexuality is a biological phenomenon—an abnormality or variance with anatomic, evolutionary, hormonal, or genetic causes—has a long history and vigorous present.[24] Do you think your own sexual orientation, if you have one, is more essence or role? more body or mind? If gender is the social form sex takes, is sexuality more properly understood as part of sex or gender, or as some of both? Is the thesis that sexual orientation is biologically determined an ideologically attractive one under male supremacy? Could attribution to natural determinants blunt what might otherwise be, in a lesbian and gay politics, a critique of the social origins and workings of the sexual element of gender roles?

The argument that homosexuality is not an inborn condition but a social role was advanced early by Professor Mary McIntosh.

> Many scientists and ordinary people assume that there are two kinds of people in the world: homosexuals and heterosexuals. Some of them recognize that homosexual feelings and behavior are not confined to the persons they would like to call "homosexuals" and that some of these persons do not actually engage in homosexual behavior. This should pose a crucial problem; but they evade the crux by retaining their assumption and puzzling over the question of how to tell whether someone is "really" homosexual or not. Lay people too will discuss whether a certain person is "queer" in much the same way as they might question whether a certain pain indicated cancer. And in much

---

methods of gratification." James G. Kiernan, "Responsibility in Sexual Perversion," 3 *Chicago Medical Recorder* 185, 197–98, 199 n.30 (1892). The "hetero" in heterosexuals thus had a meaning like that in "heterodox."

24. Anatomic approaches hypothesize that physical differences in brain structures cause differences in sexual orientation between gays and straights. *See, e.g.,* Simon LeVay, *The Sexual Brain* (1993). Evolutionary theories, such as those of Edward O. Wilson, *Sociobiology: The New Synthesis* 555 (1975), propose that homosexuality is determined by evolutionary forces. Studies of hormones claim that fetal exposure to androgens or estrogens affect sexual orientation. *See, e.g.,* John Money, *Gay, Straight, and In-Between: The Sexology of Sexual Orientation* (1988). Studies purport to find a significantly greater correlation in sexual orientation for identical than fraternal twins, suggesting that sexual orientation is genetically influenced. *See* Dean Hamer & Peter Copeland, *The Science of Desire: The Search for the Gay Gene and the Biology of Behavior* 28–29 (1994). Some genetic evidence suggests that male homosexuality may be carried on the X chromosome. *See* Dean H. Hamer et al., "A Linkage Between DNA Markers on the X Chromosome and Male Sexual Orientation," 261 *Science* 321 (1993). A summary of evidence on research on brain structure, twin studies, and X-chromosome linkage can be

found at Simon LeVay & Dean H. Hamer, "Evidence for a Biological Influence in Male Homosexuality," *Sci. Am.*, May 1994, at 44. For critical analysis, see Edward Stein, *The Mismeasure of Desire: The Science, Theory, and Ethics of Sexual Orientation* (1999), who concludes that "we need to adopt a position of cautious skepticism towards scientific research on sexual orientation." *Id.* at 228.

Very little research of this kind has been done on women. "Although research during the past decade has begun to illuminate the etiology of male sexual orientation, the causes of female sexual orientation remain largely unknown." J. Michael Bailey & Deana S. Benishay, "Familial Aggregation of Female Sexual Orientation," 150 *Am. J. Psychiatry* 272, 272 (1993). The researchers in that study found that lesbianism tended to run in families but were unable to discern a reason. *See id.* at 277. One of the few studies on women compared 108 lesbians with identical or nonidentical twin sisters and 35 lesbians with adoptive sisters, finding that almost half of the identical pairs (who share identical genes) were both lesbians, compared to only 16 percent of the nonidentical pairs and 6 percent of the genetically unrelated sisters. *See* J. Michael Bailey et al., "Heritable Factors Influence Sexual Orientation in Women," 50 *Arch. Gen. Psychiatry* 217, 219 (1993). Can you think of social conditions that might explain these results?

the same way they will often turn to scientists or to medical men for a surer diagnosis. The scientists, for their part, feel it incumbent on them to seek criteria for diagnosis. . . . [The addition of the notion of a third type of person,] the "bisexual," to handle the fact that behavior patterns cannot be conveniently dichotomized into heterosexual and homosexual . . . does not solve the conceptual problem, since bisexuality too is seen as a condition (unless as a passing response to unusual situations such as confinement in a one-sex prison). . . . [T]here is no extended discussion of bisexuality; the topic is usually given a brief mention in order to clear the ground for the consideration of "true homosexuality." . . . [The major research task has been seen as the study of [homosexuality's] etiology [producing] much debate as to whether the condition is innate or acquired. . . . The vantage point of comparative sociology enables us to see that the conception of homosexuality as a condition . . . operate[s] as a form of social control in a society in which homosexuality is condemned. . . .]

It is interesting to notice that homosexuals themselves welcome and support the notion that homosexuality is a condition. . . . It appears to justify the deviant behavior of the homosexual as being appropriate for him as a member of the homosexual category. . . . It is proposed that the homosexual should be seen as playing a social role rather than as having a condition. . . . In modern societies where a separate homosexual role is recognized, the expectation, on behalf of those who play the role and of others, is that a homosexual will be exclusively or very predominantly homosexual in his feelings and behavior. . . . [Other expectations include] the expectation that he will be effeminate in manner, personality, or preferred sexual activity; the expectation that sexuality will play a part of some kind in all his relations with other men; and the expectation that he will be attracted to boys and very young men and probably willing to seduce them. The existence of a social expectation, of course, commonly helps to produce its own fulfillment. But the question of how far it is fulfilled is a matter for empirical investigation rather than a priori pronouncement. Mary McIntosh, "The Homosexual Role," 16 *Soc. Probs.*, 182, 182–85 (1968).

Further social investigations since Professor McIntosh made these observations suggest that while many people's sexual scripts appear set early in life, many people's sexuality or ways of sexual lovemaking, and the place of gender in it, respond and adapt to their life experience. *See, e.g.*, Alan P. Bell & Martin S. Weinberg, *Homosexualities* 218 (1978); Laumann et al., *supra* at 3–4. Professors William Simon and John Gagnon urged the following view of sexuality in general:

Undeniably, sexuality is rooted in biological processes, capacities, and possibly even needs. But admitting this in no way provides for a greater degree of biological determinism than is true of other areas of corresponding intersection. Indeed, the reverse may be true: the sexual area may be precisely that realm wherein the superordinate position of the sociocultural over the biological level is most complete. William Simon & John H. Gagnon, "On Psychosexual Development," *in Handbook of Socialization Theory and Research* 733, 734 (David A. Goslin ed. 1969).

If sexuality itself is socially malleable and variable, would the social shaping of homosexuality be surprising? Do you think sexual orientation is a fixed propensity? If so, what or who fixes it? Does everyone have a sexual orientation? Are the answers likely to be the same for women and for men? Fundamentally, is being gay or lesbian reducible to the sex of a person with whom one has, or would like to have, sex? That is, is sexual orientation to be defined entirely or even primarily by the sex/gender of one's actual or desired sexual partners?

Many argue that there is more to being lesbian or gay than that. Many gay men and lesbian women resent the reduction of their lovemaking to sex acts and their whole lives to their sexuality, as if that is all they are or identify with and all they care about or are defined by. Professor Marc Fajer, for example, criticizes what he terms the "sex-as-lifestyle" interpretation of the relationships and communities of people who form their lives with others of the same sex. *See* Marc A. Fajer, "Can Two Real Men Eat Quiche Together?: Storytelling, Gender–Role Stereotypes, and Legal Protection for Lesbians and Gay Men," 46 *U. Miami L. Rev.* 511, 537–70 (1992). If gay life were defined by a broader concept that aimed to encompass its full range of human activity and relating, would the study of its trajectory in each individual life be confined to sex acts? Would one "become" gay or lesbian by having sex with someone of the same sex? Theorizing society's sexual definition of homosexuality, French cultural historian Michel Foucault, placing the birth of homosexuality as a "psychological, psychiatric, medical category" in 1870, Michel Foucault, 1 *The History of Sexuality* 43 (Robert Hurley trans., 1978), argued that "homosexuality" as a form of existence was constituted by the term the sexologists coined for it, hence, ironically, constructed by the discourse deployed to describe it:

> [S]odomy was a category of forbidden acts; their perpetrator was nothing more than the juridical subject of them. The nineteenth-century homosexual became a personage, a past, a case history, and a childhood, in addition to being a type of life, a life form, and a morphology, with an indiscreet anatomy and possibly a mysterious physiology.... The sodomite had been a temporary aberration; the homosexual was now a species. *Id.*

Among those who see sexuality as socially shaped, what forces in society shape sexuality remains open to considerable debate.

The term "gay," older than "homosexual" in origin, Boswell, *Christianity, Social Tolerance, supra,* at 43 & n.6 (tracing "gay" in medieval Europe); George Chauncey, *Gay New York: Gender, Urban Culture, and the Making of the Gay Male World 1890–1940,* at 14–21 (1995), came into widespread use when chosen by an open, self-respecting, political, and oppositional gay rights movement in the 1960s.[25] "Gay," like "homosexual," is gender-neutral and often applied to women and men. Nongay sexuality is termed "straight" by distinction.

The extent to which group definition should center on sexuality has been a political issue. Homosexuality as a sexual orientation has been distinguished from " 'gayness,' which was about a subversively political way of life." Jeffrey Weeks, *Sexuality and Its Discontents: Meanings, Myths and Modern Sexualities* 198 (1985). The irony that a sexual definition that

---

25. *See* Robert C. Doty, "Growth of Overt Homosexuality in City Provokes Wide Concern," *N.Y. Times,* Dec. 17, 1963, at 1, 33 ("the word 'gay' has been appropriated by the homosexual"); *see also* Lillian Faderman, *Odd Girls and Twilight Lovers: A History of Lesbian Life in Twentieth–Century America* 67 (1991) (referring to Gertrude Stein's early use of "gay" in "Miss Furr and Miss Skeene").

had been imposed as a stigma came to be resisted by flying it as a flag and invoking it as a foundation for a claim of rights has not gone uncriticized. *See id.* at 198–99. Specifically, Jeffrey Weeks argues that what was a critique directed at "a breakdown of roles, identities, and fixed expectations" was replaced by "acceptance of homosexuality as a minority experience," hence "deliberately emphasi[zing] the ghettoisation of homosexual experience and by implication fail[ing] to interrogate the inevitability of heterosexuality." *Id.* That is, to abolish the delegitimation of homosexuality as a marked status, its markedness had to be accentuated; to eliminate the denigration of the definition, the identity had to be embraced.[26] Does this mean it was depoliticized? Scrutinize the paradox through which a community, defined by the illegality of a sexual practice, resists the stigma and legal consequences of prohibition yet celebrates a sexual definition and at times romanticizes its outlaw status as identity. Is this posture ambivalent? uncritical? unreflective? appropriately complex? coopted? inevitable? Compare it with the vicissitudes of affirming women's differences in their present place, as constructed under conditions of male dominance, versus rejecting that place and criticizing its (and their) determinants.

Use of the terms "lesbian and gay" as adjectives is more recent still, having largely superseded the use of the gender-neutral term "gay" alone in some quarters. Politically, this usage attempts to remedy the invisibility of lesbians that was seen to have been promoted by the gender-neutral term "gay," which implicitly often meant gay men. "Lesbian and gay" recognizes the salience of gender by distinguishing lesbians as women from gay men as men, even as the issues common to women and men who identify with or practice same-sex sexuality remain in brigading the two. Terms such as "queer," "dyke," and "faggot" each occupy a place in the ongoing litany of homophobic defamation and in ongoing attempts by gay men and lesbian women to reclaim such markers of bigotry as badges of pride. "Queer" has gained currency in street politics and among academics, "queer theory" designating a field of scholarship on gay and lesbian and related issues. *See* Mary McIntosh, "Queer Theory and the War of the Sexes," *in Activating Theory: Lesbian, Gay, Bisexual Politics* 30 (Joseph Bristow & Angelia R. Wilson eds., 1993); Francisco Valdes, "Queers, Sissies, Dykes, and Tomboys: Deconstructing the Conflation of 'Sex,' 'Gender,' and 'Sexual Orientation' in Euro–American Law and Society," 83 *Cal. L. Rev.* 3 (1995). Is the gender neutrality of "queer" a virtue? a concern?

So, what "is" homosexuality? Is it an act, a status, a proclivity, a gene, an identification, an identity, a stigma, an experience, a politics? What, for that matter, is sexuality? Is it something one does, something one has, or someone one is? Is it inherent or chosen, biological or social, determined or free, individual or collective, routinized and ritualized or unchained and expressive, a sin or a sacrament, a practice or an essence, a response to abuse or a liberation from convention? It has been argued to be all of these. What, for legal purposes, turns on what same-sexuality "is"? In terms of arguing for or against legal protections for homosexuals from discrimination, does it matter what homosexuality "is"? The relation of sexuality to gender and gender inequality, and whether sex is better analyzed in terms

---

26. Assessing the various approaches to legal claims for gay and lesbian rights in light of the role of this dynamic in III B, see whether the politics found blunted here are sharpened if the pursuit of gay and lesbian rights is recast as the cutting edge of sex equality litigation. It certainly deghettoizes the analysis.

of sameness and difference or dominance and subordination, is implicated in the answers. Also to be considered is whether inequality takes place within as well as among the sexes, and, if so, the effects of intragender inequality on gender inequality as such.

For some people, being gay or lesbian is simply society's label for them because of the gender of someone they fell in love with. For others, it is a feeling they sense they were born with, dating back to their most primordial impulses and yearnings. Some believe it is genetic. Like some heterosexuals, some gay men and lesbian women reject sexual expression with people of the sex who sexually abused them; others, like some heterosexuals, embrace it. For many, a dissenting sexual orientation is part of chosen, conscientious political principles; for many, it is community in the sense of where one belongs, home. What do you think makes a person gay or lesbian or bisexual or heterosexual? What makes a person reject sexual contact and expression with people of their own sex? Does it matter, for purposes of securing legal rights, where the gender of one's sexuality comes from, or just that they have been discriminated against because of it? Should it matter?

If the terms "gay" and "lesbian" emerge as inadequate signifiers for a diverse range of feelings, identities, identifications, communities, and lived practices, some of the terms they modify—commonly "orientation," "preference," or "lifestyle"—can seem incomplete and reductive as well. At best they only approximate the diversity of forms of human connection and consciousness, forms that include and may center on sexual expression or affectional choice or inclinations involving gender in intimacy, but by no means end (and may or may not begin) there. Consider Minnesota's attempt to define "sexual orientation" by statute:

> "Sexual orientation" means having or being perceived as having an emotional, physical, or sexual attachment to another person without regard to the sex of that person or having or being perceived as having an orientation for such attachment, or having or being perceived as having a self-image or identity not traditionally associated with one's biological maleness or femaleness. "Sexual orientation" does not include a physical or sexual attachment to children by an adult. Minn. Stat. § 363.01(45) (1999).

Is heterosexuality a sexual orientation? Is it one, by this definition? Do only people who are not heterosexual have a sexual orientation—like only women have a sex and only nonwhites have a race? Are most sexual orientations "*without* regard to ... sex"? Whatever else they are, gay and lesbian people are a social movement, visible and invisible, organized and inchoate, a movement of consciousness and of living, many possessing a nearly tribal sense of worldwide community. Would you limit that community to "out" gays and lesbians?

What makes a relationship "lesbian"? At some times in the past, passionate friendships between women were permitted and even encouraged; the relationships, both platonic and sensual, and the women in them were seldom if ever labeled lesbian. *See* Carroll Smith–Rosenberg, "The Female World of Love and Ritual: Relations Between Women in Nineteenth–Century America," 1 *Signs* 1 (1975). Whether and when female same-sex love is sexual is debated even as the realities of those relationships challenge conventional notions (past and present) of the erotic. *See* Lillian Faderman, *Surpassing the Love of Men: Romantic Friendship and*

Love Between Women from the Renaissance to the Present 17–20, 141–43 (1981); Leila J. Rupp, " 'Imagine My Surprise': Women's Relationships in Historical Perspective," 5 *Frontiers* 61 (1981); Nancy Sahli, "Smashing: Women's Relationships Before the Fall," 8 *Chrysalis* 17 (1979); Marylynne Diggs, "Romantic Friends of a 'Different Race of Creatures': The Representation of Lesbian Pathology in Nineteenth–Century America," 21 *Feminist Stud.* 317 (1995). Professor Claudia Card says she used to want to know "what made lesbian choices attractive" and now wants to know "what makes the attractions one experiences 'lesbian.' " Claudia Card, *Lesbian Choices* 55 (1995). The extent to which genital sexual acts should be required to qualify a person or relationship as lesbian is addressed critically by historian Professor Blanche Wiesen Cook:

Blanche Wiesen Cook, "The Historical Denial of Lesbianism"

20 *Radical Hist. Rev.* 60, 64 (1979)

Even if [women in the past] did renounce all physical contact we can still argue that they were lesbians: they chose each other, and they loved each other. Women who love women, who choose women to nurture and support and to form a living environment in which to work creatively and independently are lesbians. Genital "proofs" to confirm lesbianism are never required to confirm the heterosexuality of men and women who live together for 20, or 50 years. Such proofs are not demanded even when discussing ephemeral love relations between adult women and men. We know, for example, that General Eisenhower and his friend Kay Summersby were passionately involved with each other. They looked ardently into each others' eyes. They held hands. They cantered swiftly across England's countryside. They played golf and bridge and laughed. They were inseparable. But they never "consummated" their love in the acceptable, traditional, sexual manner. Now does that fact render Kay Summersby and Dwight David Eisenhower somehow less in love? Were they not heterosexual?

Professor Cook's definition of "lesbian" as "women who love women" exposes the extent to which gay and lesbian identity tends to be reduced, not always only by the dominant society, to sexual acts, while heterosexuality—routinely dignified, the default option, assumed so valid as never to be questioned, even in the known *absence* of sex acts—seldom demands genital proof. For further discussion, see Sheila Jeffreys, "Does It Matter If They Did It?" *in Not a Passing Phase: Reclaiming Lesbians in History 1840–1985* 19 (Lesbian History Group, updated ed. 1993).

Does defining lesbian to conform to the shape of the lived realities it has taken serve to retain its critique as well as self-definition? For what purpose is it important to define who is and is not a lesbian? Some lesbian women think of being lesbian, more than as a sexual orientation, as an identity. *See* Celia Kitzinger, *The Social Construction of Lesbianism* 66–124 (1987) (researching lesbian identity accounts); Diana Majury, "Refashioning the Unfashionable: Claiming Lesbian Identities in the Legal Context," 7 *Can. J. Women & L.* 287, 297–99 (1994) (arguing that "identity" is preferable legal term for lesbians). Consider the sexual, emotional, cultural, and political dimensions of sexual identification. *See generally* Kenneth L. Karst, "Myths of Identity: Individual and Group Portraits of Race and Sexual Orientation," 43 *UCLA L. Rev.* 263 (1995). How do you rank each element in your own, if you have one? To what extent do you think genital sexual acts are necessary for a relationship to be a sexual one? Is a lesbian or gay sexuality inherently political in the sense of occupying a position in a distribution of power—whatever consciousness or action accompanies it? Does the degree to which sexuality is open and acknowledged or secret and not publicly known matter to the answer? Does sexuality inexorably affect a person's larger presence in social space, even if its discrete expressions are unknown and unseen?

The poet Adrienne Rich in 1980 addressed the issue of definition by analyzing lesbians as women under conditions of sex inequality. *See* Adrienne Rich, "Compulsory Heterosexuality and Lesbian Existence," 5 *Signs* 631 (1980). For "lesbianism," she substituted "lesbian existence," consisting of "both the breaking of a taboo and the rejection of a compulsory way of life." *Id.* at 648. Partly a "nay-saying to patriarchy" that has kept heterosexuality compulsory for women, lesbians, she pointed out, have been subsumed "as female versions of male homosexuality," which obscures the distinctiveness of women's oppression yet again by lumping them together with other stigmatized sexualities. *Id.* at 649. Instead, she contextualized lesbian women on a "lesbian continuum," a term defined to include many past and present "forms of primary intensity between and among women" including "bonding against male tyranny," whether the women identified as lesbian or not. *Id.* at 648–49. Locating lesbians in this context, she argued, exposes the way women's resistance to male tyranny in the form of imposed heterosexuality has been central in women's history. She concluded: "The denial of reality and visibility to women's passion for women, women's choice of women as allies, life companions and community ... [has] meant an incalculable loss to the power of all women *to change the social relations of the sexes*" (emphasis in original). *Id.* at 657.

Ms. Rich saw lesbians as women, not as sexual deviants. Consider the significance of this shift. Consider whether, in such an analysis, being lesbian is more an act, a feeling, an identification, an idea, a stance, or a community. What do you think makes a woman lesbian? If prior definitions of lesbian have been too fixated on sex acts, might it be argued that Ms. Rich's definition is not sexual enough? Ms. Rich's analysis situated the reality of lesbian women, including emotional attachments and political beliefs, within an analysis of all women's resistance to male dominance, combining solidarity with gay men with critique of male-dominated practices. Seeking to explain lesbian women as women while defining lesbian existence on its own terms, she gave the term "lesbian" a newly encompassing meaning. Evaluate the notion of a lesbian continuum. Is anything lost for lesbian women by broadening the term in this way? Might the term "lesbian" best be used as an adjective, modifying women partially, rather than as a noun? Consider such locutions as lesbian feelings, lesbian act (which could refer to acts of female or sisterly solidarity), lesbian novel (such as Toni Morrison's *Sula* (1974), in which two women's passionate closeness is the central theme)? Would the use of lesbian as modifier broaden lesbian politics or dilute it and deprive it of significance? Is anything lost for gay rights by emphasizing the gender differences between gay men and lesbian women? Is anything gained for sex equality? Are sexual politics in the gendered sense the authentic politics of lesbian liberation?

As to who is and is not lesbian, what is at stake in the entrance requirements? Should anyone be able to claim a lesbian identification, even in part, who is not also oppressed as such? Is there much risk of this? What would be lost and what gained if many women claimed lesbian status as a political stance without actually having sex with women? If heterosexuality were not imposed as normative, would defining lesbianism be an issue or even an intelligible project? Is the act of defining who or what is lesbian thus an act of heterosexualism? *See* Sarah L. Hoagland, *Lesbian Ethics: Toward New Values* 8 (1988) (so arguing). The group Radicalesbians argued early in the 1970s, "In a society in which men do not oppress women, and sexual expression is allowed to follow feelings, the categories of homosexuality and heterosexuality would disappear." Radicalesbians, "The Woman–Identified Woman," *in Radical Feminism* 241 (Anne Koedt et al. eds., 1973). Does Adrienne Rich's analysis similarly redefine sexuality in women's terms? Does it strike at women's inequality to men? In a cross-cultural context, the term lesbian has been considered "grossly inadequate. At best, it serves as highly imperfect shorthand for a range of identities and practices too diverse to sum up in any word or set of words." Rachel Rosenbloom, "Introduction," *in* Rosenbloom, *supra*, at xxiii. How do you think Adrienne Rich might respond to this view? Describe Ms. Rich's critique of the gender neutrality of concepts used to describe lesbians, and its significance for theories of sameness and difference in analyzing sex inequality.

Centering on the role of lesbian consciousness, sexual orientation in general is described as both a way of seeing and a way of being by philosophy professor Marilyn Frye.

> The event of becoming a lesbian is a reorientation of attention in a kind of ontological conversion. It is characterized by a feeling of a world dissolving, and by a feeling of disengagement and re-engagement of one's power as a perceiver. That such conversion happens signals its possibility to others. Heterosexuality for women is not simply a matter of sexual preference, any more than lesbianism is. It is a matter of orientation of attention, as is lesbianism, in a metaphysical context controlled by neither heterosexual nor lesbian women. Attention is a kind of passion. When one's attention is on something, one is present in a particular way with respect to that thing. This presence is, among other things, an element of erotic presence. The orientation of one's attention is also what fixes and directs the application of one's physical and emotional work. Marilyn Frye, "To Be and Be Seen," *in The Politics of Reality: Essays in Feminist Theory* 152, 171–72 (1983).

Consider the fit between this definition, Ms. Rich's, and that of Cheryl Clarke: "I, for one, identify a woman as a lesbian who says she is." Cheryl Clarke, "Lesbianism: An Act of Resistance," *in This Bridge Called My Back: Writings by Radical Women of Color* 128, 128 (Cherríe Moraga & Gloría Anzaldua eds., 2d ed., Kitchen Table: Women of Color Press, 1983) (1981).

Professor Ruthann Robson, stressing both the openness and the magnitude of the project of theorizing lesbian existence, observes that "[l]esbianism as a theory has been and is being developed diversely by lesbians. It is not merely about sexual orientation.... Lesbianism takes as its content lesbian practices, sexual and otherwise; takes culture, politics; 'just about everything.'" Ruthann Robson, "Lesbian Jurisprudence," 8 *Law & Ineq. J.* 443, 446–47 (1990). Is this definition of scope justified by the subject? In your opinion, to what extent is being lesbian political, regardless of identification or openness? Does it matter for the answer whether it is consciously embraced as a politics, or must one only experience Professor

Frye's world-dissolution and perception-reconfiguration? If the latter, is lesbianism inherently feminist on some level—say, in embodying a rejection of a gender-based norm for women that has not been made by women, or in rejecting the definition of women as sexual-for-men, or in repudiating male presence as the be-all-end-all of women's sexuality? Charlotte Bunch has argued that lesbian feminism, referring generally to opposition to male dominance on behalf of all women emerging from a consciousness and practice of being lesbian, is a political perspective. *See* Charlotte Bunch, "Not for Lesbians Only," *Quest*, Fall 1975, at 50, 50–56. What definition of the political does such an analysis claim? Does it redefine politics? Is she right?

A pathological fear or hatred of same-sexuality or of gay men or lesbian women has been termed "homophobia." *See* Wayne Dynes, *Homolexis: A Historical and Cultural Lexicon of Homosexuality* 66 (1985) (documenting origin of term "homoerotophobia" with Wainright Churchill in 1967 and spread of term "homophobia" by George Weinberg in early 1970s). It might be said that homophobia is to homosexuals as misogyny is to women (although the homophobia and misogyny may be more tightly connected than that). One part ignorance, one part dominance, possibly one part desire, homophobia functions as a form of bigotry and prejudice. The reflex, however painful and to varying degrees conscious, to shield one's same-sex sexuality from the punishments and deprivations of homophobia has produced the social institution and subjective emotive location termed "the closet." Being or coming "out," openly acknowledging a gay or lesbian identity or being visible as gay or lesbian, is continuous and complex, a matter of degree, rather than binary. One is never wholly one or the other, as even the most closeted person never knows who guesses their private secret, and even the most open person is not out in every brief encounter. While many members of social groups who are discriminated against routinely deny ever experiencing such discrimination, gay men and lesbian women, open or closeted, generally do not deny the fact of discrimination against their group. Indeed, the extent to which individuals may be shielded from such discrimination at all as a result of hiding their sexual orientation, termed being "closeted," itself evidences the existence of antigay discrimination and reveals what can be one form of its harm. Suzanne Pharr describes what was her closet this way:

> To keep my identity safe meant that I had to be constantly vigilant and lie, primarily through omission but sometimes through commission, virtually every minute of every day. I had to put one large part of myself in exile. The cost was enormous. . . . Perhaps worst of all was the damage to my sense of self, my sense of integrity. . . . And yet at the time, the cost seemed worth it. . . . But never was I easy with the choice I had made to live a life of invisibility. Suzanne Pharr, *Homophobia: A Weapon of Sexism* xiii-xiv (1988).

See also Toni A.H. McNaron, *Poisoned Ivy: Lesbian and Gay Academics Confronting Homophobia* 31–60 (1997) (discussing dilemmas of being out as a teacher). What makes visibility of one's sexual orientation important? Why is invisibility of this facet of the self a source of pain rather than, say, of private fulfillment? Why is it experienced as exile rather than as self-possession? What makes the gender of one's sexual partner(s)' being known a matter of moment?

Straight society prefers gay men and lesbian women to remain hidden, invisible, as if they do not exist. Why? It appears that heterosexuals are threatened by homosexuality. What does homosexuality, when visible, challenge or call into question? What is the difference, from the standpoint of gender differentiation or of male dominance (as two analyses of the gender system), between open and covert, ashamed and self-respecting, same-sex sexuality? From the homophobic perspective, a man and a woman holding hands and kissing on a park bench can be heartwarming, a sign of spring, an affirmation of love and youth to be celebrated. From the same perspective, two women or two men holding hands and kissing on a park bench present an act of public sex, an affront and offense to morals and family, an instigation to feelings of revulsion and contempt, a provocation to rage and rape. What is going on here? Is gender, or gender hierarchy, implicated?

"Heterosexual privilege" means not being treated unequally in the ways nonheterosexuals are. Heterosexual privilege is what the lesbian and gay rights movement terms what conventional society grants to heterosexuals as such, or to people perceived as being heterosexual.

> What makes heterosexuality work is heterosexual privilege—and if you don't have a sense of what that privilege is, I suggest that you go home and announce to everybody that you know—a roommate, your family, the people you work with—everywhere you go—that you're a queer. Try being a queer for a week. Do not walk out on the street with men; walk only with women, especially at night, for example. For a whole week, experience life as if you were a lesbian, and I think you will know what heterosexual privilege is very quickly. Bunch, *supra*, at 50, 53.

Bisexuality refers to a history of sexual activities, or desire for them, with partners both one's own sex and those not of one's own sex. Bisexuals may occupy a social status, but a bisexual sex act is a problematic notion. The definition of "bisexuality" remains in flux linguistically as well as politically, in terms of organization and mobilization. *See* Marjorie Garber, *Vice Versa: Bisexuality and the Eroticism of Everyday Life* 13–152 (1995). Because bisexuals are both and neither gay and/nor straight, they may be regarded as doubly disloyal. More accepted by heterosexuals than gays are, more accepted by gays than heterosexuals are, for those very reasons they can be stigmatized by straights as gay and repudiated by lesbians as consorting with the enemy and by both gay men and lesbian women as refusing to face their real desires and give up heterosexual privilege. How do you understand bisexuality in gender terms? How would you locate it conceptually with regard to gender neutrality? androgyny? male dominance? If there were no sexism, would bisexuality be a sexual category?

In the legal cases that follow, consider the extent to which, through use of language and inexplicit assumptions, courts tend to obscure the theoretical and political issues raised in this section. Is the term "homosexuality" used as if it had no history, carried no baggage, implied no judgments, and required no further specificity? Is it supposed that what a lesbian "is," is obvious and unproblematic? Do they tend to treat gay men and lesbian women as if their sexuality is a fixed personal essence or trait rather than existential outcome? Do they tend to sexualize all of gay and lesbian life, with negative dignitary consequences? Do the cases assume that "sexual orientation" has a politically stable referent and clear meaning? Do the courts, when analyzing questions of sexual orientation, tend to obscure issues of gender and sex inequality? Be alert to passages in which courts adopt and promote positions on the sensitive and unresolved political questions treated in this section without seeming to be aware that they have done so.

II. PRIVACY

Attacks on criminal sodomy laws as violations of the constitutional right to privacy have been the preferred legal strategy for addressing the persecution of gay men and lesbian women by the state in the United States and elsewhere. *See, e.g.*, David A. Catania, "The Universal Declaration of Human Rights and Sodomy Laws: A Federal Common Law Right to Privacy for Homosexuals Based on Customary International Law," 31 *Am. Crim. L. Rev.* 289 (1994). The presumptions, politics, and implications of the privacy right in this setting raise far-reaching and undertheorized issues. They include: Does the protection for the private realm implicitly sought in privacy rights litigation posit an inner self separate from society? Does this inner self exist? Can it be freed in social isolation? Is privacy the best legal theory to use to attack sodomy laws? Is it good for women? Does it promote or retard equality between women and men? Is the challenge that self-respecting gay and lesbian existence poses to gender roles and male dominance cabined—domesticated, depoliticized, even vitiated—when pursued as private?

"The right 'to be let alone,' " Samuel D. Warren & Louis D. Brandeis, "The Right to Privacy," 4 *Harv. L. Rev.* 193, 195 (1890) (quoting Thomas M. Cooley, *A Treatise on the Law of Torts* 29 (1879)), was originally envisioned to give rise to a tort action to protect "the sacred precincts of private and domestic life," *id.* at 195, including sexual matters, from unwanted and unauthorized intrusion and publication principally by the press. *See id.* at 195–96; Samuel H. Hofstadter & George Horowitz, *The Right of Privacy* (1964) (emphasizing New York privacy law within analysis of privacy law in general). What Warren and Brandeis had in mind is clear from their concluding sentences:

> The common law has always recognized a man's house as his castle, impregnable, often, even to its own officers engaged in the execution of its commands. Shall the courts thus close the front entrance to constituted authority, and open wide the back door to idle or prurient curiosity? Warren & Brandeis, *supra*, at 220.

That private publishers should be kept from invading what the common law kept inviolate from the state was not the most prominent direction in which the right to privacy developed, however, nor has critical awareness of the social fact that "man's castle" also domiciled "woman's place," *see* Chapter 6, affected its trajectory. What Louis Brandeis as a Supreme Court Justice later termed "the right to be let alone ... the most comprehensive of rights and the right most valued by civilized men" in his dissent in *Olmstead v. United States*, 277 U.S. 438, 478 (1928) (Brandeis, J., dissenting), first gained a foothold in constitutional law in two Fourteenth Amendment cases that limited state power over education of children. In *Meyer v. Nebraska*, 262 U.S. 390 (1923), the Supreme Court invalidated a prohibition on teaching foreign languages in elementary schools, recognizing that the "liberty" the Due Process Clause guaranteed included a general right "to enjoy those privileges long recognized at common law as essential to the orderly pursuit of happiness by free men." 262 U.S. at 399. *Pierce v. Society of Sisters*, 268 U.S. 510 (1925), invalidated on similar grounds a law requiring that all children attend public schools. One might well have wondered whether the "men" whose freedom and happiness was so guaranteed included women.

It was women's attempts to gain reproductive control that propelled the right to privacy as such to constitutional status. Although political organizing for legal and accessible contraception in the United States began in the early twentieth century, *see* Chapter 9, it was not until 1961 that the first judicial step was taken to develop what was later called "substantive due process," in which the privacy right came to be located. In *Poe v. Ullman*, 367 U.S. 497 (1961), a state's criminal law against obtaining and using contraceptives was challenged in a case found unripe by the United States Supreme Court in part because the statute had been enforced neither against the plaintiffs nor hardly anyone else. Justice Harlan dissented in terms that became formative, concluding that "a statute making it a criminal offense for *married couples* to use contraceptives is an intolerable and unjustifiable invasion of privacy in the conduct of the most intimate concerns of an individual's personal life." 367 U.S. 497 at 539. Building on a previous Fourteenth Amendment case forbidding involuntary sterilization of prisoners convicted of some crimes but not others, *Skinner v. Oklahoma ex rel. Williamson*, 316 U.S. 535 (1942) (see Chapter 9 for further discussion), he envisioned in the "larger context" of the Fourteenth Amendment's Due Process Clause a guarantee of "liberty" that extended well beyond the procedural:

> Due process has not been reduced to any formula; its content cannot be determined by reference to any code. The best that can be said is that through the course of this Court's decisions it has represented the balance which our Nation, built upon postulates of respect for the liberty of the individual, has struck between that liberty and the demands of organized society.... [This larger context] is one not of words, but of history and purposes....
>
> This "liberty" is not a series of isolated points [but] a rational continuum ... which also recognizes ... that certain interests require particularly careful scrutiny of the state needs asserted to justify their abridgment.... [T]he very inclusion of the category of morality among state concerns indicates that society is not limited in its objects only to the physical well-being of the community, but has traditionally concerned itself with the moral soundness of its people as well. Indeed to attempt a line between public behavior and that which is purely consensual or solitary would be to withdraw from community concern a range of subjects with which every society in civilized times has found it necessary to deal. The laws regarding marriage which provide both when the sexual powers may be used and the legal and societal context in which children are born and brought up, as well as laws forbidding adultery, fornication and homosexual practices which express the negative of the proposition, confining sexuality to lawful marriage, form a pattern so deeply pressed into the substance of our social life that any Constitutional doctrine in this area must build upon that basis.

It is in this area of sexual morality, which contains many proscriptions of consensual behavior having little or no direct impact on others, that the State of Connecticut has expressed its moral judgment that all use of contraceptives is improper.... Connecticut's judgment is no more demonstrably correct or incorrect than are the varieties of judgment, expressed in law, on marriage and divorce, on adult consensual homosexuality, abortion, and sterilization, or euthanasia and suicide.... [We are not presented in this case with a moral judgment] to be passed on as an abstract proposition.... Precisely what is involved here is this: the State is asserting the right to enforce its moral judgment by intruding upon the most intimate details of the marital relation with the full power of the criminal law.... In sum, the statute allows the State to enquire into, prove and punish married people for the private use of their marital intimacy.... This enactment involves what, by common understanding throughout the English-speaking world, must be granted to be a most fundamental aspect of "liberty," the privacy of the home in its most basic sense, and it is this which requires that the statute by subjected to "strict scrutiny." Skinner.... [A constitutional analysis that] forecloses any claim to Constitutional protection against this form of deprivation of privacy [does so] only if due process in this respect is limited to what is explicitly provided in the Constitution, divorced from the rational purposes, historical roots, and subsequent developments of the relevant provisions. [If] the physical curtilage of the home is protected, it is surely as a result of solicitude to protect the privacies of the life within. The home derives its pre-eminence as the seat of family life.... Of [the] whole "private realm of family life" it is difficult to imagine what is more private or more intimate than a husband and wife's marital relations.

[I]t would be an absurdity to suggest ... that offenses may not be committed in the bosom of the family or that the home can be made a sanctuary for crime. The right of privacy [is] not absolute. Thus, I would not suggest that adultery, homosexuality, fornication and incest are immune from criminal enquiry, however privately practiced.... Adultery, homosexuality and the like are sexual intimacies which the State forbids altogether, but the intimacy of husband and wife is necessarily an essential and accepted feature of the institution of marriage, an institution which the State not only must allow, but which always and in every age it has fostered and protected. It is one thing when the State exerts its power either to forbid extra-marital sexuality altogether, or to say who may marry, but it is quite another when, having acknowledged a marriage and the intimacies inherent in it, it undertakes to regulate by means of the criminal law the details of that intimacy....

[E]ven though the State has determined that the use of contraceptives is as iniquitous as any act of extra-marital sexual immorality, the intrusion of the whole machinery of the criminal law into the very heart of marital privacy, requiring husband and wife to render account before a criminal tribunal of their uses of that intimacy, is surely a very different thing indeed from punishing those who establish intimacies which the law has always forbidden and which can have no claim to social protection. *Poe v. Ullman*, 367 U.S. 497, 542–43, 545–49, 551–53 (1961) (Harlan, J., dissenting).

Assess Justice Harlan's distinction between marital and other intimacies and his concession that states can regulate "that which is consensual or solitary" on a moral basis. Should the criminal law be permitted to enforce society's idea of "moral soundness" apart from showings of harm? If not, what criminal laws would go? Has Justice Harlan accurately drawn the line between sexual relationships that society has protected from governmental intrusion and sexual relationships that harm their participants? Is a morality test different from a harm test? If so, how? Analyze Justice Harlan's reference to laws against homosexuality. Does consensual homosexual practice have "little or no direct impact on others"? Evaluate Justice Harlan's reasoning in this passage in light of the inequality between women and men in marriage and the family (see Chapter 6 for examples) and in light of an inequality between homosexual and heterosexual in society. Evaluate Justice Harlan's assertion of principle through an inequality lens. His concern with tradition subsequently became very important in limiting the reach of the right to privacy. On your reading of this passage, should it be?

Women's continuing attempts to invalidate criminal laws against contraception converged with the terms of Justice Harlan's *Poe v. Ullman* dissent in victory in *Griswold v. Connecticut*, 381 U.S. 479 (1965). There, Connecticut's prohibition on the sale to and use by married people of contraceptives was invalidated on the ground that it violated the right of marital privacy. The Court announced that "penumbras, formed by emanations" from the guarantees of the First, Third, Fourth, Fifth, and Ninth Amendments, "create zones of privacy" free from government intrusion, 381 U.S. at 484, that intercept the criminalization of contraception. Then it ruled in *Stanley v. Georgia*, 394 U.S. 557 (1969), that a state's power to regulate obscenity "simply does not extend to mere possession by the individual [of obscene materials] in the privacy of his home," 394 U.S. at 568, and invalidated under the Equal Protection Clause a state law that gave differential access to contraception to married and unmarried people otherwise similarly situated. *See Eisenstadt v. Baird*, 405 U.S. 438 (1972). The zenith of this line of authority was reached in *Roe v. Wade*'s invalidation of a state criminal abortion law. *See* 410 U.S. 113 (1973). In *Roe*, the right to personal privacy, settled in the "liberty" component of the Due Process Clause, was held "broad enough to encompass a woman's decision whether or not to terminate her pregnancy." 410 U.S. at 153. (See Chapter 9.)

During this period, and up to *Bowers v. Hardwick*, 478 U.S. 186 (1986), when the argument was rejected by the U.S. Supreme Court, repeated attempts were made to invalidate criminal sodomy laws by invoking a right to sexual privacy that combined protection of "inviolate personality" from prurient intrusions, Warren & Brandeis, *supra*, at 265, with the increasingly recognized protections for sexual intimacy, association, and autonomy in cases involving heterosexual reproduction. Legally, the point was to bring same-sex sexual acts under the same roof that sheltered heterosexual sex acts from governmental invasion. The logic was deeply egalitarian but the cases were doctrinally argued on other grounds. One attempt to secure citizenship for a gay man in spite of the sodomy prohibitions illustrates, in partial contrast to *Boutilier*, not the doctrinal claim of privacy as it was to develop under the Constitution, but the judicial use of a concept of "private conduct" to address homosexuality in the immigration setting.

In re Labady

United States District Court for the Southern District of New York.
326 F. Supp. 924 (S.D.N.Y. 1971)

■ MANSFIELD, J.

After entering the United States in 1960 petitioner engaged in homosexual activities with several consenting adults. On the average he has
been the active or passive partner in such activities about once a
month, but the last occasion was about six months before his prelimi-
nary examinations by the [Immigration and Naturalization] Service
upon his Petition for Naturalization. He has never engaged in homosexual activities with minors; all of his sexual acts have taken place in
privacy, behind locked doors in hotel rooms. He has never engaged in
such activity in any park, theatre, subway station, or any other public
or semi-public place. He is unmarried and lives with his mother. There
is no suggestion that his homosexual activities could harm a marriage
relationship. Petitioner has never been arrested. Though he has not
applied for psychiatric treatment in the United States, he did unsuccessfully undergo therapy in Cuba. . . . The Service stipulates that he
has never been in trouble and, as his employer testified, he is highly
regarded at his place of employment.

[In assessing whether respondent is of "good moral character,"
w]e believe that the most important factor to be considered is whether
the challenged conduct is public or private in nature. If it is public or if
it involves a large number of other persons, it may pose a threat to the
community. If, on the other hand, it is entirely private, the likelihood
of harm to others is minimal and any effort to regulate or penalize the
conduct may lead to an unjustified invasion of the individual's constitutional rights. . . . [P]rivate conduct which is not harmful to others,
even though it may violate the personal moral code of most of us, does
not violate public morality which is the only proper concern of § 1427.
To hold otherwise would be to encourage governmental inquisition
into an applicant's purely personal private temperament and habits
(e.g., whether he harbors hate, malice or impure thoughts; whether he
has ever engaged in masturbation, autoeroticism, fornication, or the
like, etc.) even though such attitudes or conduct would not harm
others.

Without condoning the purely private conduct here involved, we
accept the principle that the naturalization laws are concerned with
public, not private, morality. . . . There is nothing to indicate that
private conduct of the type here involved would affect petitioner's
ability to be "law-abiding and useful" to society. . . . [Petitioner has]
led a quiet, peaceful, law-abiding life as an immigrant in the United
States. Although he has engaged on occasion in purely private homosexual relations with consenting adults, he has not corrupted the
morals of others, such as minors, or engaged in any publicly offensive
activities, such as solicitation or public display. He is gainfully employed, highly regarded by his employer and associates, and he has
submitted to therapy that was unsuccessful. Under all of the circumstances, setting aside our personal moral views, we cannot say that his
conduct has violated public morality or indicated that he will be
anything other than a law-abiding and useful citizen.

The court found that Mr. Labady's homosexuality was not harmful to
others essentially because, other than occasional furtive lapses, and none

very recent, he kept his sexuality to himself. Is Mr. Labady permitted to be a U.S. citizen at the price of passing, of remaining largely closeted, of not expressing himself sexually except furtively and rarely? Is Mr. Labady permitted to be an American, where Mr. Boutilier was not, precisely because Mr. Labady kept his sexuality more private? What does "private" mean in this case? Is Mr. Labady's sex life at best sequestered? Did he have the dignity of seclusion or was his privacy that of the closet? What does it mean to seek a legal right *to* a closeted privacy? Does his privacy feel circumscribed by shame? Do we keep private what we are ashamed of having be known? Is intimacy possible without privacy? Recall that one consequence of the public/private divide has historically been the relegation of women, a sexually defined group, to the "private" realm, with attendant relative invisibility and disempowerment as full public citizens. *See* Chapter 6. Are similar dynamics at work regarding the group "homosexuals" in *Labady*?

Does the *Labady* court assume that if behavior is private, no one is hurt by it? Is this necessarily correct? Alternatively, what is harmful to others about being publicly out and self-respecting? Does the *Labady* court seem to hold out hope that Mr. Labady could convert? Does he perhaps get points for having tried therapy, if unsuccessfully? Note, as with *Boutilier*, the apparent view that one is either "active" or "passive" in sex. Where does this come from? Does it map gender stereotypes from heterosexuality onto same-sex relations? Is it a measure of progress from *Boutilier* that Mr. Labady is permitted to have his shameful secret (so long as he reveals it to the INS) and his citizenship too? Is Mr. Labady treated as an equal in this opinion? The *Labady* court found it highly unlikely that Mr. Labady would be found to have violated the law against consensual sodomy in New York because it was so seldom enforced. *See* 326 F. Supp. at 928. Not many years later, that same law—as predicted by a footnote in *Labady*, 326 F. Supp. at 929 n.4—was invalidated by a New York court as a violation of the privacy protections of the U.S. Constitution in *People v. Onofre*.

People v. Onofre

Court of Appeals of New York.
51 N.Y.2d 476, 415 N.E.2d 936 (1980)

■ JONES, J.

[The question on appeal is] whether the provision of our State's Penal Law that makes consensual sodomy a crime is violative of rights protected by the United States Constitution. We hold that it is.

Defendant Onofre was convicted in County Court of Onondaga County of violating section 130.38 of the Penal Law (consensual sodomy) after his admission to having committed acts of deviate sexual intercourse with a 17-year-old male at defendant's home.... The statutes under which [the defendant was] charged and convicted provide as follows:

§ 130.38 Consensual sodomy.

A person is guilty of consensual sodomy when he engages in deviate sexual intercourse with another person.

§ 130.00 Sex offenses; definitions of terms.

The following definitions are applicable to this article: ...

2. Deviate sexual intercourse means sexual conduct between persons not married to each other consisting of contact between the penis and the anus, the mouth and penis, or the mouth and the vulva.

Because the statutes are broad enough to reach noncommercial, cloistered personal sexual conduct of consenting adults . . . , we agree with defendant['s] contentions that it violates . . . his [federal constitutional] right of privacy. . . .

At the outset it should be noted that the [privacy] right addressed in the present context is not . . . the right to maintain secrecy with respect to one's affairs or personal behavior; rather, it is a right of independence in making certain kinds of important decisions, with a concomitant right to conduct oneself in accordance with those decisions, undeterred by governmental restraint. . . . [T]he People [contend that this protection] extends to only two aspects of sexual behavior—marital intimacy [under Griswold] and procreative choice [under Eisenstadt and Roe v. Wade]. . . . In light of [the U.S. Supreme Court's] decisions, protecting under the cloak of the right of privacy individual decisions as to indulgence in acts of sexual intimacy by unmarried persons and as to satisfaction of sexual desires by resort to material condemned as obscene by community standards when done in a cloistered setting [Stanley v. Georgia, 394 U.S. 557 (1969)], no rational basis appears for excluding from the same protection decisions—such as those made by defendants before us—to seek sexual gratification from what at least once was commonly regarded as "deviant" conduct, so long as the decisions are voluntarily made by adults in a noncommercial, private setting. . . .

Any purported justification for the consensual sodomy statute in terms of upholding public morality is belied by the position reflected in the Eisenstadt decision in which the court carefully distinguished between public dissemination of what might have been considered inimical to public morality and individual recourse to the same material out of the public arena and in the sanctum of the private home. There is a distinction between public and private morality and the private morality of an individual is not synonymous with nor necessarily will have effect on what is known as public morality. So here, the People have failed to demonstrate how government interference with the practice of personal choice in matters of intimate sexual behavior out of view of the public and with no commercial component will serve to advance the cause of public morality or do anything other than restrict individual conduct and impose a concept of private morality chosen by the State. . . .

In sum, there has been no showing of any threat, either to participants or the public in general, in consequence of the voluntary engagement by adults in private, discreet, sodomous conduct. Absent is the factor of commercialization with the attendant evils commonly attached to the retailing of sexual pleasures; absent the elements of force or of involvement of minors which might constitute compulsion of unwilling participants or of those too young to make an informed choice, and absent too intrusion on the sensibilities of members of the public, many of whom would be offended by being exposed to the intimacies of others. . . .

[N]either the People nor the dissent has cited any authority or evidence for the proposition that the practice of consensual sodomy in private is harmful either to the participants or to society in general; indeed, the dissent's appeal is only to the historical, conventional characterization which attached to the practice of sodomy. It surely does not follow that, because it is constitutionally permissible to enter the privacy of an individual's home to regulate conduct justifiably found to be harmful to him, the Legislature may also intrude on such privacy to regulate individual conduct where no basis has been shown for concluding that the conduct is harmful.

Might the right to privacy shield abuse even in a "consensual" setting—despite Justice Harlan's intent in *Poe v. Ullman* to the contrary? To the concern that the division between public and private shields violence against women in the home that was discussed in Chapter 6 IV, add the vicissitudes of the law of consent, under which submission to sex under conditions of inequality is deemed "consensual sex" by the courts, as discussed in Chapter 7.1. In fact, the sex acts for which Mr. Onofre was prosecuted came to official attention because a sexual partner of his, Mr. Russell Evans, who affirmed he had been sexual with Mr. Onofre because he wanted to be, believed that telling someone in authority that Mr. Onofre had physically harmed him during sex would stop Mr. Onofre from hurting other people in the same way. *See* Aff. of Russell Evans, App. A, People v. Onofre, 424 N.Y.S.2d 566 (N.Y. App. Div. 1980) (App. unpublished). Mr. Onofre also took sex pictures of Mr. Evans. *See id.* Mr. Evans was seventeen years old at the time. *See* 51 N.Y.S. 2d at 483, 415 N.E.2d at 937.

The lower court in *Onofre* overturned the consensual sodomy law in part as a violation of the right to privacy construed as "a person's right to control his or her own body." *Onofre*, 424 N.Y.S. 2d at 568. Given the facts, did Mr. Evans have that right in his sexual relationship with Mr. Onofre, the intervention of the authorities aside? If the New York law violated Mr. Onofre's right to privacy, is something nonetheless missing in the privacy analysis, under which the harms to Mr. Evans are rendered part of Mr. Onofre's "inviolate personality" and none of anyone's else's business? If sex is socially hierarchical, will someone often be physically harmed during it? If so, does this possibility disappear among gender equals? Does Mr. Evans have anything in common with abused women whose abuse in the "private sphere" is rendered invisible even when they complain of it in public? Under such circumstances, are both heterosexual women and gay men harmed through sex, therefore legally considered not to have been harmed, because they are defined by the sex through which they are, in some instances, harmed? If an equality analysis were applied, would the conventional distinction between public and private morality that the *Onofre* court drew be possible?

Is it fair to observe that the private is precisely the place where sexual abuse is rendered invisible as harm? Does a discourse of privacy militate against exposing sexual abuse? Does a legal right to privacy become a right to be free of accountability for abuses of power there, quintessentially in sex? If so, is the right to privacy double-edged for gay and lesbian people in much the way it is for all women? Is the effect on lesbian women and gay men part of the same problem women have? Granting that criminal sodomy laws violate privacy rights, does the privacy attack on those laws sweep too broadly, tending to make sexual abuse, along with nonabusive sex, off limits to wanted relief as well as unwanted intrusion? Why does privacy law not draw an explicit harm line? Could it? What might it look like? How did the *Onofre* court miss the evidence of harm in the specific facts of the case before it? Could it have ignored those facts without indulging stereotypes about gay men's sexuality? Could it have invalidated the sodomy law on privacy grounds without denying the harm done to Russell Evans?

Similar questions could be asked of *Dronenburg v. Zech*, 741 F.2d 1388 (D.C. Cir. 1984), in which "a 27-year-old petty officer had repeated sexual relations with a 19-year-old seaman recruit. The latter then chose to break off the relationship." 441 F.2d at 1398. Petty Officer Dronenberg unsuccessfully attacked his dismissal from the navy for homosexuality on privacy grounds. Might Petty Officer Dronenberg have abused his hierarchical authority for sexual purposes? Should sailors in his position be dismissed for sex with a subordinate—a reason that applies equally and often to heterosexuals—rather than for homosexuality? Disentangle the issues of inequality based on hierarchical position in the services from inequality between homosexuals and heterosexuals represented by the navy's prohibition on homosexuality. Once the issues are separated, are cases like *Dronenburg* privacy cases? On what facts would an appropriate resolution then depend? Would you care what sex the people who had sex were? Would you care what the nineteen-year-old seaman recruit wanted?

Judge Bork for the panel commented that "[e]pisodes of this sort are certain ... given the powers of military superiors over their inferiors, to enhance the possibility of homosexual seduction." 741 F.2d at 1398. What does "seduction" mean? Does the power of military superiors enhance their sexual access to inferiors, regardless of gender and the desires of the subordinate? Is this what "seduction" means? Does Judge Bork's formulation suggest that sex that a subordinate might *want* to have with a superior would be facilitated by that superior's relative position of power? If this is true for same-sex relationships, might it also be true for non-same-sex relationships? Does Judge Bork imply that a desired relationship might be undesirable? Might it be? Which is the more important concern for policy: desire, gender, or position of power? Which is more important for equality?

The privacy argument accepted in *Onofre* was rejected by the U.S. Supreme Court in *Bowers v. Hardwick*. Michael Hardwick, described by the U.S. Supreme Court as "a practicing homosexual," 478 U.S. at 188, was having consensual sex in his bedroom with the door partially closed in his apartment in Georgia when the police walked in—a visitor having admitted them—seeking to serve an expired arrest warrant for drinking in public that had been issued by a police officer who saw Mr. Hardwick leaving a gay bar. Mr. Hardwick suspected police harassment for being gay. The arresting officer stood and watched as Mr. Hardwick and his companion dressed. *See* Peter Irons, *The Courage of Their Convictions* 395–96 (1988) (interviewing Mr. Hardwick). Mr. Hardwick was charged and briefly jailed, but ultimately not prosecuted, under a Georgia statute that criminalized sodomy defined as: "perform[ing] or submit[ting] to any sexual act involving the sex organs of one person and the mouth or anus of another," Ga. Code Ann § 16–6–2(a) (1996), with possible punishment of up to twenty years. Mr. Hardwick challenged the constitutionality of the statute for violation of his right to privacy. For a closely divided Court, Justice White wrote that the right to privacy does not extend to "a fundamental right to engage in homosexual sodomy." 478 U.S. at 191.

Bowers v. Hardwick

Supreme Court of the United States
478 U.S. 186 (1986)

■ Justice White delivered the opinion of the Court.

The issue presented is whether the Federal Constitution confers a fundamental right upon homosexuals to engage in sodomy.... [W]e think it evident that none of the rights announced in [our prior] cases bears any resemblance to the claimed constitutional right of homosexuals to engage in acts of sodomy that is asserted in this case. No connection between family, marriage, or procreation on the one hand and homosexual activity on the other has been demonstrated.... Precedent aside ..., respondent would have us announce ... a fundamental right to engage in homosexual sodomy. This we are quite unwilling to do. It is true that despite the language of the Due Process Clauses of the Fifth and Fourteenth Amendments ... the cases are legion in which those Clauses have been interpreted to have substantive content, subsuming rights that to a great extent are immune from federal or state regulation or proscription.... It is obvious to us that [none] would extend a fundamental right to homosexuals to engage in acts of consensual sodomy. Proscriptions against that conduct have ancient roots.... Against this background, to claim that a right to engage in such conduct is "deeply rooted in this Nation's history and tradition," Moore v. East Cleveland, 431 U.S. 494, 503 (1977), or "implicit in the concept of ordered liberty," Palko v. Connecticut, 302 U.S. 319, 325 (1937), is, at best, facetious....

The Court is most vulnerable and comes nearest to illegitimacy when it deals with judge-made constitutional law having little or no cognizable roots in the language or design of the Constitution.... There should be ... great resistance to expand the substantive reach of [the Due Process] Clauses, particularly if it requires redefining the category of rights deemed to be fundamental. Otherwise, the Judiciary necessarily takes to itself further authority to govern the country without express constitutional authority. The claimed right pressed on us today falls far short of overcoming this resistance.

Respondent, however, asserts that the result should be different where the homosexual conduct occurs in the privacy of the home.... [I]t would be difficult, except by fiat, to limit the claimed right to homosexual conduct while leaving exposed to prosecution adultery, incest, and other sexual crimes even though they are committed in the home. We are unwilling to start down that road.... [Respondent further] asserts that there must be a rational basis for the law and that there is none in this case other than the presumed belief of a majority of the electorate in Georgia that homosexual sodomy is immoral and unacceptable.... The law, however, is constantly based on notions of morality, and if all laws representing essentially moral choices are to be invalidated under the Due Process Clause, the courts will be very busy indeed. Even respondent makes no such claim, but insists that majority sentiments about the morality of homosexuality should be declared inadequate. We do not agree, and are unpersuaded that the sodomy laws of some 25 states should be invalidated on this basis.[27]

■ CHIEF JUSTICE BURGER, concurring.

Decisions of individuals relating to homosexual conduct have been subject to state intervention throughout the history of Western civilization. Condemnation of those practices is firmly rooted in Judeo–Christian moral and ethical standards. Homosexual sodomy was a capital crime under Roman law. See Code Theod. 9.7.6; Code Just. 9.9.31. During the English Reformation when powers of the ecclesiastical courts were transferred to the King's Courts, the first English statute criminalizing sodomy was passed. 25 Hen. VIII, ch. 6. Blackstone described "the infamous *crime against nature*" as an offense of "deeper

---

27. [8] Respondent does not defend the judgment below based on the Ninth Amendment, the Equal Protection Clause, or the Eighth Amendment.

malignity" than rape, a heinous act "the very mention of which is a disgrace to human nature," and "a crime not fit to be named." 4 W. Blackstone, Commentaries *215. The common law of England, including its prohibition of sodomy, became the received law of Georgia and the other Colonies. In 1816 the Georgia Legislature passed the statute at issue here, and that statute has been continuously in force in one form or another since that time. To hold that the act of homosexual sodomy is somehow protected as a fundamental right would be to cast aside millennia of moral teaching. . . .

■ JUSTICE POWELL, concurring.

I join the opinion of the Court. I agree . . . that there is no fundamental right . . . such as that claimed by respondent. . . . This is not to suggest, however, that respondent may not be protected by the Eighth Amendment of the Constitution. . . . [A serious felony conviction for a single private, consensual act of sodomy would create a serious Eighth Amendment issue, but it was not raised below.][28]

■ JUSTICE BLACKMUN, with whom JUSTICE BRENNAN, JUSTICE MARSHALL, and JUSTICE STEVENS join, dissenting:

[The dissenters, criticizing the Court's "almost obsessive focus on homosexual activity," noted that the language of the statute at issue was not limited to homosexuals, so Mr. Hardwick's privacy claim and right of intimate association "do[ ] not depend in any way on his sexual orientation."][29] . . . Only the most willful blindness could obscure the fact that sexual intimacy is "a sensitive, key relationship of human existence, central to family life, community welfare, and the development of human personality," Paris Adult Theatre I v. Slaton, 413 U.S. 49, 63 (1973). The fact that individuals define themselves in a significant way through their intimate sexual relationships with others suggests, in a Nation as diverse as ours, that there may be many "right" ways of conducting those relationships, and that much of the richness of a relationship will come from the freedom an individual has to *choose* the form and nature of these intensely personal bonds. See Karst, "The Freedom of Intimate Association," 89 *Yale L.J.* 624, 637 (1980). . . . This case involves no real interference with the rights of others, for the mere knowledge that other individuals do not adhere to one's value system cannot be a legally cognizable interest, let alone an interest that can justify invading the houses, hearts, and minds of citizens who choose to live their lives differently. . . . [This decision should be overruled. We] hope that . . . the Court soon will reconsider its analysis and conclude that depriving individuals of the right to choose for themselves how to conduct their intimate relationships poses a far greater

28. [2] The history of nonenforcement suggests the moribund character today of laws criminalizing this type of private, consensual conduct. Some 26 States have repealed similar statutes. But the constitutional validity of the Georgia statute was put in issue by respondents, and for the reasons stated by the Court, I cannot say that conduct condemned for hundreds of years has now become a fundamental right.

29. [2] With respect to the Equal Protection Clause's applicability to § 16–6–2, I note that Georgia's exclusive stress before this Court on its interest in prosecuting homosexual activity despite the gender-neutral terms of the statute may raise serious questions of discriminatory enforcement, questions that cannot be disposed of before this Court on a motion to dismiss. See Yick Wo v. Hopkins, 118 U.S. 356, 373–74 (1886). The legislature having decided that the sex of the participants is irrelevant to the legality of the acts, I do not see why the State can defend § 16–6–2 on the ground that individuals singled out for prosecution are of the same sex as their partners. Thus, under the circumstances of this case, a claim under the Equal Protection Clause may well be available without having to reach the more controversial question whether homosexuals are a suspect class.

threat to the values most deeply rooted in our Nation's history than tolerance of nonconformity could ever do.

NOTES AND QUESTIONS ON *BOWERS v. HARDWICK*

1. Language:

1.1 In *Hardwick*, is the term "homosexual" in the Court's phrase "homosexual sodomy" more a noun meaning sodomite or an adjective indicating who is engaging in the sodomy? Does the Court go back and forth between the two? What turns on the difference? In the first meaning, Michel Foucault's analysis is vindicated, as act is fused with identity. In the second, the failure to prosecute heterosexual sodomy opens an equal protection fissure within the Court's analysis. For a related observation, see Janet E. Halley, "Reasoning About Sodomy: Act and Identity in and After *Bowers v. Hardwick*," 79 *Va. L. Rev.* 1721, 1739–40 (1993). Can it be that only gay sodomy is constitutionally unprotected? Does the Court here regulate people's conduct or status? Is there any real difference between the two on these facts?

1.2 The Court described Mr. Hardwick as a "practicing homosexual." (In a snappy retort to this locution, Quentin Crisp, a gay male English writer desiring to emigrate to the United States, when asked by an American Embassy official whether he was a practicing homosexual, "said I didn't practice, I was already perfect." Alex Witchel, "Nose Up, Chin Up, In a Room of his Own," *N.Y. Times*, June 12, 1997, at C1, C4.) Have you ever heard of anyone being described as "a practicing heterosexual"?

1.3 On what premises is sodomy "of worse malignity than rape"?

1.4 Professor Kendall Thomas argues that the "overheated style" of Justice White's opinion in *Bowers* is

> a sign that the claimed right ... provokes fears on the part of the Supreme Court which go far beyond the perceived threat to its judicial authority.... For the writer of this opinion, a decision in Hardwick's favor would somehow not only undermine the authority of the Court but unman ... the patriarchal (hetero)sexual ideologies and identities on which the authority ultimately rests. In *Hardwick*, the claimed right to commit "homosexual sodomy" is thought ... to be a threatened attack on patriarchal power.... [T]he Hardwick case carries a traumatic force and engenders a sense of panic among the members of the Court which may fairly be described as the judicial equivalent of castration anxiety. The psychic pressures this trauma induces find displaced expression in the figural logic by which the Hardwick Court gives voice to (homo)phobic premises that the reigning protocols of constitutional doctrine do not permit the Court explicitly to acknowledge.... Anal eroticism among men must ... be repudiated ... since it poses a threat to the phallic law of masculine heterosexuality. It is perhaps this image of male homosexuality that led Chief Justice Burger in his concurring opinion to note with apparent approval that Blackstone described sex between men "as an offense of 'deeper malignity' than rape." The "deeper malignity" of "homosexual sodomy" lies in the fact that, unlike rape, sex between men represents an assault on the normative order of male heterosexuality—indeed, an abdication of masculine identity as such. Kendall Thomas, "Corpus Juris (Hetero)sexualis: Doctrine, Discourse, and Desire in *Bowers v. Hardwick*," 1 *GLQ* 33, 38, 39–42 (1993).

Evaluate his analysis. Is a threat to masculine identity a threat to men's position in gender inequality? Might the military be threatened by the same thing Professor Thomas says the Supreme Court was threatened by in its *Hardwick* opinion: looking unmanly, hence appearing less powerful? Does this challenge the essence of institutional definition in both cases? Use Professor Thomas's insight as the basis for an equal protection attack on sodomy statutes under a sex equality rubric.

2. **Bad history?** Anne B. Goldstein argues that "the Court's opinion is bad history." See Goldstein, *supra,* at 1081–89. "No attitude toward 'homosexuals' or 'homosexuality' can really be identified before the mid-nineteenth century because the concept did not exist until then"; moreover, she maintains, oral sex, the act Michael Hardwick was found engaged in, was, she shows, not considered "sodomy" until the late nineteenth century. *Id.* at 1087, 1985–86. How often have you heard prejudice justified by history? Does intensity of feeling sometimes translate into attribution of venerability?

3. **Sex as personhood:** Consider the perspective of Professor Jed Rubenfeld on the place of sexuality in defining gay personhood implicit in the privacy argument:

> The personhood position . . . is that homosexual sex should receive constitutional protection because it is so essential to an individual's self-definition—to his identity. . . . Prohibiting homosexual sex [in this view] violates the right to privacy because homosexual sex is for homosexuals "expressive of innermost traits of being." It "touches the heart of what makes individuals what they are." . . . Without doubt, personhood's arguments for homosexual rights are intended to show and to seek the highest degree of respect for those on behalf of whom they are made. Nevertheless, in the very concept of a homosexual identity there is something potentially disserving—if not disrespectful—to the cause advocated. There is something not altogether liberating. Those who engage in homosexual sex may or may not perceive themselves as bearing a "homosexual identity." Their homosexual relations may be a pleasure they take or an intimacy they value without constituting—at least qua *homosexual* relations—something definitive of their identity. At the heart of personhood's analysis is the reliance upon a sharply demarcated "homosexual identity" to which a person is immediately consigned at the moment he seeks to engage in homosexual sex. For [the personhood argument] homosexual relations are to be protected to the extent that they fundamentally define a species of person that is, by definition, to be strictly distinguished from the heterosexual. . . . [E]ven as it argues for homosexual rights, personhood becomes yet another turn of the screw that has pinned those who engage in homosexual sex into a fixed identity specified by their difference from "heterosexuals." . . .
>
> To put it another way, the idea of a "homosexual identity" has its origin in [an invidious classification]. Homosexuality is first understood as a central, definitive element of a person's identity only from the viewpoint of its "deviancy." Indeed, there is from the outset an imbalance: within its own self-understanding, heterosexuality is merely normality, and the heterosexual must make some further, more particular decisions—pursuing certain kinds of partners or forms of sexual pleasure—before he will be said to have defined his identity according to sexual criteria. To the extent that heterosexuality does

understand itself as definitive per se, it does so only in the face of and in contradistinction to a homosexuality already classified as abnormal and grotesque. By contrast, the mere act of being homosexual is seen as definitive in itself precisely because of its supposed abnormality, and it remains categorically definitive regardless of what sort of partners or sexual encounters the homosexual pursues. In defending homosexuality because of its supposedly self-definitive character, [the personhood argument] reproduces the heterosexual view of homosexuality. . . .

To protect the rights of "the homosexual" would of course be a victory; doing so, however, because homosexuality is essential to a person's identity is no liberation, but simply the flip side of the same rigidification of sexual identities by which our society simultaneously inculcates sexual roles, normalizes sexual conduct, and vilifies "faggots." . . . We must reject the personhood thesis, then . . . ultimately because it betrays privacy's—if not personhood's own—political aspirations. By conceiving of the conduct that it purports to protect as "essential to the individual's identity," personhood inadvertently reintroduces into privacy analysis the very premise of the invidious uses of state power it seeks to overcome. Jed Rubenfeld, "The Right of Privacy," 102 *Harv. L. Rev.* 737, 777, 779–82 (1989).

How does Professor Rubenfeld operationally define "identity"? Where, according to Professor Rubenfeld, does one's sexual identity come from? What defines or creates "the person" in their innermost being in a way that sexual acts, in his view, properly should not? What is the relation between the personally claimed and the socially attributed—in identity generally? in sexual identity in particular? in Professor Rubenfeld's analysis of both?

Is his analysis antisex? Is it opposed to defining people sexually? If so, what is the objection? If sexual identities were gendered but flexible, would that answer the objection? Is heterosexuality also a sexual definition? If so, what is the difference between being defined as gay and as straight? Does Professor Rubenfeld's analysis capture that distinction? Would an equality approach ameliorate or accentuate his concerns? Would the answer depend on what kind of equality approach is employed? Does Professor Rubenfeld's analysis contain elements of a dominance analysis? Does recognizing a social category in equality law for purposes of equalization further inscribe that category, as Professor Rubenfeld objects that the personhood argument in the privacy context does? Is it the aspirations of privacy, or of equality, that a sexual definition violates? Is the personhood assumption he identifies more deeply appropriate to privacy's politics than he concludes it is? Is Professor Rubenfeld's analysis supportive of bisexuality as an identity?

4. Missing equal protection challenges:

4.1 Two heterosexual plaintiffs who said they were "chilled and deterred" from engaging in heterosexual sodomy were originally part of the challenge to Georgia's sodomy prohibition. The district court held that they were in no immediate danger of injury from enforcement, so lacked standing to sue—a ruling not challenged in the U.S. Supreme Court. *See* 478 U.S. at 188 n.2. Should this ruling in itself have been seen as evidence that the statute's enforcement violated the Fourteenth Amendment guarantee of equal protection of the laws, as Justice Blackmun's footnote implies? On what basis would it have been discriminatory? Is the state's admission of unlikelihood of prosecution of the straight couples in *Hard-*

wick, while Mr. Hardwick was arrested, an admission of what would be, if recognized, an equal protection violation on the basis of sexual orientation? Is Justice Powell's complacency in the face of a law he asserts is seldom used a satisfactory answer to the legal challenge by Mr. Hardwick? by the heterosexual plaintiffs? (Revisit the question whether criminal laws affect social life only when people are jailed under them.)

4.2 If the *Hardwick* case had contained an equal protection challenge to the statute, in addition to the due process privacy challenge, would Chief Justice Burger's opinion have been possible? Does the historical record in it support the argument that governments have historically discriminated against homosexuals? Is his opinion an instance of such discrimination, one that shows how homosexuals are denied equal protection of the laws? How did what could have been strong evidence for an equal protection argument become the cornerstone of Justice Burger's argument against the substantive due process claim? Could the presence of an equal protection challenge have turned the substantive due process loss into an equal protection victory for gay rights? (See III for further discussion.) Is the privacy argument likely to be more appealing to the members of the Court than an equality argument?

Do due process and equal protection have different norms as well as distinct standards? Is it possible that sodomy statutes are constitutional under substantive due process and unconstitutional under equal protection? Professor Cass Sunstein argues that equal protection doctrine is more promising for protecting gay rights than is substantive due process doctrine in part because substantive due process protects values that are rooted in tradition, while equal protection law can protect against those same traditions.

> The Due Process Clause often looks backward; it is highly relevant to the Due Process issue whether an existing or time-honored convention, described at the appropriate level of generality, is violated by the practice under attack. By contrast, the Equal Protection Clause looks forward, serving to invalidate practices that were widespread at the time of its ratification and that were expected to endure. The two clauses therefore operate along different tracks. Cass R. Sunstein, "Sexual Orientation and the Constitution: A Note on the Relationship Between Due Process and Equal Protection," 55 *U. Chi. L. Rev.* 1161, 1163 (1988).

See also Kenji Yoshino, "Suspect Symbols: A Literary Argument for Heightened Scrutiny," 96 *Colum. L. Rev.* 1753, 1773 (1996). Should an equal protection argument have been made in *Hardwick*?

4.3 Justice Stevens, joined by Justices Brennan and Marshall, argued in dissent that Georgia's sodomy law was meant to reach heterosexual as well as homosexual sodomy, and as such criminalized some conduct, such as oral sex between husbands and wives, that privacy law clearly protects. Since the law could not, therefore, be constitutionally enforced as it was written, he contended, the state had to justify its selective application to homosexuals: "Either the persons to whom Georgia seeks to apply its statute do not have the same interest in 'liberty' that others have, or there must be a reason why the State may be permitted to apply a generally applicable law to certain persons that it does not apply to others." 478 U.S. at 185 (Stevens, J., dissenting). Is this an equality argument in privacy disguise?

4.4 If the intrusions required to enforce a law against sodomy by heterosexuals would violate the right to privacy under *Griswold*, but that same doctrine does not protect homosexuals from the same intrusions required to enforce it against them for the same acts, does the Court's interpretation of substantive due process violate the Equal Protection Clause?

4.5 Could privacy and substantive equality be combined, such that privacy became a right to which people are entitled on an equal basis? What would such an analysis look like legally?

5. Privacy and harm:

5.1 Arguably, "the private" cannot be presumed to be a setting of equality between women and men. In this light, is it in women's interest to assert that the state should not intrude into the private sphere? into sexual relations, so long as they are conducted in private? Having read the chapter on rape (Chapter 7.1), are you satisfied that prohibitions on "nonconsensual" sex adequately protect women from forced sex in private? In light of the extent of child sexual abuse, see Chapter 7.1, are children adequately protected from harm in private? Should laws against forced sodomy remain while consensual sodomy laws are eliminated? Are you confident that the line between the forced and the consensual in sex can be properly drawn under privacy law? What if the laws against forced sodomy were also selectively prosecuted against gay men? In consensual sodomy cases, how do prosecutors know whom to prosecute?

5.2 It is further arguable that women and men as members of gender groups may not have the same interests in "the private." Are the interests of lesbian women in eliminating criminal sodomy laws the same as gay men's? Observe further that both cases cited in the *Hardwick* dissent for the key role of sexuality in human relationships are cases involving obscenity. One, *Stanley v. Georgia*, 394 U.S. 557 (1969), protects consumption of obscenity in private. What human relationship does this protect? Granting that obscenity is not necessarily pornography, *see* Chapter 10.2, but recalling the extensive harm inflicted on women in the home, should harms to women attendant to male consumption of obscenity, see Chapter 10.2, be off-limits to the state because they happen in private? Does the privacy construct tend to assume that whatever happens with obscenity in private raises no questions of harm?

5.3 The statute upheld against Mr. Hardwick was struck down on privacy grounds by the Supreme Court of Georgia in *Powell v. State*, 510 S.E.2d 18 (Ga. 1998). In this case, a man defended himself from a sodomy charge based on having intercourse and oral sex with his wife's seventeen-year-old niece on grounds that the act was consensual. She testified that the sex acts were forced and against her will and she wept during them. While these events were taking place, the defendant's eight-months-pregnant wife, the girl's aunt, slept in the next room. *See* 510 S.E.2d at 20. Advocates for gay rights cheered the result ("this is especially sweet") as heralding recognition "that we are in a day and age where the government simply does not belong in bedrooms." Kevin Sack, "Georgia's High Court Voids Sodomy Law," *N.Y. Times*, Nov. 24, 1998, at A16 (quoting Stephen R. Scarborough, lawyer for Lambda Legal Defense and Education Fund, which had filed an amicus brief in the case advocating invalidating the law). Evaluate the relation between the rights of Mrs. Powell's seventeen-year-old niece and the gay rights groups advocating elimination of the sodomy law. Does the result in this case suggest that men have a common interest across the gay/straight divide in strengthening the right to privacy, and with it the public/private line? If so, why did it take so long for the state to recognize it? Do women, including those who are lesbian, have an interest in weakening or strengthening the current interpretation of the privacy right? Do some members of each group have crosscutting interests? If so, what are they and what circumstances give rise to them? Does government belong in bedrooms where abuse is inflicted?

6. A right to be sexual? No constitutional right to be sexual is expressly recognized. Should it be? Is this what the right to privacy, as argued by the plaintiff in *Hardwick*, was substantively reaching toward? Professor Mary Dunlap suggested, prior to *Hardwick*, that a "right to be sexual as an affirmative, essential source of personal liberty" might be implicit in privacy decisions, which "offer the only presently articulated judicial link between the idea that government cannot be left unaccountably free to compel particular basic choices by individuals, and the idea that an individual's sexual choices are basic." Mary C. Dunlap, "Toward Recognition of 'A Right to Be Sexual,'" 7 *Women's Rts. L. Rep.* 245, 248, 247 (1982). Presumably such a right would require eliminating laws like Georgia's sodomy law as applied to situations like that of Mr. Hardwick. What about the parts of the statutes that prohibit sex with animals?

Professor Dunlap cautions that it would be difficult to prevent a right to be sexual from institutionalizing gender stereotypes. *See id.* at 246–47. She also acknowledges that limiting the right would be challenging, given "the realities of sexual violence, exploitation, and repressiveness in our society, and the tendency of 'rights' to become chiefly the possession of those empowered to define them." *Id.* at 248. If there were a constitutional right to be sexual, how would you recommend that state laws against sexual assault, statutory rape, incest, child sexual abuse, adultery, fornication, prostitution, pimping, obscenity, and sadomasochism be treated? How would you anticipate responding to defendants, prosecuted for such offenses, that their constitutional right to be sexual was being denied? Do some of these laws address abuse, some not? Are some, in effect, laws against inequality in sexual interaction, some not? Are some pure morals infractions? Evaluate which offenses regard consent as meaningless and which do not. Consider how laws against sexual harassment and the Violence Against Women Act might be challenged and defended under such a constitutional right. Compare the affirmative "right to be sexual" approach with the negative privacy approach to eliminating sodomy laws. Do women yet have a right *not* to be sexual?

7. Privacy and the closet: Being forced to remain "closeted" hence invisible as a gay man or lesbian woman is well known to be destructive and painful to many individuals as well as damaging to a movement for equal rights. "Passing" as heterosexual is also a survival mechanism under hostile conditions. Professor Eve Kosofsky Sedgwick observes that "[t]he closet is the defining structure for gay oppression in this century. The legal couching, by civil liberties lawyers, of *Bowers v. Hardwick* as an issue in the first place of a Constitutional right to privacy [is among other things an extension of], and testimony to the power of, the image of the closet." Sedgwick, *supra*, at 71. Evaluate her analysis. Is there a difference between being private and being closeted? Is it the tension of a disreputable secret that makes the closet damaging? Why seek a right to keep a secret private if it is not disreputable? If there were no discrimination against nonhetero-sexuals, would a right to privacy as sought in *Hardwick* be necessary? Would there be a closet? If there were no discrimination against women, would the private sequester inequality? Would there be a private sphere? Would sexuality be perceived as shameful to the extent it is under conditions of sex inequality?

8. The military closet: The debate during the Clinton administration that produced the "Don't Ask, Don't Tell, Don't Pursue" policy—a so-called compromise, under which gay men and lesbian women, formerly prohibited from being in the military at all (see III A for discussion of prior policies) were supposed to be permitted to remain in the military so long as no one knows they are there—provides an evocative setting for exposing the dynamics of the closet.

The regulations, as formerly, prohibit homosexual conduct by service-members; unlike prior regulations, they purport not to prohibit homosexual status per se. However, they make "coming out" virtually a sex act, probative of orientation and grounds in itself for exclusion.[30] If acts, including verbal acts, come to light, the servicemember has the burden of disproving "propensity or intent to engage in homosexual acts." If one is not gay or lesbian, how could this negative be proven? Under this policy, imagine the risks of Charlotte Bunch's political experiment of "being queer for a week."

Does this policy constitute both act and status discrimination? Do the rules amount to allowing gay and lesbian servicemembers to serve and be sexual so long as no one knows? Why is the military's issue whether or not it is apparent that its members are lesbian or gay: not their presence, not their sex acts—their *known* presence? Why, in other words, is image, not reality, the concern? Why is furtiveness and denial acceptable, openness

---

30. The rule provides:

A member of the armed forces shall be separated [if]:

(1) . . . the member has engaged in, attempted to engage in, or solicited another to engage in a homosexual act or acts unless there are further findings . . . that the member has demonstrated that—(A) such conduct is a departure from the member's usual and customary behavior; (B) such conduct, under all the circumstances, is unlikely to recur; (C) such conduct was not accomplished by use of force, coercion, or intimidation; (D) under the particular circumstances of the case, the member's continued presence in the armed forces is consistent with the interests of the armed forces in proper discipline, good order, and morale; and (E) the member does not have a propensity or intent to engage in homosexual acts.

(2) . . . the member has stated that he or she is a homosexual or bisexual, or words to that effect, unless there is a further finding . . . that the member has demon-

strated that he or she is not a person who engages in, attempts to engage in, has a propensity to engage in, or intends to engage in homosexual acts.

(3) . . . the member has married or attempted to marry a person known to be of the same biological sex. 10 U.S.C. § 654(b) (1994).

The actual "Don't ask" part, which barred the forces from asking new recruits and servicemembers whether they were gay, is not statutory but is buried in policy guidelines and implementing regulations, and lacks any substantive or procedural rights if breached. Questions tantamount to "Are you gay?" can be asked and reports of information found credible can be pursued. *See* Janet E. Halley, "The Status/Conduct Distinction in the 1993 Revisions to Military Anti–Gay Policy: A Legal Archaeology," 3 *GLQ* 159, 179–80 (1996) (documenting regulations). The "Don't tell" part arguably "gags servicemembers' explicitly political speech." *Id.* at 181. (For rulings on the constitutionality of this provision over free speech attacks, see III A, note 3.3 to *Gay Law Students*.)

and pride unacceptable? Is furtiveness and denial what "keeping it private" means?

Does the "Don't Ask, Don't Tell" policy make the closet, by statute, the price of military service? Is "Don't Ask, Don't Tell" privacy with a vengeance? Of this policy, Professor Francisco Valdes comments: "[T]he insistence that only lesbian, gay, and bisexual service members keep their sexualities 'private' (and secret) works like a sword that beats back the expression of sexual minority identity while, at the same time, the 'privacy' of the sexual majority is waved as if shielding legitimate concerns and social justice." Valdes, *supra*, at 370–71 (1995). Is a law and discourse of privacy conducive to making a shield into a sword against the purportedly shielded? Does Professor Valdes's analysis state an equality argument against the policy? If everyone equally had to keep their sexuality equally "private," would that materially improve the lives of the nonheterosexuals? Would you predict that more or fewer gay men and lesbian women might be eliminated from the military under the supposedly more tolerant "Don't Ask, Don't Tell" policy than under prior absolute prohibitions on gay sex acts? In fact, nearly twice as many servicemembers have been discharged under this policy than the former one of absolute prohibition for status as well as act. *See* Office of the Under Secretary of Defense (Personnel and Readiness), *Report to the Secretary of Defense: Review of the Effectiveness of the Application and Enforcement of the Department's Policy on Homosexual Conduct in the Military* tbl. I (1998) (documenting 617 discharged in 1994, 997 discharged in 1997); Jim Garamone, "DoD Clarifies 'Don't Ask, Don't Tell' Policy," *Armed Forces Information Service* (last modified Aug. 13, 1999) (documenting 1,145 discharged in 1998).

Is privacy under the "Don't Ask, Don't Tell" policy a protection or a cage? If coming out is a form of speech, is enforced privacy a form of silencing? Does the policy differentially "dictat[e] what people must always keep to themselves"? Anita L. Allen, "Coercing Privacy," 4 *Wm. & Mary L. Rev.* 723, 755 (1999). Is what is being dictated be kept silent under the policy separable from the way in which the speech that is silenced is differentially dictated to some people and not to others? Does privacy doctrine promote equality under these circumstances? Does this policy expose a deep meaning of privacy under conditions of inequality or exploit the private for unequal ends?

9. Privacy in Europe: The European Court of Human Rights has interpreted the European Convention for the Protection of Human Rights and Fundamental Freedoms's provision guaranteeing respect for privacy and family life to prohibit criminalization of private consensual homosexual activity, *see Dudgeon v. United Kingdom*, (1981) 45 Eur. Ct. H.R. (ser. A) at 4; *Norris v. Ireland*, (1989) 142 Eur. Ct. H.R. (ser. A) at 186; *Modinos v. Cyprus*, (1993) 259 Eur. Ct. H.R. (ser. A) at 5, extending the same holding to the military services, *see Case of Lustig–Prean and Beckett v. The United Kingdom*, Applications nos. 31417/96 and 32377/96, Judgment, 27 Sept. 1999. Why does Europe embrace the insight that the United States Supreme Court rejects? While the dominant trend among countries around the world is to eliminate their sodomy laws, many countries, particularly in Asia and Africa, retain them. *See* James D. Wilets, "The Human Rights of Sexual Minorities," *Hum. Rts.*, Fall 1995, at 22–24.

10. Privacy under international law: In 1994, the General Assembly of the United Nations adopted the submission of its Human Rights Committee that the privacy protection in Article 17 of the International Covenant on Civil and Political Rights, 999 U.N.T.S. 171, 177, G.A. Res. 2200, U.N. GAOR, 21st Sess., Supp. No. 16, at 55, U.N. Doc. A/6316 (1966) ("ICCPR"), prohibits a provision of the Tasmanian Criminal Code in Australia that criminalized various forms of sexual contact between men, including all sexual contact between consenting adult men in private. *See* Communication No. 488/1992, Nicholas Toonen v. Australia, U.N. GAOR Hum. Rts. Comm., 49th Sess., Supp. No. 40, at 226, U.N. Doc. A/49/40 (1994). The ruling found that the provisions

> specifically target acts [but that] their impact is to distinguish an identifiable class of individuals and to prohibit certain of their acts. Such laws are thus clearly understood by the community as being directed at male homosexuals as a group. Accordingly, if the Committee were to find the Tasmanian laws discriminatory which interfere with privacy, the State party concedes that they constitute a discriminatory interference with privacy. *Id.* at 231 (¶ 6.13).

Does this reasoning both obliterate the act/status distinction and the discrimination/privacy line? Is it valid? Is the Tasmanian law simple sex discrimination in applying only to homosexual acts between men? What if Tasmania prohibited the same acts between women? The ruling for Mr. Toonen was predicated more on privacy than equality, *see id.* at 235 (¶ ¶ 9, 11). However, the committee expressly stated without further discussion that "the reference to 'sex' in articles 2, paragraph 1, and 26 is to be taken as including sexual orientation." *Id.* For commentary on *Toonen*, see generally George Selvanera, "Gays in Private: The Problems with the Privacy Analysis in Furthering Human Rights," 16(2) *Adel. L. Rev.* 331 (1994) (criticizing the use of privacy argument in *Toonen* as furthering antigay sentiment); Wayne Morgan, "Identifying Evil for What It Is: Tasmania, Sexual Perversity and the United Nations," 19 *Melb. U. L. Rev.* 740 (1994) (recognizing importance of decision but arguing that privacy analysis cannot address crucial issues of violence and discrimination). *See also* Carl F. Stychin, "Prohibitions and Promotions: A Comparative Analysis of Legal Interventions," 5 *Australasian Gay & Lesbian L.J.* 42 (1995) (analyzing attempts to control sexual expression in England and the United States).

The United States has ratified the ICCPR, but the Senate declared the treaty non-self-executing, raising the question whether it gives rise to a private right of action in U.S. courts. *See* Laurence R. Helfer & Alice M. Miller, "Sexual Orientation and Human Rights: Toward a United States and Transnational Jurisprudence," 9 *Harv. Hum. Rts. J.* 61, 77–78 (1996) (arguing that *Toonen* can help U.S. courts apply the ICCPR if self-executing, or if not, can help resolve unsettled questions of state and federal law); *see also* David A. Catania, "The Universal Declaration of Human Rights and Sodomy Laws: A Federal Common Law Right to Privacy for Homosexuals Based on Customary International Law," 31 *Am. J. Crim. L. Rev.* 289 (1994) (advocating a federal common law right to privacy based on customary international law to invalidate state sodomy statutes). Should an international standard, which when ratified is the supreme law of the land, be permitted decisive weight in a domestic issue of law previously decided the other way, as it was in *Hardwick*? Could international law be particularly helpful in construing equality guarantees domestically, which, in the United States, have not been decisively ruled upon in cases like

Hardwick? Would invalidating sodomy prohibitions violate American culture?

11. Evaluate this argument: Heterosexuality has a closet. It keeps sexual abuse in there. Because this reality remains hidden, hierarchical sex can flourish and masquerade as equal sex. (For evidence, see Chapter 7.) The inviolability of this closet is guarded by, inter alia, the law, norm, and discourse of privacy. Denying privacy to "homosexuals" amounts to defining their sexuality as a form of abuse, when it is not, while at the same time approving heterosexuality as nonabusive by definition, when it often is abusive in fact. Seeking a right to privacy, as it has been defined, for homosexuality thus amounts to seeking a right to exploit inequality and to abuse others with impunity, as is routinely done heterosexually on the basis of gender, age, race, and class hierarchies, reified and eroticized as "differences." If denying privacy rights to homosexuality promotes and symbolizes powerlessness, seeking privacy rights is a form of assimilation with dominance. To the extent that the right to privacy translates into a right to sexually abuse, winning the right to privacy for gay men and lesbian women guarantees that they will join heterosexuals in the closet of sexual abuse. Haven't both been closeted long enough?

As it has developed in law, then, privacy, both structural (federalism) and substantive (substantive due process liberty), works to hide systemic inequality enforced through abuses of power in civil society. Privacy law has been a "closeted" approach to gay rights, but it is heterosexuality's closet—containing the shame of hierarchical sex and sexual abuse—that it ultimately protects and seeks to enter. As a legal approach, equality, by contrast, is "out": it exposes abuse and claims a place of respect and dignity for presently unequal groups in the light of day.

III. EQUALITY ISSUES IN LESBIAN AND GAY RIGHTS

The realities of gay and lesbian experience raise anew every fundamental question of social and legal equality analysis, as well as provoke new questions for equality theory. Conventional equality questions, to which answers indigenous to same-sexuality are called for, include: Is this a group? If so, how is the collectivity created and defined? Is it subject to inequality? If so, to whom is it unequal, in what ways, and why? Because equality is a group-based claim, even as inequalities are inflicted on individuals, defining the contours and experiences of the group or groups is more crucial to equality claims than it is, for instance, to privacy claims. If discrimination occurs, on what basis? in what relation to other grounds for discrimination? is the group divided by sex? with what history and consequences? For instance, is the group excluded from the political process? How does law participate—past, present, and potentially—in this asserted inequality? What can and should law do to promote equality in this realm?

Some of the deeper equality questions raised concern the nature of groups in society and law, the determinants and functions of sexuality as an identity, social status ordering and force for and against social change, and the potential of equality law to address inequalities that take diverse forms. In exposing intersecting and interlocking as well as crosscutting and at times ambiguous or elusive grounds and classifications for inequality, with attendant subordinations that are often hardly ambiguous or elusive, the quest of these groups for social and legal equality raises issues at the crux of, and in the interplay between, individual identity, social group definition, social structure, and legal entitlement. The materials that follow raise questions of how social behavior, social labeling, and self-identification interact to define collectivities, both for purposes of discrimination and for purposes of ending discrimination. How would you construct an affirmative action program for gay, lesbian, and bisexual employees or students— or would you? Is anyone lesbian or gay or bisexual who experiences discrimination as such? How would you promote an environment in which same-sexuality was not punished? Fundamentally, this section asks what, in this context and generally, power is made of, what its deprivation consists in, and what its redistribution would take.

For purposes of the present discussion, the first question is whether lesbian women and gay men are treated unequally from heterosexual men and women. The next question is whether such discrimination is, or should be treated as, a basis for discrimination in itself, or whether it is integral to, and should be argued as a form of, discrimination on the basis of sex. In either case, a third question concerns whether same-sex discrimination should be analyzed in terms of sameness and difference, or dominance and subordination. In a sex equality approach, gay men and lesbian women can be argued to be either the same as other men and women, different from them and to be equally valued, or subjected to gender-based dominance that should be prohibited in public and private life. Should "homosexuals" be argued to be "the same" as heterosexuals for relevant purposes—the "We're just like you" appeal? Or does this distort and blunt the critical, distinctive, and self-respecting edge of gay politics? Women's experience with these realities and arguments may provide lessons as to whether "homosexuals" are best conceived as "different" from heterosexuals, or whether homosexuality's "difference" is a construct of heterosexuality's dominance, under which all women, including lesbian women as such, as well as gay men are subordinated. The relation between privacy and equality arguments, actual and potential, is also raised.

Cases challenging discrimination against homosexuality have typically argued that homosexuals as a group are discriminated against on grounds of sexual orientation or preference, notably in challenges to discrimination in employment, the military, the political process, and the family. *See* III A. Less frequently but increasingly, discrimination against gay men and lesbian women has been argued to be a form of discrimination on the basis of sex. *See* III B. With your assessment of the comparative social validity and legal potency of each analysis, consider where each argument seems stronger as well as the possibilities for combining their social insights and strategic merits, toward a legal theory directed at ending discrimination against sexualities other than standard heterosexual.

A.   SEXUAL ORIENTATION DISCRIMINATION

A growing body of case law concludes that sexual orientation is a ground for discrimination from which homosexuals as a group should be legally protected. The central legal issue is whether sexual orientation discrimination as such should be prohibited. Beneath this issue lies the question of the nature of legal and social categorization in equality law. Discrimination law, as we have seen, *see* Chapter 4, conventionally proceeds by categories, and equality law traditionally proceeds through asking whether likes have been treated unalike, or unalikes alike, *see* Chapter 1. The movements for lesbian and gay rights not only challenge the limits and validity of categorizing people on a sexual basis—a protest congenial to individualism's resistance to collective definition—they also to some extent question the stability and possibility of so doing, while at the same time observing that category-based discrimination can be unambiguous and tenacious in real life. In this connection, recall the discussions in Chapter 2 of racial identity and race-based inequality. As you read the cases, consider the structure of the argument being made against discrimination on the basis of sexual orientation: what implicit requisites it is being held to, whether it meets them, and what standards it calls into question.

Ask whether it is possible to give equality rights to a group that is not visually definable, indeed is largely self-defined, and has membership that is neither practically ascertainable nor empirically falsifiable, even fluctuates in life. By the same token, ask how it is possible to deny them rights. Do some approaches to same-sex discrimination tend to try to solve this conundrum by privileging genetic or other fixed determinants of sexual identity? Do doctrine and ideology encourage this resolution? Should anyone be entitled to an antidiscrimination claim who encounters differential treatment on this basis, whether they (by some yet-to-be-stabilized criterion) "are" gay or lesbian or not? How can a person's claim to be bisexual, for example, be challenged? Yet is the reality of discrimination against bisexuals in doubt? What would be the implications of premising equality guarantees on experiences of subordinated peoples, as suggested in Chapter 4, rather than on abstract grounds that in turn give rise to categories?

In conceptualizing the category, it is common to begin from the premise that "no one is a heterosexual or a homosexual independently of culture," Mary McIntosh, "Queer Theory and the War of the Sexes," *in Activating Theory: Lesbian, Gay, Bisexual Politics* 30, 34 (Joseph Bristow & Angelia R. Wilson eds., 1993). Commonly, " 'gay' is best seen as a *social* label, not a *biological one*; it is a shorthand description of how people who are attracted to members of the same sex are generally understood, and understand themselves, in Western societies in the current era." Nicholas Bamforth, *Sexuality, Morals and Justice: A Theory of Lesbian and Gay Rights Law* 80 (1997). If sex were not understood as a biological label in the first place, would "people who are attracted to members of the same *sex*" be an intelligible group descriptor? If the disadvantage of same-sex sexual orientation, rather than same-sex sexual orientation itself, were seen as the inequality problem, "homosexuals" would clearly be understood as a socially defined class. It is in this nonessentialist vein that Kenneth Plummer argued that hostility to homosexuality is key to understanding homosexuality as a social experience.

> The single most important factor about homosexuality as it exists in this culture is the perceived hostility of the societal reactions that surround it.... [This one critical factor] renders the business of becoming a homosexual a process that is characterized by problems of access, problems of guilt and problems of identity. It leads to the emergence of a subculture of homosexuality. It leads to a series of interaction problems involved with concealing the discreditable stigma. And it inhibits the development of stable relationships among homosexuals to a considerable degree. Homosexuality as a social experience simply cannot be understood without an analysis of the societal

reactions to it. Kenneth Plummer, *Sexual Stigma: An Interactionist Account* 102 (1975).

Is anyone who is not heterosexual subject to the disadvantages described? For purposes of Mr. Plummer's analysis, does it matter if homosexuality is biological or social in origin, or whether it is chosen or involuntary? If the group "homosexuals" is defined by a hostile society, in much the way the philosopher Jean–Paul Sartre once observed that anti-Semites define "the Jew," Jean–Paul Sartre, *Anti-Semite and Jew* 143 (George J. Becker trans., Schocken Books 1948), how homophobia and heterosexuality construct "the homosexual" is a proper object of inquiry and target for change in their status.

In his influential and definitive analysis of stigma, sociologist Erving Goffman analyzes how a stigmatic identity is socially shaped and a stigmatized group is socially treated. In his analysis, normal and stigmatized are not people but perspectives "generated in social situations during mixed contacts by virtue of the unrealized norms that are likely to play upon the encounter." Erving Goffman, *Stigma: Notes on the Management of Spoiled Identity* 138 (1963).

Erving Goffman, *Stigma: Notes on the Management of Spoiled Identity*

1–7, 19, 42, 65, 138 (1963)

The Greeks, who were apparently strong on visual aids, originated the term *stigma* to refer to bodily signs designed to expose something unusual and bad about the moral status of the signifier.... Today, the term is widely used in something like the original literal sense, but is applied more to the disgrace itself than to the bodily evidence of it.... The term stigma [refers] to an attribute that is deeply discrediting, but ... a language of relationships, not attributes, is really needed.... A stigma ... is really a special kind of relationship between [an] attribute and stereotype.... First there are abominations of the body—the various physical deformities. Next there are blemishes of individual character perceived as weak will, domineering or unnatural passions, treacherous and rigid beliefs, and dishonesty, these being inferred from a known record of, for example, mental disorder, imprisonment, addiction, alcoholism, homosexuality, unemployment, suicidal attempts, and radical political behavior. Finally there are the tribal stigma of race, nation, and religion.... In all of these various instances of stigma ... the same sociological features are found: an individual who might have been received easily in ordinary social intercourse possesses a trait that can obtrude itself upon attention and turn those of us whom he meets away from him, breaking the claim that his other attributes have on us. He possesses a stigma, an undesired differentness.... We and those who do not depart negatively from the particular expectations at issue I shall call the *normals*....

By definition ... we [normals] believe the person with a stigma is not quite human. On this assumption we exercise varieties of discrimination, through which we effectively, if often unthinkingly, reduce his life chances.... We construct a stigma-theory, an ideology to explain his inferiority and account for the danger he represents.... [W]e may perceive his defensive response to his situation as a direct expression of his defect, and then see both defect and response as just retribution for something he or his parents or his tribe did, and hence a justification of the way we treat him....

The stigmatized individual tends to hold the same beliefs about identity that we do.... His deepest feelings about what he is may be his sense of being a "normal person," a human being like anyone else, a person, therefore, who deserves a fair chance and a fair break.... Yet he may perceive, usually quite correctly, that whatever others profess, they do not really "accept" him and are not ready to make contact with him on "equal grounds." Further, the standards he has incorporated from the wider society equip him to be intimately alive to what others see as his failing, inevitably causing him, if only for moments, to agree that he does indeed fall short of what he really ought to be. Shame becomes a central possibility, arising from the individual's perception of one of his own attributes as being a defiling thing to possess....

[A] discrepancy may exist between an individual's virtual and actual identity. This discrepancy, when known about or apparent, spoils his social identity; it has the effect of cutting him off from society and from himself so that he stands a discredited person facing an unaccepting world.... The stigma and the effort to conceal it or remedy it become "fixed" as part of personal identity.... [W]hen his differentness is not immediately apparent, and is not known beforehand (or at least known by him to be known to the others) ... [t]he issue is ... of managing information about his failing. To display or not to display; to tell or not to tell; to let on or not to let on; to lie or not to lie; and in each case, to whom, how, when, and where.

To what extent does Professor Goffman's analysis apply to "homosexuals" as a group? Has homosexuality ascended Professor Goffman's stigmatic types, moving from being socially defined by a supposed bodily defect, to a character defect, to a social defect? Is the construction of a gay identity from a stigmatized status a process Professor Goffman would describe as integral to stigmatization itself? If so, does that observation call the validity of the identity into question? Are nonstigmatized identities also explicable in social terms? Is resistance to stigmatization possible within the confines of Professor Goffman's analysis? What are the implications of his analysis for seeking gay rights as such? Put another way, from what perspective, in Professor Goffman's analysis, is the homosexual stigmatized, making homosexuality a basis for identity, hence, in the present inquiry, for rights-seeking? Do some legal doctrines acquiesce in the perspective through which homosexuality is stigmatized, others demystify and resist it? Are the "unrealized norms" that create the stigma of homosexuality gender norms?

What are the social stigmata—in the sense of the outward and visible signs of the "inner disgrace"—of homosexuality? Are they sexual? dignitary? In light of the place of visual assignment in imposing stigma on many socially unequal groups, how do you analyze the fact that the sex of one's sexual orientation, if any, is not definitely determinable on sight? Is the stigma of being female under male dominance also sexual if "[w]omen are the sex that is sex"? Sheila Jeffreys, *The Lesbian Heresy* 52 (1993). Are women, like homosexuals, at once defined and subordinated by society's judgment that they possess, in Goffman's term, "differentness"? Is this question coherent, since lesbian women are on both sides of the comparison, as women of color are on both sides of the problematic "women, like Blacks" analysis? What are the consequences of your answer for analyzing the situation of lesbian women? Why are heterosexual men neither considered different nor sexually defined? Are the social realities, hence trajectories of liberation, of all sexually defined groups intertwined? Is male dominance a common fountainhead of their subordination? Is femaleness a stigma?

Building a legal analysis of equality rights on Professor Goffman's concept, Professor Kenneth Karst argues that

> the principle of equal citizenship presumptively insists that the organized society treat each individual as a person, one who is worthy of respect, one who "belongs." Stated negatively, the principle presumptively forbids the organized society to treat an individual either as a member of an inferior or dependent caste or as a nonparticipant. Accordingly, the principle guards against degradation or the imposition of stigma. The inverse relationship between stigma and recognition as a person is evident. . . . The relationship between stigma and inequality is also clear: while not all inequalities stigmatize, the essence of any stigma lies in the fact that the affected individual is regarded as an unequal in some respect. A society devoted to the idea of equal citizenship, then, will repudiate those inequalities that impose the stigma of caste and thus "belie the principle that people are of equal ultimate worth." Kenneth L. Karst, "The Supreme Court, 1976 Term—Foreword: Equal Citizenship Under the Fourteenth Amendment," 91 *Harv. L. Rev.* 1, 4 (1977) (quoting Goffman, *supra*, at 6, and Robert E. Rodes Jr., *The Legal Enterprise* 163 (1976)).

See also Kenneth L. Karst, "Boundaries and Reasons: Freedom of Expression and the Subordination of Groups," 1990 *U. Ill. L. Rev.* 95, 117, 119–20 (1990). Consider throughout this section the extent to which Professor Goffman has captured the problem of homosexuality for purposes of a sexual orientation discrimination claim, and the extent to which Professor Karst's formulation has captured that reality in a legally workable equality theory. Is Professor Karst's formulation of "the stigma of caste" closer to an Aristotelian sameness/difference analysis or a dominance/subordination approach? Professor Karst has argued that the equal citizenship principle "can be reduced to a claim to be free from stigma." Kenneth L. Karst, "Why Equality Matters," 17 *Ga. L. Rev.* 245, 249 (1983). Is whether a group is stigmatized, hence unequal, an abstract or a substantive determination? Can you think of an inequality that does not stigmatize? What is the relation between stigma and the more material features of discrimination against disadvantaged groups? Is there more to discrimination against lesbian women and gay men than stigma? Are gay men stigmatized differently than lesbian women are? Is there a material basis for the stigma of homosexuality? If so, what is it?

Most laws that guarantee equality in employment in the United States do not prohibit discrimination on the basis of sexual orientation. One exception is the State of California's Equal Protection Clause, which has been interpreted to prohibit sexual orientation discrimination by public employers in a decision that also recognized "coming out" as a political act of speech.

Gay Law Students Ass'n v. Pacific Telephone & Telegraph Co.

Supreme Court of California
24 Cal. 3d 458; 595 P.2d 592 (Cal. 1979)

■ TOBRINER, J.

The complaint alleges that "PT&T has maintained and enforced a policy of employment discrimination against homosexuals," and that "PT&T has, since at least 1971, had an articulated policy of excluding homosexuals from employment opportunities with its organization." ... [W]e have concluded that ... the equal protection clause of the California Constitution (art. I, § 7, subd. (a)) places special obligations on a state-protected public utility, such as PT&T, to refrain from all forms of arbitrary employment discrimination....

Article I, section 7, subdivision (a) of the California Constitution provides simply that: "A person may not be ... denied equal protection of the laws." ... [T]he question with which we are presented is a narrow but important one: Is the California constitutional equal protection guarantee violated when a privately owned public utility, which enjoys a state-protected monopoly or quasi-monopoly, utilizes its authority arbitrarily to exclude a class of individuals from employment opportunities? [W]e conclude that arbitrary exclusion of qualified individuals from employment opportunities by a state-protected public utility does, indeed, violate the state constitutional rights of the victims of such discrimination.

In California a public utility is in many respects more akin to a governmental entity than to a purely private employer.... Under [the] circumstances, we believe that the state cannot avoid responsibility for a utility's systematic business practices....

For a number of reasons arbitrary discrimination in employment particularly flouts constitutional principles when it is practiced by a state-protected public utility. First, from the point of view of the individual seeking employment, both the injurious effect of arbitrary exclusion and the risk of such exclusion loom significantly larger in the case of a monopolistic or quasi-monopolistic public utility than in the case of an ordinary employer. An individual who is arbitrarily rejected by a single private employer is generally free to seek a job with that employer's competitors.... Arbitrary rejection from employment by a public utility with a state-protected monopoly such as PT&T, however, frequently leaves an individual no comparable option.... Moreover, because PT&T has no competition to fear, it does not face the inherent, if limited, check which the free market system places on employment discrimination. Thus, from the standpoint of the individual employee, the potential for employment discrimination by a public utility is high, and the effect of such discrimination when it occurs is devastating. Second, unlike discrimination by a private employer, employment discrimination by a public utility can be particularly pernicious because, in light of the utility's position, the general public cannot avoid giving indirect support to such discriminatory practices.... Finally, employment discrimination by a public utility is particularly incompatible with the values underlying our constitutional equal protection guarantee because a public utility's monopolistic or quasi-monopolistic authority over employment opportunities derives directly from its exclusive franchise provided by the state....

[W]e conclude that in this state a public utility bears a constitutional obligation to avoid arbitrary employment discrimination.... [W]e believe that the relevant United States Supreme Court authorities are consistent with this conclusion.... [T]hose decisions have made it clear that when the state grants a private entity monopoly power over employment opportunities, the private entity—like the state itself—may not use such power in an unconstitutional fashion.... [A claim is stated under article I section 7 (a) and also for "unfair discrimination" by public utilities, a state statutory provision deriving from the medieval common law obligation on enterprises that exercise monopoly power not to discriminate.]

[In addition Labor Codes sections 1101 and 1102 forbid any employer from controlling, or threatening employment sanctions for, the political activities or affiliations of employees. By existing legal standards under state and federal law, t]he struggle of the homosexual community for equal rights, particularly in the field of employment, must be recognized as a political activity. Indeed the subject of the rights of homosexuals incites heated political debate today, and the "gay liberation movement" encourages its homosexual members to attempt to convince other members of society that homosexuals should be accorded the same fundamental rights as heterosexuals. The aims of the struggle for homosexual rights, and the tactics employed, bear a close analogy to the continuing struggle for civil rights waged by blacks, women, and other minorities....

A principal barrier to homosexual equality is the common feeling that homosexuality is an affliction which the homosexual worker must conceal from his employer and his fellow workers. Consequently one important aspect of the struggle for equal rights is to induce homosexual individuals to "come out of the closet," acknowledge their sexual preferences, and to associate with others in working for equal rights. In light of this factor in the movement for homosexual rights, the allegations of plaintiffs' complaint assume a special significance. Plaintiffs allege that PT&T discriminates against "manifest" homosexuals and against persons who make "an issue of their homosexuality." ... [The] allegations can reasonably be construed as charging that PT&T discriminates in particular against persons who identify themselves as homosexual, who defend homosexuality, or who are identified with activist homosexual organizations [in violation of sections 1101 and 1102].

[To fail effectively to sanction PT&T] for its alleged arbitrary discriminatory practices, we would ... empower any public utility to engage in an infinity of arbitrary employment practices. To cite only a few examples, the utility could refuse to employ a person because he read books prohibited by the utility, visited countries disapproved by the utility, or simply exhibited irrelevant characteristics of personal appearance or background disliked by the utility. Such possible arbitrary discrimination, casting upon the community the shadow of totalitarianism, becomes crucial when asserted by an institution that exerts the vast powers of a monopoly sanctioned by government itself. We do not believe a public utility can assert such prerogatives in a free society dedicated to the protection of individual rights.

NOTES AND QUESTIONS ON *GAY LAW STUDENTS*

1. Equality and privacy compared: Compare the choice of doctrine in *Gay Law Students* with the privacy line of cases in II.

1.1 Consider the line that divides the "public" discrimination that is prohibited from the "private" discrimination that, under *Gay Law Students*, the state constitution's equal protection provision would not reach. Compare this line with the "private" acts that are sought to be protected from state intervention in the cases seeking a right to privacy. Are antidiscrimination and privacy theories in tension? Do they draw the line between the public and the private in the same place? Do they take the same position on state intervention? If the state, under the Due Process Clause, were to be kept out of what was sought as private in *Hardwick*, could the state prohibit discrimination under the Equal Protection Clause or by statute within that same private sphere? If sexual acts are off limits to government because they are sexual, is a law against discrimination by means of sexual acts also off limits? Is banning criminal law from the bedroom and gaining civil rights in public life consistent or inconsistent in this context? If the right to privacy had prevailed in *Hardwick*, would it have eliminated the kinds of discrimination alleged in *Gay Law Students*? Are the two strategies in tension? distinct but complementary? Would a privacy analysis militate for or against recognizing "coming out" as a political act? Does privacy analysis pull in the direction of protecting the closet or eliminating the need for it?

1.2 Would the right to equality recognized by the *Gay Law Students* court tend to invalidate the sodomy laws permitted in *Hardwick*? If consensual sodomy among adults was still a crime when *Gay Law Students* was decided, would the decision have been possible? likely? In fact, in 1975 California amended its 1872 ("the infamous crime against nature") sodomy law to prohibit "sexual conduct consisting of contact between the penis of one person and the anus of another person," Cal. Penal Code § 286(a) (West 1999), limited to acts with minors, against the will of the other person, or among prisoners. *See* Act of Sept. 18, 1975, c. 877, 1975 Cal. Stat. 1957. Later amendments prohibited sodomy with incompetent persons and added a penetration requirement to the definition. *See* Act of Sept. 27, 1981, 1981 Cal. Stat. 896 and Act of July 22, 1991, 1991 Cal. Stat. 184.

2. Equality implications: Does *Gay Law Students* adopt what at the federal level would be minimal scrutiny, resulting in a rational basis invalidation? Does the decision presuppose what it neither argues nor holds: that discrimination by a public entity on the basis of sexual orientation would necessarily violate at least that state's principle of equal protection of the laws? Would that court's analysis of the reasons that a public utility should not be permitted to discriminate arbitrarily apply with equal or greater force to the state police? to the state's family courts?

3. Coming out as political speech: *Gay Law Students* suggests that coming out is political speech, an act protected from official disadvantage.

3.1 Consider what acts could constitute "coming out." What makes coming out political? Is it because coming out is sexual and the politics of gay rights are sexual politics? because being gay is discriminated against? Is "passing"—i.e., not coming out—equally political? Would all sexual speech, according to the Supreme Court of California's analysis, be "political" under the statute? even if it met the standards for sexual harassment? (*See* Chapter 7.2.) Does Justice Tobriner's analysis of the political have an inequality dimension? That is, if homosexuals and heterosexuals were social equals, would what PT&T was alleged to have done to homosexual workers be political?

3.2 In *NGTF v. Board of Education of the City of Oklahoma City*, 729 F.2d 1270 (10th Cir. 1984), the Tenth Circuit held that a provision prohibiting the employment of teachers who engage in "public homosexual conduct" defined as "advocating, soliciting, imposing, encouraging or promoting public or private homosexual activity in a manner that creates a substantial risk that such conduct will come to the attention of school children or school employees" violated the First Amendment's protections for advocacy. 729 F.2d at 1274. This result was affirmed by an equally divided Supreme Court. *See* 470 U.S. 903 (1985). Can a person engage in the prohibited acts without being gay or lesbian? Might a teacher's factual classroom comment that a well-known writer is gay or lesbian be regarded as engaging in public homosexual conduct? Evaluate the statutory definition in equality terms. If sexual orientation discrimination were prohibited under the Fourteenth Amendment, would this provision, or parts of it, be permissible? Do any of its terms overlap laws against sexual harassment in education? Does it violate equality concerns that are specific to an environment of teaching and learning? Might gay or lesbian youth be discriminated against in school because of or by this provision?

3.3 The legal argument pioneered in *Gay Law Students* that homosexuality constitutes a form of expression protected under the First Amendment has since been pursued in varying forms with varying results in the employment context, particularly in the military and public teaching settings. *See, e.g., BenShalom v. Marsh*, 703 F. Supp. 1372 (E.D. Wis. 1989) (holding unconstitutional army regulation barring reenlistment of servicewoman who admitted to being lesbian as unreasonably chilling free speech), *rev'd*, 881 F.2d 454 (7th Cir. 1989); *Able v. United States*, 880 F. Supp. 968 (E.D.N.Y. 1995) (holding statute unconstitutional that allowed discharge for coming out), *vacated and remanded*, 88 F.3d 1280 (2d Cir. 1996), *on remand*, 968 F. Supp. 850 (E.D.N.Y. 1997), *rev'd*, 155 F.3d 628 (2d Cir. 1998) (reversing district court ruling that found unconstitutional as violation of equal protection a provision permitting discharge of servicemember for homosexual acts, having previously held that the provision prohibiting statements was constitutional if the provision prohibiting acts was constitutional); *Holmes v. Calif. Army National Guard*, 920 F. Supp. 1510 (N.D. Cal. 1996) (holding that military's "Don't Ask, Don't Tell" policy violated First Amendment), *rev'd*, 124 F.3d 1126 (9th Cir. 1997). Some cases have been brought outside the military context. *See, e.g., Acanfora v. Board of Educ.*, 491 F.2d 498 (4th Cir. 1974) (finding for plaintiff on First Amendment right to come out but affirming denial of relief on other grounds); *Aumiller v. University of Delaware*, 434 F. Supp. 1273 (D. Del. 1977) (holding university lecturer could not lose job for media interviews about his homosexuality); *Weaver v. Nebo Sch. Dist.*, 29 F. Supp. 2d 1279 (D. Utah 1998) (holding school district's restriction on teacher's rights to express her sexual orientation outside class impermissibly infringed First Amendment rights). In *Rowland v. Mad River Local School District*, 730 F.2d 444, 450 (6th Cir. 1984), the court held that the school could fire the plaintiff for her statements about her bisexuality. An ambiguous special verdict question did not permit separating her equal protection theory (on which, they said, she was not entitled to protection) from her speech theory: "[I]t is impossible to tell whether the jury found that plaintiff was suspended and transferred merely for being bisexual or for talking about it. All the jury found was that this discipline was imposed for a combination of being bisexual and of making statements to others of her sexual preference." 730 F.2d at 450. *See also Fricke v. Lynch*, 491 F. Supp. 381, 384–86 (D.R.I. 1980) (holding male plaintiff's decision to invite another boy to high school prom had "significant expressive content" for equal rights, thus was First Amendment protected).

The position that being gay is a statement protectable as such has also invalidated recognition of equality rights on the basis of sexual orientation. In two cases, the U.S. Supreme Court held that First Amendment rights of groups seeking to exclude homosexuals prevailed over the equality rights states had protected from antigay discrimination. In *Hurley v. Irish–American Gay, Lesbian, and Bisexual Groups*, 515 U.S. 557 (1995), although the Massachusetts public accommodations law forbidding discrimination on grounds of sexual orientation had been held to require that an Irish–American Day parade include gay and lesbian marchers, the Court held unanimously that their presence altered the speech content of the parade, so violated the First Amendment to enforce by law. Similarly, in *Boy Scouts of America v. Dale*, 120 S.Ct. 2446 (2000), the Court held that New Jersey's guarantee against discrimination because of sexual orientation in public accommodations violated First Amendment "expressive association" rights if applied, as the Supreme Court of New Jersey had, to protect the rights of gay men and boys to be members of the Boy Scouts, 120 S.Ct. at 2449. The Scouts' position that homosexuality is not (as Scouts said they were required to be) "clean" and "morally straight" was a viewpoint the Scouts were entitled to express publicly and privately through their membership rules, the Court held. 120 S.Ct. at 2452–54. "The forced inclusion of an unwanted person in a group infringes the group's freedom of expressive association if the presence of that person affects in a significant way the group's ability to advocate public or private viewpoints." 120 S.Ct. at 2451 (citing *New York State Club Assn. v. City of New York*, 487 U.S. 1, 13 (1988)). In both cases, sexual orientation's expressive dimension was recognized, with the result that its expressive content authorized exclusion on the basis of sexual orientation, over state laws that had required inclusion of gay men and lesbian women without discrimination.

How do you suppose Mr. Dale, a gay Eagle Scout and the plaintiff, feels about having become a position his presence expresses about scouting? Is the *Gay Law Students'* argument that being gay is speech hoist on its own petard? What do you make of the fact that the gay-as-speech argument—what the existence of gay men and lesbian women says—destroyed rights that the nondiscrimination argument—how they are treated—would have protected? Does the absence of a recognized role for Fourteenth Amendment equality in the equality/speech balance have strategic implications? Does the absence of the recognition of gay rights under international law in U.S. courts as well? For further discussion on the intersection between equality and speech issues, see Chapter 10.2.

4. Outcome: The claims of the *Gay Law Students* class were subsequently settled for $5 million and adoption by defendant of an antidiscrimination policy. *See* Arthur S. Leonard, "Protecting 'Openly Gay' Californians," *in Sexuality and the Law* 410, 417 (1993). The California legislature in 1992 amended its Labor Code to provide explicit protection against discrimination based on sexual orientation in all public and private employment, except nonprofit organizations. *See* Cal. Lab. Code § 1102.1 (West Supp. 1999).

The armed forces have provided a distinctively charged site for debate over the status and rights of gay men and lesbians in society. Why? Is it perhaps more because of symbolic place than functions performed? Is the military's role in masculinity part of the answer? Unlike state sodomy laws, the military's exclusions of "homosexuals" have been enforced often. Also unlike state sodomy laws, the military has criminalized a category of people, not only particular acts, making violation easier to prove. An analytically if not practically far-reaching rejection of the military's exclusion of homosexuals was provided by the army's discharge of Perry Watkins for homosexuality. Mr. Watkins, when inducted into the army in 1967, answered "yes" to the question whether he had "homosexual tendencies." *Watkins v. United States Army*, 837 F.2d 1428, 1429 (9th Cir. 1988). He was accepted as qualified then and later became, his commanding officer said, "one of our most respected and trusted soldiers." *Id.* at 1424. His homosexuality was common knowledge; indeed, he told the army about his sexual preference at every required official opportunity. He also performed as a female impersonator in various revues with the permission of his commanding officer. His brilliant soldiering received consistent rave reviews. The army was glad to keep him and continued to accept his reenlistment. *See* Randy Shilts, *Conduct Unbecoming: Lesbians and Gays in the U.S. Military, Vietnam to the Persian Gulf* 63–64, 79, 161–62, 218, 347 (1993). In 1981, the army passed regulations mandating discharge of all homosexuals regardless of merit, *see id.* at 376–80, and a board was convened to consider Mr. Watkins's discharge.

Although lacking evidence that Mr. Watkins engaged in "homosexual acts," the board recommended his separation from the service "because he has stated that he is a homosexual." *Id.* at 348. Mr. Watkins sued to stop his discharge or compel acceptance of his reenlistment, on grounds, among others, that the regulations discriminated on the basis of sexual orientation in denial of equal protection of the laws in violation of the Fifth Amendment. In the opinion excerpted below, a panel of the Ninth Circuit Court of Appeals found that the regulations were pure status discrimination and recognized sexual orientation as a suspect classification for constitutional equality purposes. Many legal proceedings later, *see, e.g., Watkins v. United States Army*, 847 F.2d 1329 (9th Cir. 1988), Mr. Watkins, as an individual, was accepted back into the army on equitable estoppel grounds, since the army had knowingly permitted him to serve for so long. *See Watkins v. United States Army*, 875 F.2d 699 (9th Cir. 1989) (en banc), *cert. denied*, 498 U.S. 957 (1990).

Watkins v. United States Army

United States Court of Appeals for the Ninth Circuit
837 F.2d 1428 (9th Cir. 1988)

■ Norris, J.

Do the Army's regulations discriminate based on sexual orientation? The portion of the Army's reenlistment regulation that bars homosexuals from reenlisting states . . . :

> Applicants to whom the disqualifications below apply are ineligible for RA [Regular Army] reenlistment at any time. . . .
>
> c.   Persons of questionable moral character and a history of antisocial behavior, sexual perversion or homosexuality. A person who has committed homosexual acts or is an admitted homosexual but as to whom there is no evidence that they have engaged in homosexual acts either before or during military service is included. . . .
>
> k.   Persons being discharged under AR 635–200 for homosexuality. . . .
>
> *Note:* Homosexual acts consist of bodily contact between persons of the same sex, actively undertaken or passively permitted, with the intent of obtaining or giving sexual satisfaction, or any proposal, solicitation, or attempt to perform such an act. Persons who have been involved in homosexual acts in an apparently isolated episode, stemming solely from immaturity, curiosity [sic], or intoxication, and in the absence of other evidence that the person is a homosexual, normally will not be excluded from reenlistment. A homosexual is a person, regardless of

sex, who desires bodily contact between persons of the same sex, actively undertaken or passively permitted, with the intent to obtain or give sexual gratification. Any official, private, or public profession of homosexuality, may be considered in determining whether a person is an admitted homosexual. AR 601–280, ¶ 2–21. . . .

[The discharge standards are "essentially the same" as the reenlistment standards.] We conclude that these regulations, on their face, discriminate against homosexuals on the basis of their sexual orientation. Under the regulations any homosexual act or statement of homosexuality gives rise to a presumption of homosexual orientation, and anyone who fails to rebut that presumption is conclusively barred from Army service. In other words, the regulations target homosexual orientation itself. The homosexual acts and statements are merely relevant, and rebuttable, indicators of that orientation.

Under the Army's regulations, "homosexuality," not sexual conduct, is the operative trait for disqualification. For example, the regulations ban homosexuals who have done nothing more than acknowledge their homosexual orientation even in the absence of evidence that the persons ever engaged in any form of sexual conduct. The reenlistment regulation disqualifies any "admitted homosexual"—a status that can be proved by "[a]ny official, private, or public profession of homosexuality" even if "there is no evidence that they have engaged in homosexual acts either before or during military service." Since the regulations define a "homosexual" as "a person, regardless of sex, who *desires* bodily contact between persons of the same sex, actively undertaken or passively permitted, with the intent to obtain or give sexual gratification," a person can be deemed homosexual under the regulations without ever engaging in a homosexual act. Thus, no matter what statements a person has made, the ultimate evidentiary issue is whether he or she has a homosexual orientation. Under the reenlistment regulation, persons are disqualified from reenlisting only if, based on any "profession of homosexuality" they have made, they are found to have a homosexual orientation. Similarly, under the discharge regulation a soldier must be discharged if "[t]he soldier has stated that he or she is a homosexual or bisexual, *unless* there is a further finding that the soldier is not a homosexual or bisexual." In short, the regulations do not penalize all statements of sexual desire, or even only statements of homosexual desire; they penalize only homosexuals who declare their homosexual orientation.

True, a "person who has committed homosexual acts" is also presumptively "included" under the reenlistment regulation as a person excludable for "homosexuality." But it is clear that this provision is merely designed to round out the possible evidentiary grounds for inferring a homosexual orientation. . . . [T]he regulations barring homosexuals from the Army cover any form of bodily contact between persons of the same sex that gives sexual satisfaction—from oral and anal intercourse to holding hands, kissing, caressing and any number of other sexual acts. Indeed, in this case the Army tried to prove at Watkins' discharge proceedings that he had committed a homosexual act described as squeezing the knee of a male soldier, but failed to prove it was Watkins who did the alleged knee-squeezing. Moreover, even non-sexual conduct can trigger a presumption of homosexuality: The regulations provide for the discharge of soldiers who have "married or attempted to marry a person known to be of the same sex . . . *unless* there are further findings that the soldier is not a homosexual or bisexual." With all the acts and statements that can serve as presumptive evidence of homosexuality under the regulations, it is hard to think of any grounds for inferring homosexual orientation that are *not* included. The fact remains, however, that homosexual orientation, not homosexual conduct, is plainly the object of the Army's regulations.

Moreover, under the regulations a person is not automatically disqualified from Army service just because he or she committed a homosexual act. Persons may still qualify for the Army despite their homosexual conduct if they prove to the satisfaction of Army officials that their *orientation* is heterosexual rather than homosexual. To illustrate, the discharge regulation provides that a soldier who engages in homosexual acts can escape discharge if he can show that the conduct was "a departure from the soldier's usual and customary behavior" that "is unlikely to recur because it is shown, for example, that the act occurred because of immaturity, intoxication, coercion, or a desire to avoid military service" *and* that the "soldier does not desire to engage in or intend to engage in homosexual acts." The regulation expressly states, "The intent of this policy is to permit retention *only* of *nonhomosexual* soldiers who, because of extenuating circumstances engaged in, attempted to engage in, or solicited a homosexual act." ... [Under the regulations i]f a straight soldier and a gay soldier of the same sex engage in homosexual acts because they are drunk, immature or curious, the straight soldier may remain in the Army while the gay soldier is automatically terminated. In short, the regulations do not penalize soldiers for engaging in homosexual acts; they penalize soldiers who have engaged in homosexual acts only when the Army decides that those soldiers are actually gay.

In sum, the discrimination against homosexual orientation under these regulations is about as complete as one could imagine. The regulations make any act or statement that might conceivably indicate a homosexual orientation evidence of homosexuality; that evidence is in turn weighed against any evidence of a heterosexual orientation. It is thus clear in answer to our threshold equal protection inquiry that the regulations directly burden the class consisting of persons of homosexual orientation....

[Bowers v. Hardwick does not foreclose Watkins's equal protection challenge to the Army's regulations, as the Army has argued it does. Its concerns about substantive due process, and specifically the right to privacy,] have little relevance to equal protection doctrine.... [Hardwick does not approve discrimination against homosexuals.] ... Hardwick held only that the constitutionally protected right to privacy does not extend to homosexual sodomy. But we see no principled way to transmogrify the Court's holding that the state may criminalize specific sexual conduct commonly engaged in by homosexuals into a state license to pass "homosexual laws"—laws imposing special restrictions on gays because they are gay.... In sum, we conclude that no federal appellate court has decided the critical issue raised by Watkins' claim: whether persons of homosexual orientation constitute a suspect class under equal protection doctrine....

We now address the merits of Watkins' claim that we must subject the Army's regulations to strict scrutiny because homosexuals constitute a suspect class under equal protection jurisprudence. The Supreme Court has identified several factors that guide our suspect class inquiry.

The first factor the Supreme Court generally considers is whether the group at issue has suffered a history of purposeful discrimination. As the Army concedes, it is indisputable that "homosexuals have historically been the object of pernicious and sustained hostility." Rowland v. Mad River Local School Dist., 470 U.S. 1009, 1014 (1985) (Brennan, J., dissenting from denial of cert.). More recently, Judge Henderson echoed the same harsh truth: "Lesbians and gays have been the object of some of the deepest prejudice and hatred in American society." High Tech Gays v. Defense Industrial Security Clearance Office, 668 F. Supp. 1361 (N.D. Cal. 1987) (invalidating Defense Department practice of subjecting gay security clearance applicants to more exacting scrutiny than heterosexual applicants). Homosexuals have been the frequent victims of violence and have been excluded from jobs, schools, housing, churches, and even families. In any case, the discrimination faced by homosexuals in our society is plainly no less pernicious or intense than the discrimination faced by other groups already treated as suspect classes, such as aliens or people of a particular national origin.

The second factor that the Supreme Court considers in suspect class analysis is . . . whether the discrimination embodies a gross unfairness that is sufficiently inconsistent with the ideals of equal protection to term it invidious. . . . In giving content to this concept . . ., the Court has considered (1) whether the disadvantaged class is defined by a trait that "frequently bears no relation to ability to perform or contribute to society," [Frontiero]; (2) whether the class has been saddled with unique disabilities because of prejudice or inaccurate stereotypes; and (3) whether the trait defining the class is immutable. . . . Sexual orientation plainly has no relevance to a person's "ability to perform or contribute to society." Indeed, the Army makes no claim that homosexuality impairs a person's ability to perform military duties. Sergeant Watkins' exemplary record of military service stands as a testament to quite the opposite. Moreover, as the Army itself concluded, there is not a scintilla of evidence that Watkins' avowed homosexuality "had either a degrading effect upon unit performance, morale or discipline, or upon his own job performance."

This irrelevance of sexual orientation to the quality of a person's contribution to society also suggests that classifications based on sexual orientation reflect prejudice and inaccurate stereotypes. . . . We agree with Justice Brennan that "discrimination against homosexuals is 'likely . . . to reflect deep-seated prejudice rather than . . . rationality.' " Rowland, 470 U.S. at 1014. The Army does not dispute the hard fact that homosexuals face enormous prejudice. Nor could it, for the Army justifies its regulations in part by asserting that straight soldiers despise and lack respect for homosexuals and that popular prejudice against homosexuals is so pervasive that their presence in the Army will discourage enlistment and tarnish the Army's public image. Instead, the Army suggests that the public opprobrium directed towards gays does not constitute prejudice in the pejorative sense of the word, but rather represents appropriate public disapproval of persons who engage in immoral behavior. The Army equates homosexuals with sodomists and justifies its regulations as simply reflecting a rational bias against a class of persons who engage in criminal acts of sodomy. In essence, the Army argues that homosexuals, like burglars, cannot form a suspect class because they are criminals.

The Army's argument . . . rests on two false premises. First, the class burdened by the regulations is defined by the sexual *orientation* of its members, not by their sexual conduct. To our knowledge, homosexual orientation itself has never been criminalized in this country. Moreover, any attempt to criminalize the status of an individual's sexual orientation would present grave constitutional problems. Second, little of the homosexual *conduct* covered by the regulations is criminal. The regulations reach many forms of homosexual conduct other than sodomy such as kissing, handholding, caressing, and hand-genital contact. Yet, sodomy is the only consensual adult sexual conduct that Congress has criminalized, 10 U.S.C. § 925. Indeed, the Army points to no law, federal or state, which criminalizes any form of private consensual homosexual behavior other than sodomy. The Army's argument that its regulations legitimately discriminate solely against criminals might be relevant if the class at issue were limited to sodomists. But the class banned from Army service is not composed of sodomists, or even of homosexual sodomists; the class is composed of persons of homosexual orientation whether or not they have engaged in sodomy. . . .

[T]he Army has no proof that Watkins has ever engaged in any act of sodomy—homosexual or heterosexual. Nonetheless, the regulations mandated his discharge and the denial of his reenlistment application.

Finally [as to immutability, t]he Supreme Court has never held that only classes with immutable traits can be deemed suspect.... Although the Supreme Court considers immutability relevant, it is clear that by "immutability" the Court has never meant strict immutability in the sense that members of the class must be physically unable to change or mask the trait defining their class. People can have operations to change their sex. Aliens can ordinarily become naturalized citizens. The status of illegitimate children can be changed. People can frequently hide their national origin by changing their customs, their names, or their associations. Lighter skinned blacks can sometimes "pass" for white, as can Latinos for Anglos, and some people can even change their racial appearance with pigment injections. See J. Griffin, Black Like Me (1977). At a minimum, then, the Supreme Court is willing to treat a trait as effectively immutable if changing it would involve great difficulty, such as requiring a major physical change or a traumatic change of identity. Reading the case law in a more capacious manner, "immutability" may describe those traits that are so central to a person's identity that it would be abhorrent for government to penalize a person for refusing to change them, regardless of how easy that change might be physically. Racial discrimination, for example, would not suddenly become constitutional if medical science developed an easy, cheap, and painless method of changing one's skin pigment....

[W]e have no trouble concluding that sexual orientation is immutable for the purposes of equal protection doctrine. Although the causes of homosexuality are not fully understood, scientific research indicates that we have little control over our sexual orientation and that, once acquired, our sexual orientation is largely impervious to change.... Scientific proof aside, it seems appropriate to ask whether heterosexuals feel capable of changing *their* sexual orientation. Would heterosexuals living in a city that passed an ordinance banning those who engaged in or desired to engage in sex with persons of the *opposite* sex find it easy not only to abstain from heterosexual activity but also to shift the object of their sexual desires to persons of the same sex? It may be that some heterosexuals and homosexuals can change their sexual orientation through extensive therapy, neurosurgery or shock treatment. But the possibility of such a difficult and traumatic change does not make sexual orientation "mutable" for equal protection purposes. To express the same idea under the alternative formulation, we conclude that allowing the government to penalize the failure to change such a central aspect of individual and group identity would be abhorrent to the values animating the constitutional ideal of equal protection of the laws.

The final factor the Supreme Court considers in suspect class analysis is whether the group burdened by official discrimination lacks the political power necessary to obtain redress from the political branches of government.... In evaluating whether a class is politically underrepresented, the Supreme Court has focused on whether the class is a "discrete and insular minority." United States v. Carolene Products, 304 U.S. 144, 152–53 (1938). The Court has held, for example, that old age does not define a discrete and insular group because "it marks a stage that each of us will reach if we live out our normal span." Massachusetts Bd. of Retirement v. Murgia, 427 U.S. 307, 313 (1976). By contrast, most of us are not likely to identify ourselves as homosexual at any time in our lives. Thus, many of us, including many elected officials, are likely to have difficulty understanding or empathizing with homosexuals. Most people have little exposure to gays, both because they rarely encounter gays and because the gays they do encounter may feel compelled to conceal their sexual orientation. In fact, the social, economic, and political pressures to conceal one's homosexuality commonly deter many gays from openly advocating pro-homosexual legislation, thus intensifying their inability to make effective use of the political process. "Because of the immediate and severe opprobrium often manifested against homosexuals once so identified publicly, members of this group are particularly powerless to pursue their rights openly in the political arena." Rowland, 470 U.S. at 1014.

Even when gays overcome this prejudice enough to participate openly in politics, the general animus towards homosexuality may render this partic-ipation wholly ineffective. Elected officials sensitive to public prejudice may refuse to support legislation that even appears to condone homosexuality. Indeed, the Army itself argues that its regulations are justified by the need to "maintain the public acceptability of military service," AR 635–200, ¶ 15–2(a), because "toleration of homosexual conduct ... might be understood as tacit approval" and "the existence of homosexual units might well be a source of ridicule and notoriety." These barriers to political power are underscored by the underrepresentation of avowed homosexuals in the decisionmaking bodies of government and the inability of homosexuals to prevent legislation hostile to their group interests.

[O]ur analysis of the relevant factors in determining whether a given group should be considered a suspect class for the purposes of equal protection doctrine [with the principles that gave rise to these factors in the first place] ineluctably leads us to the conclusion that homosexuals constitute such a suspect class. . . .

[Subjected to strict scrutiny, the Army's regulations must be necessary to promote a compelling governmental interest. Many of the Army's justifications illegitimately cater to private biases. The Army cannot justify] its ban on homosexuals on the ground that private prejudice against homosexuals would somehow undermine the strength of our armed forces if homosexuals were permitted to serve. [Nor can majoritarian morality justify laws that discrimi-nate against suspect classes.] Laws that limit the acceptable focus of one's sexual desires to members of the opposite sex, like laws that limit one's choice of spouse (or sexual partner) to members of the same race [Loving v. Virginia], cannot withstand constitutional scrutiny absent a compelling governmental justification. . . .

[The remaining justifications offered bear little relation to the regulations, such as] the Army's professed concern with breaches of security. . . . [H]omo-sexuality poses a special risk of blackmail only if a homosexual is secretive about his or her sexual orientation. The Army regulations do nothing to lessen this problem. . . . The Army's concern about security risks among gays could be addressed [better] by adopting a regulation banning only those gays who [unlike Watkins] had lied about or failed to admit their sexual orientation. In that way, the Army would *encourage*, rather than discourage, declarations of homosexuality, thereby reducing the number of closet homosexuals who might indeed pose a security risk. . . . [The regulations are void on their face. The Army is ordered] to consider Watkins' reenlistment application without regard to his sexual orientation.

■ Reinhardt, J., dissenting

With great reluctance, I have concluded that I am unable to concur in the majority opinion. . . . Because Hardwick did not challenge the Georgia sodomy statute under the Equal Protection Clause, and neither party presented that issue in its briefs or at oral argument, the Court limited its holding to due process. . . . However, the fact that Hardwick does not address the equal protection question directly does not mean that the case is not of substantial significance to such an inquiry.... The answer to the meaning of Hardwick is not difficult to find. There are only two choices: either Hardwick is about "sodomy," and heterosexual sodomy is as constitutionally unprotected as homosexual sodomy, or it is about "homosexuality," and there are some acts which are protected if done by heterosexuals but not if done by homosexuals.... In my opinion, Hardwick must be read as standing precisely for the proposition the majority rejects. To put it simply, I believe that after Hardwick the government may outlaw homosexual sodomy even though it fails to regulate the private conduct of heterosexuals.... The anti-homosexual thrust of Hardwick, and the Court's willingness to condone anti-homosexual animus in the actions of the government, are clear.... The majority opinion concludes that under the criteria established by equal protection case law, homosexuals must be treated as a suspect class. Were it not for Hardwick, I would agree, for in my opinion the group meets all the applicable criteria. However, after Hardwick, we are not longer free to reach that conclusion.

NOTES AND QUESTIONS ON *WATKINS v. ARMY*

1. Act versus status:

1.1 Is sexuality who one is, or what one does, or what one wants to do? What does the army regulation at issue in this case define it as? Can you separate who you "are" sexually, or who you think of yourself as "being" sexually, from what you "do" sexually, or what you feel you would like to do? Can you, in other words, separate your sexual identity from your sexual practices and feelings? Does a law that makes that division make any sense in life?

Judge Norris's determination that homosexuality, under the army regulations at issue, is a status, not an act, is the basis for his ruling that the regulations discriminate against homosexuals on the basis of who they are, not what they do. Under Judge Norris's defense of their presence, are gay soldiers allowed to be in the military only on sufferance of being nonpracticing? Impliedly, must gays be celibate while heterosexuals can have sex? Does such a standard satisfy the guarantee of equal protection of the laws?

1.2 Under the army's rules at the time of *Watkins*, how many times do you suppose one can be curious, how old is no longer young, and how often is drunkenness an excuse, do you suppose, before a straight person becomes a gay person through what they do—in other words, before acts define status? How many heterosexual acts might it take to outweigh those acts? (This could keep one quite busy.)

1.3 Would the army's regulations be improved if any same-sex sexual *act* resulted in disqualification from service, while status was irrelevant? Could Judge Norris's approach address such a rule? Why is sexual orientation seen as an aspect of "moral character," as status-based definitions would have it? What, in real life, transforms the adjectives "lesbian" and "gay" into nouns for purposes of legal classification? Do you have any reservations about the validity of the noun form "lesbian" or "gay," or "homosexual"—or "straight," or "heterosexual," or "bisexual" for that matter—coupled with the existential verb "is" in this setting? Compare the definition of "homosexual" in the policy adjudicated in *Watkins* with the "Don't Ask, Don't Tell" policy that replaced it. How different are they?

1.4 What, really, is "a homosexual act"? Is a hug and a kiss between two women or two men "a homosexual act" where a hug and a kiss between a man and a woman is not? Does the answer depend on whether one or both in the same-sex case otherwise "is" lesbian or gay? What if the two are former lovers, one of whom is now sexual with a partner of the other sex? Does the sexual orientation of an act vary with the gender of those who engage in it?

2. *Hardwick*: Who has the better reading of *Hardwick*, Judge Norris or Judge Reinhardt? Does resting his invalidation of the army's rule on status help Judge Norris distinguish *Bowers v. Hardwick*? Or is *Hardwick* exactly the equal protection violation Judge Norris says it is not: a ruling that permits the law, facially and as applied, to prohibit "homosexual sodomy," meaning sodomy as and when engaged in by homosexuals only? Does *Hardwick* precisely permit sodomy to be a crime only for persons of the same sex? Does the army's definition do precisely the same thing?

Reconsider whether a rule like that in *Watkins* could be legal under substantive due process standards but violate the Equal Protection Clause. Does the army's pointing to criminal laws against sodomy as a basis for their rules excluding homosexuals from the service show the error of Justice Powell's apparent belief that sodomy laws, as largely unenforced, are harmless? What does substantive due process privacy have to do with equality? Could the Supreme Court have made a decision under one clause that violates the rights of people under another? If *Hardwick* had been a lower court decision, could it be appealed to the U.S. Supreme Court as a violation of the guarantee of equal protection of the laws?

3. Immutability: Judge Norris defines "immutable" not as preexisting in nature but as a stable and deep feature of the self that is worthy of constitutional regard.

3.1 Some cases have suggested that sexual orientation cannot be a suspect classification because sexual orientation is mutable.[31] What is the "immutability" criterion about in equality law in general? Does it have anything to do with the sameness/difference model? Are shades of *Plessy* discernible in immutability's place in equality discourse? Does an immutability requirement essentialize dominance, suggesting that social hierarchy is biologically based? If women could readily become men, would that make discrimination against women who declined the honor constitutionally acceptable?

3.2 Applying an immutability requirement to sexual orientation tends to force a choice between seeing sexuality as either immutable, meaning inborn and unchosen, such that people are incapable of making choices about who they have sex or make love with, or mutable, meaning capable of being embraced or discarded like consumer goods with alternate brand

31. *See, e.g., Woodward v. United States*, 871 F.2d 1068, 1076 (Fed. Cir. 1989) ("Homosexuality, as a definitive trait, differs fundamentally from those defining any of the suspect or quasi-suspect classes. [Suspect classes] exhibit immutable characteristics, whereas homosexuality is primarily behavioral in nature"); *Hrynda v. U.S.*, 933 F. Supp. 1047, 1053 (M.D. Fla. 1996); *see also Steffan v. Cheney*, 780 F. Supp. 1, 6 & n.12 (D.D.C. 1991) ("The Court is, however, convinced that homosexual orientation is neither conclusively mutable nor immutable since the scientific community is still quite at sea on the causes of homosexuality, its permanence, its prevalence, and its definition.... Without a definitive answer at hand, yet confident that some people exercise some choice in their own sexual orientation, the Court does not regard homosexuality as being an immutable characteristic"), *aff'd sub nom Steffan v. Perry* 41 F.3d 677 (D.C. Cir. 1994) (en banc) (rejecting suggestion that homosexuals are suspect class without discussing immutability).

names. Is sexuality either? Does the immutability criterion conventionally suggest that since you can't do anything to change who you are, the government will protect you from mistreatment for it? Is this insulting? Why is the focus on who one "is," and whether that is subject to change, rather than on being discriminated against for who one is or is thought to be? Does an immutability requirement (assuming arguendo that it is required, which is dubious) suggest that the problem of discrimination originates with the groups who are discriminated against, rather than with those who discriminate against them? Is gender immutable in the conventional sense? Transgendered people change theirs. Is sex immutable? Transsexuals change theirs. Does this make sex or gender "mutable"? Intersexed people are not necessarily male or female. *See* Alice Domurat Dreger, *Hermaphrodites and the Medical Invention of Sex* (1998); *Intersex in the Age of Ethics* (Alice Domurat Dreger ed., 1999); Cheryl Chase, "Hermaphrodites with Attitude: Mapping the Emergence of Intersex Political Activism," 4 *GLO* 189 (1998). If sex is capable of this ambiguity on the biological level, does it have the fixity some "immutability" models require? Unknown numbers of people, this literature shows, have been subjected, often without their knowledge or consent, to "normalizing" surgical procedures. Is the "immutability" of sex a social judgment in the guise of a biological fact? Does Judge Norris's socially based definition of mutability address these issues? To what extent does Judge Norris's rendition of immutability recognize being gay or lesbian as a practice, a position and identification, rather than an essence? For further discussion, see Janet Halley, "Sexual Orientation and the Politics of Biology: A Critique of the Argument from Immutability," 46 *Stan. L. Rev.* 503 (1994).

3.3   Does Judge Norris treat homosexuals more or less on the racial model—in effect substituting sexuality for color, as if sexual orientation were an ethnicity? Fernando J. Gutierrez, "Gay and Lesbian: An Ethnic Identity Deserving Equal Protection," 4 *Law & Sexuality* 195 (1994), has argued that sexuality is an ethnicity. Ethnic discrimination has been held prohibited by the laws against racial discrimination. *See Saint Francis College v. Al–Khazraji*, 481 U.S. 604 (1987) and *Shaare Tefila Congregation v. Cobb*, 481 U.S. 615 (1987) (so holding in case regarding discrimination against Arabs and Jews). Evaluate this concept.

3.4   Does the *Watkins* definition of immutability apply to bisexuals? Is heterosexuality immutable by the *Watkins* definition? If so, what makes it so, nature or privilege? Does its immutability, supposed or actual, have anything to do with gender status?

3.5   Compare the treatment of immutability in *Watkins* with that in *Andrews*. Compare the two approaches to category-construction in equality law more generally. Does *Andrews* privilege immutability in the creation of grounds it will recognize as analogous to the enumerated grounds? Does its opposition to disadvantage see social categories as intrinsically historically contingent and subject to change? Does the *Andrews* Court see disadvantaged groups as constructed in society and by history, or as presocial and metahistorical? Does it see that categories, hence grounds themselves, are an ideological construct of inequality, if nonetheless socially real? Does it reify or deconstruct categories? Would it be likely to recognize that compulsory heterosexuality constructs the category "homosexual" as an unequal group—indeed as a group at all? To what degree is a dominance analysis an advance over *Andrews* in this respect?

3.6 If cross-sex identification were to become possible, would it be because the feminine is no longer the devalued term—perhaps because its contents are no longer rigid nor prescribed, are not attached to or seen as fixed in the biology of sex, and are no longer invitations to, consequences of, or flags for powerlessness and victimization? If, in other words, gender roles no longer meant what they mean, to what degree might the (to Judge Norris unacceptable) personal cost of changing sexual orientation disappear?

4. Military masculinity: Judge Norris does not address *why* the bigotry and systemic disadvantage that he documents against homosexuals exists in the military. Might the answer lie with male dominance? Professor Kenneth Karst argues that the military's historic segregation of African American men, combined with its expulsion of gay men and lesbian women and its exclusion of women from combat, derive from a common "cult of masculinity" of the male warrior:

> For those who want to keep the public's gaze fixed on "the manliness of war," the tensions of male bonding demand a clear expression of the services' rejection of homosexuality. This expression is not just a by-product of the policy that purports to exclude gay men and lesbians from the armed forces; it is the policy's main function. When a gay soldier comes to the Army's official attention, the real threat is not a hindrance of day-to-day operations, but rather the tarnishing of the Army's traditionally masculine image. Kenneth L. Karst, "The Pursuit of Manhood and the Desegregation of the Armed Forces," 38 *UCLA L. Rev.* 499, 545–46 (1991).

Do you think this is right? Does expulsion of lesbian women preserve the military's "cult of masculinity"? What concretely is the army afraid of, should its image include a recognition of the reality of the gay and lesbian soldiers who are already there? Does its fear help explain the considerable sex segregation of the armed forces?

5. Social attitudes: Is the rigidity of the military hierarchy and the notion of following orders a particular problem in accommodating acknowledged same-sex sexuality? A German case holding that gay soldiers were not denied equality when not permitted to be officers reasons that many actions of a gay soldier might be taken as problematic that would be seen as normal if done by a heterosexual officer. *See* BVERWG 86, 355, NVwZ–RR 1998 at 244. (Wehrdienstsenat, 18.11.1997). Can you imagine what such acts might be? *See also* BVerfGE, 389, 421–22 (1957) (finding that heterosexuals and homosexuals are different in nature, not similarly situated and not factually comparable, so the equality clauses of the constitution do not apply). Is the young age of recruits relevant? (The German court thought that young soldiers could not be expected to be tolerant.) Is facing death? Can you see how each of these factors could be argued the other way? Should social prejudice be permitted to overcome equality assertions under the auspices of the military, because it is military? Is the military a culture? Should prejudice be presumed to exist, to predominate, and to be unchangeable? Is there something militarily wrong with an army of lovers?

Sharper focus on the military's fears, and its view of the interactive role of homosexual "desire" and sex acts in defining the group and the ground, was achieved in litigation over Joe Steffan's discharge from the Naval Academy six weeks short of graduation for telling the commandant, on direct inquiry, that he is gay. Chief Judge Mikva wrote for a panel of the D.C. Circuit an opinion that was rapidly overturned, *see Steffan v. Perry*, 41 F.3d 677 (D.C. Cir. 1994) (en banc), holding that there was no rational basis for the navy's directives under which Mr. Steffan was removed.

Steffan v. Aspin

United States Court of Appeals for the District of Columbia Circuit
8 F.3d 57 (D.C. Cir. 1993)

■ MIKVA, CHIEF JUDGE.

There is no "military exception" to the Constitution.... This Court has only had occasion to rule on the suspect status of homosexuals as defined by homosexual *conduct*. Padula v. Webster, 822 F.2d 97 (D.C. Cir. 1987); Dronenburg v. Zech, 741 F.2d 1388 (D.C. Cir. 1984). In that context, we have noted the anomaly of according special protection to a class whose defining characteristic, homosexual conduct, can be made illegal. Padula, 822 F.2d at 103 (citing Bowers v. Hardwick). This is a different case: the class at issue is defined by homosexual *orientation*, not conduct. The Secretary does not allege that Mr. Steffan ever engaged in homosexual conduct.... Whether an agency of the federal government can discriminate against individuals merely because of sexual orientation [is an] open question that we must begin to answer today in deciding ... whether Mr. Steffan's unequal treatment was rationally related to a legitimate military purpose....

According to the Secretary ..., the primary purpose of the regulations is to exclude from the military those individuals who have a propensity to engage in unlawful conduct. The Directives define "homosexual" as "a person ... who engages in, desires to engage in, or intends to engage in homosexual acts." DOD Directives § H.1.b(1).[32] ... By excluding [servicemembers on this basis,] the military claims it is excluding those with a "propensity" to engage in forbidden conduct, and it is that conduct—and not merely a person's orientation—that has a deleterious effect upon the morale of the armed forces.... [Mr. Steffan's] superiors never asserted that Mr. Steffan had engaged in homosexual conduct, and he never admitted to any. On its face, therefore, his discharge seems unrelated to any conduct—his statement revealed nothing more than a sexual orientation. But the Secretary argues that even if Mr. Steffan had a "homosexual orientation" he could have rebutted the presumption that he was a "homosexual" by showing that he did not "engage[ ] in, desire[ ] to engage in, or intend[ ] to engage in homosexual acts." To explain how this might be, counsel for the Secretary attempted at oral argument to draw a distinction between "attraction" and "desire." A person might be attracted to members of the same sex, and thus have a "homosexual orientation," yet that person might not "desire" to engage in homosexual conduct. Counsel for the Secretary described individuals fitting this description as "celibate homosexuals." ... Evidently, the Navy believes that the difference between "attraction" and "desire" determines whether a servicemember has a propensity to engage in misconduct, and it is only this misconduct, and not the mere presence of persons of homosexual orientation, that the Navy fears.... Even accepting the existence of the "celibate homosexual" defense, the Directives as a whole are far more concerned with status—with thoughts and

---

32. Under the regulation then in effect, "[a] homosexual act means bodily contact, actively undertaken or passively permitted, between members of the same sex for the purpose of satisfying sexual desires." 32 C.F.R. 41, App. A H.1.b.(3); DOD Directives 1332.14, E3.A4.1.2.4.1.

desires—than with conduct. And ... a presumption of misconduct based solely on status is insupportable even under rationality review....

As a factual matter [the proposition that] a person who "desires" to engage in misconduct will do so—is hardly self-evident. Many of us "desire" in the abstract to do things and yet refrain from doing them simply because they are against the rules. Nonetheless, under rationality review, the Secretary need not show a perfect means-ends fit, but only a reasonable relation between the means (excluding persons of homosexual orientation) and the end (preventing homosexual conduct). But there is no such rational relation here.... [T]he Secretary's justification for the gay ban presumes that a certain class of persons will break the law or the rules solely because of their thoughts and desires. This is inherently unreasonable.... A person's status alone, whether determined by his thoughts or by his membership in a certain group, is an inadequate basis upon which to impute misconduct. Accordingly, we find that the Secretary's "propensity" argument, which presumes that "desire" will lead to misconduct, is illegitimate as a matter of law. It cannot provide a rational basis for the DOD Directives....

The Secretary apparently also fears the impact that the mere presence of persons of homosexual orientation will have on ... vital military interests. The Directives state, in part:

> The *presence* in the military environment of persons who ... by their statements, demonstrate a propensity to engage in homosexual conduct, seriously impairs the accomplishment of the military mission. The *presence* of such members adversely affects the ability of the Military Services to maintain discipline, good order, and morale; ... [and] to recruit and retain members of the Military Services.... DOD Directives § H.1.a...

[T]he Secretary fears that ... grievous consequences will arise because heterosexual soldiers will be appalled at the requirement that they serve alongside homosexuals.... [T]hese fears are patently insufficient to justify a discriminatory policy, even under rationality review, because each depends solely upon the prejudice of third parties.... Forcing them to serve with homosexuals[, it is contended,] will lower their morale, impair their discipline, and discourage them from enlisting. Similar objections were voiced by opponents of President Truman's 1948 executive order requiring racial integration of the armed forces.... But a cardinal principle of equal protection law holds that the government cannot discriminate against a certain class in order to give effect to the prejudice of others. Even if the government does not itself act out of prejudice, it cannot discriminate in an effort to avoid the effects of others' prejudice. Such discrimination plays directly into the hands of the bigots; it ratifies and encourages their prejudice....

The Secretary also argues, and the Directives state, that the presence of homosexuals in the military will invade the privacy of heterosexual servicemen. DOD Directives § H.1.a (presence of homosexuals impairs military's ability "to facilitate assignment and worldwide deployment of servicemembers who frequently must live and work under close conditions affording minimal privacy"). This argument can mean one of two things: either (1) that homosexual servicemembers will ogle and stare at their heterosexual counterparts in the shower or other close quarters; or (2) that heterosexuals will fear such staring and feel an invasion of privacy. The argument that homosexuals will stare is very similar to the argument that they will engage in homosexual acts. Again, it equates thoughts and desires with propensity to engage in misconduct. The argument that heterosexuals will fear such staring is, in turn, a version of the argument that government should be allowed to give effect to the irrational fears and stereotypes of third parties....

The DOD Directives, the military regulations in effect when the Navy compelled Joseph Steffan to resign solely because he admitted his homosexual orientation, are not rationally related to any legitimate goal.... The constitutional requirement of equal protection forbids the government to disadvantage a class based solely upon irrational prejudice, whatever the standard of review.... America's hallmark has been to judge people by what they do, and not by who they are.

NOTES AND QUESTIONS ON *STEFFAN*

1.   The problem with acts: The D.C. Circuit, reversing the panel and upholding Mr. Steffan's exclusion en banc, stated that "removing from the military all those who admit to being homosexual furthers the military's concededly legitimate purpose of excluding from service those who engage in homosexual conduct." *Steffan*, 41 F.3d at 677, 687. Why is excluding those who engage in homosexual conduct a legitimate purpose as opposed to a blatantly discriminatory one? Can it withstand rational basis review? Is the military's problem in this connection related to its problem with excluding women from combat or the draft? Its former exclusion of women from military academies? What about same-sex sexual acts is inconsistent with the image or reality of being a good soldier, with which heterosexual acts are consistent? What about being a good soldier and being a practicing heterosexual go together? Chief Judge Mikva's opinion does not need to address this question, because it finds that the rules under which Mr. Steffan was discharged, as well as his discharge itself, turned on pure status, not conduct. But are the two ultimately as separable as the panel opinion says they are? Why don't gay men and lesbian women have as much right to sexual expression, meaning noncelibate sexuality, consistent with military service as anyone else?

2.   Spectral safety: What, precisely, is the injury of the dreaded look in the shower? Does it rise to the level of national security? The prospect of having the gaze reversed, such that heterosexual men are visually objectified by men, is clearly experienced as unsettling and violating by some. What do the men feel vulnerable to? Are they seeking "protection" under the military's rules in the sense that word is sometimes used to describe what women seek from law? Can you think of other settings in which a right not to be looked at in a sexual way might be asserted? Compare them. Does privacy law guarantee this right? Professor Kendall Thomas argues that male heterosexuality is constituted when men reject imagining themselves as objects of male sexual desire—the military's shower and closet providing the opportunity both for the imagining and its rejection. *See* Kendall Thomas, "Shower/Closet," 20 *Assemblage* 80–81 (1993). Evaluate his analysis. Why might some men resist and resent seeing themselves as objects of sexual desire by other men? What does it mean for women if men feel that their human status is at stake in being looked at the way men look at women?

3.   Animus: Similar to the military's arguments in *Steffan* and other cases, General Colin Powell, noting in support of the "Don't Ask, Don't Tell" policy that the military has "successfully mixed over the years blacks and whites, rich and poor, urban and rural," said that the military hierarchy believes, "considering where our society is right now and what is best for military effectiveness and for the force," that "open homosexuality ... is something quite different than the acceptance of benign characteristics such as color or race or background" in that it involves "matters of privacy and human sexuality that, in our judgment, if allowed to openly exist within the force, will create serious issues having to do with cohesion and having to do with the well-being of the force." Assessment of the Plan to Lift the Ban on Homosexuals in the Military: Hearings Before the Military Forces and Personnel Subcomm. of the Comm. on Armed Servs., House of Representatives, 103d Cong. 32 (1994) (testimony of Gen. Colin Powell, Chairman, Joint Chiefs of Staff). Women were not mentioned on the list of successful mixings. Do you see prejudice in the military's rules? in this justification for them?

One result of the enforced invisibility of lesbian women and gay men has been their relative lack of political power as a group. Colorado tried to foreclose their assertion of rights by passing Amendment 2, a statewide referendum to amend the state constitution that preemptively invalidated all legislative, executive, or judicial action at any level of state or local government designed to prohibit discrimination on the basis of "homosexual, lesbian or bisexual orientation, conduct, practices or relationships." Colo. Const. art. II, § 30b. In an action against the state by homosexual citizens, the U.S. Supreme Court concluded that Amendment 2 violated the Equal Protection Clause. Making it illegal for a class of people to get legal protection was termed unprecedented and found to deny equal protection of the laws in the most literal sense. The Court also inferred, given the incoherence of Colorado's defense, that Amendment 2 was born of animosity toward the class it affected. Lacking a legitimate purpose, Amendment 2 was found to be an impermissible status-based classification of persons for its own sake.

Romer v. Evans

Supreme Court of the United States
517 U.S. 620 (1996)

■ Justice Kennedy delivered the opinion of the Court.

One century ago, the first Justice Harlan admonished this Court that the Constitution "neither knows nor tolerates classes among citizens." *Plessy v. Ferguson*, 163 U.S. 537, 559 (1896) (dissenting opinion). Unheeded then, those words now are understood to state a commitment to the law's neutrality where the rights of persons are at stake. The Equal Protection Clause enforces this principle and today requires us to hold invalid a provision of Colorado's Constitution.... Amendment 2 ... has the peculiar property of imposing a broad and undifferentiated disability on a single named group, an exceptional and ... invalid form of legislation. Second, its sheer breadth is so discontinuous with the reasons offered for it that the amendment seems inexplicable by anything but animus toward the class that it affects; it lacks a rational relationship to legitimate state interests.

Taking the first point, even in the ordinary equal protection case calling for the most deferential of standards, we insist on knowing the relation between the classification adopted and the object to be attained.... In the ordinary case, a law will be sustained if it can be said to advance a legitimate government interest, even if the law seems unwise or works to the disadvantage of a particular group, or if the rationale for it seems tenuous.... By requiring that the classification bear a rational relationship to an independent and legitimate legislative end, we ensure that classifications are not drawn for the purpose of disadvantaging the group burdened by the law.

Amendment 2 confounds this normal process of judicial review. It is at once too narrow and too broad. It identifies persons by a single trait and then denies them protection across the board. The resulting disqualification of a class of persons from the right to seek specific protection from the law is unprecedented in our jurisprudence. The absence of precedent for Amendment 2 is itself instructive.... It is not within our constitutional tradition to enact laws of this sort. Central both to the idea of the rule of law and to our own Constitution's guarantee of equal protection is the principle that government and each of its parts remain open on impartial terms to all who seek its assistance. " 'Equal protection of the laws is not achieved through indiscriminate imposition of inequalities.' " Sweatt v. Painter, 339 U.S. 629, 635 (1950) (quoting Shelley v. Kraemer). Respect for this principle explains why laws singling out a certain class of citizens for disfavored legal status or general hardships are rare. A law declaring that in general it shall be more difficult for one group of citizens than for all others to seek aid from the government is itself a denial of equal protection of the laws in the most literal sense. "The guaranty of 'equal protection of the laws is a pledge of the protection of equal laws.' " Skinner v. Oklahoma ex rel. Williamson, 316 U.S. 535, 541 (1942) (quoting Yick Wo)....

A second and related point is that laws of the kind now before us raise the inevitable inference that the disadvantage imposed is born of animosity toward the class of persons affected. "[I]f the constitutional conception of 'equal protection of the laws' means anything, it must at the very least mean that a bare ... desire to harm a politically unpopular group cannot constitute a *legitimate* governmental interest." Department of Agriculture v. Moreno, 413 U.S. 528, 534 (1973).... Amendment 2, ... in making a general announcement that gays and lesbians shall not have any particular protections from the law, inflicts on them immediate, continuing, and real injuries that outrun and belie any legitimate justifications that may be claimed for it. We conclude that ... the principles it offends ... are conventional and venerable; a law must bear a rational relationship to a legitimate governmental purpose, and Amendment 2 does not.

The primary rationale the State offers for Amendment 2 is respect for other citizens' freedom of association, and in particular the liberties of landlords or employers who have personal or religious objections to homosexuality. Colorado also cites its interest in conserving resources to fight discrimination against other groups. The breadth of the amendment is so far removed from these particular justifications that we find it impossible to credit them. [Amendment 2] is a status-based enactment divorced from any factual context from which we could discern a relationship to legitimate state interests; it is a classification of persons undertaken for its own sake, something the Equal Protection Clause does not permit. "[C]lass legislation ... [is] obnoxious to the prohibitions of the Fourteenth Amendment...." Civil Rights Cases, 109 U.S. at 24....

We must conclude that Amendment 2 classifies homosexuals not to further a proper legislative end but to make them unequal to everyone else. This Colorado cannot do. A State cannot so deem a class of persons a stranger to its laws.

■ JUSTICE SCALIA, with whom THE CHIEF JUSTICE and JUSTICE THOMAS join, dissenting.

The Court has mistaken a Kulturkampf for a fit of spite. The constitutional amendment before us here is not the manifestation of a " 'bare . . . desire to harm' " homosexuals but is rather a modest attempt by seemingly tolerant Coloradans to preserve traditional sexual mores against the efforts of a politically powerful minority to revise those mores through use of the laws. . . . This Court has no business imposing upon all Americans the resolution favored by the elite class from which the Members of this institution are selected, pronouncing that "animosity" toward homosexuality is evil. . . . The people of Colorado have adopted an entirely reasonable provision which does not even disfavor homosexuals in any substantive sense, but merely denies them preferential treatment. Amendment 2 is designed to prevent piecemeal deterioration of the sexual morality favored by a majority of Coloradans, and [is] an appropriate means to that legitimate end.

NOTES AND QUESTIONS ON *ROMER v. EVANS*

1.   The breakthrough:

1.1   *Romer v. Evans* is remarkable both for how much and how little it does. The case marks the first time a law against same-sex sexual orientation was found to fail the rational relationship test, thus the first time the Court offered any constitutional protection for gays and lesbians or bisexuals as such. To what extent is this step limited to the specific facts of the case? Does *Romer* signal a broader willingness to recognize gay and lesbian rights, even a sea change? How far might it go?

1.2   *Romer* found that the provision it invalidated was not even rational. Is a great deal of discrimination against gay men and lesbian women lacking in rational basis? Does the case make rational basis review look promising as a lesbian and gay rights legal strategy? It might be said that most discriminations against "homosexuals" are utterly irrational. *See* Toni M. Massaro, "Gay Rights, Thick and Thin," 49 *Stan. L. Rev.* 45 (1996) (arguing for "thin" rational basis review and the use of "thicker" narrative to encourage empathy). How difficult is it to show that the government acts lack rational basis?

1.3   Race cases were cited but not explicitly discussed in the majority opinion. What is your evaluation of this submerged foundation? Is there a parallel between discrimination based on race and discrimination based on sexual orientation? What is the effect on your answer of recognizing the real-world overlap in the categories?

1.4   Draft an opinion under *Andrews* on the legal issues raised by Amendment 2.

2.   What *Romer* did: The *Romer* opinion has been read as standing for a variety of propositions. Professor Andrew Koppelman summarizes some leading ones:

Some think that the Court was *sub silentio* following the Colorado Supreme Court's theory that the Amendment impaired gays' "right to participate equally in the political process." Ronald Dworkin and Robert Bork, who rarely agree, both think that *Romer* holds that the law may not draw moral distinctions based on the sexual practices of consenting adults. Cass Sunstein similarly thinks "[t]he underlying judgment in *Romer* must be that, at least for purposes of the Equal Protection Clause, it is no longer legitimate to discriminate against homosexuals as a class simply because the state wants to discourage homosexuality or homosexual behavior." . . . [Akhil Amar and Laurence Tribe] think that the law's problem is that it singles out a named class to suffer a disadvantage. Andrew Koppelman, *"Romer v. Evans* and Invidious Intent," 6 *Wm. & Mary Bill Rts. J.* 89, 90–91 (1997).

What do you think the Court thought was wrong with Colorado's initiative? Can *Romer* be reconciled with *Hardwick*? Is a morality rule an equality rule? Revisit the question of the relationship between substantive due process and equal protection in the *Romer* setting. Must the two precedents be reconciled? Did the Colorado initiative treat homosexuals by law as, in Professor Kenneth Karst's terms, "nonparticipants" in the democratic process? Did it impose stigma? Are these realities salient to substantive due process privacy?

Equal protection, we have seen, was not raised in *Hardwick*. Specifically, means of discouraging sodomy other than criminalization, such as depriving a group imagined to practice it of civil rights, were not in the case. Given this distinction, on what assumptions is a conflict between *Hardwick* and *Romer* predicated? Is *Hardwick* about acts, *Romer* about status? Is substantive due process where we adjudicate (to appropriate Justice Scalia's words) culture wars and fits of spite; equal protection where we dispense equal justice under law? Does it matter, for equality purposes, whether Amendment 2 was passed as part of a culture war or a fit of spite? What is the effect of the law of intent under the Fourteenth Amendment on your answer?

3. Specialness: Justice Scalia presents homosexuals as scarily powerful, all the more so for being not readily identifiable, as well as possessing political power and economic wealth beyond their numbers. He saw the creation of "special rights" in the Court's elimination of what Justice Kennedy saw as "special animus" against homosexuals. Which is it? *See* Robert F. Nagel, "Playing Defense," 6 *Wm. & Mary Bill Rts. J.* 167 (1997) (showing animus in fight on the ground over Amendment 2). Situate their disagreement in the larger debate over affirmative action. Is a right to equal treatment a "special" right?

In fact, as to economic status, the best available evidence suggests that bisexual and gay male workers earn between 11 and 27 percent less money than heterosexual male workers with the same experience, education, occupation, marital status, and region of residence; a difference between the earnings of heterosexual women and of lesbian and bisexual women was found, but it was not statistically significant. *See* M.V. Lee Badgett, "The Wage Effects of Sexual Orientation Discrimination," 48 *Indus. & Lab. Rel. Rev.* 726, 737 (1995) (analyzing pooled data from national random sample, defining orientation "behaviorally"); *see also* Christopher Kendall & Brian Eyolfson, " 'One in Ten' but Who's Counting?: Lesbians, Gay Men and Employment Equity," 27 *Ottawa L. Rev.* 281 (1995) (arguing that the lesbian and gay community suffers from "systematic and direct discrimination in employment"). How do you explain the gender disparity? Reconsider whether sexual behavior is a good proxy for identity for women and for men. Given the lack of empirical foundation for Justice Scalia's attribution of vast economic power to this group, is it right to ask what he is afraid of?

4. Strategy: Colorado's Amendment 2 was a law against making laws to guarantee the equality of lesbian women and gay men. The Supreme Court's majority responded, in essence and in quite strong language, you must be kidding. Did the Colorado initiative overreach tactically? After *Romer*, what can states still do to "homosexuals"?

Fired from his job because he is gay, Delwin Vriend challenged Alberta's human rights code for failing to prohibit the discrimination against his sexual orientation and for failing to provide him an avenue to complain of it. Recall that *Egan v. Canada*, [1995] 2 S.C.R. 513 (*see* Chapter 1), previously recognized discrimination against sexual orientation as an analogous ground protected by the Charter's discrimination prohibitions. In *Vriend*, the Supreme Court of Canada held that Alberta's human rights code violated the Charter by failing to include a prohibition on the basis of sexual orientation, so a right not to be discriminated against on this ground must be "read in" to the act.

Vriend v. Alberta

Supreme Court of Canada
[1998] 1 S.C.R. 493

■ Cory, J.

Despite repeated calls for its inclusion [under the Individual Rights Protection Act, R.S.A., ch. 1–2 (1980) (IRPA),] sexual orientation has never been included in the list of those groups protected from discrimination.... [Its omission] was deliberate and not the result of an oversight. The reasons given ... include the assertions that sexual orientation is a "marginal" ground; that human rights legislation is powerless to change public attitudes; and that there have only been a few cases of sexual orientation discrimination in employment brought to the attention of the Minister....

[Mr. Delwin Vriend had permanent full-time employment as a laboratory coordinator at King's College in Edmonton, Alberta. Responding to an inquiry by the President of the College, Mr. Vriend disclosed that he is homosexual and was terminated solely on that basis. The Alberta Human Rights commission informed Mr. Vriend, when he tried to complain, that the IRPA did not include sexual orientation as a protected ground.] The appellant[] challenged the constitutionality of [sections] of the IRPA on the grounds that [they] contravene § 15(1) of the Charter because they do not include sexual orientation as a prohibited ground of discrimination....

[Does § 15 cover legislative omissions?] ... The notion of judicial deference to legislative choices should not ... be used to completely immunize certain kinds of legislative decisions from Charter scrutiny.... The fact that it is the underinclusiveness of the Act which is at issue does not alter the fact that it is the legislative act which is the subject of Charter scrutiny.... It is said ... that this case is different because [it] centres on the legislature's failure to extend the protection of a law to a particular group of people. This position assumes that it is only a positive act rather than an omission which may be scrutinized under the Charter.... If an omission were not subject to the Charter, underinclusive legislation which was worded in such a way as to simply omit one class rather than to explicitly exclude it would be immune from Charter challenge. If this position was accepted, the form, rather than the substance, of the legislation would determine whether it was open to challenge. This result would be illogical and more importantly unfair....

The concept and principle of equality is almost intuitively understood and cherished by all.... The difficulty lies in giving real effect to equality.... It is easy to say that everyone who is just like "us" is entitled to equality. Everyone finds it more difficult to say that those who are "different" from us in some way should have the same equality rights that we enjoy. Yet so soon as we say any enumerated or analogous group is less deserving and unworthy of equal protection and benefit of the law all minorities and all of Canadian society are demeaned.... If equality rights for minorities had been recognized, the all too frequent tragedies of history might have been avoided. It can never be forgotten that discrimination is the antithesis of equality and that it is the recognition of equality which will foster the dignity of every individual....

The respondents have argued that because the IRPA merely omits any reference to sexual orientation, this "neutral silence" cannot be understood as creating a distinction.... It is the respondents' position that if any distinction is made on the basis of sexual orientation that distinction exists because it is present in society and not because of the IRPA. These arguments cannot be accepted. They are based on that "thin and impoverished" notion of equality referred to in Eldridge v. British Columbia, [1997] 3 S.C.R. 624 at ¶ 73.... The respondents concede that if homosexuals were excluded altogether from the protection of the IRPA in the sense that they were not protected from discrimination on any grounds, this would be discriminatory.... [But t]he fact that a lesbian and a heterosexual woman are both entitled to bring a complaint of discrimination on the basis of gender [for example] does not mean that they have *equal* protection under the Act. Lesbian and gay individuals are still denied protection under the ground that may be the most significant for them, discrimination on the basis of sexual orientation....

It is clear that the IRPA, by reason of its underinclusiveness, does create a distinction ... along two different lines. The first is the distinction between homosexuals, on the one hand, and other disadvantaged groups which are protected under the Act, on the other. Gays and lesbians do not even have formal equality with reference to other protected groups, since those other groups are explicitly included and they are not. The second distinction, and, I think, the more fundamental one, is between homosexuals and heterosexuals. [Formal equality exists on the surface, but] the exclusion of the ground of sexual orientation, considered in the context of the social reality of discrimination against gays and lesbians, clearly has a disproportionate impact on them as opposed to heterosexuals. Therefore the IRPA in its underinclusive state denies substantive equality to the former group....

The "silence" of the IRPA with respect to discrimination on the ground of sexual orientation is not "neutral." ... It is apparent that the omission ... creates a distinction [that results] in a denial of the equal benefit and equal protection of the law.... [Homosexuals] are excluded from the government's statement of policy against discrimination, and they are also denied access to the remedial procedures established by the Act.... The exclusion sends a message to all Albertans that it is permissible, and perhaps even acceptable, to discriminate against individuals on the basis of their sexual orientation. The effect of that message on gays and lesbians is one whose significance cannot be underestimated.... Perhaps most important is the psychological harm which may ensue.... Fear of discrimination will logically lead to concealment of true identity and this must be harmful to personal confidence and self-esteem. Compounding that effect is the implicit message conveyed by the exclusion, that gays and lesbians, unlike other individuals, are not worthy of protection.... The potential harm to the dignity and perceived worth of gay and lesbian individuals constitutes a particularly cruel form of discrimination. Even if the discrimination is experienced at the hands of private individuals, it is the state that denies protection from that discrimination. Thus the adverse effects are particularly invidious.

NOTES AND QUESTIONS ON *VRIEND*

1. Method: Can you imagine a U.S. court ruling as the Supreme Court of Canada did in *Vriend*? Is *Vriend* audacious? heroic? principled? Analyze what would be in a U.S. court's way. Would the absence of a precedent like *Egan*, [1995] 2 S.C.R. 513, make it more difficult? a precedent like *Andrews*? With what in the *Vriend* Court's logic concerning underinclusiveness would the U.S. Supreme Court take issue? Would legislative supremacy preclude the constitutional recognition that a group is denied equal protection of the laws when its disadvantage is not recognized by a state's antidiscrimination laws? Is there any difference, for equal protection purposes, between adding a ground to discrimination legislation and adding a group to an antidiscrimination interpretation of other legislation? Is the *Vriend* ruling light-years ahead of *Romer*? Draft a dissent in *Vriend* for Justice Scalia.

2. Substance: Which comes first in *Vriend*, the substantive recognition that the group is, in fact, a group and discriminated against in society, or the more processlike equality reasoning that compels the conclusion that the statute is underinclusive? Is the Supreme Court of Canada "legislating," hence invading the proper realm of the legislature, when it compels the provinces to include sexual orientation discrimination in their antidiscrimination provisions? Or is it adjudicating constitutional equality in the simplest sense, as it suggests? Given *Egan*'s recognition that sexual orientation is an analogous ground under Section 15(1), *see Egan*, [1995] 2 S.C.R. at 513 (*see* Chapter 1), was it open to the *Vriend* Court to permit the provinces to omit discrimination against gays and lesbians under their human rights codes? What is left of the *Egan* plurality ruling that the distinction between same-sex and different-sex couples, for purposes of the federal benefit of old-age spousal benefits, was not a denial of equality rights?

3. Discrimination and the closet: Does the Court in effect recognize that both homosexuals and heterosexuals have a sexual orientation, only one of which is made into a social disadvantage? Consider how the harm of official enforcement of the closet through lack of explicit protection against discrimination functions in the opinion to support a requirement that human rights codes must include a protection from sexual orientation discrimination. Could an analogous argument be made under the Equal Protection Clause that Title VII, or similar state provisions, are discriminatory without a sexual orientation discrimination prohibition?

The rights of gay men and lesbian women to family with all its benefits and recognition have been vigorously contested. In invalidating a facially heterosexual definition of "spouse" governing access to Ontario's support provisions after the breakdown of a relationship, the Supreme Court in *Ontario v. M & H.* took a long step in the direction of recognizing same-sex family rights. The opinion also demonstrates in action the Court's equality jurisprudence since Andrews.[33]

---

33. The parties settled the financial aspects of the case before it was argued to the Supreme Court, *Ontario v. M. & H.* [1999] 171 D.L.R. (4th) 577, 600, and the Attorney General for Ontario conceded that the provision defining "spouse" violated the Charter Section 15(1). *Id.* at 670.

Ontario v. M. & H.

Supreme Court of Canada
[1999] 171 D.L.R. (4th) 577

■ CORY and IACOBUCCI JJ.[34]—

The principal issue raised in this appeal is whether the definition of "spouse" in § 29 of the Family Law Act, R.S.O. 1990, c. F.3 ("FLA") infringes § 15(1) of the Canadian Charter of Rights and Freedoms, and, if so, whether the legislation is nevertheless saved by § 1 of the Charter.... Essentially, the definition of "spouse" in § 29 ... extends the obligation to provide spousal support ... beyond married persons to include individuals in conjugal opposite-sex relationships of some permanence. Same-sex relationships are capable of being both conjugal and lengthy, but individuals in such relationships are nonetheless denied access to the court-enforced system of support provided by the FLA. This differential treatment is on the basis of a personal characteristic, namely sexual orientation, that, in previous jurisprudence, has been found to be analogous to those characteristics specifically enumerated in § 15(1).

The crux of the issue is that this differential treatment discriminates in a substantive sense by violating the human dignity of individuals in same-sex relationships.... [T]he inquiry into substantive discrimination is to be undertaken in a purposive and contextual manner.... The exclusion of same-sex partners from the benefits of the spousal support scheme implies that they are judged to be incapable of forming intimate relationships of economic interdependence, without regard to their actual circumstances.... [I]t is clear that the human dignity of individuals in same-sex relationships is violated....

This infringement is not justified under § 1 ... because there is no rational connection between the objectives of the spousal support provisions and the means chosen to further this objective. The objectives [are] ... providing for the equitable resolution of economic disputes when intimate relationships between financially interdependent individuals break down, and alleviating the burden on the public purse to provide for dependent spouses.... If anything, these goals are undermined by this exclusion.... [In our joint reasons, Cory J. has addressed § 15(1), Iacobucci J. has addressed § 1.] ...

■ CORY J.—

M. and H. are women who met while on vacation in 1980. It is agreed that in 1982 they started living together in a same-sex relationship that continued for at least five years.... During that time they occupied a home which H. had owned since 1974. H. paid for the upkeep of the home, but the parties agreed to share living expenses and household responsibilities equally. At the time, H. was employed in an advertising firm and M. ran her own company. In 1982, M. and H. started their own advertising business. The business enjoyed immediate success and was the main source of income for the couple during the relationship. H.'s contribution to this company was greater than that of M.... [T]he trial judge observed that this disparity was probably due to the fact that M. had no previous experience in advertising, and, as time went on, she was content to devote more of her time to domestic tasks rather than the business. Nevertheless, the parties continued to be equal shareholders in the company.

In 1983, M. and H. purchased a business property together. In 1986, they purchased as joint tenants a vacation property in the country. They later sold the business property and used the proceeds to finance the construction of a home on the country property. As a result of a dramatic downturn in the

---

34. Chief Justice Lamer and Justices L'Heureux–Dubé, McLachlin, and Binnie JJ. joined the opinion for the Court. Mr. Justice Major wrote a separate concurring opinion.

advertising business..., the parties' debt increased significantly. H. took a job outside the firm and placed a mortgage on her home to pay for [their] expenses.... M. also tried to find employment but was unsuccessful. Her company, which she had continued to run on a casual basis throughout the relationship, produced very little income. By September of 1992, M. and H.'s relationship had deteriorated. H. was concerned about what she perceived to be an unfair disparity in their relative financial contributions. H. presented M. with a draft agreement to settle their affairs. The same day that the agreement was presented, M. took some of her personal belongings and left the common home. Upon M.'s departure, H. changed the locks on the house....

M. alleged that she encountered serious financial problems after the separation.... [, claimed support under the FLA, and] ... challeng[ed] the validity of the definition of "spouse" in § 29 of the Act.

[The trial judge held that § 29 violates § 15(1) and is not saved by § 1. H. appealed joined by Ontario. The Ontario Court of Appeal upheld the decision but suspended its implementation for a year to give the Ontario legislature time to amend the FLA. Neither H. nor M. appealed. Ontario was granted leave to appeal to the Supreme Court.] ...

In Law v. Canada [1999] 1 R.C.§ 497, 524, Iacobucci J ... summarized the basic elements of this Court's approach [to § 15(1) following Andrews and Egan (*see* Chapter 1)]....

> First, does the impugned law (a) draw a formal distinction between the claimant and others on the basis of one or more personal characteristics, or (b) fail to take into account the claimant's already disadvantaged position within Canadian society resulting in substantively differential treatment between the claimant and others on the basis of one or more personal characteristics? If so, there is differential treatment for the purpose of § 15(1). Second, was the claimant subject to differential treatment on the basis of one or more of the enumerated and analogous grounds? And third, does the differential treatment discriminate in a substantive sense, bringing into play the *purpose* of § 15(1) of the Charter in remedying such ills as prejudice, stereotyping, and historical disadvantage? ...

[T]he FLA draws a distinction by specifically according rights to individual members of unmarried cohabiting opposite-sex couples, which by omission it fails to accord to individual members of same-sex couples who are living together.... [T]he definition of "spouse" in § 29 ... specifically allows persons who became financially dependent in the course of a lengthy intimate relationship some relief from financial hardship resulting from the breakdown of that relationship.... It is true that women in common law relationships often tended to become financially dependent on their male partners because they raised their children and because of their unequal earning power. But the legislature drafted § 29 to allow either a man *or* a woman to apply for support, thereby recognizing that financial dependence can arise in an intimate relationship in a context entirely unrelated either to child-rearing or to any gender-based discrimination existing in our society....

[The FLA imposes] an obligation on persons to support themselves and their dependants. A "dependant" can be the spouse, child or parent of the person who must fulfil the support obligation. The definition of "spouse" in § 29 ... includes a person who is actually married, and also: "either of a man and woman who are not married to each other and have cohabited, (a) continuously for a period of not less than three years, or (b) in a relationship of some permanence, if they are the natural or adoptive parents of a child."

Section 1(1) defines "cohabit" as "to live together in a conjugal relationship, whether within or outside marriage."

The definition clearly indicates that the legislature decided to extend the obligation to provide spousal support *beyond* married persons ... to include those relationships which: (i) exist between a man and a woman; (ii) have a specific degree of permanence; (iii) are conjugal.... Same-sex relationships are capable of meeting the last two requirements. Certainly same-sex couples will often form long, lasting, loving and intimate relationships. The choices they make in the context of those relationships may give rise to the financial dependence of one partner on the other. Though it might be argued that same-sex couples do not live together in "conjugal" relationships, in the sense that they cannot "hold themselves out" as husband and wife, on this issue I am in agreement with the reasoning and conclusions of the majority of the Court of Appeal[:]

> [T]he generally accepted characteristics of a conjugal relationship [include] shared shelter, sexual and personal behaviour, services, social activities, economic support and children, as well as the societal perception of the couple.... In order to come within the definition, neither opposite-sex couples nor same-sex couples are required to fit precisely the traditional marital model to demonstrate that the relationship is "conjugal." ...

Obviously the weight to be accorded the various elements ... will vary widely and almost infinitely. The same must hold true of same-sex couples.... [T]here is nothing to suggest that same-sex couples do not meet the legal definition of "conjugal." [The distinction to which the section gives rise is not] between opposite-sex and same-sex *couples*.... Section 29 defines "spouse" as *"either* of a man and a woman" who meet the other requirements of the section ... [thus] explicitly refers to the *individual* members of the couple. Thus the distinction of relevance must be between individual persons in a same-sex, conjugal relationship of some permanence and individual persons in an opposite-sex, conjugal relationship of some permanence.... Under § 29 ..., members of opposite-sex couples ... are able to gain access to the court-enforced system of support.... Members of same-sex couples are denied access to this system entirely on the basis of their sexual orientation....

In Egan, this Court unanimously affirmed that sexual orientation is an analogous ground to those enumerated in s.15(1). Sexual orientation is "a deeply personal characteristic that is either unchangeable or changeable only at unacceptable personal costs." Egan [1995] 2 S.C.R. at 528. In addition, a majority of this Court explicitly recognized that gays, lesbians and bisexuals, "whether as individuals or couples, form an identifiable minority who have suffered and continue to suffer serious social, political and economic disadvantage." Id. at 602.... The relevant [§ 15(1) purposive and contextual] inquiry is whether the differential treatment imposes a burden upon or withholds a benefit from the claimant in a manner that reflects the stereotypical application of presumed group or personal characteristics, or which otherwise has the effect of perpetuating or promoting the view that the individual is less capable or worthy of recognition or value as a human being or as a member of Canadian society, equally deserving of concern, respect, and consideration.... When a relationship breaks down, the support provisions help to ensure that a member of a couple who has contributed to the couple's welfare in intangible ways will not find himself or herself utterly abandoned.... [Thus § 29] creates a distinction that withholds a benefit from the respondent M. The question is whether this denial of a benefit violates the purpose of § 15(1).

In Law, Iacobucci J. explained that ... [four contextual factors may influence this] determination ... [and that the court in examining them] must adopt the point of view of a reasonable person, in circumstances similar to those of the claimant.... One factor ... is the existence of preexisting disadvantage, stereotyping, prejudice, or vulnerability experienced by the individual or group at issue.... In this case, there is significant preexisting disadvantage and vulnerability, and these circumstances are exacerbated by the impugned legislation. [By denying access to the potential benefit of a judicially enforced] measure of protection for their economic interests[,] ... a person in the position of the claimant is denied a benefit regarding an important aspect of life in today's society. Neither common law nor equity provides the remedy of maintenance that is made available by the FLA.... [This denial] contributes to the general vulnerability experienced by individuals in same-sex relationships.

A second contextual factor ... is the correspondence, or the lack of it, between the ground on which a claim is based and the actual need, capacity, or circumstances of the claimant or others.... [T]he legislation at issue ... fails to take into account the claimant's actual situation.... [A]ccess to the court-enforced spousal support regime ... is given to individuals in conjugal relationships of a specific degree of permanence. Being in a same-sex relationship does not mean that it is an impermanent or a non-conjugal relationship.

A third contextual factor [in Law] is ... whether the impugned legislation has an ameliorative purpose or effect for a group historically disadvantaged in the context of the legislation:

> An ameliorative purpose or effect which accords with the purpose of § 15(1) of the Charter will likely not violate the human dignity of more advantaged individuals where the exclusion of these more advantaged individuals largely corresponds to the greater need or the different circumstances experienced by the disadvantaged group being targeted by the legislation.... Law [1999] 1 S.C.R. at 502.

[We] reject the idea that the allegedly ameliorative purpose of this legislation [for women in married or opposite-sex relationships] does anything to lessen the charge of discrimination in this case.

A fourth contextual factor [in Law] was the nature of the interest affected by the impugned legislation.... [We must ask] whether the distinction in question restricts access to a fundamental social institution, or affects a basic aspect of full membership in Canadian society, or constitutes a complete non-recognition of a particular group. In the present case, the interest protected by § 29 ... is fundamental, namely the ability to meet basic financial needs following the breakdown of a relationship characterized by intimacy and economic dependence. Members of same-sex couples are entirely ignored by the statute.... The societal significance of the benefit conferred by the statute cannot be overemphasized. The exclusion of same-sex partners from the benefits of § 29 ... promotes the view that M., and individuals in same-sex relationships generally, are less worthy of recognition and protection. It implies that they are judged to be incapable of forming intimate relationships of economic interdependence as compared to opposite-sex couples, without regard to their actual circumstances. As the intervener EGALE [Equality for Gays and Lesbians Everywhere] submitted, such exclusion perpetuates the disadvantages suffered by individuals in same-sex relationships and contributes to the erasure of their existence.

Therefore I conclude that ... the human dignity of individuals in same-sex relationships is violated by the impugned legislation [and thus that] the definition of spouse in § 29 of the FLA violates § 15(1).

■ IACOBUCCI J—

Same-sex couples are ... excluded from [the § 29 definition of "spouse"] thereby giving rise to the charge that the legislation is underinclusive. In Vriend, this Court found that where a law violates the Charter owing to under-inclusion, the first stage of the § 1 analysis is properly concerned with the object of the legislation as a whole, the impugned provisions of the Act, and the omission itself. . . .

[Appellant argues that] the underlying purpose of [the provision at issue was] to remedy the systemic inequality associated with opposite-sex relation-ships, including the economic dependence of women on men resulting from women assuming primary responsibility for child care and from gender-based inequality in earning power. . . . [It is also] said to reflect a concern for children and the conditions under which they are raised. Although I do not dispute the claim that economically dependent heterosexual women and children are well served by the spousal support provisions. . . , in my view, there is insufficient evidence to demonstrate that the protection of these groups informs the fundamental legislative objectives. . . . Indeed, the thrust of the OLRC's 1975 remarks which preceded the new legislation emphasize the importance of a gender-neutral scheme . . . [and] encouraged the government to premise sup-port obligations on need and actual dependence. . . . [Other provisions of the Act are also cast in gender-neutral terms, and are] silent with respect to the economic vulnerability of heterosexual women, their tendency to take on primary responsibility for parenting, the greater earning capacity of men, and systemic sexual inequality. . . . [That most claimants are women does not establish that the goal was] to address the special needs of women in opposite-sex relationships. The terms of the spousal support provisions . . . are also inconsistent with the [goal of supporting children, since the Act] imposes spousal support obligations on opposite-sex couples irrespective of whether or not they have children[, expressly including in] cohabiting opposite-sex part-ners who are not the parents of a child . . . the § 29 definition of "spouse" after three years of cohabitation. . . . In Moge v. Moge, [1992] 3 S.C.R. 813, 848, 849 L'Heureux-Dubé J. [for the Court] . . . [noted] that "[w]hat the Act requires is a fair and equitable distribution of resources to alleviate the economic conse-quences of marriage or marriage breakdown for both spouses, regardless of gender." . . .

Providing for the equitable resolution of economic disputes when intimate relationships between financially interdependent individuals break down, and alleviating the burden on the public purse to provide for dependent spouses, are to my mind pressing and substantial objectives. . . . Even if I were to accept that . . . the Act is meant to address the systemic sexual inequality associated with opposite-sex relationships, the required nexus between this objective and the chosen measures is absent in this case. In my view, it defies logic to suggest that a gender-neutral support system is rationally connected to the goal of improving the economic circumstances of heterosexual women upon relation-ship breakdown. In addition, I can find no evidence to demonstrate that the exclusion of same-sex couples from the spousal support regime of the FLA in any way furthers the objective of assisting heterosexual women. Although there is evidence to suggest that same-sex relationships are not typically character-ized by the same economic and other inequalities which affect opposite-sex relationships, this does not, in my mind, explain why the right to apply for support is limited to heterosexuals. . . . [I]t is no answer to say that same-sex couples should not have access to the spousal support scheme because their relationships are typically more egalitarian. . . .

The second of the objectives put forth by the appellant, namely, the protection of children, also fails the rational connection test.... [It is] overinclusive because members of opposite-sex couples are entitled to apply for spousal support irrespective of whether or not they are parents and regardless of their reproductive capabilities or desires.... [It is] underinclusive [because a]n increasing percentage of children are being conceived and raised by lesbian and gay couples as a result of adoption, surrogacy and donor insemination. Although their numbers are still fairly small, it seems to me that the goal of protecting children cannot be but incompletely achieved by denying some children the benefits that flow from a spousal support award merely because their parents were in a same-sex relationship....

[Further] it is nonsensical to suggest that the goal of reducing the burden on the public purse is advanced by limiting the right to make private claims for support to heterosexuals. The impugned legislation ... [drives] a member of a same sex couple who is in need of maintenance to the welfare system.... Indeed, the *inclusion* of same-sex couples in § 29 ... would better achieve the objectives of the legislation while respecting the Charter rights of individuals in same-sex relationships.... I conclude that the exclusion of same-sex couples from § 29 of the Act is simply not rationally connected to the dual objectives of the spousal support provisions of the legislation. Given this lack of a rational connection, § 29 of the FLA is not saved by § 1....

I acknowledge that some individuals in same-sex relationships, including H. herself, have expressed reservations about being treated as "spouses" within the family law system.... [However,] given that the members of equality-seeking groups are bound to differ to some extent in their politics, beliefs and opinions, it is unlikely that any § 15 claims would survive § 1 scrutiny if unanimity with respect to the desired remedy were required before discrimination could be redressed.... [G]overnment incrementalism ... is generally an inappropriate justification for Charter violations.... None of the reforms [in the FLA] ... has addressed the equal rights and obligations of individuals in same-sex relationships.... If the legislature refuses to act so as to evolve towards Charter compliance then deference as to the timing of reforms loses its raison d'être.... [Section 29 is declared of no force and effect, but suspended for six months to give the legislature latitude to redefine "spouse" in a more comprehensive fashion.]

■ Bastarache J—

[E]ven if most individual partners in same-sex relationships are not in a position more typical of a woman in an opposite-sex relationship, some are.... I agree that the failure to provide same-sex couples with any consensual avenue for mutual and public recognition perpetuates a legal invisibility which is inconsistent with the moral obligation of inclusion that informs the spirit of our Charter.... In truth, [the] opposite-sex family form is a product of socialization. In recognition of the significance of the procreative and socializing role of the opposite-sex family, the modern state has created a host of inducements for this family form, in addition to the obligations between the parties which are intended to mitigate the insecurities created by traditional patterns of gender inequality and specialization. Both ... confer an objective benefit to society by creating a regime in which opposite-sex partners will suffer the least harm by virtue of engaging in the sometimes risky enterprise of a family.... I am satisfied, however, that the government's legitimate interest in setting social policies designed to encourage family formation can be met without imposing through exclusion a hardship on non-traditional families....

It would be consistent with Charter values of equality and inclusion to treat all members in a family relationship equally and all types of family relationships equally. It is, however, inconsistent with § 15 to deny equal treatment to a member of a family relationship *on the basis of an analogous ground* . . . . Even though most same-sex couples do not experience economic imbalance, some do. What is the purpose in excluding them? This exclusion is not a valid means of achieving the positive purpose of § 29, economic equality within the family. By defining restrictively the scope of the family concept, § 29 in effect is restricting the reach of equality.

■ GONTHIER J., dissenting—

Plainly, this appeal raises elemental social and legal issues. Indeed, it is no exaggeration to observe that it represents something of a watershed. . . . [T]he nature of my disagreement with the majority in this case is basic. . . . In my opinion, this legislation seeks to recognize the specific social function of opposite-sex couples in society, and to address a *dynamic* of dependence unique to both men and women in opposite-sex couples that flows from three basic realities. First, this dynamic of dependence relates to the biological reality of the opposite-sex relationship and its unique potential for giving birth to children and its being the primary forum for raising them. Second, this dynamic relates to a unique form of dependence that is unrelated to children but is specific to heterosexual relationships. And third, this dynamic of dependence is particularly acute for women in opposite-sex relationships, who suffer from pre-existing economic disadvantage as compared with men. Providing a benefit (and concomitantly imposing a burden) on a group that uniquely possesses this social function, biological reality and economic disadvantage, in my opinion, is not discriminatory. Although the legislature is free to extend this benefit to others who do not possess these characteristics, the Constitution does not impose such a duty on that sovereign body. . . .

It is plain to any observer that same-sex couples may, and do, form relationships which are similar in many ways to those formed by opposite-sex couples. . . . However . . . [i]ndividuals in same-sex relationships do not carry the same burden of fulfilling the social role that those in opposite-sex relationships do. They do not exhibit the same degree of systemic dependence. They do not experience a structural wage differential between the individuals in the relationship. In this sense, individuals in same-sex relationships are an advantaged group as compared to individuals in opposite-sex relationships. As such, there is no need to consider whether the legislation aggravates or exacerbates any preexisting disadvantage. Nor can it be said that the ameliorative legislation excludes a group which is disadvantaged in relation to the subject-matter of the legislation. The main targets of the ameliorative legislation, partners in opposite-sex relationships (particularly women), suffer a structural disadvantage which is unknown to individuals in same-sex relationships. Just because one form of disadvantage is addressed by this legislation does not mean that all forms of disadvantage must be addressed by it. . . . [I]t is clear that there is an impact on the claimant's group. . . . However . . . the claimants are not deprived of *access* to support, but rather, they are not forced to participate in a mandatory support regime. The cost of receiving this benefit is the imposition of a burden on a class of people. The burden is not only a reduction in autonomy, but also is an imposition of financial obligations. It is a departure from the general principle in Western societies that individuals enjoy freedom and are expected to provide for themselves. . . . While the legislature does not force individuals in same-sex relationships to provide support, it also does not prevent them from doing so. Individuals in same-sex relationships are free to formulate contracts which impose support obligations upon themselves, just as the FLA does for some opposite-sex couples. I do not understand how it could be said that individuals in same-sex relationships are rendered "invisible" by non-inclusion in a regime merely because they have the same rights and obligations as all persons other than certain opposite-sex couples, particularly as they can impose equivalent support obligations by way of contract....

Human dignity is the lifeblood of the equality guarantee.... [I]t is not a denial of human dignity to recognize difference; to the contrary, acknowledging individual personal traits is a means of fostering human dignity. By recognizing individuality, and rejecting forced uniformity, the law celebrates differences, fostering the autonomy and integrity of the individual.... [S]hould a reasonable person in circumstances similar to the claimant feel her dignity is demeaned? ... I cannot see how she could.... Although the claimant is a member of a group that suffers pre-existing, historical disadvantage, the claimant's group is relatively advantaged in relation to the subject-matter at hand.... [T]he legislation takes into account accurate differences between that group and the claimant in a manner which respects the claimant's human dignity by not relying on a stereotype.

NOTES AND QUESTIONS ON *M. & H.*

1. Rationality review: *M. & H.* holds that there is no rational relation between excluding same-sex partners and any legitimate purpose served by the family law statutory support regime. Does the Section 1 analysis of the majority amount to what, in the United States, might be called rationality with bite? Are legal disadvantages imposed on gay men and lesbians often irrational? Would American definitions of "spouse" be rational by Canadian lights? If *M. & H.* manifests rationality review, is any higher degree of scrutiny needed to ensure gay rights?

2. What is sexual orientation? Is what Mr. Justice Iacobucci calls discrimination "on the basis of their sexual orientation" actually discrimination on the basis of the sex of one's sexual partner(s)? Is an orientation toward loving and forming intimate partnerships with persons of a certain sex necessarily a *sexual* orientation, even if it is often expressed sexually? In other words, which comes first, one's feelings for another person, the sex of the person with whom one is or wants to be sexual, or one's sexuality and its expression? Does the term "sexual orientation" make assumptions about the answer? Does it tend to assume, for example, that if M. was not with H., she would be with another woman? If M. married a man after separating from H., would her "sexual orientation" have changed—or only the sex of her partner? How does gender fit in here?

3. Sex specificity and gender neutrality: Mr. Justice Iacobucci's invalidation of Section 29's exclusion of same-sex couples is argued on grounds of gender neutrality, while Mr. Justice Gonthier's attempted defense of confining the FLA regime to heterosexuals is argued in sex-specific terms. Is Mr. Justice Gonthier's analysis what a substantive sex equality standard looks like? Is his solicitude for women in the traditional family role likely to alter their dependence or to enforce it? Is it protectionist? Is he celebrating women's dependency or criticizing it? Does he see it as inevitable? Does the FLA regime become, in his defense of it, necessary to keep women dependent in the family, or to free them from it? In his analysis, is women's inequality in the family to some degree biologically based in gestation? Would cloning dissolve his bottom line?

Might it have been possible for the majority to grant same-sex couples spousal support without negating Ontario's, and the Court's, concerns for substantive gender hierarchy? Is it possible to read the FLA's gender-neutral language, after *Andrews*, in light of a commitment to ending structural gender inequality, rather than as indifference to it? Does Mr. Justice Gonthier ignore *Andrews* and slip the Aristotelian equality calculus in by the back door when he argues, for example, that "taken as a group, same-sex relationships simply do not resemble opposite-sex relationships on this fundamental point"?

What is your view of Mr. Justice Gonthier's analysis of social causation—specifically, of his view of the relationship between women's economic status and their role in the family? Assess his view of women's "choice" and his spirited defense of homosexuality's "difference." How, in Mr. Justice Gonthier's opinion, does including gay and lesbian couples as spouses "sweep away" the institution of the family, rather than, for example, expand and extend its reach? Do Mr. Justice Gonthier and Ontario remind you of *Lochner v. New York*, 198 U.S. 45 (1905) (*see* Chapter 3.1), when they argue that subjection to the FLA spousal support regime restricts the freedom and autonomy of the less needy spouse? Is there a perhaps unintended irony in Mr. Justice Gonthier's defense of "special treatment" for the heterosexual family? Does Mr. Justice Gonthier's opinion show that this case was a battle in a Kulturkampf that gays and lesbians won?

4. The heterosexual woman: How do you explain the rush to champion the heterosexual woman's interests in this case? Who does it best? Do Ontario and Mr. Justice Gonthier attempt to play off heterosexual women against gay men and lesbian women? Do they succeed? If not, why not? Does Mr. Justice Gonthier think that a good reason for remedying discrimination against heterosexual women creates a good reason to discriminate against gays and lesbians? Consider the often jaw-dropping concessions to the disadvantages for women in the heterosexual family in each opinion. Compare them with U.S. paeans to the glories of the family in opinions in Chapter 6. Explain the difference. Which is closer to the real family? All in all, does the family sound like an institution that, given options, a woman would want to join? Does the majority contribute to privatizing women's dependency by keeping them off the welfare rolls, hence reducing pressure for systemic change? *See generally* Martha L.A. Fineman, "Masking Dependency: The Political Role of Family Rhetoric," 81 *Va. L. Rev.* 2181 (1995) (criticizing use of family to privatize dependency); Ariela R. Dubler, "Governing Through Contract: Common Law Marriage in the Nineteenth Century," 107 *Yale L.J.* 1885 (1998) (rethinking law's role in privatization of women's dependency historically).

5. Equality as a reason to deny equality rights:

5.1 Why does Mr. Justice Gonthier see the relative equality of gay and lesbian relationships as a reason to deny them access to the benefits of the legal support regime, rather than as a reason that not much money will be transferred to many of them under that regime? That is, why is he so against doing so little for so few? Heterosexual spouses who have relatively equal financial lives while married do not pay each other alimony on dissolution, but that is not seen as a reason that these less traditional spouses have no rights under the family law regime, or are not spouses at all. It may be the case that, if and as society becomes more equal, there will be less need for spousal support on breakdown, but does that support a gay/straight legislative line in providing it through law, especially after *Egan*? Does Mr. Justice Iacobucci's analysis have an implicit due process dimension, much like *Stanley v. Illinois*, 405 U.S. 645 (1972) (*see* Chapter

6), granting in effect equal access to due process of law in providing spousal support?

5.2 Recall the difficulty in justifying the award of spousal support at all (see Chapter 6 III). If alimony had been more explicitly justified as a promotion of sex equality in *Moge*, would it have been easier or harder to support the result in *M. & H.*? Is Mr. Justice Gonthier saying, because long-term same-sex relationships are not systematically unequal in the way that opposite-sex relationships are, because they are not institutions of male advantage and female disadvantage the way the heterosexual family is, they need not be recognized as family for purposes of support? If the heterosexual family were more equal, would the basis for his rationale disappear? Does he seem very concerned about this eventuality? Is his approach likely to reach it? Should gay men and lesbian women have fewer rights under equality guarantees because their relationships may be more equal? Does describing gays and lesbians as "advantaged" for purposes of the support regime seem respectful or mocking, persuasive or perverse? Are gays and lesbians advantaged for purposes of spousal recognition and support the way Allen Bakke was advantaged by being white for purposes of admission to medical school?

5.3 Locate and describe the role of the "one step at a time" rationale in the majority and the dissenting opinions. Compare it with American judicial discussions of the same doctrine. Does the U.S. law contain the element of moving in the direction of greater equality? Now consider "one step at a time" as a possible rationale for affirmative action.

6. Stereotyping: Evaluate Mr. Justice Gonthier's use of "objective reality" and "real differences." Are the values that are driving his analysis more stereotyped on the basis of gender than he appears to be aware? Is his analysis a defense of layer cake jurisprudence?: nature on the bottom, society building on that, law on top? If each layer reflects the other, we have law as the perfect mirror of nature. Has anything moved since *Bradwell* and *Plessy*? Is Mr. Justice Gonthier's "woman" reminiscent of Justice Bradley's "woman," to whom those who do not conform are dismissed as "exceptions" that law need not consider?

Does Mr. Justice Gonthier appear to understand that stereotypes can create reality, that discrimination can be based on stereotypes when they have become real by constructing society in their image? Why are "exceptional" families excluded from law's protection in his analysis only when they are gay or lesbian? Can his analysis of the exceptionality of gay and lesbian unions be squared with his purported adherence to a rule of dignity that treats individuals as they really are? Are those he would exclude as exceptional, exceptional not only to stereotypes but to a reality that largely conforms to stereotypes? Would he impose through law the reality of the stereotypes he purports to oppose? How does his purported opposition to stereotyping accommodate his view that mere need in an individual case, unrelated to systemic factors, is insufficient?

Both the majority and the dissent claim to reflect reality, the majority the "actual circumstances" and "actual situation" of the individuals in the unions at issue, the dissent "biological reality" and "objective reality." Whose reality is more real? Is the answer a matter of counting heads? Is it the policy consequences of reality that count for promoting equality?

7. Dignity and equality: Rethink in this setting, and in light of contemporary developments in equality law, the connections between equality and dignity raised in connection with the analysis of Immanuel Kant in Chapter 1. To what extent has equality been transmuted into dignity in the Canadian equality tradition? Is this a positive development? Is dignity part of equality? Is equality reducible to dignity? Trace how private support after dissolution of a relationship became a dignitary aspect of being equal. Has equality been reduced to dignity in *M. & H.*? If so, is it a sufficiently capacious concept of dignity to swallow all of equality? Is there more to equality than dignity, however conceived?

8. Choice of comparison: What is the significance of the disagreement over whether it is individuals or couples who are protected? The European Parliament's legislation prohibiting discrimination on the basis of sexual orientation specifically seeks to address discrimination against gay and lesbian couples as well as individuals. *See* Resolution on Equal Rights for Homosexuals and Lesbians in the E.C., 1994 O.J. (C 61) 40. What is the difference politically or analytically between protecting individuals and protecting couples? groups? To what extent does Mr. Justice Iacobucci's opinion rely on individualism? on reducing state responsibility for poverty on a collective basis?

9. Definition of family: Is the majority's approach to "conjugality" compelling? Taking an approach to the legal definition of family similar to the *M. & H.* Court's, the New York Court of Appeals held that a gay or lesbian couple could constitute a family for purposes of the law of rent control, which provided that "[n]o occupant of housing accommodations shall be evicted ... where the occupant is either the surviving spouse of the deceased tenant or some other member of the deceased tenant's family who has been living with the tenant." N.Y. Comp. Codes R. & Regs. tit. 9, § 2204.6(d) (1987).

> The intended protection against sudden eviction should not rest on fictitious legal distinctions or genetic history, but instead should find its foundation in the reality of family life. In the context of eviction, a more realistic, and certainly equally valid, view of a family includes two adult lifetime partners whose relationship is long-term and characterized by an emotional and financial commitment and interdependence. This view comports both with our society's traditional concept of "family" and with the expectations of individuals who live in such nuclear units. *Braschi v. Stahl Assoc.*, 74 N.Y.2d 201, 211, 543 N.E.2d 49, 53–54 (1989).

Is it a victory for two men or two women together to be recognized as a nuclear family? Is it a victory for the nuclear family to have gay men and lesbian women assimilated to its definitions? Ask the same questions of the definition of "spouse" in the FLA.

A few months after *Braschi*, the city revised its regulations to reflect it, "to clarify a non-traditional family member's right to remain in his or her home, particularly at a time when a significant percentage of these households may be vulnerable to the AIDS epidemic." *Rent Stabilization Ass'n. v. Higgins*, 83 N.Y.2d 156, 157, 608 N.Y.S.2d 930, 934, 630 N.E.2d 626, 630 (1993). The regulations defined "family member" as a person residing with the tenant in a primary residence who can prove "emotional and financial commitment, and interdependence. In no event would evidence of a sexual relationship between such persons be required or considered." N.Y. Exec.

Law § 104.6(d) (McKinney 1999). Evidence that could be considered included longevity of the relationship, sharing of household expenses and intermingling of finances, engaging in family-type activities and functions, formalized legal obligations to each other, holding themselves out as family, or any other behavior showing an intent to create a long-term emotionally committed relationship. *See* N.Y. Exec. Law § 2104.6(d)(3)(i). Compare this definition of family member with that of spouse in *M. & H.* What values and interests are served by precluding evidence of sexual relationship in defining family?

10. Gender and the family:

10.1 Does Mr. Justice Gonthier see the "family" as a unit that is gendered unequal, without regard to the sex of its members? In fact, not just in Mr. Justice Gonthier's view, is M. socially cast in the female role? That is, consistent with the facts, one could argue that M. entered the relationship with fewer skills and fewer material assets, her lesser economic contribution from marketplace work (regardless of her persistent attempts) gradually gave way to greater service contribution to the household as the relationship went on, her partner came to resent her financially and cut her off economically as the relationship soured, and she had an extremely difficult time subsequently subsisting on her own.

Is anyone who has an experience that conforms to these contours in a long-term dyad gendered "the woman" regardless of sex? If sex were not still ideologically tied to biology, but were seen as the social designation called gender, would this question even need to be asked? Does nonparticipation in heterosexuality necessarily insulate one from gendered-unequal social institutions? Did the U.S. Supreme Court give a negative answer in the sexual harassment case of Joseph Oncale? *See Oncale v. Sundowner Offshore Servs.*, 523 U.S. 75 (1998) (*see* Chapter 7.2). Did M.'s family remain structurally gendered without regard to the sex of its occupants? If M. and H. are insulted or offended by such an analysis, does that make it inaccurate? Does the fact that M. remained in woman's status in the labor market—and what is a woman other than an occupant of women's status?—make this analysis compelling? Is M. not seen as a woman, meaning an occupant of women's social status, by the Court because her partner is also a woman? Does the majority, in missing this point, reify gender?

Does H. object to the imposition on her of a legal structure that in part reflects and imposes, and in part is attempting to ameliorate, the heterosexual family model? Does this case impose a male (i.e., heterosexual, meaning male dominant) model of family on gay and lesbian couples? Will assimilating gay and lesbian families to the support regime further impose a male dominant family structure on more gender-equal relationships, or will the relationships' being part of the legal regime promote greater equality in all marriages and ameliorate the economic difficulties of some? Put another way, is it fair to attribute both economic dependence and persistent breakdown to the family *form* created under male dominance, such that one person is left relatively disadvantaged when it ends? If the family is an intrinsically unequal form, will parties tend to leave it more unequal than they entered it? In yet other words, if the family form is itself heterosexual, taking the unequal form of the genders in society, and the FLA is designed to try to compensate for the disadvantages intrinsic to it, shouldn't anyone who undertakes that life form have access to its compensations? Does this analysis of the system explain why relationships like M. and H.'s are "systemic," rather than "exceptional," in Mr. Justice Gonthier's terms?

10.2 Assuming that, despite disclaimers, the logic of *M. & H.* moves in the direction of legalizing same-sex marriage, consider the argument of Professor Nancy Polikoff against making the right to marry a priority for the lesbian and gay rights movement:

> I believe that the desire to marry in the lesbian and gay community is an attempt to mimic the worst of mainstream society, an effort to fit into an inherently problematic institution.... [Professor William] Eskridge's compilation [of same-sex marriages across cultures and historical time] is filled with ... examples of same-sex relationships whose structure reinforces traditional notions of marriage as gendered and hierarchical.... [H]ierarchy was a component of all such ostensibly same-sex marriages, with the partner embodying the most male characteristics accorded higher status and greater control.... Similarly, the political and public relations campaign to legalize same-sex marriage would likely contend that our relationships are no different from heterosexual marriages. In other words, the pro-marriage position would accept, rather than challenge, the current institution of marriage.... [Just as t]hose challenging the military exclusion neither critique the military as an institution nor acknowledge the transformative potential of allowing lesbians and gay men to serve openly, ... those campaigning for lesbian and gay marriage would adopt a similar strategy, neither critiquing the institution of marriage nor acknowledging the transformative potential of allowing lesbians and gay men to enter into state-sanctioned unions....
>
> Long-term, monogamous couples would almost certainly be the exemplars of the movement, sharing stories of adversity resulting from their unmarried status: a partner who lacked health care because he was not eligible for spousal employee benefits, or who was denied hospital visitation rights because she was not family, or who was unable to make burial arrangements after her partner's death. Marriage would be touted as the solution to these couples' problems; the limitations of marriage, and of a social system valuing one form of human relationship above all others, would be downplayed.... Advocating lesbian and gay marriage will detract from, even contradict, efforts to unhook economic benefits from marriage and make basic health care and other necessities available to all. It will also require a rhetorical strategy that emphasizes similarities between our relationships and heterosexual marriages, values long-term monogamous coupling above all other relationships, and denies the potential of lesbian and gay marriage to transform the gendered nature of marriage for all people. Nancy D. Polikoff, "We Will Get What We Ask For: Why Legalizing Gay and Lesbian Marriage Will Not 'Dismantle the Legal Structure of Gender in Every Marriage,' " 79 *Va. L. Rev.* 1535, 1536, 1539–41, 1543, 1546, 1549 (1993).

Do the facts, the language, the logic, and the result of *M. & H.*, interpreted as a step toward legalization of same-sex marriages, bear out or contradict Professor Polikoff's analysis?

11. The future of marriage: Consider the relationship between *Egan*, [1995] 2 S.C.R. 513 (*see* Chapter 1), and *M. & H.* What is left of *Egan*'s result after *M. & H.*? That is, how possible is it to hold, as *Egan* did, that a law that detrimentally distinguishes members of a disadvantaged group on an analogous ground may still not constitute discrimination under Section

15(1)? If the analysis of "spouse" of *M. & H.* controls federally as well as provincially, how can the two men in *Egan* still be denied old-age spousal benefits? Mr. Justice Iacobucci recognized that *Egan* also treated the opposite-sex definition of "spouse" in provincial legislation, but said that the FLA is unique so must be evaluated on its own merits. Did he change his mind? Both writers for the majority of the Court repeatedly stated that their opinions had no implications for any other provisions where the term "spouse" is used, and imply nothing about marriage as such. For example, Mr. Justice Iacobucci noted that "arguments based on the possible extension of the definition of 'spouse' beyond the circumstances of this case are entirely speculative and cannot justify the violation of the constitutional rights of same-sex couples in the case at bar." *M. & H.*, 171 D.L.R. 4th at 641. Can its implications be contained? Should they be? After *M. & H.*, what reasons are left to support the view that a statute governing the economics of family breakdown can define "spouse" one way, a statute governing who can create legally recognized families can define "spouse" another way? Mr. Justice Gonthier finds "Cory J.'s statement that 'this appeal has nothing to do with marriage per se' entirely unconvincing." *M. & H.*, 171 D.L.R. (4th) at 679. Are you convinced?

M. & H. holds that the FLA, by confining its definition of spouse to "either of a man or a woman," exacerbates a preexisting arbitrary social disadvantage by contributing to the general vulnerability of same-sex relationships, that it fails to take into account actual situations by declining to give legal protection to relationships of dependency and permanence, and that it affects fundamental interests of individuals by institutionalizing the view that some are less worthy of social recognition in their capacity to form intimate conjugal relationships—all to the detriment of their dignity on the basis of a recognized analogous ground for prohibited discrimination. Can you distinguish a case that challenges the same definition of spouse in a marriage law? Can legal gay and lesbian marriage be far behind?

In invalidating South Africa's male-only sodomy prohibition as a violation of equality, dignity, and privacy rights under the 1996 Constitution, the South African Constitutional Court treated the social and legal issues of gay rights with sweep and nuance. In *National Coalition for Gay and Lesbian Equality v. Minister of Justice*, 1999 (1) SALR 6 (CC), that Court found that the statutory offense of sodomy—defined as "a male person [committing] with another male person ... any act which is calculated to stimulate sexual passion or to give sexual gratification," Sexual Offenses Act 1957, § 20A (1)—as well as the common law offense—defined as "unlawful and intentional sexual intercourse per anum between human males" including with consent, 1999 (1) SALR 6, 22 (CC), violated the constitutional requirement that "the state may not unfairly discriminate against anyone on ... grounds [of] sexual orientation." Section 9, 1996 Constitution (*see* Chapter 1).

The National Coalition for Gay and Lesbian Equality v. The Minister of Justice

Constitutional Court of South Africa
1999 (1) SALR 6 (CC)

■ ACKERMANN, J.

[S]ection 9 of the 1996 Constitution [does not envisage] a passive or purely negative concept of equality; quite the contrary.... [To summarize the enquiry, we ask:]

(a) Does the provision differentiate between people or categories of people? If so, does the differentiation bear a rational connection to a legitimate government purpose? If it does not then there is a violation.... Even if it does bear a rational connection, it might nevertheless amount to discrimination. (b) Does the differentiation amount to unfair discrimination? ... (i) Firstly, does the differentiation amount to "discrimination"? If it is on a specified ground, then discrimination will have been established.... (ii) If the differentiation amounts to "discrimination," does it amount to "unfair discrimination"? If it has been found to have been on a specified ground, then unfairness will be presumed.... (c) If the discrimination is found to be unfair then a determination will have to be made as to whether the provision can be justified under the limitations clause.... [citing Harksen v. Lane 1998 (1) SA 300 CC (1997 (12) BCLR 1655)]

I adopt the following definition ...: "... sexual orientation is defined by reference to erotic attraction: in the case of heterosexuals, to members of the opposite sex; in the case of gays and lesbians, to members of the same sex. Potentially a homosexual or gay or lesbian person can therefore be anyone who is erotically attracted to members of his or her own sex." Edwin Cameron, "Sexual Orientation and the Constitution: A Test Case for Human Rights," (1993) 110 SALJ 450, 452.... The desire for equality is not a hope for the elimination of all differences. "The experience of subordination—of personal subordination, above all—lies behind the vision of equality." Michael Walzer, Spheres of Justice: A Defence of Pluralism and Equality xiii (1983) ... The discriminatory prohibitions on sex between men reinforces already existing societal prejudices and severely increases the negative effects of such prejudices on their lives. "Even when these provisions are not enforced, they reduce gay men ... to what one author has referred to as 'unapprehended felons,' thus entrenching stigma and encouraging discrimination...." Cameron, supra, at 455.

[The common law offense of sodomy has had the following impact on gay men:] (a) The discrimination is on a specified ground. Gay men are a permanent minority in society and have suffered in the past from patterns of disadvantage. The impact is severe, affecting the dignity, personhood and identity of gay men at a deep level.... (b) The nature of the power and its purpose is to criminalise private conduct of consenting adults which causes no harm to anyone else. It has no other purpose than to criminalise conduct which fails to conform with the moral or religious views of a section of society. (c) The discrimination has ... gravely affected the rights and interests of gay men and deeply impaired their fundamental dignity. [This] analysis confirms that the discrimination is unfair ... and therefore in breach of section 9 of the 1996 Constitution....

In my view ... the common-law crime of sodomy also constitutes an infringement of the right to dignity which is enshrined in section 10 [and underlined in section 36] of our Constitution.... At its least, it is clear that the constitutional protection of dignity requires us to acknowledge the value and worth of all individuals as members of our society. The common-law prohibition on sodomy criminalises all sexual intercourse per anum between men.... In so doing, it punishes a form of sexual conduct which is identified by our broader society with homosexuals. Its symbolic effect is to state that in the eyes of our legal system all gay men are criminals. The stigma thus attached to a significant proportion of our population is manifest. But the harm imposed by the criminal law is far more than symbolic. As a result of the criminal offence, gay men are at risk of arrest, prosecution and conviction of the offence of sodomy simply because they seek to engage in sexual conduct which is part of their experience of being human. Just as apartheid legislation rendered the lives of couples of different racial groups perpetually at risk, the sodomy offence builds insecurity and vulnerability into the daily lives of gay men. There can be no doubt that the existence of a law which punishes a form of sexual expression for gay men degrades and devalues gay men in our broader society. As such it is a palpable invasion of their dignity and a breach of section 10 of the Constitution. . . .

The present case illustrates how, in particular circumstances, the rights of equality and dignity are closely related, as are the rights of dignity and privacy. . . . Privacy recognises that we all have a right to a sphere of private intimacy and autonomy which allows us to establish and nurture human relationships without interference from the outside community. The way in which we give expression to our sexuality is at the core of this area of private intimacy. If, in expressing our sexuality, we act consensually and without harming one another, invasion of that precinct will be a breach of our privacy. Our society has a poor record of seeking to regulate the sexual expression of South Africans. In some cases, as in this one, the reason for the regulation was discriminatory; our law, for example, outlawed sexual relationships among people of different races. The fact that a law prohibiting forms of sexual conduct is discriminatory, does not, however, prevent it at the same time being an improper invasion of the intimate sphere of human life to which protection is given by the Constitution in section 14 [privacy]. . . . The offence which lies at the heart of the discrimination in this case constitutes at the same time and independently a breach of the rights of privacy and dignity which, without doubt, strengthens the conclusion that the discrimination is unfair. . . .

[We conclude, in balancing the different interests under the limitation clause, that t]he criminalisation of sodomy in private between consenting males is a severe limitation of a gay man's right to equality in relation to sexual orientation, because it hits at one of the ways in which gays give expression to their sexual orientation[, while] the enforcement of the private moral views of a section of the community, which are based to a large extent on nothing more than prejudice, cannot qualify as . . . a legitimate purpose. . . .

[The statutory provision] amounts to unfair discrimination [for the same reasons as the common law offence and cannot be justified.] There is nothing before us to show that the provision was motivated by anything other than rank prejudice and had as its purpose the stamping out of these forms of gay erotic self-expression. [Held invalid under Section 9.]

■ Sachs J. [concurring]

Only in the most technical sense is this a case about who may penetrate whom where. At a practical and symbolical level it is about the status, moral citizenship and sense of self-worth of a significant section of the community. . . . [W]hat is really being punished by the anti-sodomy laws[?] Is it an act, or is it a person? . . . In the case of male homosexuality . . . the perceived deviance is punished simply because it is deviant. It is repressed for its perceived symbolism rather than because of its proven harm. If proof were necessary, it is established by the fact that consensual anal penetration of a female is not criminalised. Thus, it is not the act of sodomy that is denounced by the law, but the so-called sodomite who performs it; not any proven social damage, but the threat that same-sex passion in itself is seen as representing to heterosexual hegemony.

The effect is that all homosexual desire is tainted, and the whole gay and lesbian community is marked with deviance and perversity. When everything associated with homosexuality is treated as bent, queer, repugnant or comical, the equality interest is directly engaged. People are subject to extensive prejudice because of what they are or what they are perceived to be, not because of what they do. The result is that significant group of the population is, because of its sexual non-conformity, persecuted, marginalized and turned in on itself. . . .

[Applicants treated the right to privacy] as a poor second prize to be offered and received only in the event of the Court declining to invalidate the laws because of a breach of equality. Their argument may be summarised as follows: privacy analysis is inadequate because it suggests that homosexuality is shameful and therefore should only be protected if it is limited to the private bedroom; it tends to limit the promotion of gay rights to the decriminalisation of consensual adult sex, instead of contemplating a more comprehensive normative framework that addresses discrimination generally against gays; and it assumes a dual structure—public and private—that does not capture the complexity of lived life, in which public and private lives determine each other, with the mobile lines between them being constantly amenable to repressive definition.

These concerns are undoubtedly valid. Yet, I consider that they arise from a set of assumptions that are flawed as to how equality and privacy rights interrelate and about the manner in which privacy rights should truly be understood. . . . [B]oth from the point of view of the persons affected, as well as from that of society as a whole, equality and privacy cannot be separated, because they are both violated simultaneously by anti-sodomy laws. In the present matter, such laws deny equal respect for difference, which lies at the heart of equality, and become the basis for the invasion of privacy. At the same time, the negation by the state of different forms of intimate personal behaviour becomes the foundation for the repudiation of equality. Human rights are better approached and defended in an integrated rather than a disparate fashion. The rights must fit the people, not the people the rights. This requires looking at rights and their violations from a persons-centred rather than a formula-based position, and analysing them contextually rather than abstractly. . . . There is no good reason why the concept of privacy should . . . be restricted simply to sealing off from state control what happens in the bedroom, with the doleful sub-text that you may behave as bizarrely or shamefully as you like, on the understanding that you do so in private. . . .

[Viewed affirmatively] autonomy must mean far more than the right to occupy an envelope of space in which a socially detached individual can act freely from interference by the state. What is crucial is the nature of the activity, not its site. . . . [T]he Constitution . . . acknowledges that people live in their bodies, their communities, their cultures, their places and their times. The expression of sexuality requires a partner, real or imagined. It is not for the state to choose or to arrange the choice of partner, but for the partners to choose themselves. At the same time, there is no reason why the concept of privacy should be extended to give blanket libertarian permission for people to do anything they like provided that what they do is sexual and done in private. In this respect, the assumptions about privacy rights are too broad. There are very few democratic societies, if any, which do not penalise persons for engaging in inter-generational, intra-familial, and cross-species sex, whether in public or in private. Similarly, in democratic societies sex involving violence, deception, voyeurism, intrusion or harassment is punishable (if not always punished), or else actionable, wherever it takes place (there is controversy about prostitution and sado-masochistic and dangerous fetishistic sex.) The privacy interest is overcome because of the perceived harm. The choice is accordingly not an all-or-nothing one between maintaining a spartan normality, at the one extreme, or entering what been called the post-modern supermarket of satisfactions, at the other. Respect for personal privacy does not require disrespect for social standards....

[I]t is my view that the equality principle and the dignity principle should not be seen as competitive but rather as complementary. Inequality is established not simply through group-based differential treatment, but through differentiation which perpetuates disadvantage and leads to the scarring of the sense of dignity and self-worth associated with membership of the group. Conversely, an invasion of dignity is more easily established when there is an inequality of power and status between the violator and the victim. One of the great gains achieved by following a situation-sensitive human rights approach is that analysis focuses not on abstract categories, but on the lives as lived and the injuries as experienced by different groups in our society.... The commonality that unites [all different groups that are discriminated against] is the injury to dignity imposed upon people as a consequence of their belonging to certain groups. Dignity in the context of equality has to be understood in this light.... In the case of gays, history and experience teach us that ... scarring comes not from poverty or powerlessness, but from invisibility. It is the tainting of desire, it is the attribution of perversity and shame to spontaneous bodily affection, it is the prohibition of the expression of love, it is the denial of full moral citizenship in society because you are what you are, that impinges on the dignity and self-worth of a group.... Gays constitute a distinct though invisible section of the community that has been treated not only with disrespect or condescension but with disapproval and revulsion; they are not generally obvious as a group, pressurised by society and the law to remain invisible; their identifying characteristic combines all the anxieties produced by sexuality with all the alienating effects resulting from difference; and they are seen as especially contagious or prone to corrupting others....

At the heart of equality jurisprudence is the rescuing of people from a caste-like status and putting an end to their being treated as lesser human beings because they belong to a particular group.... In the case of gays it comes from compulsion to deny a closely held personal characteristic.... The present case shows well that equality should not be confused with uniformity; in fact, uniformity can be an enemy of equality. Equality means equal concern and respect across difference.... This judgment holds that in determining the normative limits of permissible sexual conduct, homosexual erotic activity must be treated on an equal basis with heterosexual, in other words, that the same-sex quality of the conduct must not be a consideration in determining where and how the law should intervene.... At the very least, what is statistically normal ceases to be the basis for establishing what is legally normative. More broadly speaking, the scope of what is constitutionally normal is expanded to include the widest range of perspectives and to acknowledge, accommodate and accept the largest spread of difference.

NOTES AND QUESTIONS ON *NATIONAL COALITION FOR GAY AND LESBIAN EQUALITY*

1. Sexual orientation: If you had been clerking for the Court, would you have recommended to your Justice that sexual orientation be defined exclusively in terms of erotic attraction in this case?

2. Race: Evaluate the Court's references to South Africa's experience with prohibiting sex between races as a foundation for understanding its prohibition of sex between men. Is there a parallel in the United States?

3. Unfair discrimination: Revisit the questions concerning the possible interpretations of South Africa's concept of "unfair discrimination" from Chapter 1 in light of the Court's more developed elaboration of its approach to assessing questions under that rubric.

4. Comparative law: The Constitutional Court cited *Dudgeon, Norris, Toonen,* and *Egan* as supporting their reasons. *Bowers v. Hardwick* was distinguished, the Court observing that the text of the United States Constitution is substantially different from South Africa's, in that the 1996 Constitution contains explicit guarantees of privacy and dignity as well as an express prohibition on unfair discrimination on the ground of sexual orientation. *See* 1998 (1) SALR 6, 37 (CC). The Court thus draws on several foreign jurisdictions both to support its conclusion and to distinguish precedents with which it disagrees. How relevant are transnational authorities in a setting such as this country, this constitution, and this case? Do these references increase or decrease the perceived legitimacy of judicial decisions such as this one? *See generally* Christopher McCrudden, "Transnational Judicial 'Conversations' on Constitutional Rights," (unpublished manuscript, 1999) (analyzing judicial citation of judgments from other jurisdictions in human rights cases). Why do the courts of South Africa and Canada consider foreign precedents in interpreting their constitutions while the United States Supreme Court virtually never does (or never says it does)? Should the United States display more openness to global developments on subjects such as gay rights? Do the textual differences between the United States and South African constitutions limit the applicability of the insights of this case in the U.S. context? How do you suggest using the rulings and analyses of the Court in addressing the constitutionality of sodomy laws in the United States?

5. Forced sodomy: The Constitutional Court invalidated the entire offense of sodomy, including not only consensual acts but sodomy that is forced and sodomy with children as well, suggesting in passing that the offense of "male rape" could be dealt with through new legislation if desired. *See* 1999 (1) SALR 6, 43 (CC). Did the Court's logic supporting the invalidation of the crime of consensual sodomy require or support this step? Does equality require a right to force sex on another adult? on a child? Does dignity? Does privacy?

6. Justice Sachs's concurrence: Justice Sachs attempts an ambitious reconciliation of privacy, dignity, and difference with an expansive, contextual, antihierarchical concept of equality under the 1996 Constitution much like that developed in Canada after *Andrews* (*see* Chapter 1). Does he succeed?

6.1 Consider his question about whether act or status is criminalized under the sodomy law. Is it more parsimonious to conclude that the act not the person is prohibited, in that a man is prohibited from engaging in the act of anally penetrating a man because of the threat that act in itself represents to male supremacy? On this reading, anal penetration of a woman is *not the same act* because that act affirms male supremacy rather than threatens it. Consider next whether heterosexual *women* have "hegemony" over gay men? If not, or not quite, or not in the same sense heterosexual men do, to speak of "heterosexual hegemony," gender neutral, is imprecise. It is, rather, the hegemony of heterosexual *men* that is threatened by sodomy. If the gay man as a person represents this threat, the distinction between person and act dissolves. Does this analysis clarify the issues raised?

6.2   Justice Sachs limits his consideration of the possible sex equality arguments to the formal sameness/difference sex equality argument. Why is the place of a sodomy prohibition in male dominance not considered?

6.3   Is Justice Sachs's concept of privacy based on equality? Does he sufficiently recognize the consequences of gender disparity on the drawing of the "private" line where it has traditionally been drawn, such that even existing prohibitions on abuse in private, particularly when sexual, are overwhelmingly not enforced? Does "perceived harm" in fact overcome the shield provided by the privacy he defends in societies of sex inequality? Or is the harm simply not perceived under unequal conditions? Does Justice Sachs display awareness of women's lack of privacy, in his sense, in private? Is his confidence in privacy as a legal value warranted by women's transcultural experience in reality? Do the facts of the provision at issue, as well as the conflation of lesbian women with gay men in the terms "gays" or "homosexuals," tend to conspire to keep women invisible in the analysis?

6.4   Is Justice Sachs's concept of privacy the same one that is in effect in the American legal system? Is the applicants' critique of privacy applicable to privacy as it exists across the law? Does Justice Sachs's attempted recoupment of privacy from an equality critique adequately address the function of privacy in reinforcing inequality in the United States? If privacy, properly understood, does not shield abuse, why didn't Justice Sachs dissent from the Court's invalidation of the prohibition on forced sodomy and sodomy with children? If Justice Sachs could adjudicate the public/private line, would it look very different than it looks now? Does he improve it? Does he provide a standard to which it could aspire?

6.5   Do Justice Sachs's principles lead to a conclusion on whether sadomasochism, understood as the sexualization of hierarchy, is one more "different" form of sexual expression that must be tolerated under law? Clearly, on his analysis, same-sex sadomasochism is to be treated no differently from heterosexual sadomasochism. But what about sadomasochism itself? Does the absence of emphasis in his analysis on an antihierarchical principle as central to substantive equality leave this question open? Further, if tradition itself is suspect as having entrenched inequalities, and an antihierarchical equality principle is incompletely articulated, what is to stop a successful equality attack on laws against intergenerational sex (sex between adults and children) as simple moralism? Does Justice Sachs recover difference from the grip of equality formalism?

B.   SEX DISCRIMINATION

Society defines lesbian women and gay men as at once sexual and inferior. Women as such are also—or so some theories of sex inequality contend—sexually defined as inferiors. Is there a connection between the two: the social definition, status, and treatment of all women on the one hand and that of lesbian women and gay men on the other? Are these two "hands" of one body dispensing inequality? One Texas judge, in sentencing a convicted murderer to thirty years rather than life in prison for killing two gay men, saw a connection: "I put prostitutes and gays at about the same level. If these boys [the defendants] had picked up two prostitutes and taken them to the woods and killed them, I'd consider that a similar case. . . . And I'd be hard put to give somebody life for killing a prostitute." Lori Montgomery, "Why Judge Went Easy on Gays' Teen Killer," *Dallas Times Herald*, Dec. 16, 1988, at A-16 (quoting Judge Hampton); *see also In re Hampton*, 775 S.W.2d 629, 630 (Tex. 1989) (citing article in subsequent censure proceeding). What do you call the belief system that finds the analogy that Judge Hampton drew, and the consequences he attached to it, legitimate and persuasive? Is it misogynistic? homophobic? both at once? Is the judge's statement discriminatory? on what ground or grounds? Is it an extreme reflection of a social ideology that is pervasive in other forms? Explain why, in the cultural view illustrated by Judge Hampton, a sexual definition lowers the value of a human life. (See also Chapter 10.1.) Do only certain sexual definitions do this, or does any definition that is sexual—or are only certain people sexually defined, so it comes to the same? Are lesbian women discriminated against as lesbian, as women, inseparably and simultaneously as both, or variously depending on the situation?

The legal issues raised by attempts to establish gay and lesbian rights raise fundamental questions for sex equality theory. The basic legal and social question is whether discrimination against gay men and lesbian women is an aspect of sex inequality, taking place on gendered terrain, or whether the two phenomena are separate and autonomous. If there were no sex roles, would society care what the sex of your sexual partner was? Or is analyzing discrimination against "homosexuals" as sex-based reductive and incomplete, reflecting a failure to grasp the issue on its own terms and as a discrete form of discrimination in itself? Does understanding same-sex discrimination as sex discrimination obscure the distinctive history and unique features of the oppression—such as persecution of both men and women, denial that such people exist, and the difficulty of telling who is who and finding each other? Choice of analysis and doctrine also presents second-order issues. Does a sex equality approach to same-sex discrimination work better for some situations and people, less well for others, promoting certain legal priorities? To what extent does the answer depend on what kind of sex equality approach is used? Can the two theories be combined, producing for example a gender-sensitive analysis of a sexual orientation ground? Might the particularities of the experience of inequality of gay men and lesbian women make an analysis of male dominance more nuanced? Might some instances of discrimination against gay men and against lesbian women yield to sex equality initiatives where prior legal avenues have failed?

The answers to these questions depend in part upon, and have major implications for, the place of sexuality in gender. If one thinks, for example, that "sexuality and sexual activity are not the primary motives" for sex discrimination but "the desire to maintain rigid gender roles is," Amelia A. Craig, "Musing About Discrimination Based on Sex and Sexual Orientation as 'Gender Role' Discrimination," 5 *S. Cal. Rev. L. & Women's Stud.* 105, 105 (1995), to the degree sexual orientation discrimination is seen as sexually motivated, sex discrimination law would not address it, while sex equality law's questioning of the rigidity of gender roles could help when same-sexuality calls those roles into question. Alternatively, if sexuality is the linchpin of the inequality of the sexes, the status and treatment of gay men and lesbian women, as sexually defined and as subordinated groups, is critical to sex inequality, and the access, control, and pleasure men receive from male sexual dominance provide an incentive and payoff for discriminating against all women in general and gay men and lesbian women in particular. Such a view is implicit in the analysis of the French writer Monique Wittig, for whom sexuality is not confined to the bedroom:

> The category of sex is the product of heterosexual society that turns half of the population into sexual beings, for sex is a category which women cannot be outside of. Wherever they are, whatever they do (including working in the public sector), they are seen (and made) sexually available to men, and they, breasts, buttocks, costume, must be visible. They must wear their yellow star, their constant smile, day and night. One might consider that every woman, married or not, has a period of forced sexual service, a sexual service which we may compare to the military one, and which can vary between a day, a year, or twenty years or more. Some lesbians and nuns escape, but they are very few. Monique Wittig, *The Straight Mind and Other Essays* 7 (1992).

Is the reality she describes sex-based? If she is right, is same-sexuality a core issue for sex equality law? Examining the social and legal treatment of same-sex sexuality, including the extent to which lesbian women are outside of the category of women who are defined as sexual beings, promises to illuminate the question of whether gender inequality is sexualized in the lives of both women and men.

1. SAME–SEXUALITY AND GENDER INEQUALITY

Activists and social theorists have long seen sexism in heterosexism. One early gay activist stated simply: "Gay liberation is a struggle against sexism." Allen Young, "Out of the Closet: A Gay Manifesto," *Ramparts*, Nov. 1971, at 52. Professor Francisco Valdes made the same observation: "Gender is the central device for the simultaneous oppression both of women and of sexual minorities under hetero-patriarchy.... Sexual orientation actually and ultimately is sex-based." Francisco Valdes, "Queers, Sissies, Dykes, and Tomboys: Deconstructing the Conflation of 'Sex,' 'Gender,' and 'Sexual Orientation' in Euro-American Law and Society," 83 *Cal. L. Rev.* 1, 324–36 (1995). (Should arguable "sexual minorities" such as pedophiles and sadomasochists be encompassed in such an analysis?) If there were no sexism, would heterosexism exist? An early movement organization said no:

> Sexism is the material, ideological and psychological oppression of women and Gay people.... In reality the whole conception of heterosexual and homosexual was created as part and parcel of the definition of sex roles.... When we say that sexuality ... is role-defined and gender-defined we mean that we are sexually and emotionally attracted to people on the basis of gender (on the basis of whether they are a woman or a man) and trained to respond in terms of roles (dominant/passive, masculine/feminine etc.) ... When no privileges are given to men or to heterosexuals a sexuality will develop which does not accord a certain role to women and a certain role to men and whether one relates to people of the same sex or the opposite sex would have no particular significance. At that point sexuality would become *non-defined*.... There is no individual solution to the problem of sexuality. As long as men and heterosexuals are given privileges and power sexuality for all of us will be "defined." *The Political Perspective of the Lavender & Red Union* 5–11 (1975) (on file with author).

What do you think?

Related insights have been explored, developed, and extended as subsequent scholars sought to illuminate the connections between the social system that positions men distinct from and over women, and the system that places heterosexual people distinct from and over nonheterosexual people. The challenge same-sexuality poses to conventional gender role behaviors and expectations has been widely observed. Professor Marc Fajer sees homophobia as substantially fueled by gender role anxiety:

> [There is] evidence that homophobia is caused, at least in part, by a desire to preserve traditional gender roles; that homophobia is a highly gendered phenomenon generally; and that homophobia has the effect of enforcing gender-role norms.... Much of the psychological literature examining homophobia has concluded that support for the traditional gender-role structure is a primary cause of homophobia.... Many stories reveal discrimination purely on the basis of failure to conform to gender stereotypes. Society is hard on "butch" women and effeminate men, whether or not they are gay.... Anti-gay violence often takes the form of attacks on men who seem effeminate.... Derogatory terms applied to gays—butch, queen, fairy—often reflect concern with gender-role variation.... A corollary to this perception is that gay men are described as not being men.... Another variation of gender-related discrimination occurs when people, having decided that gay men share female characteristics, discriminate against them in a way that mirrors discrimination against women generally.... One particularly significant form of gender-related discrimination is that non-gay people often assume that gay men prefer sexual positions associated with heterosexual females: the active role in oral sex and the passive role in anal sex. This stereotype is so powerful that men who perform sexual activity with other men, but only assume the "male" role may not be considered gay by others or by themselves. Indeed, even cultures that treat some forms of gay activity as acceptable have denigrated adult men who performed the "female" role during sexual activity. Many stories support the idea that the perception that a male is acting like a female is a significant component of some people's discomfort with male-male sexual activity.... These stories together lend support to the conclusion that homophobia is based primarily in "anxiety about the boundaries of gender." Fajer, *supra*, at 617–24 (citing Andrew Koppelman, "The Miscegenation Analogy: Sodomy Law as Sex Discrimination," 98 *Yale L.J.* 145, 159 (1988)).

Suzanne Pharr offers a dominance analysis of the same phenomena:

> [G]ay men are perceived ... as a threat to male dominance and control.... Visible gay men are objects of extreme hatred and fear by heterosexual men because their breaking ranks with male heterosexual solidarity is seen as a damaging rent in the very fabric of sexism. They are seen as betrayers, as traitors who must be punished and eliminated.... When gay men break ranks with male roles through bonding and affection outside the arenas of war and sports, they are perceived as not being "real men," that is, as being identified with women, the weaker sex that must be dominated and that over the centuries has been the object of male hatred and abuse. Suzanne Pharr, *Homophobia: A Weapon of Sexism* 18–19 (1988).

Professor Mary Becker analyzes the same realities in yet more sexually specific terms that are explicitly critical of male dominance:

Taboos on lesbian and gay relationships play a number of roles in supporting patriarchy and patriarchal privilege for heterosexual men.... First, homophobia protects men who conform to the requirement of patriarchal masculinity—men who act like real men—from sexual assault by other men. Men understand the aggressive nature of male sexuality in our patriarchal culture. They understand and *fear* it. They fear that another man might control and subordinate them sexually were they viewed as his sexual objects. Men tend to be paranoid about this danger.... This phenomenon gives all men an incentive to be normal, heterosexual men.... Second, a key aspect of women's oppression is rooted in heterosexual relations that subordinate women to men's right to sexual access and control. Lesbian relationships threaten patriarchal privileges because lesbians reject intimate relationships with men. Part of the payoff to men, after all, for being "normal" is sexual access to girls and women. Mary E. Becker, "The Abuse Excuse and Patriarchal Narratives," 92 *Nw. U. L. Rev.* 1459, 1477–78 (1998).

While recognizing the ways in which gay and lesbian existence challenges and undermines conventional sex roles and male dominance as a social system, many scholars have also observed and critically analyzed a stake in gender and male dominance found in some facets of gay culture, observing it to be no gender-free utopia. That gay men can remain male-defined, affirming patriarchy even as their existence is rejected by it and challenges it, is analyzed by Professor Marilyn Frye:

In a woman-hating culture, one of the very nasty things that can happen to a man is his being treated or seen as a woman, or womanlike. This degradation makes him a proper object of rape and derision, and reverses for him the presumption of civil rights. This dreadful fate befalls gay men. In the society at large, if it is known that a man is gay, he is subject to being pegged at the level of sexual status, personal authority and civil rights which are presumptive for women. This is, of course, really quite unfair, for most gay men are quite as fully *men* as any men: being gay is not at all inconsistent with being loyal to masculinity and committed to contempt for women. Some of the very things which lead straight people to doubt gay men's manhood are, in fact, proofs of it. One of the things which persuades the straight world that gay men are not really men is the effeminacy of style of some gay men and the gay institution of the impersonation of women.... But as I read it, gay men's effeminacy and donning of feminine apparel displays no love of or identification with women or the womanly. For the most part, this femininity is affected and is characterized by theatrical exaggeration. It is a casual and cynical mockery of women, for whom femininity is the trappings of oppression.... Some gay men achieve, indeed, prodigious mastery of the feminine.... But the mastery of the feminine is not feminine. It is masculine. It is not a manifestation of woman-loving but of woman-hating. Someone with such mastery may have the very first claim to manhood. Marilyn Frye, "Lesbian Feminism and the Gay Rights Movement: Another View of Male Supremacy, Another Separatism," *in The Politics of Reality* 128, 136–38 (1983).

Charles Silverstein concluded, based on his investigation of the attitudes of several respondents in his research, that the realities of both male homosexuality and lesbianism can be understood in the simplest of conventional gender terms:

> [M]ale homosexuality is predominantly a phenomenon of masculinity
> ... lesbianism is predominantly a phenomenon of femininity. Male
> gays are first and foremost men; they act like men and feel like men,
> and this is particularly true with regard to their sexual inclinations. In
> a sense, I am suggesting that straight men and gay men are far more
> similar than they are dissimilar when it comes to sexual behavior and
> attitudes toward sex. Similarly, lesbians are first and foremost women
> and only secondarily gay. Charles Silverstein, *Man to Man: Gay
> Couples in America* 329 (1981).

Gender has been found significant in people's beliefs about the source
of their sexual orientation. Men are more likely to report that their
sexuality is a fixed part of their being, while women are more likely to
report that their sexuality is a response to their lives, such that "choice is a
salient feature of sexuality for a significant minority of [lesbian] women."
Carla Golden, "Do Women Choose Their Sexual Orientation?" *in The Best
of the Harvard Gay & Lesbian Review* 91, 97 (Richard Schneider ed., 1997)
(reporting results of interviews). Might different notions of choice in sexual
activity for gay men and lesbian women be primarily a product of gender
socialization? Professor Marc Fajer observes:

> That the perception of choice (or lack of it) is gendered strikes me as
> unsurprising. Our culture includes an understanding that men are not
> really in control of their sexual behavior. When issues like rape and
> sexual harassment are discussed, the culture often attempts to limit
> the culpability of the male on the theory that once a woman arouses a
> man, he cannot help himself. On the other hand, we train women to
> feel responsible for sexual activity and to believe they should be in
> control of it. Thus, a gay man's perception that he has no choice and a
> lesbian's perception that she chooses are consistent with cultural
> understandings of sexuality in general. Fajer, *supra*, at 540 n.139.

Is the tacit social understanding that men "are not really in control of their
sexual behavior" a strategy for empowering men as sexual actors? Does it
seem at all paradoxical that men, whom (according to much evidence in
Chapter 7) society in fact empowers as sexual actors, are more likely to see
themselves as acted upon in their sexual orientation, regarding it as *done to*
them (in the sense of being innate hence beyond their control), while
women, whom (again according to Chapter 7 evidence) society disempowers
as passive receivers of sexual initiative, are more likely to see their
sexuality as something they actively *do*? Is it possible that both are
empirically correct: that significant numbers of gay men accept and lesbian
women reject the male-defined and masculinity-centered sexuality thrust
upon them?

Assuming sexuality is at least substantially affected by life experience,
it seems worth asking whether women become lesbian through the same
process by which men become gay, indeed whether sexuality in general is
produced through a gender-neutral process. Is sexuality as a social experience the same for those who become women and those who become men?
For that matter, do women become women through the same process
through which men become men? Might the centrality of sex acts to
defining homosexuality and the centrality of sexual partner's gender to
sexuality embody not only a heterosexual definition of sexual relating
(making gender crucial when it otherwise might not be) but also a male
definition of identity (you are whom you sleep with)? Professor Eve

Kosofsky Sedgwick, for one, is agnostic on the sources of sexual identity, content with the subjective attribution of individuals:

> If, for instance, many people who self-identify as gay experience the gender of sexual object-choice, or some other proto-form of individual gay identity, as the most immutable and immemorial component of individual being, I can see no grounds for either subordinating this perception or privileging it over that of other self-identified gay people whose experience of identity or object-choice has seemed to themselves to come relatively late or even to be discretionary. Eve Kosofsky Sedgwick, *Epistemology of the Closet* 26–27 (1990).

Does it matter where it comes from? What turns on whether sexual orientation is chosen or not? Reconsider whether the whole notion of a sexual "object-choice" is a product of sexism. Is an identity predicated on the gender of a sexual object-choice a consequence of a gender-unequal society? Is being homosexual the same thing as having a "gay identity"? If gender subordination constructs "gay identity," or even being gay, can a gay liberation movement for social and political change afford to be as indifferent to the evidence and political processes that construct these realities as Professor Sedgwick is?

The fact that the dominant society reacts differently to lesbian women and gay men at times, and the perhaps related priority placed on the suffering of gay men, have been widely observed. Professor Mary Coombs understands these experiences this way:

> The different responses to lesbians and gay men by the dominant culture, I think, can be linked in part to the different ways in which lesbians and gay men are traitors to their gender roles.... In patriarchal cultures, male homosexuality will draw hostility because it suggests the refusal of the dominant role the society offers and thus threatens the naturalness and legitimacy of male superiority.... [H]omophobia as constructed through patriarchy is gendered. Lesbians are condemned both for what we do not do as well as for what we do— engage in "unnatural" sexual practices. Lesbians are seen as women who hate men and who refuse to make themselves sexually available to men. One canard is that lesbians are simply women who have never had good heterosexual sex. Not surprisingly, heterosexual male pornography is full of images of "lesbianism," in which the women perform for men, as a foreplay to performing under men. This vision of lesbianism is used to police all women....
>
> The history suggests that lesbians and gay men are linked at least as much by their oppression as by their practices. Each is condemned for the perceived denial of true gender, but the genders to which they are disloyal are different. The demand for gender loyalty is, in turn, an essential precondition to the enforcement of patriarchy. Thus, the oppression of gay men and lesbians is linked to the oppression of women as women, whether heterosexual or lesbian. This linkage between heterosexism and patriarchy sometimes tends to disappear in discussions of gayness. One aspect of that disappearance is linguistic: Lesbians are women, but "women" often means heterosexual women; lesbians are homosexual, but "homosexual" often means homosexual men. Mary Coombs, "Comment: Between Women/Between Men: The Significance for Lesbianism of Historical Understandings of Same-(Male)Sex Sexual Activities," 8 *Yale J.L. & Human.* 241, 257–59 (1996).

Is it fair to suggest that Professor Coombs's thesis is that while both gay men and lesbian women are traitors to their sexes, because the roles of the sexes are differently crucial to the system of male dominance and female subordination, termed patriarchy, society's response to their respective betrayals varies accordingly? That is, is women's betrayal, not men's, sexualized in an attempt to repossess lesbians as normally objectified women, while gay men's betrayal cannot be recouped as male without destroying male dominance—revealing the definition of maleness as non-sexual to be central to its power?

The gendered stake in a gender-neutral politics of sexual orientation is elucidated by John Stoltenberg in these terms:

> Ultimately it is not possible to support one's belief in gender polarity (or "sex difference") without maintaining gender hierarchy (which in our culture is male supremacy). Clinging to "sex difference" *is* clinging to male supremacy. And our "sexual orientation" is one of the ways we've learned to cling. To be "oriented" toward a particular sex as the object of one's sexual expressivity means, in effect, having a sexuality that is like target practice—keeping it aimed at bodies who display a particular sexual definition above all else, picking out which one to want, which one to get, which one to have. Self-consciousness about one's "sexual orientation" keeps the issue of gender central at precisely the moment in human experience when gender really needs to become profoundly peripheral. Insistence on having a sexual orientation in sex is about defending the status quo, maintaining sex differences and sexual hierarchy, whereas *resistance* to sexual-orientation regimentation is more about where we need to be going. The sensuality that may be occasioned by intimacy, trust, and fairness is quite unlike that sexuality which is driven to hit on a particular gender embodiment. The sensuality that arises in a relational context of actual people being together and actually being themselves—not stand-ins for a gender type—is radically different from that sexuality which requires that the "other" not deviate from a particular standard of sexedness. John Stoltenberg, "What Is 'Good Sex'?" *in Refusing to Be a Man: Essays on Sex and Justice* 89, 93 (rev. ed. 2000) (1989).

In light of this analysis of gender inequality, is the concept of sexual orientation itself retrograde in gender equality terms?

The presence of gendered roles in some parts of gay and lesbian communities, and the connection of those roles to the system of male dominance over women in society at large, is evocatively analyzed by Professor Leo Bersani. Speaking of the simultaneous suspicion and acceptance of male homosexuality in ancient Greece as analyzed in the work of French social and cultural historian Michel Foucault, Professor Bersani writes:

> What the Athenians find hard to accept, Foucault writes, is the authority of a leader who as an adolescent was an "object of pleasure" for other men; there is a legal and moral incompatibility between sexual passivity and civic authority. The only "honorable" sexual behavior "consists in being active, in dominating, in penetrating, and in thereby exercising one's moral authority." In other words, the moral taboo on "passive" anal sex in ancient Athens is primarily formulated as a kind of hygienics of social power. *To be penetrated is to abdicate power.* Leo Bersani, "Is the Rectum a Grave?" 43 *October* 197, 212 (1987).

A similar observation is made by Professor Craig A. Williams of the ancient Romans:

> First and foremost, a self-respecting Roman man must always give the appearance of playing the insertive role in penetrative acts, and not the receptive role.... A Roman man was ideally ready, willing, and able to express his dominion over others, male or female, by means of sexual penetration. By contrast, men who willingly played the receptive role in penetrative acts were imagined thereby to have abrogated their masculine privilege, to have assimilated themselves to the inferior status of women. Craig A. Williams, *Roman Homosexuality: Ideologies of Masculinity in Classical Antiquity* 18 (1999).

Consider the place of gendered roles here and the implications of this analysis for women's civic and moral authority.

Professor Bersani pursues his critique into some contemporary gay and lesbian practices:

> It has frequently been suggested in recent years that such things as the gay-macho style, the butch-fem lesbian couple, and gay and lesbian sadomasochism, far from expressing unqualified and uncontrollable complicities with a brutal and misogynous ideal of masculinity, or with the heterosexual couple permanently locked into a power structure of male sexual and social mastery over female sexual and social passivity, or, finally, with fascism, are in fact subversive parodies of the very formations and behaviors they appear to ape....
>
> If licking someone's leather boots turns you (and him) on, neither of you is making a statement subversive of macho masculinity. Parody is an erotic turn-off, and all gay men know this.... Male gay camp is ... largely a parody of women.... The gay male parody of a certain femininity, which ... may itself be an elaborate social construct, is both a way of giving vent to the hostility toward women that probably afflicts every male (and which male heterosexuals have of course expressed in infinitely nastier and more effective ways) *and* could also paradoxically be thought of as helping to deconstruct that image for women themselves. A certain type of homosexual camp speaks the truth of that femininity as mindless, asexual, and hysterically bitchy, thereby provoking, it would seem to me, a violently antimimetic reaction in any female spectator.... The gay-macho style, on the other hand, is intended to excite others sexually, and the only reason that it continues to be adopted is that it frequently succeeds in doing so....
>
> The dead seriousness of the gay commitment to machismo (by which I of course don't mean that all gays share, or share unambivalently, this commitment) means that gay men run the risk of idealizing and feeling inferior to certain representations of masculinity on the basis of which they are in fact judged and condemned. The logic of homosexual desire includes the potential for a loving identification with the gay man's enemies.... [A] gay man doesn't run the risk of loving his oppressor *only* in the ways in which blacks or Jews might more or less secretly collaborate with their oppressors—that is, as a consequence of the oppression, of that subtle corruption by which a slave can come to idolize power, to agree that he should be enslaved because he is enslaved, that he should be denied power because he doesn't have any. But blacks and Jews don't *become* blacks and Jews as a result of that internalization of an oppressive mentality, whereas that internalization is in part constitutive of male homosexual desire,

which, like all sexual desire, combines and confuses impulses to appropriate and to identify with the object of desire. An authentic gay male political identity therefore implies a struggle not only against definitions of maleness and of homosexuality as they are reiterated and imposed in a heterosexist social discourse, but also against those very same definitions so seductively and so faithfully reflected by those (in large part culturally invented and elaborated) male bodies that we carry within us as permanently renewable sources of excitement. Bersani, *supra*, at 206–09.

In this analysis, are gay men both acted upon by, and actors in, male dominance? Are both true at once? Are you as sure as Professor Bersani is here that people who are Black or Jewish "don't become blacks and Jews," socially speaking, through considerable internalization of an oppressive mentality? (Assume, as Professor Bersani does, that oppressor groups impose and believe the oppressive view.) Does the parody of the feminine that Professor Bersani describes support misogyny? Is drag gender's form of blackface? If one sees sex as a role, might it be said that all women, to the extent they conform to stereotyped role, are more or less impersonating women? Do women act out women's roles, i.e., be feminine, to whatever extent they do (a) because they do not know what they look like? (b) because they think the roles are natural? (c) because men demand and reward this self-presentation? Might gay male parody of femininity be said to deconstruct the former two for a female observer, while reinforcing hostility and contempt for women in female and male observers alike? Is the observer, under the circumstances, more likely male? Are sex roles escaped, or are they refashioned and replayed, through exaggeration and parody? Is the allure of a space beyond the dynamics of power a seductive one? Does Professor Bersani's argument rely on the existence of such a space? Does any such space exist?

Do you agree that all sexual desire appropriates and identifies with its object? Are these qualities characteristic of the sexual paradigm found under gender inequality? Is the paradigm an equal one? Do women who have sex with men generally identify with and appropriate objectified men in and as sex, in the way gay men may, according to Professor Bersani? If Professor Bersani is correct that male homosexual desire is the result of the internalization of a mentality oppressive to gay men, what is female heterosexual desire under conditions of gender inequality the result of? Would a sexuality of equality embody a different sexual desire? Is it perhaps premature to announce how "all sexual desire" functions, to the degree it is constituted and experienced under conditions of gender inequality, as yet pervasive? Does love figure in here anywhere? Is it a cause, a consequence, a sentimentalization, of the dynamics described? Something else?

Picking up on the same parallel Judge Hampton made, Professor Bersani's analysis of popular culture's images of AIDS—trying to understand why male homosexuals are regarded as killers, why (especially male) homosexuality is associated with promiscuity, and specifically why a conventional family with three young hemophiliac boys with AIDS from blood transfusions was driven out of town—presents this image:

> [T]he similarities between representations of female prostitutes and male homosexuals should help us to specify the exact form of sexual behavior being targeted ... as the criminal, fatal, and irresistibly

repeated act. This is of course anal sex … and we must … take into account the widespread confusion in heterosexual *and* homosexual men between fantasies of anal and vaginal sex…. Women and gay men spread their legs with an unquenchable appetite for destruction. This is an image with extraordinary power …[, the] seductive and intolerable image of a grown man, legs high in the air, unable to refuse the suicidal ecstasy of being a woman. Bersani, *supra*, at 211–12.

Does the posture Professor Bersani describes define what "being a woman" is? If so, from what vantage point? Does he attribute this social identity to biology or society? What makes this posture, to the degree that it is, "suicidal"? Is "legs high in the air" a position in which a person is vulnerable to violation? Is the position shameful? If so, from what does the shame derive? Is this a position of dignity, socially speaking? of power? What does it mean that women are socially seen as those who occupy this position by nature? Do you think that, taken from the standpoint of a heterosexual male-dominant world view, gay men are regarded as like women, hence inferior, because some of them are sexually penetrated by men? Is this what straight men fear and loathe about gay men, i.e., about what gay men represent? Is sexual penetration the act that defines sex in both the sense of the gendered and sexualized body, that is, that defines sexuality's place in gender under male dominance? If so, why would that be the case? Does the possibility of sexual penetration of a man denature the basic rationale for women's inferiority? Is this the source of the law's obsession with retaining sodomy laws? of the military's preoccupation with distinguishing soldiers from homosexuals? of homosexuality's stigma (applied to gay men and then conflated with lesbian women as well)? Is it the threat gay male sexuality poses to male supremacy? If so, what is the threat posed by lesbian sexuality?

2. Same-Sex Discrimination, Gendered

Why is same-sex discrimination *not* sex discrimination? Who stole the sexuality in law's "sex"? Justice Ruth Bader Ginsburg recounts how "sex" was supplanted by "gender" in sex equality law:

I owe it all to my secretary … who said, "I'm typing all these briefs and articles for you, and the word sex, sex, sex is on every page…. Don't you know that those nine men (on the Supreme Court)—they hear that word, and their first association is not the way you want them to be thinking? Why don't you use the word gender? It is a grammatical term, and it will ward off distracting associations." Associated Press, "Ginsburg Tells Why She Avoids 'Sex,'" *S.F. Chron.*, Nov. 20, 1993, at A12.

What if those "distracting associations" are the essence of the problem? Has supplanting sex with gender made it easier or harder to identify and reflect critically upon the place of sexuality in women's status? Why was thinking of sexuality not the way Ruth Bader Ginsburg wanted the Justices to be thinking? Is this avoidance encouraged by the sameness/difference approach or has it merely become an artifact of it?

The sex equality canon (*see* Chapter 3) recognizes that the legal prohibition on sex discrimination encompasses arbitrary and invidious treatment based not only on biological sex but also on social gender. Sex roles have sexual elements; sexual orientation is a well recognized facet of gender definition and identification. Taking Professor Judith Butler's formulation of the standard insight that "[i]f gender is the cultural meanings that the sexed body assumes, then a gender cannot be said to follow from a sex in any one way," Judith Butler, *Gender Trouble: Feminism and the Subversion of Identity* 10 (10th anniv. ed. 2000), and accepting that sexuality is socially gendered, as few dispute, then sexual orientation discrimination is gender-based because it forces the sexual component of gender to follow only one way from a sex.

Sex equality arguments for lesbian and gay rights that have been made in courts have been confined to such sameness/difference sex equality arguments. Their strategic merits aside, might this have restricted their appeal and persuasiveness? Although gay men and lesbian women are making the least threatening of assertions from a formal equality point of view—perfectly meeting the similarly situated requirement in most instances and claiming merely individual rights, albeit on a group basis—their arguments for sex equality have failed repeatedly, as *DeSantis* and the Equal Employment Opportunity Commission ("EEOC") cases on which it relies illustrate. However, the argument succeeded in *Baehr v. Lewin*, which would legalize same-sex marriage in Hawai'i on a strict sameness/difference sex equality theory. If in highly formal terms, *Baehr* comes close to questioning the place of heterosexuality in sex-based discrimination and relies heavily on the racial analogy to *Loving v. Virginia*. Is same-sexuality a "difference" from heterosexuality in the legal sense? in the social sense? If legal, with what consequences?

DeSantis v. Pacific Tel. & Tel. Co.

United States Court of Appeals for the Ninth Circuit
608 F.2d 327 (9th Cir. 1979)

■ CHOY, CIRCUIT JUDGE:

Male and female homosexuals [sued for discrimination in employment] because of their homosexuality . . . [under Title VII and 42 U.S.C. § 1985(3)'s prohibition on conspiracy to deprive of civil rights]. DeSantis alleged that he was not hired when a [Pacific Telephone & Telegraph Co. (PT&T)] supervisor concluded that he was a homosexual. . . . Lundin and Buckley, both females, were operators with PT&T [who alleged] that PT&T discriminated against them because of their known lesbian relationship and eventually fired them [and] that they endured numerous insults by PT&T employees because of their relationship. . . . The district court dismissed their [Title VII] suit[s] as not stating a claim upon which relief could be granted. . . .

Appellants argue first that the district courts erred in holding that Title VII does not prohibit discrimination on the basis of sexual preference. They claim that in prohibiting certain employment discrimination on the basis of "sex," Congress meant to include discrimination on the basis of sexual orientation. They add that in a trial they could establish that discrimination against homosexuals disproportionately affects men and that this disproportionate impact and correlation between discrimination on the basis of sexual preference and discrimination on the basis of "sex" requires that sexual preference be considered a subcategory of the "sex" category of Title VII. . . . "Several bills have been introduced to *amend* the Civil Rights Act to prohibit discrimination against 'sexual preference.' None [has] been enacted into law. Congress has not shown any intent other than to restrict the term 'sex' to its traditional meaning. Therefore, this court will not expand Title VII's application. . . . The manifest purpose of Title VII's prohibition against sex discrimination in employment is to ensure that men and women are treated equally....'' (quoting Holloway v. Arthur Andersen & Co., 566 F.2d 659, 662–63 (9th Cir. 1977)) [W]e conclude that Title VII's prohibition of "sex" discrimination applies only to discrimination on the basis of gender and should not be judicially extended to include sexual preference such as homosexuality.

Appellants argue that recent decisions dealing with disproportionate impact require that discrimination against homosexuals fall within the purview of Title VII ... [because] discrimination against homosexuals disproportionately affects men both because of the greater incidence of homosexuality in the male population and because of the greater likelihood of an employer's discovering male homosexuals compared to female homosexuals.... [I]n passing Title VII Congress did not intend to protect sexual orientation.... Appellants now ask us to employ the disproportionate impact decisions as an artifice to "bootstrap" Title VII protection for homosexuals under the guise of protecting men generally. This we are not free to do.... It would achieve by judicial "construction" what Congress did not do and has consistently refused to do....

Appellants next contend that recent decisions have held that an employer ... may not use different employment criteria for men and women. They claim that if a male employee prefers males as sexual partners, he will be treated differently from a female who prefers male partners. They conclude that the employer thus uses different employment criteria for men and women and violates the Supreme Court's warning in Phillips v. Martin-Marietta [against] "permitting one hiring policy for women and another for men." ... While we do not express approval of an employment policy that differentiates according to sexual preference, we note that whether dealing with men or women the employer is using the same criterion: it will not hire or promote a person who prefers sexual partners of the same sex. Thus this policy does not involve different decisional criteria for the sexes....

The district courts [also] dismissed the male appellants' claims under 42 U.S.C. § 1985(3).... Appellants argue that the concerted actions of various agents of their employers and others, to effectuate the discriminatory policy of the employers constituted a conspiracy in violation of § 1985(3).... The forerunner of § 1985(3) [passed in 1871] was intended to provide special federal assistance to southern blacks and their allies in protecting their [equality] rights ... against the Ku Klux Klan and others organized to thwart reconstruction efforts. A century later the Supreme Court held that § 1985(3) applied only when there is "some racial, or perhaps otherwise class-based, invidiously discriminatory animus behind the conspirators' action." Griffin v. Breckenridge, 403 U.S. 88, 102 (1971).... In Life Insurance Co. of North America v. Reichardt, 591 F.2d 499 [at 502] (9th Cir. 1979), this court held that plaintiffs alleging a conspiracy to deprive women of equal rights could invoke § 1985(3). Appellants here claim that since Reichardt moved beyond the narrow historical perspective of 1871, homosexuals (and all groups) can now claim the special protection of § 1985(3). We disagree.... [W]e may not uproot § 1985(3) from the principle underlying its adoption: the Governmental determination that some groups require and warrant special federal assistance in protecting their civil rights.... In contradistinction to southern blacks of 1871, the blacks of Griffin, and the women of Reichardt, it cannot be said that homosexuals have been afforded special federal assistance in protecting their civil rights. The courts have not designated homosexuals a "suspect" or "quasi-suspect" classification so as to require more exacting scrutiny of classifications involving homosexuals. Cf. Doe v. Commonwealth's Attorney, 403 F. Supp. 1199, 1202 (E.D. Va. 1975) (constitutionality of Virginia sodomy law upheld ...), aff'd mem., 425 U.S. 901 (1976).... We conclude that homosexuals are not a "class" within the meaning of § 1985(3).[35]

■ SNEED, CIRCUIT JUDGE (concurring and dissenting):

I concur [except for holding] that male homosexuals have not stated a Title VII claim under the disproportionate impact theories of Griggs v. Duke Power Co.... The male appellants' complaint ... is based on the contention that the use of homosexuality as a disqualification for employment, which for Griggs' purposes must be treated as a facially neutral criterion, impacts disproportionately on *males* because of the greater visibility of male homosexuals and a higher incidence of homosexuality among males than females. To establish such a claim will be difficult because ... it will be necessary to establish that the use of homosexuality as a bar to employment disproportionately impacts on *males*.... I would permit them to try to make their case.... [A]ppellants' § 1985(3) claims ... fail because ... [§ 1985(3)] is not a writ by which the judiciary can provide comfort and succor to all groups, large and small, who feel social disapproval from time to time.

NOTES AND QUESTIONS ON *DeSANTIS*

1. Similarly situated individuals: Title VII by its language protects individuals from discrimination on the basis of sex. Is anything wrong with Mr. DeSantis's argument that had he been a *woman* worker at PT&T, in relationship with his same male partner, he would not have been subjected to discrimination? Does it simply adopt the "similarly situated" approach?

1.1 Is this the "but for sex" argument that has been developed since *DeSantis* in the sexual harassment legal setting? If so, why, after being treated as the sine qua non of discrimination (to the detriment of most women, who never will be "similarly situated" to men), can the similarly situated standard be cavalierly circumvented when a gay man notices that he is similarly situated to many women and, but for being a man, he would not be disadvantaged at work? Is he subjected to simple sexism—not really sexual orientation discrimination at all? Does the *DeSantis* court reject what the courts, in their sameness/difference mode, have said sex discrimination is fundamentally about all along?

1.2 Does any legal doctrine control the choice of comparator under the sameness/difference approach to sex equality in its application to same-sex situations? For example, what answer does sex equality doctrine give to the question whether, for purposes of assessing sex discrimination, lesbian women should be compared with straight men, since both have women partners, or lesbian women should be compared with gay men, because both have partners of the same sex? What law says that lesbian women can be as disadvantaged as gay men are, rather than requires that they be no more disadvantaged than straight men are? Logically, does one comparison have priority over the other? How do you account for the vigor with which one comparison is found more obvious and compelling than the other? What is at stake in the choice of comparison? What makes it appear that lesbian women and gay men are doing the same thing, while lesbian women and straight men are doing different things?

1.3 Much to the detriment of many women, courts have asserted that sex equality is an individual right, not a group right. Why now does detrimental treatment not qualify as sex-based because other individuals

---

35. For further discussion, see *Bray, infra.*

are subjected to the same detriment on the basis of *their* sex, when *neither* would be subject to any detriment if they were not of the sex they are? How did sex equality suddenly become not an individual right? How is an individual right to be free from discrimination based on one's sex vindicated by discriminating in the same way against an individual of another sex? If men and women are both discriminated against, each *as* a woman or *as* a man, why isn't the treatment of *both* sex-based? Do you sense a doctrinal fast one being pulled by the court here?

1.4 What about a gay- or lesbian-identified person who is in no sexual partnership with anyone? Is an individual protected, either by the *DeSantis* argument or by a sex equality argument you devise, from discrimination based on how their sexual orientation is gendered? Should people be protected from discrimination only when they are in relationships?

1.5 How do you recommend litigants make use of the argument of the *DeSantis* plaintiffs, both in light of intervening developments and in light of its application of doctrine that has often worked to the disadvantage of women (*see* Chapter 3)? Should truly disadvantaged people like gay men and lesbian women at least get the benefit of the conventional approach where it applies? Why do you think it was largely abandoned after a couple of tries, while privacy litigation against sodomy laws went on for decades, persevering after many losses?

1.6 One version of a sex equality–based argument for gay and lesbian rights is simple underinclusiveness: providing sex equality rights to some people but not others, depending in this instance on the irrelevant criterion of the gender orientation of their sexuality or the preferred gender of their sexual partner(s), violates the Equal Protection Clause. See if you can find in these cases this form of the argument, and reasons for accepting or rejecting it.

2. EEOC cases: The Equal Employment Opportunity Commission cases to which the *DeSantis* court refers held that discrimination based on what were termed by one complainant his "sexual practices" is not encompassed in Title VII's prohibition based on sex.

EEOC Decision No. 76–75

1976 Empl. Prac. Guide CCH EEOC Decisions (1983) ¶ 6495

[T]he Commission is of the opinion that when Congress used the word "sex" in Title VII it was referring to a person's gender, an immutable characteristic with which a person is born.

Thus, in the instant case Charging Party alleges unlawful employment discrimination based on his homosexuality, a condition which relates to a person's sexual proclivities or practices, not his or her gender; these two concepts are in no way synonymous. There being no support in either the language or the legislative history of the statute for the proposition that in enacting Title VII Congress intended to include a person's sexual *practices* within the meaning of the term "sex," and since the evidence in this case, viewed as a whole, indicates that Respondent Employer failed to rehire Charging Party at least in part because of his sexual practices, not his gender, the Commission must conclude that it lacks jurisdiction over the subject matter alleged.

EEOC Decision No. 76–67

1976 Empl. Prac. Guide CCH EEOC Decisions (1983) ¶ 6493

Charging Party states specifically ... that by "sex" he meant his "homosexuality (male)." ... Charging Party alleges unlawful employ-

> ment discrimination based on his homosexuality, a condition which relates to a person's sexual proclivities or practices, not to his or her gender.... [Thus, because] Respondent failed to hire Charging Party because of his sexual practices, not his gender, the Commission must conclude that it is without substantive jurisdiction to decide the issue.... The Commission is without jurisdiction over a charge of unlawful employment discrimination based on a person's homosexuality, i.e. his sexual practices.

Is sex immutable? In fact, it is a visual assignment made at birth. More precisely, is the "sex" that forms the basis for the sex discrimination found actionable under law regarded anymore as simply a biological fact? Why did it take a case raising facts of discrimination against gay men and lesbian women for the legal system first to tell us, definitively, what gender is and is not? If "sexual proclivities and practices" are part of gender identity, is discriminating based on them discriminating based on gender?

3. Application to criminal laws: The same logic of sameness and difference that was applied in *DeSantis* was used by the Supreme Court of Missouri to reverse a lower court ruling that Missouri's statute prohibiting "deviate sexual intercourse with another person of the same sex," Mo. Rev. Stat. § 566.090 (1999), deprived the man who was prosecuted for violating it (for touching a clothed undercover police officer's penis with his hand) of equal protection of the laws because "the statute would not be applicable to the defendant if he were a female." *State v. Walsh*, 713 S.W.2d 508, 509 (Mo. 1986) (en banc) (quoting trial court). Reversing, the Supreme Court of Missouri reasoned this way:

> The State concedes that the statute prohibits men from doing what women may do, namely, engage in sexual activity with men.... We believe it applies equally to men and women because it prohibits both classes from engaging in sexual activity with members of their own sex. Thus, there is no denial of equal protection on that basis. 713 S.W.2d at 510.

Analyze this reasoning formally and substantively. Compare it with the reasoning rejected by the Supreme Court in *Loving v. Virginia*, 388 U.S. 1 (1967) (*see* Chapter 4). What is your view of the racial analogy attempted and rejected concerning the application of Section 1985(3)? Is there an analogy between race and sexual orientation? between race and sex in the gay and lesbian setting? If race and sex are parts of a larger whole, and sexual orientation is part of sex, will the three phenomena be marked by similar features but never seem exactly analogous?

4. Sexual orientation as sex in disguise: In *Engel v. Worthington*, a California Court of Appeal held that David Engel had a sex equality right to have his picture with his male partner published in the memory book of his high school class reunion under the prohibition on sex discrimination in the equal accommodations provision of the Unruh Civil Rights Act, Cal. Civ. Code § 52(a) (West 1999). That court thought that homosexuality was not the issue and sex was:

> The trial court and the parties focus on Engel's homosexuality. They miss the point.... [The Act applies to sex-based classifications.] ... [I]t matters not whether Engel is homosexual or heterosexual. Had Engel's guest been female, no controversy would exist. At issue, then, is Worthington's refusal to print Engel's picture, with his guest, in the memory book because *both were male*.... Worthington maintains ...

his discriminatory policies were statutorily acceptable because everyone, regardless of gender, was treated the same: His restriction applied to any two same-sex couples whether father/son or twin sisters. . . . Worthington's services were gender dependent. Equal application of a discriminatory practice makes it no less violative of the law. Loving. *Engel v. Worthington*, 23 Cal. Rptr. 2d 329, 331 (Cal. App. 1993).[36]

Is there any defect in the *Engel* court's logic in applying the Aristotelian model? Is there a logical defect in *DeSantis*'s application of it? If the logic of each is above reproach, is the ability of the Aristotelian approach to produce diametrically opposed results with identical inputs, *through use of the same reasoning*, a virtue or vice of the theory? Is its studied indeterminacy in promoting equality a problem?

The *Engel* theory is less a gender theory of sexual orientation than a theory of how sexual orientation discrimination is simply sex discrimination misrepresented as something else. Would sexual orientation, so rendered, act like a "plus" in a "sex plus" prohibition, so that gay *men* could not be discriminated against as men simply because they are gay (an unprotected category), and lesbian *women* could not be discriminated against as women because they are lesbian? (*See* Chapter 4 for discussion of "sex plus" doctrine.) Is man-with-man and woman-with-woman rather obviously doubly sex-based? Should people's sex equality rights be permitted to be "plused" away, even if women and men both potentially lose? Note also that women together were not actually excluded from the memory book at the time; it was only asserted that they *would have been*. Does David Engel's real experience matter more than abstract nonfactual comparisons?

The *Engel* court said this in a footnote:

The concept is perhaps best understood in another context. Section 51 disallows discriminatory treatment based on religion. Could Worthington have limited his portraits to people of different religions, i.e., he would take pictures of a Jew and Catholic but not two Jews or two Catholics? To ask the question is to answer it. 23 Cal. Rptr. 2d at 331 n.6.

Is being gay or lesbian more like being a Jew or a Catholic than it is like being Black or Caucasian? Is homosexuality more like a religion—what is sacred to you, what gives life meaning, your community, your identifications, your holy practices—than like a race? Is sexuality the secular religion?

The First Amendment rights of the photographer and publisher did not justify the sex discrimination in this case. The court held that the photographer-publisher's opinion contrary to the "lifestyle and social agenda" of homosexuals did not justify violating Mr. Engel's sex equality rights, and in any event a disclaimer or an opinion could also be published. 23 Cal. Rptr. 2d at 335. Perhaps remarkably, Mr. Worthington's right of discriminating through speech was not the magic bullet that killed Mr. Engel's equality rights under California law. If "coming out" were held to be protected

---

36. The California Supreme Court, with two dissenters, denied review and ordered *Engel v. Worthington* depublished, *see Engel v. Worthington*, 1999 Cal. LEXIS 558 (Cal. Feb. 3, 1994), meaning the case may not be cited except for res judicata and akin narrow purposes. *See* Cal. R. Ct. 977.

speech, would the *Engel* result be further supported by a free-speech rationale?

4. Comparing women and men: Are gay men and lesbian women treated differently from each other in society on the basis of their sex? Are gay men, as the *DeSantis* plaintiffs argued, more visible than lesbians, therefore more subjected to the burdens of antigay discrimination? Are lesbian women subjected to distinctive often virulent forms of discrimination because they are seen as a certain kind of *woman*? If so, is that sex discrimination through gender stereotyping? Does the *DeSantis* argument seek to protect a group of men as men, hence men as such, as the dissent claims? What would be the implication of the success of such a claim for the rights of lesbian women to be free from discrimination? Who, the majority or the dissent, is correct on the application of *Griggs* to the *DeSantis* allegations?

5. Animus: Consider the analogy between race and sex on the one hand and sexual orientation on the other. Why doesn't homophobia qualify as a "class-based discriminatory animus"? Is it just that "homosexuals" are not a suspect class, or is it that the animus, homophobia, is insufficient to render them so, or are they not seen as a class at all? Do gay men and lesbian women merely feel occasional and episodic "social disapproval from time to time," as the dissent in *DeSantis* puts it, or are they systematically and cumulatively subordinated to a dominant heterosexual culture animated by homophobia? Do you see any distinctions between the homophobia directed at gay men and that directed at lesbian women? If so, what are the implications, if any, for an analysis of "class-based discriminatory animus"?

6. Europe: In *Grant v. South-West Trains Ltd.*, [1998] E.C.R. 449, 476–78, the European Court of Justice held that the refusal of an employer to give travel concessions to a person of the same sex with whom a worker has a stable relationship, where this concession is given to a worker's spouse or a person of the opposite sex with whom a worker has a stable but unmarried relationship of over two years, is not sex discrimination under Article 119 of the Treaty or under Directive 75/117 requiring equal pay for men and women. The rule (adopted by South-West Trains and embodied in Lisa Grant's employment contract) provided: "Privilege tickets are granted for one common law opposite sex spouse of staff ... subject to a statutory declaration being made that a meaningful relationship has existed for a period of two years or more." [1998] E.C.R. at 451.

Ms. Grant argued that a male employee in her circumstance would have travel concessions for his female partner, specifically that the "refusal constitutes discrimination directly based on sex [because] her employer's decision would have been different if the benefits in issue ... had been claimed by a man living with a woman, and not by a woman living with a woman." [1998] E.C.R. at 475. She further argued that not receiving the travel concession constituted sexual orientation discrimination, which is included in the concept of sex discrimination in Article 119, because "differences in treatment based on sexual orientation originate in prejudices regarding the sexual and emotional behaviour of persons of a particular sex, and are in fact based on those persons' sex." [1998] E.C.R. at 475. Is her allegation merely one of sex-based discrimination?

The European Court of Justice held that the travel benefit condition was not sex discrimination, since it applied in the same way to female and male workers, and that the term "sex" was not intended to cover sexual orientation. Was this result predictable, given Europe's predominant approach to sex discrimination, *see* Chapter 1, or is it simply wrong under that approach? How would the Supreme Court of Canada treat the same issue? How would you answer the ECJ within the sameness/difference framework? Is the difficulty of making a sameness/difference argument in this setting—in the double-is-nothing *DeSantis* logic in which discriminating twice is equality—an argument against a sex equality approach to discrimination against lesbian women and gay men, or is it an argument against the sameness/difference sex equality framework? What do you make of the European disconnect in which same-sex sex acts are protected in private, but same-sex partnerships can be legally discriminated against? Might male dominance have an interest in promoting sexual privacy but not in promoting equality on the basis of sex, in this case, of other-than-heterosexual families?

A victory was achieved for recognition of same-sex relationships through application of the sameness/difference sex equality approach in an attack on Hawai'i's Marriage Law, which, as interpreted and applied by the Department of Health, justified the refusal to issue a marriage license on the sole basis that the members of the applicant couples were of the same sex.

Baehr v. Lewin

Supreme Court of Hawai'i
852 P.2d 44 (Haw. 1993)

■ Levinson, Judge, in which Moon, Chief Judge, joins.

[W]e do not believe that a right to same-sex marriage is so rooted in the traditions and collective conscience of our people that failure to recognize it would violate the fundamental principles of liberty and justice that lie at the base of all our civil and political institutions. Neither do we believe that a right to same-sex marriage is implicit in the concept of ordered liberty, such that neither liberty nor justice would exist if it were sacrificed. Accordingly, we hold that the applicant couples do not have a fundamental constitutional right to same-sex marriage arising out of the right to privacy or otherwise.... [However,] ... HRS § 572-1, on its face, discriminates based on sex against the applicant couples in the exercise of the civil right of marriage, thereby implicating the equal protection clause of article I section 5 of the Hawai'i Constitution.... It has been held that a state may deny the right to marry only for compelling reasons.... Hawai'i's counterpart [to the Fourteenth Amendment] provides in relevant part that "[n]o person shall ... be denied the equal protection of the laws, *nor be denied the enjoyment of the person's civil rights or be discriminated against in the exercise thereof because of* race, religion, *sex*, or ancestry." Thus, by its plain language, the Hawai'i Constitution prohibits state-sanctioned discrimination against any person in the exercise of his or her civil rights on the basis of sex.

"The freedom to marry has long been recognized as one of the vital personal rights essential to the orderly pursuit of happiness by free [people]." *Loving*.... [B]y its plain language, HRS § 572-1 restricts the marital relation to a male and a female.... The non-consanguinity requisite ... precludes marriages, inter alia, between "brother and sister," "uncle and niece," and "aunt and nephew[.]" The anti-bigamy requisite ... forbids a marriage between a "man" or a "woman" as the case may be, who, at the time, has a living and "lawful wife . . . [or] husband[.]" And the requisite . . . [of licensed persons performing ceremonies] speaks in terms of "the man and woman to be married[.]" Accordingly, on its face and (as Lewin admits) as applied, HRS § 572-1 denies same-sex couples access to the marital status and its concomitant rights and benefits. It is the state's regulation of access to the status of married persons, on the basis of the applicants' sex, that gives rise to the question whether the applicant couples have been denied the equal protection of the laws [under Hawai'i's Constitution]. . . .

Lewin contends that "the fact that homosexual [sic—actually, same-sex][37] partners cannot form a state-licensed marriage is not the product of impermissible discrimination" implicating equal protection considerations, but rather "a function of their biologic inability as a couple to satisfy the definition of the status to which they aspire." Put differently, Lewin proposes that "the right of persons of the same sex to marry one another does not exist because marriage, by definition and usage, means a special relationship between a man and a woman." We believe Lewin's argument to be circular and unpersuasive. . . . The facts in Loving [v. Virginia] and the respective reasoning of the Virginia courts, on the one hand, and the United States Supreme Court, on the other, both . . . unmask the tautological and circular nature of Lewin's argument that HRS § 572-1 does not implicate [Hawai'i's sex equality guarantee] because same sex marriage is an innate impossibility. Analogously to Lewin's argument . . ., the Virginia courts declared that interracial marriage simply could not exist because the Deity had deemed such a union intrinsically unnatural, and, in effect, because it had theretofore never been the "custom" of the state to recognize mixed marriages, marriage "always" having been construed to presuppose a different configuration. With all due respect to the Virginia courts of a bygone era, we do not believe that trial judges are the ultimate authorities on the subject of Divine Will, and, as Loving amply demonstrates, constitutional law may mandate, like it or not, that customs change with an evolving social order. . . .

We hold that sex is a "suspect category" for purposes of equal protection analysis under article I section 5 of the Hawai'i Constitution and that HRS § 572–1 is subject to the "strict scrutiny" test. It therefore follows, and we so hold, that (1) HRS § 572-1 is presumed to be unconstitutional (2) unless Lewin . . . can show that (a) the statute's sex-based classification is justified by compelling state interests and (b) the statute is narrowly drawn to avoid unnecessary abridgments of the applicant couples' constitutional rights. . . . On remand, . . . the burden will rest on Lewin to overcome the presumption that HRS § 572-1 is unconstitutional.

■ WALTER M. HEEN, J., INTERMEDIATE COURT OF APPEALS JUDGE, dissenting.

HRS § 572-1 treats everyone alike and applies equally to both sexes. The effect of the statute is to prohibit same sex marriages on the part of professed or non-professed heterosexuals, homosexuals, bisexuals, or asexuals, and does not effect an invidious discrimination . . .

HRS § 572-1 does not establish a "suspect" classification based on gender because all males and females are treated alike. A male cannot obtain a license to marry another male, and a female cannot obtain a license to marry another female. Neither sex is being *granted* a right or benefit the other does not have, and neither sex is being *denied* a right or benefit that the other has. . . . In my view, the statute's classification is clearly designed to promote the legislative purpose of fostering and protecting the propagation of the human race through

37. These brackets and their contents
are in the original.

heterosexual marriage and bears a reasonable relationship to that purpose. I find nothing unconstitutional in that.

NOTES AND QUESTIONS ON *BAEHR v. LEWIN*

1. **Precedent:** Does the plurality properly apply *Loving*? Can you articulate more precisely how prohibiting laws against mixed-race marriages supports prohibiting laws against same-sex marriages? In other words, the element of heterogeneity in marriage that was prohibited on a racial basis is what is enforced on a gender basis, in the usual legal arrangement. Sameness and difference are found in a crossover position in both instances, but, in sameness/difference logic, is the sameness of race that Virginia was imposing on marriages analogous to the difference of sex that Hawai'i seeks to impose? Is the difference of race sought by Mr. Loving analogous to the sameness of sex the *Baehr* plaintiffs are seeking? In other words, if sameness and difference are the issue, is what the *Baehr* plaintiffs are seeking access to on the basis of sex—sameness in marriage partners— what Virginia was seeking to impose on a racial basis and Mr. Loving was seeking not to be a criminal for having rejected? Does this twist tell you something about sameness/difference logic? Is the way it obscures the realities of domination and exclusion exposed by its effect in this setting? By the same token, does the dissent's logic remind you of *Plessy* (*see* Chapter 1)? *of Gilbert* and *Geduldig* (*see* Chapter 3)? Can you think of additional sex equality arguments to support the majority's result? Could the sexual harassment cases help dispose of the dissent's arguments?

2. **Unexplored gender dimensions:** Do women and men in societies of gender inequality have the same objective interest in marriage? Does marriage as an institution envision a union of equals on the basis of sex? Is marriage in the interest of lesbian women? Would the availability of marriage to those couples whose members could not be presumed unequals on the basis of gender change the institution of marriage, to some degree and eventually, for everyone? Or would the availability of marriage to gay men and lesbian women coopt the critique of power as deployed through sexuality that the gay critique of heterosexuality has offered all women? Reconsider *M. & H.* in light of these queries.

3. **The *Loving* analogy:** Professor Andrew Koppelman has argued that the homosexuality taboo shares assumptions with the prior taboo on miscegenation, making the two analogous for purposes of a discrimination argument that enforces marriage by polar category:

> In the same way that the prohibition of miscegenation preserved the polarities of race on which white supremacy rested, the prohibition of homosexuality preserves the polarities of gender on which rests the subordination of women.... Both assume the hierarchical significance of sexual intercourse and the polluted status of the penetrated person. The central outrage of sodomy is that a man is reduced to the status of a woman, and that is understood to be degrading. Just as miscegenation was threatening because it called into question the distinctive and superior status of being white, homosexuality is threatening because it calls into question the distinctive and superior status of being male. Male homosexuals and lesbians, respectively, are understood to be guilty of one aspect of the dual crime of the miscegenating white woman: self-degradation and insubordination. By analogy with miscegenation, a member of the superior caste who allows his body to be penetrated is thereby polluted and degraded, and he assumes the

status of the subordinate caste: he becomes womanlike. "[M]en cannot simultaneously be used 'as women' and stay powerful because they are men." Andrea Dworkin, *Right-Wing Women* 129 (1983).

Just as miscegenation became the central symbol of the necessity of racial segregation, so today homosexuality stands as *the* signifier of the importance of maintaining male status. Lesbianism, on the other hand, is a form of insubordination: It denies that female sexuality exists, or should exist, only for the sake of male gratification. The prohibition of lesbianism is, however, less central to the taboo. In the same way that black male-white female was the paradigmatic act that the miscegenation taboo prohibited, male sodomy is the paradigmatic act that the homosexuality taboo prohibits. Andrew Koppelman, *Antidiscrimination Law and Social Equality* 159 (1996).

Evaluate the racial analogy. If both race and sex are conceived as hierarchies, as Professor Koppelman does here, or part of one larger interconnected inequality, rather than mere differences, does his analogy work better? Does Professor Koppelman offer one analysis for gay men, another for lesbian women? Is this appropriate? What are the implications of Professor Koppelman's analysis for a sexuality linchpin theory of gender inequality? (*See* Chapter 7.) How is the term "male supremacy" avoided here?

4. Doctrinal argument: Evaluate the extent to which the following post-*Hardwick*, pre-*Hopkins* sameness/difference sex equality argument against sodomy laws was adopted by the *Baehr* court.

Sodomy statutes that criminalize only acts between persons of the same sex ... discriminate on the basis of gender. Because the statutes permit a woman to engage in sodomy with a man, but prohibit a man from engaging in the same acts with a man, an act's criminality is determined solely by the actor's gender. Proponents of same-sex sodomy statutes have argued that because the statutes prohibit both sexes from engaging in same-sex sodomy, they treat both sexes equally. The Supreme Court rejected this "separate but equal" reasoning in the school segregation context, concluding that laws prohibiting both races from mixing with each other violate equal protection. The miscegenation cases extended the Court's rejection of the separate but equal rationale to interracial marriage, and held that a statute that defines conduct by a particular characteristic is not neutral with respect to that characteristic. Because same-sex sodomy statutes define the prohibited conduct by reference to gender, these statutes are gender-discriminatory rather than gender-neutral.

Not only do these statutes classify based on gender, but the classification also reinforces stereotypical sex roles, and therefore may not be sustained as a "benign" classification. The prohibition of same-sex sodomy reinforces a dichotomous view of gender in which differences between men and women are so significant that same-sex sexual conduct violates the roles assigned to each gender through cultural indoctrination. The very characterization of sodomy as a "crime against nature" implies that men and women were created to fulfill their respective procreative roles, and that their sexual options should be restricted accordingly. The acceptance of same-sex intimacy would threaten these notions of masculinity and femininity upon which traditional gender roles are based. A prohibition on same-sex sodomy also reinforces stereotypical gender roles, as stigmatizing homosexuality contributes to the bifurcation of male and female identities. In a society with a history of legal and economic subordination of women, the preservation of traditional gender roles disproportionately disadvantages women. The tendency of same-sex sodomy statutes to perpetuate traditional gender roles demonstrates that their classificatory structure is not benign, but rather discriminates based on gender and requires heightened scrutiny.

Once a court acknowledges that a same-sex sodomy statute employs a quasi-suspect or suspect classification, the state interests advanced ... will not survive heightened scrutiny. The primary state justification for punishing same-sex sodomy and not opposite-sex sodomy is a moral interest in deterring homosexual activity. The Court in *Griswold* struck down a regulation establishing procreation as the only purpose of marital sex. Consequently, *Griswold* forecloses the use of the criminal law for the sole purpose of effecting a particular sexual norm. Moreover, a desire to deter homosexuality is motivated by a belief that gay men and lesbians are inferior to non-gay persons. However, a moral interest based on prejudice toward persons within a suspect or quasi-suspect class does not rise to the level of an important state interest. Because the maintenance of traditional gender roles underlies the moral condemnation of homosexuality, a moral interest in deterring homosexuality cannot support same-sex sodomy statutes.

Non-moralistic rationales also fail heightened scrutiny. Arguments that gay men disproportionately molest children have been discredited, as have claims that anti-sodomy laws strengthen heterosexual marriage. The state's interest in the protection of public health also fails to survive heightened scrutiny [as AIDS does not disproportionately affect lesbians and even if confined to men, is] grossly overinclusive, as not all prohibited acts carry a high risk of transmission, and the risks depend on the acts themselves rather than the gender of the participants. *Sexual Orientation and the Law* 16–20 (Editors of the Harvard Law Review eds., 1990).

Is the racial analogy well made? Why might the Supreme Court of Hawai'i not have predicated its ruling on sex classification per se? Is the *Harvard Law Review*'s argument about classification consistent with sex-specific statutory rape laws, as upheld in *Michael M.*? What Supreme Court Justice or Justices can you most readily imagine writing an opinion containing the words in this excerpt? Why do you suppose this argument was not made in *Hardwick*?

5. Aftermath: After *Baehr*, the federal government passed the Defense of Marriage Act (DOMA) 110 Stat. 2419 (1996), defining marriage federally as a legal union between one man and one woman, *id.*, out of concern that same-sex couples might seek recognition of their Hawai'ian marriages in other jurisdictions; many states legislated to preclude the *Baehr* result. *See* Alba Conte, 1 *Sexual Orientation and Legal Rights* 614–16 (1998). The New York Supreme Court rejected a claim for a marriage license by a same-sex couple. *See Storrs v. Holcomb*, 168 Misc. 2d 898, 645 N.Y.S.2d 286 (Sup. Ct. 1996). The Supreme Court of Vermont legalized same-sex marriage, *see Baker v. State*, 744 A.2d 864 (Vt. 1999), and the legislature enacted a domestic partnership statute accordingly. (See Chapter 6 and *Same-Sex Marriage, Pro and Con: A Reader* (Andrew Sullivan ed. 1997) for further discussion.) What political and legal factors would you consider in strategizing a legal campaign for recognition of same-sex marriage or domestic partnership? What role, if any, would sex equality arguments play?

6.   Hypothetical: In *Longwe v. Intercontinental Hotels* [1993] 4 L. Rep. Commw. 221, the High Court of Zambia held that a hotel policy, under which a woman was refused entry to the bar of the Intercontinental Hotel on the ground that she was unaccompanied by a man, discriminated on the basis of sex contrary to the Zambian Constitution. That Court stated:

> The reason for the discrimination was that she was a female who did not have male company at the material times. Now if that is not discrimination on the basis of sex or gender, what else is it, looking at the matter in a reasonable, ordinary person's perspective? I have not been able to find any reasonable argument to persuade me into holding that this was not based on the fact that at the material time this female ... because she was a female, and nothing else, was commanded by the hotel to be accompanied by another human being, but who must be a male, in order for her to be allowed by the hotel to patronise this bar. On the other hand, an unaccompanied male i.e. a male who was not in the company of a female, was free to patronize the same bar. This was very naked discrimination against the females on the basis of their gender or sex, by the respondent hotel. [1993] 4 L. Rep. Commw. at 232.

Would this reasoning be controversial in a United States court on these facts? What if, instead of stating that women could not enter without men, the rule said that women, for safety reasons, could not enter alone or with another woman? Would the latter be treated as discrimination based on sexual orientation? based on sex? supported by a legitimate purpose? Now suppose that instead of the policy stating that only women without men were excluded, it stated that everyone must be accompanied and women may not enter accompanied by another woman. Would this be seen as sex discrimination? as sexual orientation discrimination? Next consider, what if the hotel rule was that everyone must be accompanied by someone of the other sex? (In fact, the hotel said that the reason for the rule was that patrons complained that unaccompanied women had "fights over men," [1993] 4 LRC at 233, suggesting the possibility that the actual but unacknowledged concern was prostitution, that this concern was then visited solely on women, but that the facially gender-neutral rule would serve it even better.) How distant from the latter rule are the marriage laws? From the standpoint of a woman who wants a drink without a man in tow, how different would this rule be from the hotel's actual one? Do the marriage laws similarly prescribe that a woman cannot get access to the public benefits of the married status "unless accompanied by a man"?

Most sex equality thinking in the lesbian and gay rights area that reaches beyond the sex-switching model also begins with the antistereotyping analysis. For example, I. Bennett Capers argues that

> discrimination based on sexual orientation is essentially discrimination based on sex stereotyping.... [T]he binary gender system now rewards and penalizes women and men in accordance with how well they conform with this gender system.... Extending rights to lesbians and gays, however, would subvert this schema of rewards and penalties ... [b]ecause lesbians and gays by definition undermine the notion of a binary gender system. I. Bennett Capers, "Sexual Orientation and Title VII," 91 *Colum. L. Rev.* 1158, 1187 (1991).

Many draw on *Price Waterhouse v. Hopkins*, 490 U.S. 228 (1989), as does Mary Eaton:

> The courts have recognized that the regulation of female gender role conformity constitutes sex discrimination against heterosexual women. It is illegal, for instance, to fire or fail to promote a woman because she appears "too macho" or insufficiently feminine. If cast in more general terms, the guarantee against sex discrimination could be taken to mean that no one can be legally sanctioned for failing or refusing to abide by gender role norms. Given that discrimination against lesbians and gays is rooted in the notion that they reject or are incapable of respecting gender expectations, like heterosexual women, homosexuals should also be protected under guarantees of sex equality.
>
> Interestingly, the argument linking the oppression of lesbians and gays to the transgression of gender role norms bears a striking resemblance to the lesbian feminist claim that lesbian oppression is intimately connected with the subordination of women under conditions of male supremacy. Under the system of heterosexism, the two genders, "male" and "female," are constructed as polar opposites that complement one another. Each gender is distinguished by its own set of unique traits: associated with femininity are the characteristics of nurturance, caring, reproductivity, emotionality, irrationality, relationality, softness, and passivity, while independence, rationality, detachment, hardness, logic, aggressiveness, and intelligence are correlated with masculinity. The products of this system of gender differentiation do not enjoy equal social, political or legal status. Rather, "woman" and her femininity and "man" and his masculinity are arranged in relation to one another such that maleness occupies a superior and dominant position. What distinguishes the gay sex role thesis from the lesbian one is its claim that under the gender system gay men are, in effect, "women" too. That gay men are feminized through the stereotype of the "sissy" is the most obvious evidence of the interconnection between sexual identity and gender. More generally, however, the regime of gender differentiation and hierarchization requires the normalization of heterosexuality to sustain itself. Because the naturalization of the attraction between men and women is integral to the gender system and its devaluation of females and the feminine, discrimination against homosexuals (male and female alike) is thus inextricably bound with the subordination of women. Mary Eaton, "At the Intersection of Gender and Sexual Orientation: Toward Lesbian Jurisprudence," 3 *S. Cal. Rev. L. & Women's Stud.* 183, 191–92 (1994).

Is there a sex equality argument on behalf of gay men that is consistent with Mary Eaton's description of the lesbian feminist critique? Does Professor Leo Bersani's analysis meet those specifications? Professor Eve Kosofsky Sedgwick argues that "homophobia directed by men against men is misogynistic, and perhaps transhistorically so." Eve Kosofsky Sedgwick, *Between Men: English Literature and Male Homosocial Desire* 20 (1985). Can her analysis be made into a legal argument? Consider using Professors Bersani and Sedgwick as expert witnesses in a case argued by Professor Andrew Koppelman on the legal theory that

> [t]he effort to end discrimination against gays should be understood as a necessary part of the larger effort to end the subordinate status of women, because the function of the stigmatization of homosexuality is to preserve the hierarchy of males over females.... [The taboo on homosexuality] police[s] the boundary that separates the dominant

from the dominated in a social hierarchy that rests on a condition of birth. Koppelman, *supra*, at 153–54.

What facts would be most propitious for the use of these expert resources in litigation?

No litigation located contends that compulsory heterosexuality—as embodied in same-sex marriage prohibitions, sodomy laws, lack of family benefits, refusal to prohibit employment and housing discrimination, and the "gay panic" defense to murder as just a few examples—is a feature of male dominance, therefore an instance of inequality on the basis of sex, hence a violation of statutory and constitutional sex equality guarantees. The argument that lesbian women and gay men's disadvantage are twin features of one gender system of unequal power that subordinates all women and some men remains to be made in a court of law in a gay rights case. However, it has essentially been made in a same-sex context. Review *Oncale v. Sundowner Offshore Services*, 523 U.S. 75 (1998) (*see* Chapter 7.2). Prior to *Oncale*, authority was divided on whether sexual harassment based on same-sex sexual orientation was actionable as a form of sex discrimination.[38] In *Oncale*, the Supreme Court, in permitting Joseph Oncale to sue his employer for acts of sexual aggression against him by a male supervisor and coworker, for the first time recognized sex discrimination in a same-sex setting. How long a step is it from there to the recognition that when a man harasses a man because he is gay, or harasses him as gay whether he "is" gay or not, is sexual harassment recognizable under Title VII? From there, how far is it to the recognition that discrimination based on sexual orientation is discrimination based on sex?

Prior to *Oncale*, the Court of Appeal of California ruled in *Mogilefsky v. Superior Court* that same-sex sexual harassment is sex-based discrimination under California's sex discrimination law. Consider its analysis of the place of sexual orientation discrimination in sex discrimination.

Mogilefsky v. Superior Court

Court of Appeal for the Second District
20 Cal. App. 4th 1409, 26 Cal. Rptr. 2d 116 (Cal. App. 1993)

■ Woods, J.

The issue presented . . . is whether same gender sexual harassment may be the basis of a cause of action for sexual harassment in violation of the Fair Employment and Housing Act (Gov. Code, § 12940, subdivision (h).) . . . [W]e answer this question in the affirmative. . . . [P]etition alleged that on two occasions Levy, the president of Silver Pictures, demanded petitioner [his employee] stay overnight in Levy's hotel suite. On the first occasion, Levy allegedly informed petitioner that he would receive more money if he cooperat-

---

38. *Compare, e.g.,* Carreno v. Local Union No. 226, IBEW and Shelley Electric Co., 54 FEP Cas. 81 (D. Kan. 1990) (finding harassment based on sexual preference not sex not actionable under Title VII), *and* Hopkins v. Baltimore Gas & Electric Co., 77 F.3d 745 (4th Cir. 1996) (finding same-sex harassment actionable under Title VII only against gay perpetrators), *with* Joyner v. AAA Cooper Transp., 597 F. Supp. 537 (M.D. Ala. 1983), aff'd, 749 F.2d 732 (11th Cir.1984), *and*

Wright v. Methodist Youth Serv., Inc., 511 F. Supp. 307 (N.D. Ill. 1981) (holding that plaintiffs subjected to demands by a supervisor for same-sex sexual contact have a claim for sex discrimination under Title VII); Sardinia v. Dellwood Foods, 69 FEP Cas. 705 (S.D.N.Y. 1995) (holding same-sex sexual harassment actionable under Title VII). *See* Samuel A. Marcosson, "Harassment on the Basis of Sexual Orientation: A Claim of Sex Discrimination Under Title VII," 81 *Geo. L.J.* 1 (1992).

ed, ordered petitioner to play a pornographic film on the VCR, made lewd and lascivious comments about the film, and asked petitioner how much he would charge to perform acts similar to those depicted in the film. The next morning Levy allegedly falsely implied to others that petitioner engaged in anal sex with him. On the second occasion, Levy allegedly referred to petitioner in a profane and degrading manner and inquired repeatedly into petitioner's private life, including questions regarding his prior relationships. Very early the next morning, Levy allegedly woke petitioner, requested him to take his clothes off, and told petitioner that he wanted to sleep next to him. Petitioner alleged that he went to Levy's hotel suite the second time only after being informed by others that he had no choice in the matter, that attendance at the suite was mandatory, that another male employee had been fired for not going to Levy's suite when ordered to do so, and that petitioner should consider the consequences before refusing.

These acts were alleged to be violations of ... [§ 12940,] including the prohibitions against discrimination on the basis of gender, asking for sexual favors in return for favorable treatment in the workplace.... Levy argued [that these allegations] could not state a cause of action for sexual harassment as a matter of law.... [Allegations were added that] other named defendants allowed [Levy] to surround himself with "young, attractive males and employment decisions were made and job duties were assigned on the basis of Levy's attraction to male employees. As such, a hostile environment was created in which males were treated differentially from females and plaintiff alleges he was discriminated on the basis of his gender." ...

The only reported California case dealing with alleged sexual harassment by a member of the same sex was ... Hart v. National Mortgage & Land Co., 189 Cal. App. 3d 1420 [in which the plaintiff] testified in his deposition that he had been subjected to genital grabbing, attempted mounting, sexually suggestive gestures, and crude remarks by a male coemployee named Campbell. Hart described Campbell as a "pervert" and stated that he believed Campbell was "singling him out for this treatment," but that he did not believe Campbell was interested in having sex with him. [Summary judgment was granted to employer on grounds that Hart did not allege, nor did deposition show, that he was harassed because of his sex.] Hart is of questionable value as a legal precedent. The reviewing court's failure to deal with the undeniably sexual nature of the conduct to which Hart was subjected is, to say the least, troublesome. Such conduct, whether motivated by hostility or by sexual interest, is always "because of sex" regardless of the sex of the victim.... We find no basis of support in the statutory language for the contention that the Legislature intended to limit protection from sexual harassment of male-female harassment....

Nor do we share [the] concern that allowing a cause of action for same gender sexual harassment will "make an inquiry into the sexual orientation of the male supervisor an absolute necessity." The focus of a cause of action brought pursuant to [§ 12940] is whether the victim has been subjected to sexual harassment, not what motivated the harasser. [n.7:] We are aware of the holding in Gay Law Students Assn. v. Pacific Tel & Tel. Co., that the ... predecessor [statute to the FEHA] "did not contemplate discrimination against homosexuals." We do not base our decision in this case to any degree upon the sexual preference of the harassed employee. We therefore conclude that a cause of action for sexual harassment [under the sex discrimination prohibition] may be stated by a member of the same sex as the harasser.

NOTES AND QUESTIONS ON *MOGILEFSKY*

1. Inequality among men: Do the *Mogilefsky* facts demonstrate, as Marc S. Spindelman and John Stoltenberg say the facts in *Oncale* do, that "sexual subordination between purported social equals—gender-equals—is not harmless or nongendered simply because it happens between those of the same sex"? Marc S. Spindelman & John Stoltenberg, "Introduction, *Oncale*: Exposing 'Manhood,'" 8 *UCLA Women's L.J.* 3, 6 (1997). When a man's testicles are aggressively grabbed at work, is he attacked as a man? Is the attack sexual? gendered? sexed? *See Quick v. Donaldson Co., Inc.*, 90 F.3d 1372 (8th Cir. 1996) (holding pre-*Oncale* that "bagging" is sex-based in harassment case). If you were strategizing the claim in *Mogilefsky* and *Oncale*, would you be more concerned that the cause of action could be used viciously by homophobes to advance spurious allegations against gay men, or that, without it, all men, gay men included, could harass and violate other men with impunity?

2. **First Amendment:** The *Mogilefsky* court also rejected the studio's First Amendment argument, saying that its "fear that freeing 'everyone from sexual remarks and conduct' would 'put the First Amendment right of free speech on the endangered list' reveals a superficial understanding of its protections," referring to another case as precedent (*People v. Hernandez*, 231 Cal. App. 3d 1376, 1381 (Cal. App. 1991)), in which "the statutes in question protected a legitimate state interest and proscribed conduct rather than pure speech." *Mogilefsky*, 20 Cal. App. 4th at 121. Is the claim that coming out is protected political speech preserved by this approach to same-sex harassment? If coming out is protected speech, is sexual harassment also?

3. **Gay rights as sex equality rights:** Is the *Mogilefsky* court correct to rule that the plaintiff's sexual orientation is properly irrelevant? If he had "been" gay, would what was sex-based have become sexual-orientation-not-sex-based? If Mr. Levy had confined his harassment of the plaintiff to gay slurs instead of same-sex sexual importuning, would the harassment have been based on sexual orientation rather than sex, hence not actionable as sex discrimination? In the view of *Dillon v. Frank*, 952 F.2d 403 (table), 1992 WL 5436, *4 (6th Cir. 1992), in which Mr. Dillon alleged he was discriminated against "because he was believed to be a homosexual," no relief was held possible because "Title VII does not proscribe discrimination based on sexual activities or orientation." *Id.* Is this ruling less possible or likely after *Oncale*?

Is same-sex discrimination often simply sex discrimination, as the court said it was here? Does same-sex sexual orientation work, in addition, like an ethnicity of gender, so to speak: a culture, an identity, a belief system defining a group that varies socially and can be targeted for stigma and disadvantage by more dominant cultural forms? Are the winning arguments in same-sex sexual harassment cases like *Mogilefsky* and *Oncale* instructive for developing legal arguments to protect same-sex rights under sex discrimination law in other settings, or are they confined to harassment facts?

4. **Strategy:** Explain the connection between the ruling in *Oncale* and the recognition that lesbian and gay rights are sex equality rights. Design a litigation strategy to get there. Consider the plaintiffs, injuries, and legal arguments as you would frame them.

Consider ways to adapt and incorporate the following argument, revolving around the role of sexuality in gender hierarchy, for use in the factual settings raised by the cases and materials in this chapter.

Argument: Same–Sex Discrimination Is Sex Discrimination

I.   Sexuality Is a Social Construct of Gender.

1.   Gender refers to the social meaning of sex in the sense of being a man or a woman.

2.   Sexuality is a significant dimension along which gender is defined and expressed in social life.

3.   Many social roles and rules comprise gender. They include stereotyped scripts for masculinity and femininity, including those in which the male acts, the female is acted upon, the man is superior, the woman his inferior, self-interested pursuit is masculine, deference to male pursuit or being pursued is feminine, aggression is male, being prey is female, and so on.

4.   These sex roles are socially enacted in part through sexual expression and sexual identity.

5.   These sex roles, including in their forms as sexuality, are replicated and enacted throughout society in the family, the workplace, education, and public life.

6.   Much gender identity—thinking of oneself as a man or a woman, as masculine or feminine—is rooted in the meanings socially ascribed to sexuality and in the feelings and experiences it produces. Whether society perceives a person as adequate in gender terms is also largely determined by one's conformity with sexual behaviors assigned to one's sex.

7.   Manhood and womanhood are partly constituted by how and with whom a person is sexual. Much of the social meaning of being a man, and one's status as a man in society, is learned and lived through sexual congress with women and all the social institutions that anticipate, organize, channel, and support that activity. Much of the social meaning of being a woman in society, and one's status as such, is derivative of one's sexual relations with men, and is learned and lived in response to, and in support of the appearance of receptivity to, male sexual initiative.

8.   Many of the lines of distinction between women and men as such are drawn through heterosexuality as a social experience and institution. Traditional heterosexual intercourse, for this purpose, is a cardinal social act of gender definition, crucially defining its participants as women and men in society.

9.   The norms and mores of masculinity and femininity in sexuality are socially attributed to the biology of sex, resulting in an ideology that considers them natural to men, women, and their relations.

10.   The male role in society, including in sexuality, has no necessary relation to male biology, nor does the female role have any necessary relation to female biology. The roles socially assigned to each maintain their relative status in society.

II.   Sexuality Partly Defines Gender Inequality in Unequal Societies.

11.   Societies of gender inequality are societies of male supremacy and female subordination.

12.   The male role in sexuality and society is the role of members of the sexually dominant group. Calling their role natural serves to legitimize their dominance. The female role in sexuality and society is the role occupied by members of the socially inferior gender group so long as it is kept subordinate.

The female role has no necessary relation to women's biology but is ideologically naturalized in order to make it appear inevitable and unchangeable as well as justifiable.

13.   Much of the social meaning of being a man is learned and lived through relating to women as unequals, and through all the social institutions that anticipate, organize, channel, maintain, and enforce women's subordination to men, male interests, and male desires. Much of the social meaning of being a woman is learned and lived as a quest for male approval, including in the form of heterosexual desirability. Its benefits can include, or seem to include, validation, status, resources, opportunities, and survival.

14.   In societies of gender inequality, sex between women and men is sex between social unequals. In societies of male dominance, the inequality of the sexes is backed by direct force in the form of violence against women as well as by pervasive socialization and the power of the state.

15.   The traditional and enforced roles of man as active and woman as passive in sex extend, in life and law, to justifying sexual coercion and assault as normative and natural. They also tend to define women's allegations of rape as incredible. Sex roles of masculinity and femininity, generally attached to biological males and females, normalize and naturalize this aggression as the meaning of being a man and define women as its natural target..

16.   Sexual expression in the heterosexual context is thus marked by gender inequality, specifically by the use and abuse of male power in sex. The signs range from rituals of one-sided initiation through pressure and force, to aggression. The social pattern is one of men as aggressors and women as victims of their aggression, of male dominance and female subordination.

III.   SAME-SEXUALITY CHALLENGES THE SEX ROLES OF GENDER INEQUALITY.

17.   The terms gay man and lesbian woman refer to the sexual choices, politics, culture, and community of men and women who consider the fact that they have or wish to have sex with members of their own sex, and/or claim the centrality of intimacy with members of their own sex, to be a defining part of their identity or lives.

18.   A woman whose sexual and affectional identification, expression, affirmation, or community centers on women is termed lesbian. A man is termed gay who identifies, sexually and/or affectionally, with men.

19.   The practice of this identification and expression challenges the definition of sexuality and gender in societies of gender hierarchy of men over women.

20.   Lesbians challenge male dominance by defining women as sexual actors, by rendering men sexually irrelevant to women, and by calling into question the place of sexual intercourse with men in defining women socially. They undermine the purported naturalness of the assigned sexual roles of the sexes. (These are consequences for male dominance, not motivations for being lesbian.) By not defining women in sexual relation to men, lesbianism challenges that relation as definitive of all women. Many women who resist sex inequality, including celibate women and women who are not attached to men, pose a related challenge.

21.   Often a woman's heterosexuality is called into question when she refuses to conform to the feminine role as man's inferior.

22.   Lesbians, to the degree they are women who are sexually defined, particularly when defined in terms of domination and subordination, can also participate in, even strengthen, male dominance rather than challenge it.

23. Gay men may also pose a challenge to gender inequality. Gay men present the possibility that a man can be sexually acted upon, including in being sexually penetrated. This undermines the natural foundation claimed to underlie and justify male supremacy. (This is not a reason men are gay or a definition of male sexual practice, but rather the impact that the existence of gay men has on heterosexuality as an institution of gender inequality.) If a man can be sexually treated the way male dominance prescribes for women, male dominance is unmasked as a set of arbitrarily assigned social roles—a political invention rather than a natural expression of men's superiority over women.

24. Male inviolability and female violation are cardinal tenets of gender hierarchy. If men can do to men what men do to women sexually, women's sexual place as man's inferior is not a given, natural one, because a biological male can occupy it. That male sexual aggression could be directed at a biological male vitiates the biological basis upon which gender inequality ideologically rests.

25. When gay men are visible, a primal act defined by male dominance as underlying women's socially assigned inferiority can no longer be used to define women as a sex.

26. This analysis suggests that the fear of loss of sexually dominant status—including being subject to male sexual dominance and losing women as sexually available subordinates—drives homophobia in men. Homophobia in women may be driven by fear of loss of their source of value, such as it is, in the eyes and lives of men.

IV. Sexual Orientation Discrimination is Sex Discrimination.

A. Formal Equality

27. Under the "sameness/difference" approach to sex equality, when a lesbian woman or gay man is discriminated against because of that status, she or he is discriminated against because of sex.

28. Gay men and lesbian women are arguably situated similarly to heterosexual counterparts in every respect but their sex or the sex of their sexual partners. If they had sex with, or identified sexually as available for sex with, the same partners but were themselves of the other sex biologically, they would not be discriminated against. If, say, Pat and Mike are treated one way if Pat is Patricia and another if Pat is Patrick, sex discrimination pure and simple has occurred.

29. Sex equality is an individual right, statutorily and constitutionally. Discriminating against lesbian women because they are women with women, and gay men because they are men with men, is discriminating against them because they are women and men. But for their sex, they would not be so treated.

30. Most people who are discriminated against on the basis of their sex— i.e., women—do not have the opportunity to become similarly situated enough to claim discrimination under the standard approach. Gay men and lesbian women *are* similarly situated with comparators. Gay men's rights from discrimination should be especially easily recognized in light of sex equality law's consistent recognition of men's individual rights under sex equality rubrics.

B. Substantive Equality

31. Lesbians are denied civil benefits and human rights as lesbians, that is, as women who resist and challenge the sexual definition of women that male dominance imposes.

32.   Gay men are denied the full benefits society accords to men, and are deprived of human rights, because they fail to conform to the sexual rules and roles prescribed as masculine in societies of male dominance. Gay men are disadvantaged as men, including by stigma, aggression, and other forms of punishment and deprivation.

33.   It is unnecessary that individual gay men and lesbian women consciously position themselves as resisters to gender inequality for their discrimination to serve that function. When perceived and punished as gay men and lesbian women, they are discriminated against for flouting gender hierarchy, for failing to conform to male-dominant society's requirements for women and femininity, men and masculinity. The open existence of gay men and lesbian women undermines women's role as men's natural subordinates.

34.   Homosexuality is abhorred by straight society, homosexuals reviled, excluded and attacked in it, because they are seen to stand against sexuality between gender unequals, and for a sexuality of potential gender equals, hence against a primary feature of sex inequality as created and practiced.

V.   LAWS AGAINST SEX DISCRIMINATION PROHIBIT DISCRIMINATION AGAINST GAY MEN AND LESBIAN WOMEN.

35.   Unequal sex roles enforce gender hierarchy. Sex inequality as a social system disadvantages gay men and lesbian women prior to the operation of law, a disadvantage that is compounded every time law collaborates with it.

36.   To deprive lesbian women and gay men as such of equality under law, or to allow their human rights to be flouted because they stand against the gender system, is to enforce sex inequality by law.

37.   Prohibiting discrimination against lesbian women and gay men grants them sex equality and promotes equality of the sexes.

NOTES AND QUESTIONS ON ARGUMENT

1.   Gender: Evaluate the Argument. Is same-sex sexuality gendered? Does it participate in gender hierarchy? Does homosexuality have a stake in gender? Does it have a sexual stake in gender inequality? Given that most individuals in societies of male dominance learn their sexuality, as such, under conditions of unequal power, does homosexuality have a sexual stake in unequal sex, albeit differently gendered from heterosexuality's? Does same-sexuality also challenge material dimensions of the gender system? Consider, in a context of gender inequality, possible differences between the interests of gay men as men, and lesbian women as women, revealed by your answers. Compare the above argument with the sexual-orientation–based argument against sexual-orientation discrimination—strategically, legally, politically, and on principle.

2.   The critique of heterosexuality: Professor Sheila Jeffreys, among others, has argued that heterosexuality eroticizes the power difference between women and men under conditions of inequality of the sexes:

> Heterosexual desire is defined here as sexual desire that eroticises power difference. It originates in the power relationships between the sexes and normally takes the form of eroticising the subordination of women. In heterosexual desire our subordination becomes sexy for us and for men. Heterosexual desire can exist also in same sex relationships, because women and men do not escape the heterosexual construction of their desire simply by loving their own sex. We all grow up in the political system of heterosexuality. Sheila Jeffreys, *Anticlimax: A Feminist Perspective on the Sexual Revolution* 2 (1990).

Does this analysis converge with that of Professor Bersani? What experiences are likely to eroticize hierarchy? Does same-sex sexuality give equality more of a chance in interpersonal relationships than opposite-sex sexuality does? Does it guarantee that equality? If dominance as such is sexualized under the ruling sexual script in sex-unequal societies, what difference does the gender of individuals make to their participation in its sexuality?

3. Sexual abuse and sexual orientation: Suppose that the question is not what makes people gay but how hierarchical sexuality comes to be experienced as sexuality itself. In this inquiry, the origins of sexual orientation to power and powerlessness would be the question, its interface with gender a second-order issue. The stigma of degradation attached to being the passive/powerless/object other, and the mapping of those features onto the feminine/female/subordinate, would be a consequence.

The gender of one's sexual orientation in itself, in this view, says nothing about one's erotic investment in dominance. But does it make sense, given widespread sexual abuse of girl children by adult heterosexual men and the widespread conflation of maleness with power and femaleness with powerlessness in society, that many girls, imprinted by male dominant sex from a young age through abuse, would grow up heterosexual? What else are they likely to know as their own sexuality? How else would they have learned to get approval, resources, and what passes for power? Does it also make sense that many young boys, abused by heterosexual men, would reject everything to do with femininity once they learned that, by being men, they could never be sexually abused again? Might their revulsion at their own abuse (where it exists) help explain their misogyny as well as the militancy of their heterosexuality and intensity of their homophobia (where they exist)? Does it also make sense that some women would decide to avoid their experiences of violation by choosing not to be open to sex with men ever again? and that some men, like women who grow up heterosexual, would seek to repeat their prior violation by powerful men *as* sex, having eroticized these violations from an early age?

Not everyone who has a sexual orientation is sexually abused in childhood, but a large percentage of children of both sexes is. What empirical realities would it take to make such abuse sufficiently culturally pervasive and sufficiently culturally normative to produce the results on which this suggested analysis is predicated? Do these realities exist? (*See* Chapter 7.1.) Could these realities be shifting in the direction of more, rather than less, hierarchy in sexuality, producing both more violent subordination of women by men and more violent responses to gay men and lesbian women? What cultural forces might produce such a shift? (*See* Chapters 7.1 and 10.2.) What effects, if any, might such a shift have on sexual orientations?

If gender identity "is performatively constituted by the very 'expressions' that are said to be its results," Butler, *supra*, at 25, what gender identity does performing sexual abuse constitute?

3. Bisexuality: Many people are or identify as bisexual, meaning they are intimate and sexual, or desire to be so, with both women and men.

3.1 Consider Professor Mary Becker's description of some women's sexuality:

[M]any women do not have a sexual orientation in the sense of one fixed sexual preference for lovers with either the same or the opposite physical sex. For these women, sexuality is very fluid, though most are likely to assume that they are heterosexual because they feel normal and our society teaches that normal women are heterosexual. Many of these women might have strong preferences for relationships with men or women, but this preference would not be based on the partner's physical sex, but rather on the many differences between being the intimate partner—emotionally as well as sexually—of a man versus being the intimate partner of a woman. Becker, *supra*, at 1475.

See also Mary Becker, "Women, Morality, and Sexual Orientation," 8 *UCLA Women's L.J.* 165, 207–12 (1998). Is she describing what is usually (without her nuance and texture) termed bisexuality?

3.2 Bisexual women and men are often discriminated against. *See generally* Ruth Colker, *Hybrid: Bisexuals, Multiracials, and Other Misfits Under American Law* (1996). Typically, bisexuality is legally treated as an add-on in a prohibited list that reads "gay, lesbian, or bisexual"; bisexuality is most often legally treated, as it were, as a lesser-included offense of homosexuality.

In adoption and custody cases, bisexual men have been denied family rights to children based on same-sex sex acts. *See, e.g., In re Appeal in Pima County Juvenile Action B-10489*, 727 P.2d 830 (Ariz. Ct. App. 1986) (denying adoption to bisexual man due to homosexual conduct and possibility of such unlawful conduct after adoption); *Glover v. Glover*, 586 N.E.2d 159, 164–65 (Ohio Ct. App. 1990) (reversing trial court's grant of custody to bisexual father based on one gay encounter seven years prior and availability of heterosexual mother as custodian).

Bisexual orientation, usually meaning in practice same-sex sex acts, is also admissable in criminal cases to show potential for having committed various crimes.[39] Servicemembers can be discharged for bisexuality, usually meaning having engaged in same-sex sex acts but refusing to disavow having also other-sex histories and desires. *See, e.g.,* SECNAVINST 1900.0D; *Schowengerdt v. United States*, 944 F.2d 483, 489–90 (9th Cir. 1991) (permitting discharge of man from naval reserve for bisexuality); *Beller v. Middendorf*, 632 F.2d 788 (9th Cir. 1980) (permitting discharge of Mr. Beller, an "avowed" bisexual, as well as James Miller, who refused to have his sexuality defined in gender terms, for engaging in admitted same-sex activity). Is discrimination against bisexual women and men conceivable without discrimination against lesbians and gays? Is it a distinguishable category at all, or does its heart lie in its fluid edges?

3.3 Is discrimination against bisexuals gender-based discrimination or does bisexuality's lack of, as courts seem to imagine it, discrimination on

---

39. *See, e.g., Wellborn v. State*, 372 S.E.2d 220, 221 (Ga. 1988) (holding evidence of bisexual orientation admissible to show "intent, motive, plan, scheme, and bent of mind" in appeal of malice murder conviction for male victim found nude with multiple stab wounds); *Williams v. State*, 420 S.E.2d 781, 781–83 (Ga. Ct. App. 1992) (holding admissable evidence of bisexuality in appeal of conviction for aggravated child molestation of three-year-old boy); *Montana v. Ford*, 926 P.2d 245, 250–51 (Mont. 1996) (holding evidence of bisexuality admissible on appeal of conviction of male defendant for rape of male victim); *see also Simon v. State*, 743 S.W.2d 318, 325 (Tex. Ct. App. 1987) (holding prosecutor's attempt to use wife's bisexuality as impeachment did not warrant mistrial where judge instructed jury to disregard, in conviction of husband and wife in sexual assault of fifteen-year-old child).

gender grounds eliminate that claim of right? Do homosexuality and heterosexuality by definition share the principle of organizing sexual life around the gender of the partner? Is bisexuality a less gendered sexuality than either heterosexuality or homosexuality? Consider whether it is gender-nondiscriminating or, rather, less sex-based, in the sense of organizing sexuality around the biological sex of a sex partner. Could bisexuality equally well be doubly sex-based? Bisexual women and men are not sexually indiscriminate. As a way of sexual life, does bisexuality as such have less, or no less, stake in gender than either homosexuality or heterosexuality? Does bisexuality challenge gender inequality or potentially participate in it from two locations? Does the answer depend upon one's degree of orientation to hierarchy? One can be bisexual but sexually consistently either dominant or subordinate. Would this pattern challenge gender difference but not sexualized hierarchy hence leave gender hierarchy in place? Does bisexuality, and its defense under law, have a special role to play in promoting gender equality?

3.4 How would you frame an argument that a bisexual person, fired from employment as such, was discriminated against under existing sex equality law and theory? Do sexual harassment cases provide any leads in arguing against discrimination against bisexual people? Revisit the doctrinal skirmishes over the mainly fictional bisexual harasser in Chapter 7.2 in light of your analysis.

3.5 Evaluate this analysis: A woman's sexual relations with men tend to immunize her from being defined by her sexual relations with women, making her seen as bisexual at most. A man's sexual relations with men can trump his sexual history with women, making him seen as gay, period. That is, having sex with a man locates femininity but dislocates masculinity; having sex with a woman does neither in a way that can't be displaced by sex with a man. Thus, the defining issue of sexual orientation under male dominance is one's sexual history with men.

4. Shunning sex equality: Why does the sex equality argument, particularly the version that criticizes male dominance as the source of the inequality of both all women and gay men, tend to be shunned in legal attempts to secure lesbian and gay rights?

4.1 Marilyn Frye offers this potential answer.

One might have hoped that since gay men themselves can be, in a way, victims of woman-hating, they might have come to an unusual identification with women and hence to political alliance with them. This is a political possibility which is in some degree actualized by some gay men, but for most, such identification is really impossible. They know, even if not articulately, that their classification with women is based on a profound misunderstanding. Like most other men who for one reason or another get a taste of what it's like to be a woman in a woman-hating culture, they are inclined to protest, not the injustice of anyone ever being treated so shabbily, but the injustice of *their* being treated so when *they* are not women. The straight culture's identification of gay men with women usually only serves to intensify gay men's investment in their difference and distinction from the female other. What results is not alliance with women but strategies designed to demonstrate publicly gay men's identification with men, as over and against women. Frye, *supra*, at 138–39.

Does Professor Frye's analysis suggest that a sex equality analysis is rejected by some gay men because it jettisons their claim to status as men? Does the privacy strategy for gay rights "demonstrate publicly gay men's identification with men, as over and against women"? If sex inequality is not biological, and fundamentally sexual, is the classification of gay men with women not a misunderstanding?

4.2 Evaluate this analysis: Reasons for neglect of the sex equality argument in gay rights litigation doubtless include the appeal of the "none of your business" dimension of privacy law in its reference to matters sexual as well as the elevating gender neutrality of the argument for equal treatment based on sexual orientation. Both arguments rely on a "We are just like you" comparison with heterosexuality, thus may be experienced as dignifying as well as strategically comparatively unthreatening to heterosexual dominance. Both arguments also avoid making common cause with all women.

But the fundamental dynamic is misogynistic, thus ultimately against gay men's interests, because they as well as all women are under the boot of male dominance. Sex equality is perceived as a risky argument because women are a low-status people and pointing fingers at the realities of male power makes men angry, hostile, and aggressive. Too, the presence of men in any group raises the status of that group, hence the likelihood it will be taken as human, hence the possibility that disadvantage to the group will be taken as discrimination. Avoiding sex equality arguments for gay rights is yet another discriminatory approach to nondiscrimination, blunting the transformative potential of gay and lesbian liberation and abandoning women in the bargain, particularly lesbian women, who are sexually defined twice over.